The Handbook
of Behavioral Operations
Management

The Handbook of Behavioral Operations Management

Social and Psychological Dynamics in Production and Service Settings

EDITED BY ELLIOT BENDOLY

WOUT VAN WEZEL

AND

DANIEL G. BACHRACH

OXFORD
UNIVERSITY PRESS

Oxford University Press is a department of the University of Oxford.
It furthers the University's objective of excellence in research, scholarship,
and education by publishing worldwide.

Oxford New York
Auckland Cape Town Dar es Salaam Hong Kong Karachi
Kuala Lumpur Madrid Melbourne Mexico City Nairobi
New Delhi Shanghai Taipei Toronto

With offices in
Argentina Austria Brazil Chile Czech Republic France Greece
Guatemala Hungary Italy Japan Poland Portugal Singapore
South Korea Switzerland Thailand Turkey Ukraine Vietnam

Oxford is a registered trade mark of Oxford University Press
in the UK and certain other countries.

Published in the United States of America by
Oxford University Press
198 Madison Avenue, New York, NY 10016

© Oxford University Press 2015

All rights reserved. No part of this publication may be reproduced,
stored in a retrieval system, or transmitted, in any form or by any means,
without the prior permission in writing of Oxford University Press,
or as expressly permitted by law, by license, or under terms agreed with the
appropriate reproduction rights organization. Inquiries concerning reproduction
outside the scope of the above should be sent to the Rights Department,
Oxford University Press, at the address above.

You must not circulate this work in any other form
and you must impose this same condition on any acquirer.

Library of Congress Cataloging-in-Publication Data
The handbook of behavioral operations management : social and psychological dynamics
in production and service settings / edited by Elliot Bendoly, Wout van Wezel,
and Daniel G. Bachrach.
p. cm.
Includes bibliographical references and index.
ISBN 978-0-19-935721-5 (alk. paper) — ISBN 978-0-19-935722-2 (alk. paper)
1. Production management. 2. Management science—Psychological aspects. I. Bendoly, Elliot.
II. Wezel, Wout van. III. Bachrach, Daniel G.
TS155.H28133 2015
658.5—dc23
2014046429

9 8 7 6 5 4 3 2

Printed in the United States of America on acid-free paper

CONTENTS

CONTRIBUTORS

Daniel G. Bachrach, *University of Alabama*
Elliot Bendoly, *Ohio State University*
Thomas Callahan, *Michigan State University*
David E. Cantor, *Iowa State University*
Jaime A. Casteneda, *University of Lugano*
Yi-Su Chen, *Michigan State University*
Sander de Leeuw, *VU University Amsterdam & Nottingham Trent University*
David del Rio Vilas, *UDC–Universidade da Coruña*
Karen Donohue, *University of Minnesota*
Miguel Estrada, *IPADE Business School*
George Easton, *Emory University*
Karen Eboch, *Bowling Green State University*
Stephanie Eckerd, *University of Maryland*
Paul Gonçalves, *University of Lugano*
Miguel Guzman, *IPADE Business School*
Stefan J. Hoogervorst, *Involvation*
Khuong Ngoc Mai, *International University, Vietnam*
Pamela Manhart, *Iowa State University*
Kenneth N. McKay, *University of Waterloo*
Tung Nhu Nguyen, *International University, Vietnam*
Arturo Orozco, *IPADE Business School*
Anton Ovchinnikov, *Queen's University*
Diego Crespo Pereira, *UDC–Universidade da Coruña*
Young K. Ro, *Michigan State University*
Michael Alan Sacks, *Emory University*
Tsai-Shan Shen, *Eastern Michigan University*
Michaela Schippers, *Rotterdam School of Management*
John Sterman, *Massachusetts Institute of Technology*
Louis St. Peter, *Georgia State University*
Wout van Wezel, *University of Groningen*

Toni Wäfler, *University of Applied Sciences, Northwestern Switzerland*
Walter L. Wallace, *Georgia State University*
Steve V. Walton, *Emory University*
Yusen Xia, *Georgia State University*
Yinghao Zhang, *Salisbury University*

INTRODUCTION

ELLIOT BENDOLY ■

Let's start with a definition:

> *Behavioral operations management* explores the interaction of human behaviors and operational systems and processes. Specifically, the study of behavioral operations management has the goal of identifying ways in which human psychology and sociological phenomena impact operational performance, as well as identifying the ways in which operations policies impact such behavior.

In 2013, the following question was posed by an academic scholar trained in the normative mathematical modeling of operations research:

> *How much knowledge of Behavioral Operations (BeOps) is necessary for the field?*

Such a question would strike most people as odd. One might as well as ask how much knowledge of genetics is needed. The answer's simple: All of it. Effective decisions in a real-world context require understanding of the key elements of that context. And as any operations manager worth her salt would tell you, PEOPLE are key to OPERATIONS. Or more directly put, as a counter to the original question:

> *If we don't account for the human factor in the operational contexts we hope to manage, how can we possibly hope to manage them?*

A LITTLE BACK HISTORY

As a point of fact, the academic field of operations has long suffered from a disconnect with practical application. Many of the mathematical models, which have been the hallmark of OR scholarship, are not being applied (or even referenced) by practice. It's not a "newly recognized" problem either. The identification of and attempts to resolve this deficit go back to the founding of journals such as

Interfaces in the 1970s. Nevertheless . . . the operations scholarship-application gap remains.

To be fair, the issue is not that the models developed by OR researchers lack sophistication or complexity. There's certainly plenty of sophistication and complexity that can be built into models, and that has certainly not been ignored. What matters, though, is whether these additions actually make the models more practically relevant (read: more than incremental practical contributions). It's a selection problem, really. In the mindset of Goldratt, scholars should be looking for what is constraining the applicability of model prescriptions and actually target and address those issues, rather than modifying other aspects that do not improve throughput (think of model throughput = financially or broad, socially relevant returns on applications of that model).

We can't blame practitioners. It's not as if they are not skilled enough to interpret OR models (though granted, OR researchers often don't make it easy). Unfortunately many scholars don't find contributions to practice critical to their careers, a problem in itself that has roots in an academic reward system that tends to change at only a glacial speed. As a result, there hasn't been much of a driving force pushing practical modeling in operations. In an associated sense, there also hasn't been a push to considering the findings of other fields keenly interested in human factors (psychology and sociology fields) that could be critical to ensuring that practicality. As a result, once again . . . the operations scholarship-application gap remains.

Interestingly, this also might be argued to be the case for certain domains of operations than for any other management discipline. Given that scholarship in the other managerial fields has been growing in applicability, while at the same time characterized by a richer appreciation of the study of psychology and sociology, one has to wonder, "When did they figure this out?"

MOVING FORWARD

Thankfully the climate is changing for operations scholarship, largely through changes in the external business environment. The greatest force now augmenting operations management scholarship is the broad availability of large quantities of data. From enterprise bolt-ons that are finally effectively tapping into the vast reserves of operational data (the foundations for which were only nascent in the late 1980s), to large-scale Internet sales traffic, to ubiquitous peer-to-peer interactions and mobile applications. It's a very different place today. Practitioners see big data everywhere. They expect to see it in the recommendations they received, as evidenced by the strong analytical shift in consulting practice. Managers aren't about to blink at yet another purely math-theoretic model that isn't substantiated by their own data. They need proof that it's relevant to their particular context.

The rub is that the last decade of research into behavioral operations, leveraging this bounty of data, has shown that many of the long-standing assumptions foundational to OR models are in fact flawed, or at least significantly lacking. As a group of scholars we are finally seeing what practice has been seeing since the 1970s: The need for operations scholarship to closely re-examine and scrutinize their approach to managerial prescription. This is critical if scholars hope to stay on par with the relevance of the other managerial disciplines. Operations scholars with any interest in practice must assess which "state of the art" OR models can still be salvaged for robust application, and in which practical contexts. In all other cases (i.e., the majority), they must strive to provide modifications toward context specific application.

How to make these modifications? This goes back to the original question regarding the behavioral operations knowledge base. If human actors are present in operational contexts we are attempting to model and prescribe for, we clearly need to better understand how they create deviations from preexisting assumptions (i.e., how are they different in this context from the homogeneous, nonsocial, boundedly rational, profit-maximizing automatons that are typically assumed for model tractability).

Of course the call for change has not gone unheeded. Those scholars active in the study of behavioral operations to date have clearly demonstrated value added to the operations field as a whole. The visibility and impact of their contributions has grown in leaps and bounds over the last decade. They have led a revolution that has spawned conference colleges, top-level journal departments, and entire research centers devoted to the study. It stands as one of the most dramatic foundational shifts operations has seen in its history.

And this also is where pure scholars can learn from the best instructors in operations, who have been willing to cross the boundary into other disciplines and comment on how basic economic order quantity (EOQ) is one thing, and practice is something entirely different. The best operations management instructors follow a gainful path, incorporating psychological and sociological phenomena in their descriptions of the most fundamental aspects of the operations field, from the basics of process control to revenue management, all the way up the supply chain. It is to them that we tip our hats, since many undertook this challenge far ahead of everyone else.

GOAL AND CONTENT

The chapters contributed in this handbook represent exemplars of the efforts made by broad-minded and practice-oriented instructors and scholars, willing to break from the confines of standard models and flawed assumptions. The exercises capture aspects of the best of teaching approaches in modern practice-oriented operations management, as upheld by the top management degree programs in the world. The intention is threefold:

1. Augment core content, by offering exercises that span and expand on topics typical of core operations management instruction
2. Support elective content by offering multiple related exercises specific to a focal topic
3. Support training in practice, ensuring that the descriptions of the exercises are available and easy to leverage by those already in practice

With these goals in mind we broadly distinguish between two categories of experiential lessons: intraorganizational (i.e., phenomena characteristic of internal operations) and interorganizational dynamics (i.e., phenomena specifically characteristic to supply chain activity). We make this separation not to suggest that intraorganizational phenomena are limited to the walls of a single organization, but rather because we recognize and wish to emphasize that the supply chain-level phenomena often the subject of discussion are often fundamental artifacts of these internal phenomena. One would have a difficult time understanding supply chain-level behavioral dynamics without a grounding in the behavioral dynamics that characterize the inner workings of firms.

Our first set of learning-activity chapters (Part Two) therefore takes care to delineate a wide range of contexts in which cognitive limitations and behavioral tendencies lead to deviations in simplified economically rational behavior. In chapter 3, we start with a simple example of how a lack of experience with the interplay between fundamental operational constraints and process variance can lead to false expectations regarding system performance, and ostensibly to corrective actions that yield less than stellar results. In chapter 4 we continue to demonstrate broadly the nature of operational systems and the impact of anchoring and bias, using a unique application of a well-established Harvard Business case. Motivation is then formally introduced as an issue relevant in the design of operational work schedules in chapter 5.

Chapter 6 takes the behavioral concepts discussed in the preceding chapters and applies them to the context of quality management. The learning activity discussed demonstrates the critical role of attribution and feelings of ownership that can emerge through experience, and how expectations and subsequent behavior can be shaped by such experience. Related issues are confronted in a revenue management context in chapter 7, with a consideration of how multiple agents with distinct and often opposing objectives further complicate the dynamics observed in operations.

With the experiences from these chapters we shift gears slightly to consider more introspective, and richly descriptive, approaches to thinking about design. Chapters 8 and 9 discuss the design of processes in production and service settings, outlining activities that force participants to consider in tandem the many issues addressed in the earlier chapters. This break is intended to provide a platform for considering in more depth how various issues contribute to the complexity of the operational settings in which critical management decisions are made. Finally we capitalize on those composite descriptions and close this part with a prelude to the broader interorganizational discussions of Part Three. Chapter 10 provides and activity in which group behavioral is simulated and even the most classic of behavioral telltales (e.g., Parkinson's Law of work expansion) can be witnessed.

Part Three, focusing on activities particularly relevant to the study of supply chains, begins with a contemporary discussion of the highly popular Beer Game, by none other than the originator of the game itself (chapter 11). Chapters 12 and 13 provide activities that formally discuss biases such as pull-to-center tendencies, loss aversion, risk aversion, and mental accounting in supply chain management contexts. The relevance of framing effects on the nature of bias is also discussed. We then take a bit of a different direction in chapter 14, considering how issues such as fairness, justice, and altruism can impact the relationships and decisions made between partners in many real-world supply chain contexts.

Equity is once again discussed in an illustrative supply chain negotiation activity in chapter 15, building on considerations of framing and bias from the earlier chapters. Chapter 16 provides an intriguing discussion of Schumpterian economics and strategic core theory in an activity leveraging a supply chain-focused enterprise system simulation. We conclude the part with two capstone activity chapters (chapters 17 and 18) providing descriptions of activities intended to demonstrate the culmination of the various behavioral phenomena discussed across organizational functions and across interorganizational partnerships.

In total these sixteen chapters represent some of the best tried-and-tested methods for illustrating behavioral phenomena that we know of. We supplement each chapter with online content where possible and encourage readers to reach out to those that have designed these games with questions as well as novel extensions designed to elicit experiences that we may not have considered. The hope here is not to suggest that these are the only means by which to effectively inform practice of issues often overlooked by standard OM discussions, but rather to simply open as many doors as possible to further discussion beyond that standard.

There is a fourth, perhaps more covert, intention, though nevertheless a critical one. By making available exercises that clearly demonstrate the role of human factors in operations contexts, we hope to further inspire scholars in operations to delve deeper into the phenomena so clearly critical to assisting practice. Our concluding chapter (19) provides some thoughts to that end. We hope to advance the ideas of scholars already in the behavioral operations domain, as well as convert other operations scholars to the belief that, yes, we still have a lot to learn from (and about) other humans—even, and especially, those outside our own field. The greatest threat to the burgeoning BeOps research and instructional effort is being co-opted by those who in the name of progress simply apply early empirical findings to one-time model enhancements, declaring the human factor question CLOSED. To this we say to all others truly interested in elevating the field of operations: Keep doubting, keep asking, keep testing, keep observing, and keep the field on its toes!

PART ONE

Background and Theoretical Considerations

CHAPTER 1

The Study of Behavioral Operations

STEPHANIE ECKERD AND ELLIOT BENDOLY ■

Core to the study and consideration of behavioral operations management (BeOps) in practice and the classroom is a firm understanding of the foundations of operations management. A range of contexts is encompassed by OM research and managed in practice, including but not limited to service operations, manufacturing, supply chain, and project management. Regardless of the context in focus, certain key factors and principles receive regular attention by scholars and practitioners that bear on critical decision-making. These include the role of variability and constraints in operating processes, the impact of interdependencies among those processes, the general dynamics of stocks and flows, and the costs/return trade-offs of decision-making subject to these factors. This focus feeds the application of methods for modeling and optimizing processes, selecting the best managerial options from available options, and broadly connecting tactics to long-term strategy.

Models developed to facilitate managerial identification of problems and solutions in this domain necessarily incorporate assumptions. As George Box so aptly stated, "All Models are Wrong . . . Some are Useful" (1987). The framing traditionally undergirding operations model development encompasses the norm of rationality employed in the fields of psychology and economics. This framing describes the "rational man" as one who (1) is self-interested and concerned with wealth accumulation; (2) makes conscious, cognitive, and deliberate decisions; (3) makes decisions with full information, and can discriminate useful information from that which is not; and (4) is optimizing (Simon 1986).

More specifically, Boudreau and coauthors (2003) offered the following summary of common behavioral assumptions underlying operations models:

People are not a major factor.
People are deterministic and predictable.
Workers are independent.
Workers are "stationary" (no learning, fatigue, or problem-solving occurs).
Workers are not part of the product or service.
Workers are emotionless.
Work is perfectly observable.

While some of these assumptions appear extreme or even absurd at first blush, it is worth recognizing that traditional models would have had little hope of incorporating any kind of departure from this rational foundation given the dearth of empirical evidence bearing on these contexts at the time. Many of the results evolving from these assumptions have been useful to practice. Of course, many also fell far short of being applicable. Times have changed, spearheaded by efforts to more effectively incorporate the human element into these settings.

Behavioral operations management, as a branch of operations management, adopts a critical approach toward traditional modeling simplifications with the understanding that they are largely predicated on more fundamental assumptions regarding the capabilities of actors in these systems. People make decisions and process work—and the approaches they adopt can neither be assumed to be constant nor easily anticipated. In taking this position, BeOps aspires both (1) to identify behaviors that deviate from rational, normative theory to better design systems requiring human judgment and decision-making and (2) to advance the incorporation of behavioral or affective responses (e.g., motivation; individual differences) into operations management models to improve work outcomes such as productivity and satisfaction.

THE REFERENCE DISCIPLINES OF BEOPS

The goal of BeOps is to study human behavior as it is both impacted by and drives the effectiveness of operational designs. Although interest in these issues has been present for decades, only sporadic attention has been paid to them in research. Methodical exploration of these issues in research focused on practice is essentially nil. However, conditions for such exploration have changed in both research and practice. The emergence of large-scale data collection efforts and technologies facilitating the mining of data not previously practicably obtainable has been vital in furthering these efforts. Within this new empirical landscape researchers must be mindful of preexisting theory to guide them in these targeted explorations. Toward that end, the three principal conceptual domains that augment the BeOps knowledge-base (Bendoly et al. 2010) include cognitive psychology, social/group psychology, and system dynamics / systems thinking (figure 1.1). We examine each

Cognitive Psychology	Social / Group Psychology	System Dynamics / Thinking
Cognitive limitations on the abilities of individuals to process information make it difficult for individuals to clearly grasp true cause-effect relationship. As a result they operate with imperfect mental models of reality, and act guided by inherent biases and available heuristics.	Multiple actors complicate information processing, compelling individuals to consider the thoughts of others they collaborate or compete with, depending on incentive structures. Incomplete pictures of the mental models of others augment individual biases and the use of heuristics.	Operational process structure, constraints and variation, as well as Feedback mechanisms, reduce the likelihood of accurate mental models of cause and effect. Hence, particularly in complex operating environments, the tendencies for problematic biases and heuristics increase.
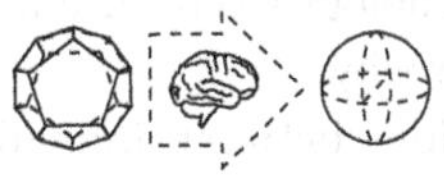 *Cognitive limits lead to limited (and often critically flawed) mental models of work contexts*	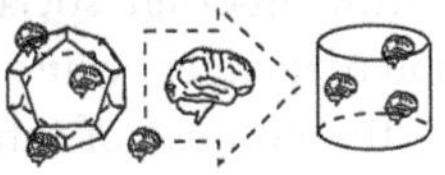 *Multiple actors + cognitive limits lead to limited views of actors and still more limited mental models of work contexts*	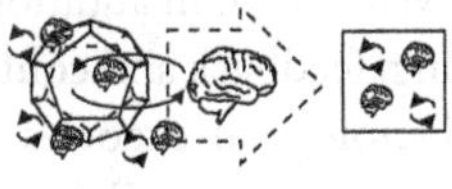 *Multiple actors in complex systems + cognitive limits (i.e. many real-world settings) lead to extremely limited mental models of work contexts*

Figure 1.1 Foundational Disciplines Supporting the Behavioral Operations Knowledge Base

of these domains in turn to illustrate the kinds of nuanced considerations typical of exploration in behavioral operations.

Cognitive Psychology

The cognitive revolution in psychology was foundational because it recognized an "operant" individual acting between a stimulus and response, capable of moderating the relationships between stimuli and responses that previously were believed to be mechanistic (Seligman and Maier 1967). Psychological and organizational behavior models (see below) had to be developed to account for unobservable, affective, and seemingly irrational individual responses. In particular, cognitive psychology addresses individuals' decision-making biases and use of heuristics to overcome bounded rationality. Heuristics are mapped to deviations in decision-making processes, and often lead to biases mapped to deviations in decision outcomes (Bendoly et al. 2010). The anchoring and insufficient adjustment heuristic falls under this domain, and is employed when people attempt to estimate unknown data points. In an operations management context, orders for inventory may be anchored to the previous period's demand and then insufficiently adjusted for in the current period (Schweitzer and Cachon 2000). Other behavioral regularities falling within the realm of cognitive psychology include framing effects and the overconfidence effect.

Social and Group Psychology

Social psychology describes how individuals relate to other individuals, and how individuals' actions are influenced by emotions (Loch and Wu 2005) and motivation (Bendoly et al. 2010). Social behavioral theories illuminate why individuals act competitively or cooperatively with one another. For example, those seeking status make decisions consistent with the achievement of recognition or position as an end goal. Status seeking as a social preference in operations management is observed in laboratory experiments where subjects are shown to be willing to sacrifice supply chain profits and efficiency in response to aggressive pricing by their supply chain partner. They reveal a willingness to forfeit profits to prevent aggressors from achieving status (Loch and Wu 2008). In addition to status, important social psychology facets include goal setting, feedback and controls, interdependency, and reciprocity.

Sociological theories define the context of interactions between individuals and groups, as well as the interactions between multiple groups, referred to as group dynamics (Forsyth 2010). The concept of groupthink fits within this body of knowledge, where individuals change their beliefs to conform to group consensus. A strong group identity, and associated groupthink, is common in team life-cycles and can prevent teams from accepting outside advice and incorporating external ideas. In operations management, product development teams can fall prey to this phenomenon and thus stall in creative and innovative efforts. Examinations of organizational and national cultural variations also are important facets of work in this area.

Organizational behavior is an applied branch of psychology that focuses on understanding human behavior in organizational settings. Organizational behavior researchers have recognized that many of the variables studied in operations management, such as process-enabling technology, lean inventories, and cross-training, are essential to understanding that setting. However, organizational behavior researchers tend to take the operations management variables as given contexts in their study of behavioral variables, such as motivation, job satisfaction, and individual differences (in, e.g., responses to technology). Although operations management researchers as far back as the 1960s (such as Norman Dudley and Ezey Dar-El) sometimes worked at the intersection between organizational behavior and operations management, an extended period of focus on normative models ignoring human behavior (as described above) characterized operations management research until the late 1990s (Doerr et al. 1996; Hayes and Hill 2001; Schultz et al. 1998). Currently in behavioral operations, researchers seek to understand the implications of behavior (and the findings of organizational behavior research) for the design of the "context" variables within the domain of traditional operations management.

System Dynamics and Systems Thinking

Consider the modeling of complex and often time-lagged interactions in systems characterized by dynamic stocks and flows, feedback loops (either human or automated), floating and variable constraints, and in some cases tipping points beyond which reinforcement can have long-term performance implications. This is all standard within the field of system dynamics. Relatedly, the study of systems thinking focuses on individuals' ability to grasp and willingness to leverage the salient features of such systems when making decisions and selecting actions. As Senge (1990, 314) put it, systems thinking involves "seeing interrelationships rather than linear cause and effect chains, and in seeing processes of change rather than snapshots."

Contemporary work in BeOps has accounted for synergies present between these two fields of study, and has leveraged their contributions in OM contexts. The relationship between system dynamics and systems thinking, as well as the potential value they bring to the study of behavioral operations, is emphasized by Bendoly (2014), who proposed that

> The literature focusing on system dynamics in particular emphasizes the importance of how system components interact, evolve, and provide a structured analytical form to these processes (Forrester 1968; Sterman 2000). Scholars of systems thinking tend to support the goals of this structuring because it suggests that the availability of "purposeful holons" (constructed abstract models of "the whole") is fundamental to the process of systems thinking. The argument is that these constructed mental and computational models of reality can be used to formally check assumptions and explicitly outline prescriptions for action (Checkland 1981; Zexian and Xuhui 2010).

Not only can the development of comprehensive systems models offer insights in the analysis of operational systems, the study of behavioral operations also critically benefits from a systematic understanding how people in those settings think about the work context in which they operate. Indeed Bendoly (2014) found that the basic tendency of project group members to think holistically can significantly benefit project-specific performance. Further, similarity in such thinking across members in project groups facilitates information and social exchanges and provides additional benefits, including psychological safety and collaborative efforts.

We argue here that systems thinking also provides an appropriate vehicle for conceptualizing the field of research in behavioral operations itself. The flow chart (figure 1.2) provides a general schematic of some of the most prevalent factors and dependencies discussed in BeOps. Note in particular the presence of feedback among these factors, dynamics that are thought to appear in some form, albeit varying in magnitude, regardless of the specific operating context or topic considered.

Operational design features are portrayed as providing levers for managers to manipulate the dynamics of any system, subject to intermediate contextual outcomes (social climate, worker skill sets, levels of work challenge) they can give rise to. However, most critically, the appropriate use of these levers cannot be determined without appreciation of the role of human behavior. The fundamental conceptual drivers of behavior include feelings of motivation and stress, perceptions and evolving mental models of the work context, and the biases and heuristics these lead to, which, in turn, govern action and performance (highlighted and broadly

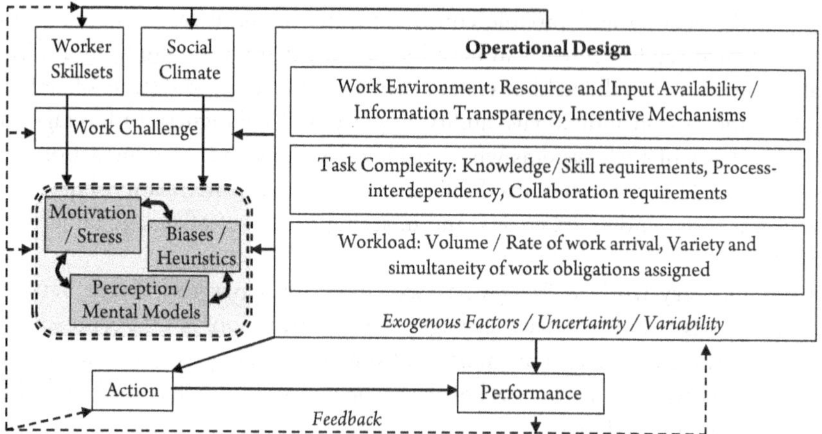

Figure 1.2 Unified Theory: Operational Design, Individual Traits, Behavior, and Action

characterized in gray in figure 1.2). These elemental concepts, fundamental to the field, are outlined in more detail in the next section, with references to contemporary applications.

ELEMENTAL BEHAVIORAL CONCEPTS IN BEOPS

Within the field of behavioral operations management, a number of concepts have been leveraged to help explain individual decision-making, among them motivation and stress, perceptions and mental models, biases, and heuristics (areas in gray highlighted in figure 1.2). Examples of motivational mechanisms include "pure" rationality, concerning monetary incentives, but also social utilities. Stress represents one of the dangerous consequences associated with incentives and other institutionalized decisions in work settings that detract from gains that motivation otherwise catalyzes. Perceptions and mental models in the presence of feelings of motivation and stress shape individuals' evolving contextual understanding, and lead to biases and heuristics as well as reinforce motivation and strain responses. Biases that result from improperly formed mental models lead to systematic deviations in decision-making, as do associated heuristics (rules of thumb) that often oversimplify the mental calculations necessary to properly evaluate scenarios and form decisions.

While much of the literature to date treats biases and heuristics as a liability, some scholars contend that these behavioral shortcuts can lead to improved decision-making (Katsikopoulos and Girgerenzer 2013). These are evolutionary mental mechanisms critical to the historical success of the human race. There is reason to believe these efficiencies can, under certain circumstances, also have utility in modern business settings. As a domain of study, behavioral operations must remain open to both the advantages and the disadvantages of human cognition and behavior.

Motivation and Stress

Motivation drives people to take action, and motivational factors can be classified into extrinsic and intrinsic motivators. Extrinsic motivators lead to a separable outcome, such as money or praise, whereas intrinsic motivators are associated with internally driven values such as learning or enjoyment (Ryan and Deci 2000). Interestingly, extrinsic motivators are not always successful in eliciting desired actions. They can actually be interpreted as dehumanizing (Etzioni 1971), insulting (Gneezy and Rustichini 2000), or possibly even "crowd out" otherwise more effective intrinsic motivations (Baron and Kreps 1999). As Alfie Kohn noted, in the book *Punished by Rewards* (1993, 243), "Like any other tool for facilitating the completion of a questionable task, rewards offer a 'how' answer to what is really a 'why' question." Some motivators intended to raise motivation also may inadvertently result in high levels of stress, with effects that run counter to—and may in fact overwhelm—any beneficial motivational gains. By better understanding workers' motivation, as well as when they experience stress, operational systems can be designed to emphasize realistic goals that are critical for success, and provide appropriate rewards and feedback to elicit desirable actions.

Research on goal setting is voluminous and expansive. To be effective, goals should be specific and not of the "do your best" variety, difficult yet reasonably attainable, and measurable (Bendoly et al. 2009). The impact of appropriate goal setting is evident in the results reported by Doerr and Gue (2013) who showed that a goal-setting procedure applied to an order fulfillment operation led to more customers receiving their orders sooner. The way in which goals are designed and implemented also can influence the development of strong norms within interdependent work groups, which enhance group effectiveness (Schultz, Juran, and Boudreau 1999). Finally, how problem-solving goals are framed at the organizational level also can lead to differential results. In a study of automotive assembly plants, those plants that positively framed problem-solving as an opportunity to learn rather than an opportunity to assign blame saw improved effectiveness of process quality improvement efforts (MacDuffie 1997).

Feedback also can have a substantive motivating effect. Consider the findings by Schultz and coauthors (1998), in which workers' output was influenced by feedback concerning the processing speeds of co-workers and inventory levels, which called into question previous modeling assumptions of independent processing times in low-inventory contexts. Moreover, feedback of this nature encourages stronger group cohesiveness (Schultz, Juran, and Boudreau 1999). However, feedback alone is not always sufficient to improve outcomes, as evidenced by Bolton and Katok (2008). In their newsvendor experiments, simply providing information regarding forgone payoffs did not drive improvements in subjects' decision-making behavior. In the forecasting literature, too much feedback, in the form of frequent updating of soft orders, often leads to counterproductive buyer outcomes; suppliers become unwilling to dedicate capacity to what they perceive as unreliable order information (Terwiesch et al. 2005).

Indeed, contemporary research in BeOps shows that the availability of regularly updated information regarding workload and other dynamic features of work contexts also can have negative behavioral effects. Bendoly and Swink (2007) demonstrated the significant magnification effect that constraint visibility can have on perceptions and sharing in controlled project management settings. Bendoly (2013) showed that certain forms of regular performance feedback can inspire stress and instigate less than optimal approaches to revenue management tasks. Bendoly and coauthors (2014) further demonstrated the deleterious effects of feedback as a driver of switching in project management settings, while Bendoly and Prietula's seminal (2008) work demonstrated the detractions that direct visibility into workload levels can have on stress and performance. The interplay of motivation and stress brought on by any variety of motivators and associated work conditions gives rise to one of the most frequently reexamined macro-phenomena of modern BeOps research—the behavioral hill (inverted U), discussed later in this chapter.

Perception and Mental Models

The extent to which individuals (and groups) feel motivated or experience stress not only can have a significant impact on their immediate work; it also can have more lasting consequences, shaping perceptions of the surrounding context and form or reinforce increasingly limited and or even critically flawed mental models of these contexts. Artifacts of these mental models include the wide variety of human biases and heuristics we now recognize as present in real-world work settings.

A mental model, or schema, is a "prototypical abstraction of a complex concept, one that gradually develops from past experience, and subsequently guides the way new information is organized" (Rousseau 2001, 513). Mental models evolve over time as individuals receive relevant information and incorporate this into the schema, but over time the mental model stabilizes and is quite resistant to change. Capturing thought processes via verbal protocol and similar process-mapping techniques can provide insight into how individuals cope and approach solutions to complex problems, as demonstrated by Gavirneni and Isen in their work with the newsvendor problem (2010). Laying this groundwork is critical if research is to identify ways in which mental models can be changed or improved. Early work by Senge (1993) highlights the importance of building shared mental models for creating a learning organization—one that is adept at sharing tacit knowledge between organizational members rather than experiencing conflict as a result of differing perspectives. This collaborative learning approach runs counter to "defensive routines" that often creep into complex problem-solving efforts, driven by an innate fear of failure (Argyris 1991). Most recently the value of such sharing has been observed empirically in the work of Bendoly (2014).

However, the sharing of mental models, and having similar systems thinking perspectives, can have drawbacks. Like all models, mental models are never perfect and can be critically flawed. If extreme similarity is present, flaws can lead to groupthink, inappropriate biases, and insufficient heuristics. This threat can be just as severe as that of extremely disparate mental models (Abilene dilemma, for example). Just as there are trade-offs between overly complex unwieldy models and those that are frugal and field-practical, there also are trade-offs between shared mindsets (ensuring psychological safety and collaboration) and conflicting mindsets (ensuring checks and balances). This golden middle ground for groups can reduce the risks individual biases and heuristics introduce. Although certainly not completely eliminating the translation of mental models into biases and the application of heuristics, effective mental model sharing can help emphasize the most effective (least problematic) available heuristics. In turn it also can help ensure that feedback mechanisms between bias and heuristic application do not (or only minimally) reinforce flawed facets of mental models.

Forms of Human Bias

Human biases are both outcomes of mental models (shared or otherwise) and mechanisms through which updates to mental models can emerge. Scholars have identified a wide range of biases that can influence decision-making tasks: *overconfidence, confirmation bias,* and *framing bias,* to name a few. Research in behavioral operations management has only begun to explore the role of biases within the span of decisions or judgments that can explain or predict behavior. Numerous research calls have pointed out myriad ways in which this research area can be moved forward.

Overconfidence occurs when individuals subjectively believe they know more than they objectively do know. One facet of the overconfidence bias is when individuals believe that their information is more precise than it actually is, called overprecision bias. This bias has the potential to impact forecasting decisions, particularly when forecasters underestimate the variance of a demand distribution (Lee and Siemsen 2014). The overprecision bias also has been analytically incorporated in the newsvendor model to demonstrate a propensity for underordering behavior with high-margin items and overordering behavior with low-margin items (Croson, Croson, and Ren 2011). Follow-on work by Ren and Croson (2014) showed direct experimental evidence of the link between overprecision and order bias. Responses on these estimation tasks show improvement from the overprecision bias when individuals are primed to think more deeply about the full distribution of their estimates before making decisions, using a technique developed by Haran and coauthors (2010).

Empirical evidence also suggests that individuals exhibiting high cognitive reflection may be less prone to ordering bias within the context of high-margin newsvendor problems (Moritz, Hill, and Donohue 2013). Researchers have identified the overconfidence bias as similarly relevant to the bullwhip problem, where its manifestation is complicated by the dynamic setting in which multiple decision-making individuals interact and feedback integrity is tenuous (Diehl and Sterman 1995; Sterman 1989a; Croson and Donohue 2006). Specific forms of overconfidence also emerge in *intellectual attribution bias* and *emotional attribution bias, situational attribution bias* and *dispositional attribution bias* (Shermer 2011).

Confirmation bias describes individuals' tendency to seek out information confirming or reinforcing their own hypotheses. Applications of confirmation bias are common in the business literature, where, for example, it has been shown to explain escalation behavior in product development decisions (Biyalogorsky, Boulding, and Staelin 2006), and is thought to be a driving factor in entrepreneurs' failure to promptly drop technologies not showing commercial promise (Lowe and Ziedonis 2006). Other opportunities for confirmation bias to influence operations management decisions include supplier selection, where metrics and data sources used to rate a favorably viewed supplier are strictly confirmatory in nature, and forecasting, where similar data sources can be selectively searched (Gino and Pisano 2008). Interestingly, even the best applied intelligence—carefully designed to avoid such confirmation bias—can upon failure be subject to poorly constructed criticism in the form of *hindsight bias*, or the advent of failure brushed aside through *self-justification bias*. Damned if you don't, damned if you do, and "damned if you could do better!"

The effects of confirmation bias also can be extended to group conditions. For example, collective confirmation bias of individual members may lead to groupthink or the Abilene Paradox. In groupthink, group members with previously disparate viewpoints come to a consensus on a decision, whereas in the Abilene Paradox verbal consensus about a decision emerges although the underlying beliefs of group members are not in cohesion. The implications to practice can be devastating. Bendoly and Cotteleer (2008) showed evidence within the context of an ERP (enterprise resource planning) implementation that members without earnest "buy-in" find passive and overt ways to buck the system, negating the benefits of implementation. Finally, in an interesting application of the system dynamics perspective, Rudolph, Morrison, and Carroll (2009) examined the problem of medical diagnoses in an operating room crisis. They developed a generalizable model demonstrating that reinforcing loops with moderate degrees of confirmation bias can actually be beneficial to problem-solving processes (2009).

Framing bias demonstrates that the way information is conveyed can impact individuals' choices. In particular, identical expected values can be presented as either gains or losses, and people tend to make risk-averse choices in gains and risk-seeking choices in losses (Tversky and Kahneman 1981). A framing bias is particularly relevant in supply chain contracting, where buyers can offer suppliers incentives framed as either bonuses or penalties. The framing has an effect on supplier effort. Specifically, contract recipients (i.e., employees, but may be generalized to suppliers) prefer contracts framed as bonuses because they are perceived as more fair (Luft 1994), but will exhibit greater effort under penalty contracts as the influence of loss aversion dominates any increases in effort achieved through fairness or reciprocity (Hannan, Hoffman, and Moser 2005). In a related negotiation setting, positively framed negotiations are more cooperative and achieve settlements with greater profitability than negatively framed negotiations (Bazerman et al. 1985; Neale and Bazerman 1985; Neale et al. 1987).

A number of other biases have been recognized in the literature, among them *central tendency bias*, *sunk-cost bias*, *risk aversion*, *status quo bias*, and *immediacy bias*. For example, participants in newsvendor experiments exhibit a clear bias of placing orders toward the demand distribution mean, acknowledged as a "central tendency bias" (Benzion et al. 2008; 2010). Risk aversion influences decision-making in a variety of contexts. Research has evaluated optimal two-part pricing strategies given buyers' degree of risk aversion (Png and Wang 2010), incorporation of consumer risk attitudes in retailer's advance-selling strategies (Prasad, Stecke, and Zhao 2011), and the implications of risk on capacity investment decisions (Van Mieghem 2003). Finally, immediacy bias has been used to explain how projects run over schedule and over budget by emphasizing immediate costs and hyperbolically discounting future costs (Loch and Wu 2005). Su (2009) also used hyperbolic time preferences to explain why "pay now, consume later" arrangements may contribute to consumer inertia. Many of these biases are intimately tied to the heuristics individuals use in decision-making.

Features of Human Heuristics

Although it is not uncommon for scholars to lump the concept of heuristics together with cognitive biases, BeOps researchers tend to distinguish heuristics as "methods through which solutions are arrived at." This is in contrast to biases, which are more meaningfully classified as "lenses through which problems and solutions are viewed." Clearly the two are intertwined byproducts of, as well as recursive accelerators of, the mental models individuals hold. In operations management, heuristics have proven practically essential because of the complexity and information requirements of many real-world decision-making contexts. The field has a rich history of heuristics research, including very well-known applications to lot-sizing problems and line balancing, for example. Early work in the management sciences concerned itself with identifying solutions to complex problems in the face of limited computing power. The development of heuristics to solve these problems represented a deviation from optimal processing, even though the heuristic solutions often still were quite complex and required computing power to solve.

Contemporary behavioral operations management continues to evaluate solutions to these classic operations problems. For example, in line balancing, *cherry-picking* occurs when underutilized resources at one workstation are deployed to assist a bottleneck workstation in order to increase system capacity. This is in line with Goldratt's Theory of Constraints (Goldratt and Cox 1992), which has been a prominent point of philosophical departure within the field for several decades. Recent research has analyzed the effectiveness of the cherry-picking approach to a novel skill-chaining method under varying environmental conditions, finding the skill-chaining method generally more robust and efficient (Hopp, Tekin, and Van Oyen 2004). Contemporary research also has begun to incorporate more well-known heuristics, such as those established in the seminal work of Tversky and Kaheman (1974): the *anchoring and adjustment heuristic* and *availability heuristic,* and apply them to a broader set of operations problems.

Anchoring and adjustment has played a key role in the emerging behavioral operations management research stream. This heuristic characterizes how people estimate information. They first start with an anchor (often an artifact itself of a shortcut referred to as the *representativeness heuristic,* and which is further often irrelevant to the decision at hand). Then, they insufficiently adjust this initial value to their final estimate. In one of the earlier contributions to the behavioral movement in OM, Schweitzer and Cachon (2000) analyzed the data from newsvendor experiments. They did this to highlight reliance on an anchoring and adjustment heuristic process in determining order quantities, anchoring on mean demand and then adjusting insufficiently toward the optimal. Since that seminal work, a flood of follow-on papers has furthered our knowledge of the "pull to center" effect in the newsvendor problem and various means of mitigating it. For example, aggregating orders over longer time periods (Bolton and Katok 2008; Lurie and Swaminathan 2009) has been identified as an effective approach.

In addition, the anchoring and adjustment heuristic has proven or may prove useful for explaining anomalies in alternate problem-solving domains, including forecasting (Harvey 2007), time estimates (and potentially cost estimates, for that matter) within product development or project development (Aranda and Easterbrook 2005), and negotiations with external supply chain partners and internally in competition over limited resources (Gino and Pisano 2008).

The *availability heuristic* leads individuals to assess the frequency or probability of an event by how readily such information is recalled or imagined. In decisions involving risk management, it is easy to see how this heuristic might come into play. While events like a labor strike at a major port or a fire completely disrupting supply of a critical component are low-probability events, the widespread and hypersensationalized news coverage of such events makes them particularly vivid and salient (i.e., available) to shareholders and managers who make decisions using this information (Hendricks and Singhal 2003; 2005). Another possible application of the availability heuristic bears on its role in individuals' perceptions of the moral intensity surrounding an ethical issue and the impact on ethical decision-making and behavior (Jones 1991; Hayibor and Wasieleski 2009). This is a topic that has particular relevance in supplier selection and management decisions, and also is subject to some of the same exaggerated media coverage as disruption events.

Another heuristic making its way into recent operations management research has been the *affect heuristic*. The affect heuristic encompasses the influence that emotions can have in the process of judgment or decision-making (Finucane et al. 2000). The role of emotions in operations contexts has been explored in the emotional contagion of groups (Yee et al. 2008), as a regulatory mechanism in social transactions (Urda and Loch 2013), and in response to conflict in the supply chain (Eckerd et al. 2013). In reality, the affect heuristic is a form of the availability heuristic, where the term "available" applies to increasingly limited cognitive resources, mental models, and heightened biases that may be salient when certain emotions (fear, pleasure, surprise, etc.) are heightened.

COMPOSITE (MACRO) PHENOMENA IDENTIFIED IN BEOPS

While motivation and stress, perception and mental models, biases and heuristics all are fundamental to theory and empirical examination in BeOps, they also are often only building blocks in the development of larger theoretical propositions and explanations of observed phenomena. Because they are present in combination in real-world settings, their combined consideration tends to yield the greatest insights into the complex nature of human behavior, decision-making, and performance. While there have been several instances published in contemporary BeOps literature in which empirical observations have been predicted or explained through the explicit additive consideration of these concepts, only a handful to date have gained much traction in the field. Nevertheless, those that have received attention highlight the potential impact that such composite theory offers. In this section we review three composite or macrophenomena that have proven particularly useful in explaining empirical observations in research and practice: the bullwhip effect, the behavioral hill (or inverted U), and resonant dissonance (see figure 1.3).

The *bullwhip effect* is far and away the most established of these macrophenomena, and illustrates a classic, complex dynamic system with feedback loops, delays, stocks-and-flows, and nonlinearity. This bullwhip phenomenon, first introduced by Forrester in 1958, is typified by an increase in order variability moving upstream in a multiechelon supply chain. Much of what we have learned about the bullwhip effect has been derived from the famous Beer Distribution Game, which models a sequential four-tier inventory system with order and fulfillments delays. Subjects in the game each assume the role of one of the echelons (retailer, wholesaler, distributor, or manufacturer), and place orders where in some executions of the game demand is nonstationary and unknown, and in others distribution is stationary and known (typically uniform [0,8]). A recent study reported by Croson and coauthors (2014) even used demand that was both known and constant, representing the most significant simplification of the game to date, yet evidence of the bullwhip effect remained.

Phenomenon	Theoretical Rationale	Empirical Studies
The Bullwhip Effect 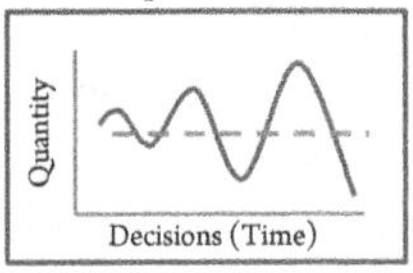 (Quantity / Decisions (Time))	Anchoring and adjustment, limited/flawed mental models, risk aversion and overconfidence. Greater information transparency and systematic understanding can significantly reduce systematic variance introduced by players.	Foundational research (Forrester. 1958, Sterman 1989a, Sterman 2000, Metters 1997) Contemporary findings (Croson et al. 2014, Shan et al. and 2014, Croson and Donohue 2006)
The Behavioral Hill (Inverted-U) 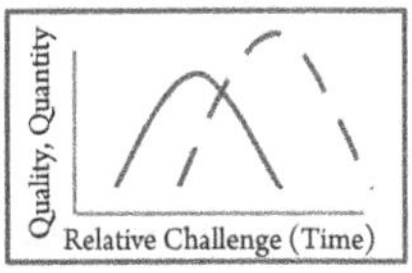 (Quality, Quantity / Relative Challenge (Time))	Goal theory, Parkinson's Law, motivation/stress, learning. Work challenges that maximize performance balance motivational gains with losses from demotivating factors (stress, work excess) and change as skill levels evolve.	Foundational research (Bendoly and Hur 2007, Linderman et al. 2007, Bendoly and Prietula 2008) Contemporary findings (Bendoly 2011, Staats and Gino 2012, Bendoly 2013, Tan and Netessine 2015)
Resonant Dissonance 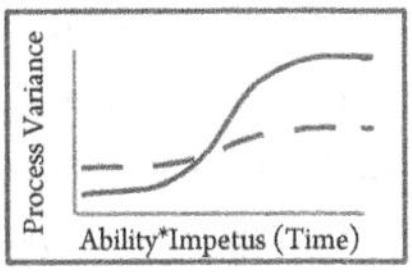 (Process Variance / Ability*Impetus (Time))	Cognitive dissonance, motivation, availability heuristic, learning. The sooner dissonance can be resolved the less the negative impact on long-run performance.	Foundational research (Festinger 1957; Bendoly and Cotelleer 2008) Contemporary findings: Bendoly et al. 2015

Figure 1.3 Popularized Composite or Macrophenomena in Behavioral Operations

Early research efforts on the bullwhip effect revealed that individuals create deficient mental models of the system in which they operate (Sterman 1989b). Because they do not accurately understand the system, individuals make orders that fail to incorporate appropriate or complete information. In the beer game, individuals consistently underweight the supply line, and this bias creates conditions of extreme inventory holdings and backlogs. Of course, individuals do not know that their mental models are flawed. In fact, Sterman (2000) reported that most players in the game blame their poor performance on the decisions of those playing the other roles. This attribution bias prevents them from updating their mental models in ways that could otherwise improve their own ordering accuracy. Further, because players' decisions depend on the decisions of others, issues of coordination risk are present. This uncertainty, similar to the uncertainties associated with demand or lead times, may provide the rationale for individuals to hold a form of safety stock—coordination stock—to hedge against it, and this stock can be successful in improving performance (Croson et al. 2014).

Bullwhip research has evaluated various additional ways in which the system could be improved, for example by enhancing feedback quality. Croson and Donohue (2003; 2006) found that sharing point-of-sale data and retailer's inventory position up the supply chain can help decrease the impact of bullwhip for those at the far upstream echelons, although these tactics do not fully mitigate the effect. The effect of shortened order and delivery lead times also has been evaluated. Results reported by Kaminsky and Simchi-Levi (1998) and Gupta and coauthors (2001) support the notion that reduced lead times lower costs across the entire supply chain. However, these findings have not been tied to reductions in the bullwhip effect derived from better decision-making.

The *behavioral hill*, or *inverted U*, is actually no less established in the field of management in general than the bullwhip effect, although the attention it has gained in the domain of operations management has been particularly heightened only in recent years. The increasing attention paid to this phenomenon has emerged as a result of recent access to large-scale operational archival data, and the blossoming of rigorous laboratory studies that the behavioral operations movement has inspired.

In simple terms, the behavioral hill, or inverted U, describes the existence of peak productivity conditions for a given worker, such that increases or decreases in a contextual factor (which in contemporary work typically boils down to the level of work challenge faced by that individual) ceteris paribus lower productivity. Empirical observations of this relationship are now common in the BeOps literature, and references to this phenomenon are now emerging in practitioner outlets (Bendoly and Sacks 2013). Bendoly and Hur (2007) provided perhaps the most definitive theoretical discussion of the kinds of competing forces that give rise to the behavioral hill.

Fundamentally, human beings respond to a range of motivators. Various motivators are present simultaneously in the context in which we work. Many are in fact correlated such that as one increases, others decline, though often this relationship is not linear. Further, certain "motivators" have multiple effects on individuals, some of which are in fact demotivating. The issue is one of magnitude. When positive effects outweigh negative effects, these seemingly "bipolar" contextual factors benefit performance. Beyond a limit, however, their negative consequences are more influential, and higher levels of such factors only further diminish motivation. The classic example that Bendoly and Hur (2007) drew on is that of work challenge. Goal Setting Theory (Locke 1968; Latham and Locke 2006) maintains that increases to the challenge of work assigned are positively related to performance, provided those challenges are viewed as falling within the capabilities of the individual set the goal. As challenge increases to become more representative of capabilities individuals feel they have, the more they are motivated to take on that apparently well-suited challenge.

In contrast, at lower levels individuals are less motivated and can display less productivity (as per Parkinson's Law). At levels seen to exceed individuals' capabilities, however, once again the lack of fit is likely to be demotivating. The overwhelming nature of excessive challenges also can lead to stress with additional detrimental performance consequences. Bendoly and Prietula (2008) demonstrated that performance-maximizing levels of challenge are not only individually sui generis, but also dynamic such that as skill levels advance, so do both performance and the performance-maximizing level of challenge.

Fit, or lack thereof, also factors into the most nascent of these macrophenomena —*resonant dissonance*. First suggested by Bendoly and Cotteleer (2008), the phenomenon is predicated on the established theoretical concept of cognitive dissonance (Festinger 1957), considered in tandem with other behavioral concepts such as motivation and the availability heuristic, in the presence of systematic feedback and learning. In its original application, resonant dissonance was used to explain how process change following an ERP implementation failed to sustain anticipated operational cost reductions, but rather saw increased workarounds and reversions to earlier process patterns. Case examinations revealed sustained dissonance held by workers regarding the perceptions of an ideal process and that which the ERP system promoted.

Initially faced with a lack of understanding (available know-how) regarding ERP-process circumvention options, which might have otherwise resolved the dissonance immediately and triggered early corrective action by management, workers viewed compliance as their only choice. However, through this forced acquiescence, dissonance was not resolved and in fact resonated across time. It served as a motivator for a specific form of learning that the firm had not counted on—dissonance deconstrainment (lifting of constraints on dissonance resolution) in the form of circumvention learning. Ultimately workers learned how to only marginally utilize the planned schema of the ERP system, and resorted to actions much more aligned with preimplementation norms. Dissonance can be temporarily buried from an operational perspective, but if not resolved can emerge in often unexpected forms that eventually degrade operational performance.

More recently Bendoly, Swink, and Shaw (2015) have observed a similar long-term behavioral role played by cognitive dissonance in multiproject settings. Faced with dissonance between tasks worked on and preferred task conditions, individuals naturally attempt to resolve dissonance via switching. Seeking out alternatives serves as a learning mechanism making the comparison of task options possible. However, switching does not always reveal superior options, and thus does not always provide the means to entirely resolve dissonance. When only perceptually inferior alternatives exist, the availability of limited (and often short-term) comparative information regarding options can lead to switchbacks (switch-and-balk activity) and the transfer or propagation of dissonance to later task work. This is work that must be dealt with at some later point. This resonant dissonance and the reencountering of undesired work passed on in previous searches is fatiguing and demotivating, consuming scarce resources. Negative performance consequences are increasingly noticeable after many failed attempts to resolve such dissonance. Resonant dissonance over time not only has the potential to motivate circumvention away from work design, but also can give rise to demotivating work-choice spirals for that same designed work.

COMMON THREADS

In consideration of the interplay among theoretical concepts in BeOps, as well as the nature of the macrophenomena in focus, it is clear that a common factor that is woven throughout: Dynamics, or perhaps more fundamentally, Time. As humans we are subject in everything we do to the consequences of time. We are present in contexts that change in time, the decisions we have to make vary in time, and critically we ourselves change through time based on what we experience, what we do, and feedback between these events. Because business operations depend on human activity, it is not surprising that the variance in performance experienced by firms is largely unaccountable if changes associated with human actors are ignored. Yet we are faced with a very long tradition of studying businesses not in a dynamic, but rather a largely static, way. We have sought differences between contexts, but have been less focused on differences within contexts over time. The vast majority of studies to date that do happen to incorporate longitudinal data operate at such high levels or with such low frequency that they offer little hope of providing understanding of the role of human behavior.

Behavioral operations has seen so much success in contributing to research and practice in recent years not because it has stayed true to these traditional methods, but because it has capitalized on two related paradigm changes: the availability of large sources of archival data rich with records of individual activity, and the availability of a variety of user-friendly computerized laboratory design applications and methods coupled with rigorous design protocols. The behavioral operations research community has been quick to adopt, seek out, and in some cases improve upon best practices in computerized laboratory design. Indeed the same principles that prove effective in collecting data on behavior in the lab also have proven useful in the classroom. The activities discussed throughout this text not only demonstrate highly effective ways of illustrating the importance of BeOps concepts to students and practitioners, they also provide a glimpse into the kinds of approaches that have been used to study human behavior.

References

Aranda, J., Easterbrook, S. 2005. Anchoring and adjustment in software estimation. Eur. Software Engineering Conference/ACM SIGSOFT Symposium. Foundations of Software Engineering, Lisbon, Portugal.

Argyris, C. 1991. Teaching smart people how to learn. Harvard Business Review, May–June, 99–109.

Baron, J., Kreps, D. 1999. Strategic Human Resources. New York: John Wiley.

Bazerman, M. H., Magliozzo, T., Neale, M. A. 1985. Integrative bargaining in a competitive market. Organizational Behavior and Human Decision Processes 35, 294–313.

Bendoly, E. 2011. Linking task conditions to physiology and judgment errors in RM systems. Production and Operations Management 20 (6), 860–876.

Bendoly, E. 2013. Real-time feedback and booking behavior in the hospitality industry: Moderating the balance between imperfect judgment and imperfect prescription. Journal of Operations Management 31 (1–2), 62–71.

Bendoly, E. 2014. Systems dynamics understanding in project execution: Information sharing quality and psychological safety. Production and Operations Management 23 (8), 1352–1369.

Bendoly, E., Cotteleer, M. J. 2008. Understanding behavioral sources of process variation following enterprise system deployment. Journal of Operations Management 26 (1), 23–44.

Bendoly, E., Croson, R., Gonçalves, P., Schultz, K. 2010. Bodies of knowledge for research in behavioral operation. Production and Operations Management 19 (5), 432–452.

Bendoly, E., Hur, D. 2007. Bipolarity in reactions to operational "constraints": OM bugs under an OB lens. Journal of Operations Management 25 (1), 1–13.

Bendoly, E., Prietula, M. 2008. In "the zone": The role of evolving skill and transitional workload on motivation and realized performance in operational tasks. International Journal of Operations and Production Management 28 (12), 1130–1152.

Bendoly, E., Sacks, M. 2013. Reducing human error in revenue management decision-making. Ernst & Young: Performance 5 (4), 30–35.

Bendoly, E., Swink, M. 2007. Moderating effects of information access on project management behavior, performance and perceptions. Journal of Operations Management 25 (3), 604–622.

Bendoly, E., Swink, M., Shaw, R. 2015. Take it or leave it: Searching, balking and dissatisfaction switching-traps in multi-project work. Working paper.

Bendoly, E., Swink, M., Simpson, W. 2014. Prioritizing and monitoring in concurrent project work: Effects on switching behavior and productivity. Production and Operations Management 23 (5), 847–860.

Benzion, U., Cohen, Y., Peled, R., Shavit, T. 2008. Decision-making and the newsvendor problem: An experimental study. Journal of the Operational Research Society 59 (9), 1281–1287.

Benzion, U., Cohen, Y., Peled, R., Shavit, T. 2010. The newsvendor problem with unknown distribution. Journal of the Operational Research Society 61 (6), 1022–1031.

Biyalogorsky, E., Boulding, W., Staelin, R. 2006. Stuck in the past: Why managers persist with new product failures. Journal of Marketing 70 (2), 108–121.

Bolton, G. E., Katok, E. 2008. Learning by doing in the newsvendor problem: A laboratory investigation of the role of experience and feedback. Manufacturing and Service Operations Management 10 (1), 519–539.

Boudreau, J., Hopp, W., McClain, J. O., Thomas, L. J. 2003. On the interface between operations and human resources management. Manufacturing and Service Operations Management 5 (3), 179–202.

Checkland, P. B. 1981. Systems Thinking, Systems Practice. Chichester, UK: John Wiley & Sons.

Croson, R., Croson, D., Ren, Y. 2011. The overconfident newsvendor. Working paper.

Croson, R., Donohue, K. 2003. Impact of POS data sharing on supply chain management: An experimental study. Production and Operations Management 12 (1), 1–11.

Croson, R., Donohue, K. 2006. Behavioral causes of the bullwhip effect and the observed value of inventory information. Management Science 52 (3), 323–336.

Croson, R., Donohue, K., Katok, E., Sterman, J. 2014. Order stability in supply chains: Coordination risk and the role of coordination stock. Production and Operations Management 23 (2), 176–196.

Diehl, E., Sterman, J. D. 1995. Effects of feedback complexity on dynamic decision making. Organizational Behavior and Human Decision Processes 62 (2), 198–215.

Doerr, K. H., Gue, K. R. 2013. A performance metric and goal-setting procedure for deadline-oriented processes. Production and Operations Management 22 (3), 726–738.

Doerr, K. H., Mitchell, T. R., Klastorin, T. D., Brown, K. A. 1996. The impact of material flow policies and goals on job outcomes. Journal of Applied Psychology 81 (2), 142–152.

Eckerd, S., Hill, J. A., Boyer, K. K., Donohue, K., Ward, P. T. 2013. The relative impact of attribute, severity, and timing of psychological contract breach on behavioral and attitudinal outcomes. Journal of Operations Management 31 (7–8), 567–578.

Etzioni, A. 1971. Modern Organizations. Englewood Cliffs, NJ: Prentice-Hall.

Festinger, L. 1957. A Theory of Cognitive Dissonance. Stanford, CA: Stanford University Press.

Finucane, M. L., Alhakami, A., Slovic, P., Johnson, S. M. 2000. The affect heuristic in judgments of risk and benefits. Journal of Behavioral Decision Making 13, 1–17.

Forrester, J. W. 1958. Industrial dynamics: A major breakthrough for decision makers. Harvard Business Review 36, 37–66.

Forrester, J. W. 1968. Principles of Systems. Cambridge, MA: MIT Press.

Forsyth, Donelson R. 2010. Group Dynamics. Cengage Learning.

Gavirneni, S., Isen, A. M. 2010. Anatomy of a newsvendor decision: Observations from a verbal protocol analysis. Production and Operations Management 19 (4), 453–462.

Gino, F., Pisano, G. 2008. Toward a theory of behavioral operations. Manufacturing and Service Operations Management 10 (4), 676–691.

Gneezy, U., Rustichini, A. 2000. Pay enough or don't pay at all. Quarterly Journal of Economics 115 (3), 791–810.

Goldratt, E. M., Cox, J. 1992. The Goal: A Process of Ongoing Improvement. 2nd ed. Croton-on-Hudson, NY: North River Press.

Gupta, S., Steckel, J., Banerji, A. 2001. Dynamic decision making in marketing channels: An experimental study of cycle time, shared information and customer demand patterns. A. Rapoport, R. Zwick (eds.) in Experimental Business Research. Boston, MA: Kluwer Academic Publishers.

Hannan, R. L., Hoffman, V. B., Moser, D. V. 2005. Bonus versus penalty: Does contract frame affect employee effort? Experimental Business Research 2, 151–169.

Haran, U., Moore, D. A., Morewedge, C. K. 2010. A simple remedy for overprecision in judgment. Judgment Decision Making 5 (7), 467–476.

Harvey, N. 2007. Use of heuristics: Insights from forecasting research. Thinking Reasoning 13 (1), 5–24.

Hayibor, S., Wasieleski, D. 2009. Effects of the use of the availability heuristic on ethical decision-making in organizations. Journal of Business Ethics 84, 151–165.

Hays, J. M., Hill, A. V. 2001. A preliminary investigation of the relationships between employee motivation/vision, service learning, and perceived service quality. Journal of Operations Management 19 (3), 335–349.

Hendricks, K. B., Singhal, V. R. 2003. The effect of supply chain glitches on shareholder wealth. Journal of Operations Management 21 (5), 501.

Hendricks, K. B., Singhal, V. R. 2005. An empirical analysis of the effect of supply chain disruptions on long-run stock performance and equity risk of the firm. Production and Operations Management 14 (1), 35–52.

Hopp, W. J., Tekin, E., Van Oyen, M. P. 2004. Benefits of skill chaining in serial production lines with cross-trained workers. Management Science 50 (1), 83–98.

Jones, T. M. 1991. Ethical decision making by individuals in organizations: An issue-contingent model. Academy of Management Review 16 (2), 366–395.

Kaminsky, P., Simchi-Levi, D. 1998. A new computerized beer game: A tool for teaching the value of integrated supply chain management. H. Lee, S. M. Ng (eds.) in Global Supply Chain and Technology Management. Miami, FL: Production and Operations Management Society.

Katsikopoulos, K. V., Girgerenzer, G. 2013. Behavioral operations management: A blind spot and a research program. Journal of Supply Chain Management 49 (1), 3–7.

Kohn, A. 1993. Punished by Rewards: The Trouble with Gold Stars, Incentive Plans, A's, Praise, and Other Bribes. Boston: Houghton Mifflin.

Latham, G. P., Locke, E. A. 2006. Enhancing the benefits and overcoming the pitfalls of goal setting. Organizational Dynamics 35 (4), 332–340.

Lee, Y. S., Siemsen, E. 2014. Task decomposition and newsvendor decision making. Working paper.

Linderman, K., Choo, A., Schroeder, R. 2007. Social and method effects on learning behaviors and knowledge creation in Six Sigma projects. Management Science 53 (3), 437–450.

Loch, C. H., Wu, Y. 2005. Behavioral operations management. Foundations and Trends in Technology, Information and Operations Management 1 (3), 121–232.

Loch, C. H., Wu, Y. 2008. Social preferences and supply chain performance: An experimental study. Management Science 54 (11), 1835–1849.

Locke, E. A. 1968. Toward a Theory of task motivation and incentives. Organizational Behavior and Human Performance 3 (2), 157–189.

Lowe, R. A., Ziedonis, A. A. 2006. Overoptimism and the performance of entrepreneurial firms. Management Science 52 (2), 173–186.

Luft, J. 1994. Bonus and penalty incentives: Contract choice by employees. Journal of Accounting and Economics 18 (2), 181–206.

Lurie, N. H., Swaminathan, J. M. 2009. Is timely information always better? The effect of feedback frequency on decision making. Organizational Behavior and Human Decision Processes 108 (2), 315–329.

MacDuffie, J. P. 1997. The road to "root cause": Shop-floor problem-solving at three auto assembly plants. Management Science 43 (4), 479.

Metters, R. 1997. Quantifying the bullwhip effect in supply chains. Journal of Operations Management 15 (2), 89–100.

Mortiz, B. B., Hill, A. V., Donohue, K. L. 2013. Individual differences in the newsvendor problem: Behavior and cognitive reflection. Journal of Operations Management 31 (1–2), 72–85.

Neale, M. A., Bazerman, M. 1985. The effects of framing and negotiator overconfidence on bargaining behaviors and outcomes. Academy of Management Journal 28 (1), 34–47.

Neale, M. A., Huber, V. L., Northcraft, G. B. 1987. The framing of negotiations: Contextual versus task frames. Organizational Behavior and Human Decision Processes 39, 228–241.

Png, I. P. L., Wang, H. 2010. Buyer uncertainty and two-part pricing: Theory and applications. Management Science 56 (2), 334–342.

Prasad, A., Stecke, K. E., Zhao, X. 2011. Advance selling by a newsvendor retailer. Production and Operations Management 20 (1), 129–142.

Ren, Y., Croson, R. 2014. Overconfidence in newsvendor orders: An experimental study. Management Science 59 (11), 2502–2517.

Rousseau, D. M. 2001. Schema, promise, and mutuality: The building blocks of the psychological contract. Journal of Occupational and Organizational Psychology 74 (4), 511.

Rudolph, J. W., Morrison, J. B., Carroll, J. S. 2009. The dynamics of action-oriented problem-solving: Linking interpretation and choice. Academy of Management Review 34 (4), 733–756.

Ryan, R. M., Deci, E. L. 2000. Intrinsic and extrinsic motivations: Classic definitions and new directions. Contemporary Educational Psychology 25 (1), 54–67.

Schultz, K. L., Juran, D. C., Boudreau, J. W. 1999. The effects of low inventory on the development of productivity norms. Management Science 45 (12), 1664–1678.

Schultz, K. L., Juran, D. C., Boudreau, J. W., McClain, J. O., Thomas, L. J. 1998. Modeling and worker motivation in JIT production systems. Management Science 44 (12), part 1 of 2, 1595–1607.

Schweitzer, M. and Cachon, G. 2000. Decision bias in the newsvendor problem. Management Science 46 (3), 404–420.

Seligman, M. E. P. and Maier, S. F. 1967. Failure to escape traumatic shock. Journal of Experimental Psychology 74, 1–9.

Senge, P. M. 1990. The Fifth Discipline: The Art and Practice of the Learning Organization. London: Random House Business.

Senge, P. M., 1993. Transforming the practice of management. Human Resource Development Quarterly 4 (1), 5–32.

Shan, J., Yang, S., Yang, S., Zhang, J. 2014. An empirical study of the bullwhip effect in China. Production and Operations Management. Forthcoming.

Shermer, M. 2011. The Believing Brain. New York: St. Martin's Press.

Simon, H. A. 1986. Rationality in Psychology and Economics. Chicago: University of Chicago Press.

Staats, B., Gino, F. 2012. Specialization and variety in repetitive tasks: Evidence from a Japanese bank. Management Science 58 (6), 1141–1159.

Sterman, J. D. 1989a. Modeling managerial behavior: Misperceptions of feedback in a dynamic decision making experiment. Management Science 35 (3), 321–339.

Sterman, J. D. 1989b. Misperceptions of feedback in dynamic decision making. Organizational Behavior and Human Decision Processes 43 (3), 301–335.

Sterman, J. 2000. Business Dynamics: Systems Thinking and Modeling for a Complex World. New York: McGraw-Hill.

Su, X. 2009. A model of consumer inertia with applications to dynamic pricing. Production and Operations Management 18 (4), 365–380.

Tan, T., Netessine, S. 2015. When does the devil make work? An empirical study of the impact of workload on server's performance. Management Science, forthcoming.

Terwiesch, C., Ren, Z. J., Ho, T. H., Cohen, M. A. 2005. An empirical analysis of forecast sharing in the semiconductor equipment supply chain. Management Science 51 (2), 208–220.

Tversky, A., Kahneman, D. 1974. Judgment under uncertainty: Heuristics and biases. Science 185 (4157), 1124–1131.

Tversky, A., Kahneman, D. 1981. The framing of decisions and the psychology of choice. Science 211 (4481), 453–458.

Urda, J., Loch, C. H. 2013. Social preferences and emotions as regulators of behavior in processes. Journal of Operations Management 31 (1–2), 6–23.

Van Mieghem, J. A. 2003. Capacity management, investment, and hedging: Review and recent developments. Manufacturing and Service Operations Management 5 (4), 269–302.

Yee, R. W. Y., Yeung, A. C. L., Cheng, T. C. E. 2008. The impact of employee satisfaction on quality and profitability in high-contact service industries. Journal of Operations Management 26 (5), 651–668.

Zexian, Y., Y. Xuhui. 2010. A revolution in the field of systems thinking: A review of Checkland's system thinking. Systems Research and Behavioral Science 27, 140–155.

CHAPTER 2

The Virtuous Cycles of Experimental Learning

ELLIOT BENDOLY ■

One of the characteristics of research in behavioral operations is that it capitalizes on an extremely wide range of methods. Moreover, the willing combination of diverse research methodologies has allowed behavioral operations research to blossom over the last decade in its innovativeness. This integrative multi-method and multidisciplinary orientation also serves the broader operations management field. It safeguards the field from becoming too introspective (an issue it has certainly faced in the past). Where mathematical models can help to improve suboptimal human decision-making, behavioral models can help to explain why humans do not act like mathematical models predict or why people find it difficult to interact with decision support systems. The behavioral methodologies provide input to further improve current operations models, not from the point of view of optimization but for increasing the quality of application in practice.

Illustrations of the multimethod and multidisciplinary perspective maintained by BeOps also can be found embedded in the lessons we teach in the classroom. The learning activity chapters within this book provide testimony to the value gained through integration of a variety of vantage points in considering the work we do in the field. In light of this emphasis it is important to take stock of the variety of methods generally applied within behavioral operations contexts. Broadly, Bendoly and coauthors (2010) classified common methods applied in behavioral operations research into five types: *normative modeling, survey methods, empirical experiments, system simulation,* and *field case studies.*

Common Methods	**Cognitive Psychology**	**Social / Group Psychology**	**System Dynamics / Systems Thinking**
Normative Modeling	◊◊◊◊◊	◊	◊◊
Survey/Archival Methods	◊◊◊◊	◊◊◊	◊◊
Empirical Experiments	♦♦♦♦♦	♦♦♦♦♦	♦♦♦
System Simulation	◊◊	◊◊	◊◊◊◊◊
Field Case Studies	◊	◊◊◊	◊◊◊◊◊

Figure 2.1 Research methods and typical alignment with reference literature applications
Adapted from Bendoly et al. (2010). Above, more diamonds represent more predominant applications of methods.

The tendency for BeOps research to apply these methods in large part depends on the primary reference literature from which the theory is drawn from (figure 2.1). Notably the robustness of empirical experimentation (in-lab or in-field; controlled, action, or natural) as a methodology allows it to support strong applications regardless of theoretical orientation. Empirical experimentation is thus positioned as an appealing complimentary method in multimethod research, and not merely a highly accessible means of demonstration (as attested to later chapters). The other methods listed above also provide unique vantage points, and thus influence the complimentary role played by empirical experimentation. We discuss each of these methods in turn and offer suggestions for the most effective complimentary application of empirical experimentation.

NORMATIVE MODELING

The method perhaps most characteristic of industrial engineering, management science, and the nonempirical branches of operations (operations research as opposed to operations management) is theoretically developed normative mathematical modeling. This includes both deterministic and stochastic forms. Philosophically, this approach to research is most akin to Aristotelian views of science, which fully leverage established (bounded) assumptions and advance models predicated on those assumptions. In general, perhaps counterintuitively, normative modeling does not require empirical justification or support. Although throwing darts doesn't fundamentally require the gift of sight . . . it does help if you want to hit the target. Certainly in more recent years the tradition of simply "building the more sophisticated theoretical model" has been replaced with the goal of "building the more practical model." The latter goal, of course, has been made possible through the combination of modeling sophistication with empirical parameterization and validation in the field.

Much contemporary examination of normative models in fact has been accomplished through controlled empirical experiments designed to provide parameters and modeling outcomes. Research has progressed this way so that the accuracy of these models as predictive of real-world cause-and-effect relationships might be substantiated. More often than not these combined methods in fact reveal flaws in normative modeling assumptions and avenues for additional research (cf. Bendoly 2011; 2013). The combination of normative modeling and laboratory-based empirical experimentation has created a virtuous cycle in which models are formed, tested, modified, and retested. The same principles can apply to classroom instruction of related topics.

FIELD CASE STUDIES

In sharp contrast to normative modeling is the field case approach, which is more akin to the Galilean observational scientific perspective ("Look then try to explain"). Often highly exploratory, field case studies approach contexts without extensive preset suppositions regarding how those contexts operate. The greatest potential of field case studies lies in the potential access they offer to extremely rich contextual details. Relationships between researchers and contacts within contexts studied often provide additional avenues of inquiry that can help to further clarify researchers' mental models. The hope is that the empirical observations themselves may illuminate phenomena otherwise not evident through purely theoretical contemplation. Indeed case studies have formed the basis of grounded models of phenomena in operations settings, contributing extensively to more targeted examinations.

These grounded models can give rise to laboratory-based empirical experimentation designed to help validate emergent theoretical reasoning from case analysis (cf. Bendoly and Cotteleer 2008). The findings of these subsequent experiments have the potential to raise new questions about the dynamics of case contexts. Thus, the relationship between researcher and their contacts remains vital. As with the empirical experimentation and normative modeling cycle, a virtuous learning cycle also can emerge between case-based grounded model development, empirical experimentation, further case examination, and subsequent experimentation.

SYSTEM SIMULATIONS

Compromises between the Aristotelian assumption that dynamics are fully understood (and thus only need mathematical examination through sensitivity analysis prior to prescription), and the kind of theoretical blank-slate that case studies empirically support, are methods that capture the spirit of each in degrees: survey/archival and simulation methodologies. System simulations continue a tradition of strong dependence on functional assumptions. But these are designed to permit examination of dynamics over time without restrictions and often without fixed assumptions regarding how causal relationships emerge. Although strong assumptions regarding the microdynamics of systems are still required (e.g., whether a specific flow is present and what laws it follows), there is often a high level of exploration associated with complex system simulations.

Contemporary research has, again, allowed these micro-level assumptions to be rigorously examined in certain contexts. This in turn has allowed for more meaningful macro-depictions through overall system simulation analysis. Validation of the presence of otherwise assumed stocks and flows, feedback loops, and constraints and the estimation of their characteristic mathematical representations (parameterizations, etc.) is supported by a variety of empirical methods including case-based, survey, and archival approaches. In recent years, given advancements in experimental design and observation, the use of empirical experiments has proven particularly valuable to this end (cf. Croson et al. 2014). In fact in the absence of this coupling with empirical experimentation, it is unlikely that system simulation as a general methodology would have generated as much contemporary interest as it has.

SURVEY AND ARCHIVAL METHODS

In contrast to simulations, survey and archival methods begin with the proposition that although theory can strongly inform the causal linkages within a model, it is the researcher's fundamental responsibility to provide empirical evidence in support of (not rejecting) the existence of those linkages among others that might alternately explain variance. This fundamental requirement is a core for developed hypotheses, whereas implications drawn from the specific magnitude of estimated effects are secondary. Hypothesized relationships between factors that are buttressed by empirical evidence subsequently become the means by which initial assumptions are strengthened, model connections refined, saliency focused upon, and prescription developed.

Unfortunately, though there are some striking examples of well-developed studies using either longitudinal survey or longitudinal archival data, the vast majority of these studies still focus on snapshot comparisons and variance analysis. While a handful of these studies are open to the consideration of nonlinear dependencies between model factors, the most characteristic relationships investigated remain linear. This stands in stark contrast to system simulation methods, which maintain a variety of nonlinear assumptions regarding the rates by which flows occur and stocks are augmented. However, survey methods can find strong synergies with empirical experimentation through a variety of approaches. Most contemporary empirical experiments are flanked by pre- and postexperimental questionnaires designed to capture data that would otherwise not be captured by the structure and specificity of the experimental design itself. Survey data collected in association with empirical experiments can be used to test against traditional risks to experimental validity and interpretation (manipulation checks, confounding checks, Hawthorne checks, etc.). They also can serve as controls in model estimation through which experimental data are otherwise designed to provide insight (cf. Bendoly et al. 2014).

In contrast, large-scale surveys often arrive at conclusions that are at odds with hypotheses initially posed. Post hoc alternative theoretical explanations are typically given to help explain why observed results differ from initial assumptions. Can follow-up empirical experiments further substantiate post hoc arguments? Can initial empirical experiments have provided advanced insight into alternative theoretical lenses before the survey was conducted? The value of multimethod research approaches can only be fully appreciated if the insight generated through one approach is used to enhance understanding that emerges through another. When research approaches are done right, contributions to the advancement of both research and practice can be substantial.

THE BEST ASPECTS OF LEARNING EXPERIMENTS

It is difficult to develop a case against the benefits of empirical experimentation, either as a primary or as a supplementary method. However, it is not our intention here to provide a primer on experimentation. Some very good sources in BeOps already exist on various aspects of experimental design (cf. Bachrach and Bendoly 2011; Katok 2011; Rungtusanatham et al. 2011, etc.). Instead, here we focus on some of the attributes of experimental best-practice to determine what these might suggest for learning activities in the classroom.

- *Identify a behavioral phenomenon of importance that is not fully understood.*

In research the benchmark for such understanding is often other researchers. Simultaneous, direct informing of practice has become increasingly appreciated in the academic literature. In teaching and training, outcomes for students and employees-in-practice have become the benchmark for learning activities. If they already "get it," there's not much point in conducting in-class activities designed to illustrate the prevalence of a particular phenomenon (e.g., if students already understand the Gamblers Fallacy, and how they—and others—might be subject to it, there's little utility in activities focusing on that issue alone). If they don't "get it" or think they do but don't, this represents an opportunity to use an engaging activity to illustrate the issue and also to collect data for further consideration.

Here it is also critical to consider the appropriate selection of participants. Just as the results of an empirical experiment can prove of little use if carried out with a sample unlikely to face the context in question, instructors need to carefully select their classroom activities to match the profile and needs of their students and trainees. Clearly, force-fitting a convenient learning activity with the wrong audience is generally poor practice. It is a waste of the instructor's and the audience's time.

- *Define specifically what you want to measure to help advance understanding.*

The adage "You can't manage what you don't measure" has been applied variously and has seen both its share of support and criticism. In practice, people manage what they don't measure all the time, just not necessarily in the best way (and sometimes fatally). Ignorance isn't bliss in this regard. Moreover, ultimately it's extremely difficult to understand unmeasured phenomena. Once again, if we are to accept that purely theoretical (or gut-feel) approaches to understanding and management are fundamentally risky, as researchers and practitioners we must recognize that at some level measurement of things that take place in the world around us is essential. Choosing the right things to measure and the right way to measure them is equally critical.

Data, if collected and examined faithfully, don't lie, even if they don't provide an entirely clear picture. Even an unclear picture is useful because it can help us determine how to change our observational approaches. Ultimately the opportunities for observation and active learning through discussion of observation can be plentiful, provided the most salient aspects of the exercise are effectively measured for the benefit of researchers, students, and instructors. When data do offer a clear picture, either in research or in the classroom, we can form understanding or adjust our mental models and have a much better chance of more intelligently managing reality. Data advance discussion and create a history upon which further discussion can build.

- *Carefully design how you plan to cleanly measure and impart understanding.*

Once you've identified what you'd like to measure, the act of measurement itself isn't simple. If a data collection is designed to operate beyond tunnel vision, the act of measurement can offer far more insights than you may have originally intended. Most methods, with the exception of case analysis and empirical experimentation, run a high risk of operating with functional blinders. Focusing on only a subset of assumed relationships and explicitly asking only a predefined set of questions (again arguing for multimethod approaches) limits the emergence of broader insight. The beauty of empirical experimentation is the opportunity to collect the kind of specific information you might need to calculate measures of interest, while also collecting a wide array of related data. In the least, these associated data can once again serve in a design check and control of analysis capacity. But it can also be examined variously to provide richer descriptions of what is actually happening.

The emergence of these benefits is predicated on designs that can meaningfully identify what the main and ancillary data represent. It is critical that accurate, unambiguous, and appropriate data are collected at the right point in time throughout an experiment. The same caution broadly applies to in-class activities designed to illustrate behavioral phenomena. If observations are not made at the right time, or if they involve data that are only tenuously related to the phenomena you are trying to portray and discuss, then both portrayal and discussion (and associated learning) will most likely fail. Pretesting a classroom activity with a characteristic set of students is just as important as pretesting an experimental protocol with a set of characteristic subjects.

With these issues in focus, we'd like to encourage instructors and trainers using this reference to be selective in their choice of in-class activities. Preview the options. Find the right mix that works for you, and of course feel free to experiment. If you find novel improvements on the activities, please let us know. We'll post recommended variants on the book's site so that other instructors can benefit from your insights. To those intrepid researchers intending to use these activities to advance the science, we make the same pledge. Here we have a fantastic and unique opportunity for both research and teaching to support and evolve in conjunction with one another. Let's take advantage of this opportunity, and let's have some fun while doing it!

References

Bachrach, D. G., Bendoly, E. 2011. Rigor in behavior experiments: A basic primer for SCM researchers. Journal of Supply Chain Management 47 (3), 5–8.

Bendoly, E. 2011. Linking task conditions to physiology and judgment errors in RM systems. Production and Operations Management 20 (6), 860–876.

Bendoly, E. 2013. Real-time feedback and booking behavior in the hospitality industry: Moderating the balance between Imperfect Judgment and Imperfect Prescription. Journal of Operations Management 3 (1–2), 62–71.

Bendoly, E., Cotteleer, M. J. 2008. Understanding behavioral sources of process variation following enterprise system deployment. Journal of Operations Management 26 (1), 23–44.

Bendoly, E., Croson, R., Gonçalves, P., Schultz, K. 2010. Bodies of knowledge for research in behavioral operations. Production and Operations Management 19 (4), 434–452.

Bendoly, E., Swink, M., Simpson, W. 2014. Prioritizing and monitoring in concurrent project work: Effects on switching behavior and productivity. Production and Operations Management 23 (5), 847–860.

Croson, R., Donohue, K., Katok, E., Sterman, J. 2014. Order stability in supply chains: Coordination risk and the role of coordination stock. Production and Operations Management 23 (2), 176–196.

Katok, E. 2011. Using laboratory experiments to build better operations management models. Foundations and Trends in Technology, Information and Operations Management 5 (1), 1–86.

Rungtusanatham, M., Wallin, C., Eckerd, S. 2011. The vignette in a scenario-based role-playing experiment. Journal of Supply Chain Management 47 (3), 9–16.

PART TWO

Lessons in Production and Service Contexts

CHAPTER 3

Synch and Swim

Managing and Mismanaging Process Constraints and Variability

ELLIOT BENDOLY ■

Note: In this the first of a series of "activity chapters," the discussion and associated activity are designed to be both concise and fairly basic. The concepts described here are built upon in later chapter discussions. It is recommended that instructors and students begin their exploration with this chapter before moving on to others.

OVERVIEW

The works of Eliahu Goldratt have had an enduring impact on the way in which many operations managers and scholars think about process design. Goldratt's Theory of Constraints emphasizes the core importance of identifying process bottlenecks, key constraints that limit system throughput. It also emphasizes potential tactics for dealing with identified constraints. This frame highlights the potentially dynamic nature of constraints, and the complex interplay between process variation and systematic constraints. "The Goal" (Goldratt and Cox 1984) describes an activity aimed at illustrating this complex relationship in a serial processing system. In reality the fundamentals of the activity can be applied to describe a wide range of operating contexts, from computer repair, to insurance claim processing, to sandwich assembly.

In this chapter the focus is on a jewelry restoration process, which illustrates these constraint and variance dynamics. A general description of the activity is provided, and two stages in which students can interact within the activity are detailed. This is followed by a brief consideration of the often counterintuitive results that can emerge from the activity. In order to help frame these results a simple computer simulation is offered to demonstrate the overall sensitivity of the system to changes in variability and constraint severity. Additional interesting modifications to the activity that have been known to redirect these dynamics are offered. Finally, additional, related behavioral phenomena that further complicate the dynamics of even the simplest of operational processes are discussed.

THEORETICAL PERSPECTIVE

In any discussion of how human behavior impacts operations, it's critical to distinguish between what is and what is not actually subject to human influence, as well as who if anyone is the source of that influence. As it turns out, there is a great deal that we, as humans, can influence within even the most automated of operational settings. Much of this influence is managerial and ultimately trickles down into the dynamics lower-level workers experience, impacting their ability to perform. Some of this human influence comes through the behavior of those workers, acting under conditions set up by managers (for better or worse). Often operational processes amplify the effects of human behavior, and obscure the connections we'd like to be able to make between action and outcomes. Unfortunately, because both higher- and lower-level human behavior can influence operational performance, we sometimes misattribute performance success and failure to the wrong actors. This can lead to blame or praise (punishment and reward) that can set yet additional behavior and action into motion, often with substantively negative consequences.

Attribution errors are in fact fairly common, and have been examined extensively in the social psychology research literature. It is now well established that as the complexity and opacity of the association between cause and effect increases, individuals are increasingly at risk of falsely attributing certain actions (and actors) with beneficial outcomes (Onifade et al. 1997). There are numerous modern explanations associated with these attribution errors, many predicated on the fact that humans have certain unavoidable cognitive limitations. These impair our ability to connect evidence in forming true understandings (correct mental models) of cause and effect.

As complexity increases, we're less likely to get it right. This is because factors such as delays between actions and outcomes (Sterman 1987; 1989) and difficulty actually measuring outcomes with a single gauge obscure complex relationships. Many real-world outcomes have many different dimensions and are difficult to sum up with a discrete metric (Diehl and Sterman 1995; Schweitzer and Cachon 2000; Bendoly 2013). Conditions also change. Even if causality is fairly fixed, changing conditions in which actions are taken and outcomes observed (characteristic of real-world dynamics) can further obscure relationships, making it still harder to develop strong models of what's actually happening (Kleinmuntz and Thomas 1987; Massey and Wu 2005).

The result of this "causal ambiguity" and potential causal misperception (Sterman 1989) can play havoc with management and also can create significant problems for workers. This is particularly true if they have any interest in resolving problems where there has been a misattribution of causal impact. Under these conditions, managers and workers may not consider unanticipated side-effects of their actions, trade-offs between subsystems and the broader system, or trade-offs between short-term and long-term performance (Forrester 1971; Sterman 2000; 2001; Bendoly 2014). Because of this, actions taken within real-world complex management settings often are viewed as having counterintuitive results. Worse yet, if the full impact of such actions can only be measured later in time, the slightest hint of positive feedback (or a lack of immediate negative feedback) can itself be misinterpreted—and acted upon—reinforcing the belief that a model of reality, although faulty, is correct. This can further serve as the foundation of an adverse phenomenon referred to as a capability trap, in which misperceived strengths are reinforced and critical capabilities starved (Repenning and Sterman 2002). In associated literature the same mechanisms can lead to what is more generally referred to as superstitious learning (Levitt and March 1988; Zolo 2009).

That having been said, there also are good reasons that we as humans are susceptible to belief in flawed causal relationships (Shermer 2012). From an evolutionary perspective, we've benefited from falling for false positives (there's a tiger in the bush, though there really isn't) rather than false negatives (there's no tiger in the bush, but there really is). False positives allow us to follow lines of thought even if eventually we are proven wrong, which is better than believing no relationships exist worth testing out. Where would the creative process be without this bias?

As managers, we also can learn from initial models. We may find we are entirely off base, but also learn new things about our setting that we would never have figured out without running with our mental models, for all their possible weaknesses. It's likely we'll be surprised, and once in a while pleasantly. If nothing else, we learn lessons about how to more finely assess our surroundings, account for delays that might connect cause and effect, and more effectively determine who's hand is really the one steering variations in performance.

CASE EXAMPLE

To examine these ideas a little further, we'll begin with a very simple setting—but one that proves effective for illustration—art or jewelry restoration. As it turns out, some art restoration projects don't take days, as often popularized in television documentaries, but rather merely hours. Hand-size metallic statuettes, pocket-sized profile paintings, antique rings, small stone carvings, glassware—all of these represent small, fairly manageable projects. They also tend to come in "sets" (collections of jewelry, sets of glass goblets, etc.). Restoration can be time consuming simply as a consequence of volume. Because many steps need repeating, regular managers of the restoration process often try to assign only specific steps to individual restoration experts (steps that they are best at).

However, workers in this setting are typically cross-trained so that if needed they can also assist with other tasks. The result is a kind of flexible restoration assembly line. The complexity that arises in these settings stems in part from the serial nature of the work, but also from inherent variation in workers' productivity and the associated constraints. It is further made more complex by the discretion workers have over what they work on. The question is whether such discretion helps or hinders the process, and whether there are more meaningful ways to target and improve the performance of the process/system as a whole.

LEARNING ACTIVITY

We'll try to get a feeling for the dynamics of this kind of a serial process by breaking a class of students into multiple groups (ideally four or more), each of five individuals (fewer would require multiple roles to be played by each individual, which also is doable). Participants are asked to imagine themselves in roles that are characteristic of one of these jewelry collection restoration processes. In this stylized rendition, the following five steps are distinguished and handled separately at their own "stations":

- **A. Disassembly**
- **B. Gem cleaning**
- **C. Metal fitting repair**
- **D. Metal polishing**
- **E. Reassembly**

All pieces of jewelry need to pass through each station in strict sequence (e.g., metal fitting repair cannot be done until gems are cleaned and remeasured). However, the time needed per station will vary (i.e., is uncertain) and in reality depends on factors such as worker skill, piece complexity, and the amount of restoration need for that piece at each particular step. There are two main consequences of this:

1. Sometimes delays at one station will mean the next station has nothing to do.
2. Those same delays can mean a buildup of incomplete work (in "buffer") at that station, which can prove cumbersome (and potentially costly if parts go missing as a result; read "shrinkage").

One potential setup for this activity might involve a multislot pill-case game board to represent each of five buffers behind each station as well as a sixth space we'll call "Completed." A paper-marquee can provide labels for stations A–E. Red bingo chips can be used to represent jewelry available for work (in buffer) by each station (as depicted in figure 3.1). A simpler setup could involve a single piece of paper divided into six sections with straight-drawn lines, with sticky-notes serving to represent pieces of jewelry at various stages of processing or having been completed. Ultimately either setup should suffice to demonstrate the system dynamics.

A six-sided die can be used to determine the amount of work each station can do in a given "turn." Each station gets a separate roll of the die, starting with station E and then moving backward to station A (completing a "round"). If the number rolled is equal to or less than the number of pieces available to the station

Figure 3.1 Layout for Process Dynamics Activity

(i.e., in the buffer behind it), then that same number of pieces will be removed from that buffer and passed forward to the buffer behind the next station. The flow of piece is therefore opposite to the flow of the die: Why? Because in a given round, station E, for example, should only have material processed in the *previous round* available to work on.

For example, if station B has four pieces in buffer and the group member at station B rolls a 3, then three pieces would be passed through station B and to the buffer behind station C. *However*, if the number rolled is greater than the number of pieces before the station (e.g., a 6 is rolled), then all of the pieces (four) from that buffer are passed on to the next station, *but no additional work* is done. Pieces processed by station E are placed on the "Completed" page.

Each group should be asked to play this out for six rounds. Before the first round begins, stations B–E should start with four pieces in buffer available, and station A will have the rest (unlimited work potential). Record each round completed by writing how many units were completed (moved to completion by the individual at station E) in a tally-bar such as the one presented in figure 3.2.

Thinking about the Initial Results

Looking at the performance of all groups in this "training" exercise may reveal something surprising. The average value of a six-sided die roll is 3.5. If that was in fact the average rolled at station E, and if there was always sufficient material to process from D on those roles, we would expect that the average throughput of six rounds to be about 6 × 3.5, or 21 units. However, a quick examination of the results (provided groups follow directions and the dice are not weighted toward the high end) typically shows the total completed by every group to be significantly lower than this number. But why?

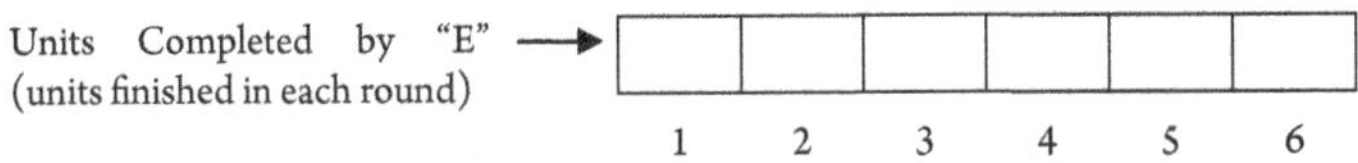

Figure 3.2 Throughput Record Form for Base Activity

Certainly there were some cases where stations/workers were partially idle, where they could have done more if had they more to work on. That in itself should raise a red flag. We missed something. In our little demonstration, we haven't really played with all the conditions that describe the setting. After all, the workers are supposed to be cross-trained, right? Couldn't one otherwise idle worker lend a hand (in this case, give her station's die roll) to another player that might have a lot more work available? In the Theory of Constraints, the elevation of constrained capacity and the subordination of other activities are suggested as possible options for improvement. The ability of workers to use discretion to shift around capacity as needed might provide a perfect setting for testing out this logic.

Modification 1: Incentive Effects

When managers see a solution (e.g., float capacity in this case) they seldom just leave it up to workers to leverage it as a mere recommendation. Managers tend to motivate such solutions one way or another. One factor that likely influences discretionary capacity reallocation by individual workers is the incentive structure under which they work (Schultz et al. 1998). For example, workers rewarded based purely on the amount of work they accomplish at their own station/step might act differently from those whose pay depends on system throughput (Bendoly et al. 2010). To test this, we could split the class in two at this point and impose one of these two distinct incentive schemes on one half, and the other scheme on the rest of the teams. Playing out the game once again, for another 10 rounds, allowing individuals to choose at each round whether they wish to use their die roll for themselves or lend it to another, should produce some interesting results. To track what takes place and how it impacts performance, a slightly more complex record-keeping system should be used, possibly along the lines as those presented in figure 3.3.

How did we do? Typical runs of 10 rounds of this version of the activity lead to fewer than 35 completed units (10 times the average roll on a six-sided die). At this point it is worth asking teams why they think "most teams" failed to achieve "average" performance.

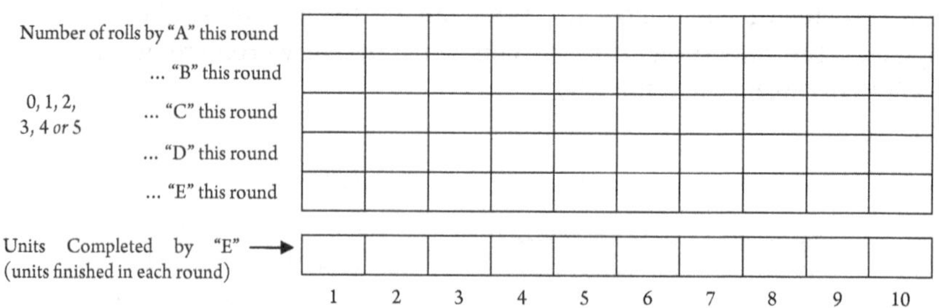

Figure 3.3 Record Sheets for Augmented Tasks

Demystifying through Simulation: Clarifying Dynamics and Sensitivity

This isn't simply a matter of uniformly bad luck, and it's not entirely the fault of people choosing to share their capacity with others. It's more fundamentally a function of the process. The fact is that there is some uncontrollable variability in worker productivity, as depicted by these die rolls. That and the fact that the serial process structure, and limited initial buffers, fundamentally constrain the work that can be processed. In fact, if we gave this same task to a computer to play out, we'd see the same results that were encountered in the class setting. It's surprisingly simple to illustrate.

The Excel workbook titled Synch&Swim.xls contains a simulation tool designed to help illustrate the general dynamics associated with this kind of a serial system in the presence of productivity variability (as in the training exercise). An image of this tool, following a simulation of 20 teams playing 20 rounds with a fair die, is presented in figure 3.4. The results should be very similar to what emerged in the class trials. Twenty rounds of an average die roll of 3.5 would lead to an average completion of 70 units, provided the final station always had enough work from D to process. Again, that's an "average." Under such myopic conditions, half of the time performance would be higher.

Of course the process we've examined is more nuanced because of the interdependency of the various steps. In fact, a typical simulation will show not a single group completing 70 units over 20 rounds. It turns out the typical 20-round completion under these conditions is only around 56 units.

How much of this is the variability is associated with the die? To figure this out, we can manipulate the range of values each die can take on with equal probability (cells D25:H26 in the first spreadsheet shown in figure 3.3). If we keep the average the same (3.5) but reduce the possible range of values (e.g., a four-sided die with the values 2, 3, 4, 5; or a coin with a 3 on one side and a 4 on the order)

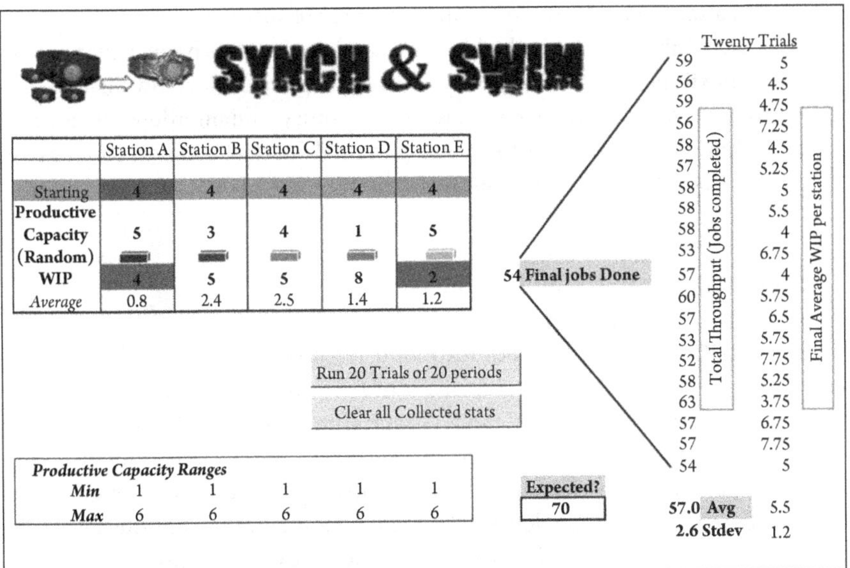

Figure 3.4 Illustration of a Simple Dynamics Simulator for This Process

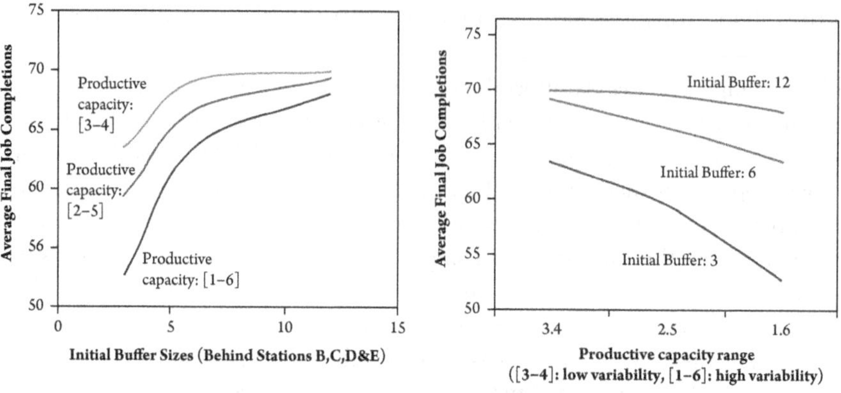

Figure 3.5 Sensitivity of Throughput to Constrain and Variability Interaction

we see the total system throughput increase markedly, particularly when the initial buffer size is fairly low (3 or 4). However, if this initial buffer is increased, we can also improve throughput. The effects of such manipulations are shown in figure 3.5 (and the second worksheet of the Excel workbook).

If we can root out inherent variability or increase inventory buffers (essentially an effort to exploit sources of constraint), we can significantly improve the performance of the process. However, neither comes free. Buffers require storage, and storage of any kind carries inherent costs. Even when units don't take up much space, they may become lost or damaged the longer they remain in unfinished storage. There's also some evidence from real-world settings that the presence of inventory can reduce effort on the part of those doing the work (hence actually reducing throughput). Reducing variability in productivity isn't simple either. Whatever tactic is used to reduce variability (e.g., training, controls, etc.) also comes with attached costs, and often no guarantee of success.

However, thinking "outside the box," we can imagine alternatives that can increase the flexibility of this kind of system. Perhaps such flexibility is all that's needed to deal with the mix of constraints, variability, and interdependency that otherwise limit the system's performance potential. With this expectation, we introduce two modifications of the in-class activity.

Modification 2: Ownership Effects

As an alternative to the first modification, it is interesting to consider an alternative behavioral dynamic. Specifically, if individual workers simply appreciate the value of system-wide performance, something indicative of efforts made by all members of a workgroup in a serial process, this in itself may influence their willingness to share (and forfeit) their own capacity. In extremely complex processes, different fundamental levels of system dynamics understanding alone can have a significant impact in this respect (Bendoly 2014). In simpler process settings, such as this, sufficient system dynamics understanding can be assumed.

However, differences in workers' perceptions of ownership may still be relevant. In particular, perceptions of ownership that extend to the work of the team as a whole can have effects similar to those of an incentive scheme.

There are various ways to create different feelings of ownership among the teams in a classroom activity of this kind. The first six rounds of the activity (the training rounds) can involve incentives to help focus half of the class on individual performance and the other half on system-wide throughput (no sharing of capacity allowed, as per the original description of the training rounds). After a simulation analysis, the incentive structure is leveled such that all teams receive incentives based 50% on individual productivity, and 50% on that of the system as a whole. The distinctions made in the training rounds may play out in surprising ways in the sharing and system performance of the final 10 rounds of play. Once again a sophisticated structure for capturing and comparing group dynamics could be useful, similar perhaps to that posed in the first modification (figure 3.3).

Additional Behavioral Factors: Relative Workload, Arousal, and Stress

As preview to some of the alternate behavioral phenomena examined in later chapters, it is worth also considering further complications to the dynamics of even simple human-managed processes. For example, recent work has shown strong evidence of an inverted-U relationship between productivity and motivation (Bendoly and Prietula 2008). When individuals are not given enough challenging work to motivate them, they tend to be uninterested and work below their processing potential (Locke and Latham 1990). This pattern has given rise to observations of "work filling time" (Parkinson 1957). In multiworker systems it also is possible that such workers voice frustration to others (whether truly warranted or not), thus encouraging higher upstream productivity to reduce the risk of insufficient work (Shultz et al. 1999). Excessive work, however, can be similarly deleterious, as this acts as a stressor and leads to inefficient handling, errors, and shutdown. These effects are not simply psychological. They are observable physiologically (Bendoly 2011; 2013). Peak performance occurs when individuals are sufficiently aroused by the challenge of their work, but not so much as to overwhelm them. What level of challenge is most suitable varies by individual and skill level (Bendoly and Prietula 2008) and these dependencies can be observed in even the simplest process. How, then, do these issues emerge in the many more complex processes that organizations manage on a daily basis?

Questions

- How did the examined modification (1 or 2) impact capacity allocation?
- How did it impact the productivity of individuals and the system as a whole?
- Can you recommend any additional policies/rules that might make capacity reallocation more effective?

DISCUSSION

The dynamics illustrated by this activity and its subsequent modifications are characteristic of effects observed in practice in much more complex settings. Too often managers focus on the nonhuman elements of systems, or attempt to reduce human psychology and sociological dynamics simply to "noise." Aside from doing a disservice to the individuals involved, this response essentially ignores the possibility of leveraging these very human characteristics. On the other hand, it's clearly easy to misinterpret the cause-and-effect relationships between human action and long-term performance. While it is widely held that incentives impact the way people approach work, the true consideration of incentives in specific operating settings is seldom rigorously assessed; often the "kind" of behavior in work that incentives encourage doesn't quite yield the results intended. If managers are intent on truly leveraging the lessons revealed by authors such as Goldratt, they need to expand their considerations to the softer elements of these systems and both the self-correcting and impeding phenomena that they imply. They need to be cautious with the mental models they form regarding human behavior, but more fundamentally they can't ignore the implications of these models. Trying new policies that attempt to influence human behavior to resolve operational problems can serve as vital lesson both about the people being managed and the inherent dynamics of the process in focus. These lessons can then be applied toward the development of more accurate mental models. Indeed the approach to mental model development, incorporating both industrial process rules and structure, as well as the predictably irrational patterns of the human agents within them (Ariely 2008), should be considered as much a process of continuous improvement as is the effort to improve operational performance in general.

References

Ariely, D. 2008. Predictably Irrational. New York: Harper Collins.

Bendoly, E. 2011. Linking task conditions to physiology and judgment errors in RM systems. Production and Operations Management 20 (6), 860–876.

Bendoly, E. 2013. Real-time feedback and booking behavior in the hospitality industry: Moderating the balance between imperfect judgment and imperfect prescription. Journal of Operations Management 31 (1–2), 62–71.

Bendoly, E. 2014. Systems dynamics understanding in project execution: information sharing quality and psychological safety. Production and Operations Management 23(8), 1352–1369.

Bendoly, E., Croson, R., Gonçalves, P., Schultz, K. L. 2010. Bodies of knowledge for behavioral operations management. Production and Operations Management 19 (4), 434–452.

Bendoly, E., Prietula, M. 2008. In "the zone": The role of evolving skill and transitional workload on motivation and realized performance in operational tasks. International Journal of Operations and Production Management 28 (12), 1130–1152.

Diehl, E., Sterman, J. D. 1995. Effects of feedback complexity on dynamic decision making. Organizational Behavior and Human Decision Processes 62 (2), 198–215.

Forrester, J. W. 1971. Counterintuitive behavior of social systems. Technology Review 73 (3), 52–68.

Goldratt, E. M., Cox, J. 1984. The Goal: A Process of Ongoing Improvement. 2nd ed. Great Barrington, MA: North River Press.

Kleinmuntz, D. N., Thomas, J. B. 1987. The value of action and inference in dynamic decision making. Organizational Behavior and Human Decision Processes 39, 341–364.

Levitt, B., March, J. G. 1988. Organizational learning. Annual Review of Sociology 14, 319–340.

Locke, E. A., Latham, G. P. 1990. A Theory of Goal Setting and Task Performance. Englewood Cliffs, NJ: Prentice-Hall.

Massey, C., Wu, G. 2005. Detecting regime shifts: The causes of under and overreaction. Management Science 51 (6), 932–947.

Onifade, E., Harrison, P. D., Cafferty, T. P. 1997. Causal attributions for poorly performing projects: Their effect on project continuation decisions. Journal of Applied Social Psychology 27, 439–452.

Parkinson, C. N. 1957. Parkinson's Law, or The Pursuit of Progress. Cutchogue, NY: Houghton Mifflin.

Repenning, N., Sterman, J. D. 2002. Capability traps and self-confirming attribution errors in the dynamics of process improvement. Administrative Science Quarterly 47, 265–295.

Schultz, K. L., Juran, D. C., Boudreau, J. W. 1999. The effects of low inventory on the development of productivity norms. Management Science 45, 1664–1678.

Schultz, K. L., Juran, D. C., Boudreau, J. W., McClain, J. O., Thomas, L. J. 1998. Modeling and worker motivation in JIT production systems. Management Science 44, 1595–1607.

Schweitzer, M. E., Cachon, G. P. 2000. Decision bias in the newsvendor problem with a known demand distribution: Experimental evidence. Management Science 46 (3), 404–420.

Shermer, M. 2012. The Believing Brain: From Ghosts and Gods to Politics and Conspiracies—How We Construct Beliefs and Reinforce Them as Truths. New York: St. Martin's Griffin Press.

Sterman, J. D. 1987. Testing behavioral simulation models by direct experiment. Management Science 33 (12), 1572–1592.

Sterman, J. D. 1989. Modeling managerial behavior: Misperceptions of feedback in a dynamic decision making experiment. Management Science 35, 321–339.

Sterman, J. D. 2000. Business Dynamics: Systems Thinking and Modeling for a Complex World. New York: McGraw-Hill.

Sterman, J. D. 2001. System dynamics modeling: Tools for learning in a complex world. California Management Review 43, 8–24.

Zollo, M. 2009. Superstitious learning with rare strategic decisions: Theory and evidence from corporate acquisitions. Organization Science 20 (5), 894–908.

CHAPTER 4

Process and Perception

Kristen's Cookie Company from a Behavioral Point of View

STEVE V. WALTON AND MICHAEL ALAN SACKS

OVERVIEW

Historically, we teach process analysis from a rational point of view. The underlying assumption of this approach is that if you understand the math, then you understand process analysis. Many of us have used an excellent case, Kristen's Cookie Company, to teach process analysis. The problem with the rational approach, and thus how we tend to teach Kristen's, is that it risks validating a set of common misconceptions about operations in general, and process analysis in particular—that people, as part of complex operating systems, are deterministic, predictable, independent, emotionless, and interchangeable (Boudreau et al. 2003).

The relatively new discipline of behavioral research in operations management acknowledges the "predictably irrational" nature of people as part of complex operating systems. Thus, teaching Kristen's from a behavioral point of view helps avoid the mistake of ignoring the dynamism inherent in the people element in process analysis. In this chapter we describe approaches to expand on the traditional way Kristen's is typically taught, including the addition of behavioral elements.

State of Management Practice

The state of management practice is bimodal in its acknowledgment of the implications of behavioral issues on process analysis. At one extreme, the position of service businesses, or service functions within manufacturing businesses, is that their work is so human-centered that it is inappropriate to apply process analysis approaches. At the other extreme, the position of mechanistic operations is that their work is so automated that there is no need to consider human implications at all. Between these extremes, many organizations tend to think of their processes mostly as machines to be optimized, even if these involve considerable human input.

In general, this leads to a set of negative behaviors, including a failure to manage interdependencies or consider variance, and doing only limited risk analysis. These behaviors in turn lead to a number of practical challenges including the misallocation of resources, unreasonable expectations placed on the operations function, missed targets, lower morale, and weakened performance.

Interestingly, a group of organizations have taken advantage of behavioral aspects in operations: those that have adopted lean, total quality management, Six Sigma, or other worker-oriented process improvement approaches. These tend to emphasize the role of human behavior in process performance and improvement, so organizations that have adopted these approaches in a meaningful way are more familiar with the implications of people in process management.

The challenge associated with the current state of management practice is that managers either tend to ignore the role of human behavior entirely, or "routinely dose their organizations with strategic snake oil: discredited nostrums, partial remedies or untested management miracle cures" (Pfeffer and Sutton 2006). People in general, and managers in particular, are unduly influenced by behavioral issues such as falling for vivid hype and marketing, overemphasizing dogma and belief over evidence, and overrelying on the results of benchmarking despite availability biases. Integrating a behavioral perspective into traditional models will enhance understanding and ultimately improve business decision-making.

THEORETICAL PERSPECTIVE

Traditional OM Theory

Boudreau, J. (2003) provided an excellent review of traditional OM theory by describing a set of embedded OM assumptions, which include the following:

1. The role of people is not an important part of OM models. In fact, many OM models look at machine performance and scheduling rules and completely ignore the fact that people are involved.
2. If people are to be considered in a model, the people are presumed to be more like the machines than people: interchangeable, with the identical skill sets, able to execute a task predictably and consistently every time, and available any time machines are available—not taking breaks.
3. There are no interpersonal dynamics between the people. There are no power struggles or agendas. People share a common vision about what the work is and how important it is.

4. There are no individual personal issues. No one is crazy, stubborn, mean, or embarrassed.
5. And from these assumptions comes a belief that human work can be modeled and measured without error.

Many sophisticated models within the operations literature routinely employ these assumptions about the role of people in their computations.

Limitations of the Traditional Approach

Assumptions such as these can greatly simplify the mathematics and enhance the power of predictive models. However, the unrealistic nature of these assumptions when applied to practice quickly becomes apparent when made explicit. In practice, people are boundedly rational, are impacted by emotion, react differently to motivations and incentives, and live and work in social systems. These complexities violate the assumptions of the more rational approach to behavior in systems, greatly weakening the effective application of such models in practice. Worse yet, managers risk significant operational problems by applying these models based on false assumptions in running their operations. A better approach would take advantage of deterministic analytical approaches while placing results firmly within the social context in which they belong.

Psychological and Sociological Studies of Human Behavior in Systems

Scholars within the fields of sociology and psychology have produced rich literature streams illuminating the many ways in which people do not behave rationally in the workplace. These approaches tend to focus on the negative or harmful ways in which human behavior disrupts operational systems. A common goal of these approaches is to critique the unrealistic nature of "hyperrational" approaches to studying human behavior within organizations. Two examples of these trends lie in the areas of economic decision-making and operations.

The popular field of economic sociology emerged as a critique of neoclassical economic arguments about human behavior in economic decision-making. The emergence of dominant economic figures such as Milton Friedman, Gary Becker, and many others focused economic arguments on elegant models of rational decision-making. The foundations of rationality in their models—that people's central goal in decision-making is to maximize short-term profit—opened the door to new literature streams dedicated to disproving this assumption. Twenty years of subsequent research in psychology followed, demonstrating that individuals are prone to common psychological biases that cause them to behave in irrational ways when making economic decisions (Ariely, Lowenstein, and Prelec 2003; Bazerman 1986; Kahneman 1992; Tversky and Kahneman 1986). In addition, economic sociology focused on "embeddedness," whereby economic decisions are embedded within social systems that shape economic behavior differently across distinct cultural settings (Granovetter 1985; Uzzi 1996).

A parallel focus took place in response to scientific management approaches within the field of operations. The scientific management movement sought to maximize the efficiency of human work through routinization of human labor processes. Popular examples include Fordism and Taylorism, which emerged as assembly lines, and other methods of mass production became commonplace. However, this trend led to new streams of research in psychology and sociology challenging the notion that human behavior can be routinized efficiently. The most famous early critique of scientific management produced the "Hawthorne Effect," whereby workers behaved differently on similar tasks depending on the extent that managers engaged in open conversations with them (Landsberger 1958). Subsequent research continued to demonstrate the many ways in which human behavior is far from efficient and scientific in operational processes (Biggart 1977; Selznick 1996).

Limitations of These Psychological and Sociological Approaches
Organizational studies have produced rich and fascinating results in the myriad ways that human behavior veers from idealized hyperrational assumptions. However, these paradigms have been criticized for their inability to replace unrealistic approaches with a substitute. This weakness has produced many calls for organizational theory to provide real-world solutions, rather than merely offering critiques. A second limitation is the inherently negative focus of these research streams. By focusing on inefficiency, irrationality, and workplace oppression, among other negative workplace experiences, these approaches have left open the question of how these legitimate concerns can be focused in a positive way. The recent emergence of positive organizational scholarship seeks to fill this void by studying the ways in which deviations from idealized behavior can lead to positive organizational outcomes (Dutton et al. 2006; Rynes et al. 2012).

Based on the review of both the operations literature and the literature in sociology and psychology, business practice in operations can be improved by incorporating insights from both literatures into the teaching of operations approaches. By relaxing the assumption that people can be modeled in ways similar to machines, research and practice can more accurately describe the impact of human behavior on process performance. We describe how one might teach process analysis in light of the fact that people naturally inject behavioral dimensions into the process.

CASE EXAMPLE

As an example of how to integrate operations with a behavioral approach, consider the maintenance operations of a major international airline. The maintenance hangar is a typical job shop, with departments ranging from engine assembly to engine testing to painting. The traditional operations focus might emphasize issues such as which departments should be closest to each other, and the optimal routing of a fixed number of maintenance jobs through a subset of the departments (e.g., five jobs through four departments).

While these are important issues, the lack of human consideration creates significant challenges. For example, the work to disassemble, overhaul, and repair and then test an engine is complex and requires trust and teamwork in the overhaul/repair and engine-testing departments. For this reason, in practice, the maintenance operation creates work teams that cross departments. Making these teams successful requires great attention to how they work with one another. When an engine is done in overhaul and repair, it doesn't simply enter the queue in engine testing. The worker that has completed the overhaul and repair has a partner in engine testing. This pair of workers always passes projects to one another, leading to the development of a relationship between these two workers. The maintenance operation is able to better meet its business objectives by explicitly acknowledging the important role of teams and the organizational culture in which the operations are embedded.

LEARNING ACTIVITIES

Teaching behavioral aspects of Kristen's begins with an assumption—that students have only limited knowledge of behavioral issues. This assumption is important, as the contribution of the approach we describe is to link behavioral issues with process analysis using Kristen's as the context. If your students are already deeply familiar with behavioral issues, then you can reduce the time spent on the behavioral aspects of the activity.

A Simulation to Set the Scene

The first activity is a small Excel simulation of a four-server waiting line. The simulation is used to draw out the fact that the basic relationship between utilization and time in line is not linear, although people typically assume that it is. The simulation can be executed in as little as 10 minutes or as long as 15, depending on whether instructors include variability in the discussion.

The simulation begins with four servers, average service rate of 36 per hour and an average arrival rate of 70 per hour, and shows the deterministic results that derive from queuing theory (time in line of 0.13 minutes, utilization rate of 49%; see figure 4.1). Students take the role of the manager of this operation and are asked whether they are satisfied with the performance of the operation. Typically someone points out that the time in line is excellent, but the utilization is too low. It doesn't take long for the group to decide they want to increase utilization, and drive up time in line, but reduce the number of servers from four to three (some students may argue that the system should be reduced to two servers, and the instructor should deflect this argument).

The instructor changes the number of servers from four to three, but, prior to pressing Enter, asks the students to speculate about what will happen to the time in line ("It will go up") and about the utilization rate ("It will go up as well"). Ask the students to speculate on how high the utilization rate will go. They will quickly settle on a number around 70%. Once they have, press Enter and the students will see that

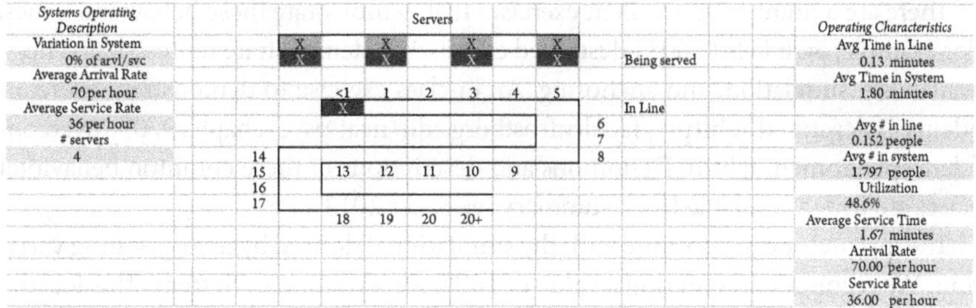

Figure 4.1 The Initial Setup of the Simulation

the time in line has risen to 0.66 minutes and utilization has risen to 65%. This first step sets up the surprise that comes in a moment.

Many students will feel that a 65% utilization rate is still too low and argue that the number of servers should now be reduced to two. The instructor agrees and asks the same two questions, but now in reverse order: What will happen to utilization rate? What will happen to time in line? Reverse the order because the change in time in line is so unexpected that the students find it shocking. The students will offer numbers around 90 seconds for the time in line. Press them to offer their "worst case" estimates. As the estimates creep up to two minutes and even five minutes, the instructor will be able to see the students getting uncomfortable that these worst-case estimates seem unrealistically high.

This comes from the fact that the students fall into three traps: they impose a linear model on an exponential relationship (between utilization and time in line), they are anchored on a very low number for time in line (0.66 minutes), and they exhibit overconfidence in their ability to think about what the worst-case scenario really looks like.

As the instructor presses Enter to change the number of servers from three to two, the visual representation of the queue (the red snake visible in figure 4.2) causes the students to verbally express disbelief. They all but cry out in surprise as the time in line jumps to nearly 29 minutes!

At this point, the instructor should emphasize that having a deterministic model is helpful, but it also is important to understand the behavioral issues that relate to the deterministic model. Specifically, the instructor can explain anchoring, overconfidence, and the tendency for people to presume that any relationship that they don't know about must be a linear relationship.

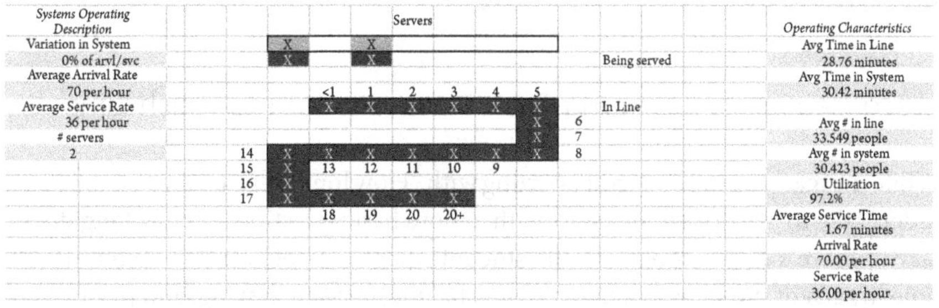

Figure 4.2 The Two-Server Model

There are a number of excellent exercises that demonstrate these behavioral issues. For example, Swinkels (2003) described exercises to demonstrate representativeness, availability, simulation, and anchoring. An in-class exercise to demonstrate overconfidence is described at http://faculty.frostburg.edu/ncat-psyc/chapter9/09_overconfidencephenomenon.htm. Definitions and descriptions of these common behavioral biases are widely available (for a summary see Sacks 2013).

The instructor can continue with the simulation if desired by incorporating variation. We recommend entering a value of 100% for Variation in System. This lets the service rate vary randomly between 36 and 72, and independently lets arrival rate vary between 70 and 140. Recalculating the spreadsheet simulates another day for the operation. We add this portion of the simulation to the class when we have more than 90 minutes to teach the case, as adding variability typically takes an additional five minutes.

Kristen's Cookie Company and Behavioral Operations

The next part of the class moves to teaching Kristen's. There are multiple versions of the case. For this discussion we refer to the case Kristen's Cookie Company (A1), HBS Case Number 9-686-093, which includes the "key questions" around which the teaching note is organized. We do this because the way that we teach Kristen's is quite similar to the teaching note, with the addition of important behaviorally oriented misperceptions that we draw out at four different points.

The general flow of the analysis is to teach (1) the basics of cycle time and start to finish time, then (2) to teach capacity measures, followed by (3) determining bottlenecks and concluding with (4) spotting shifting bottlenecks. Each of these four big ideas from the case has an associated misconception of how processes behave. (For further detail on how to teach the traditional operations models using Kristen's Cookies see Harvard Business School Teaching Note 5-688-024.) One important detail not developed in the teaching note is that for the approach described here to work, instructors must start with a "base case" of one dozen cookies per order. While the mixing bowl is big enough for three dozen, in order to best draw out the behavioral aspects the analysis must reserve the notion of an order being two or three dozen for a later point in the analysis. When a student raises the fact that the bowl holds more than one dozen, acknowledge this and suggest that it is best to begin by establishing the base case; we can expand the analysis to include multiple dozen cookies per order later in the analysis.

Misconception 1: Confusing Cycle Time with Start-to-Finish Time

While the teaching note suggests starting with "How long will it take you to fill a rush order?" the instructor should start with a more basic question—"How long does it take to make a dozen cookies?" The students quickly recognize that if you sum the time in each of the steps (mixing, traying, baking, cooling, boxing, and paying) you get a measure of how long it takes to make a dozen cookies, start-to-finish time.

However, in virtually every class, someone will suggest that the length of time it takes to make a dozen cookies depends on whether it is the first batch of the night or not. Use this issue as a way to develop the idea of cycle time, which is by definition determined by the bottleneck. Only with start-to-finish time and cycle time defined should the instructor ask how long it would take to make a rush order. By saving the question of how long to make a rush order until after the students have determined start-to-finish time, the instructor sets the stage to draw out the first misconception.

The instructor can expect the class to be nearly evenly split in thinking that it will take 26 minutes (start-to-finish time) or 10 minutes (cycle time) to complete a rush order, which demonstrates the misconception of confusing cycle time with start-to-finish time. This first misconception is used as a way to introduce the idea of flaws in thinking and their impact on how managers use process analysis results. At this point, the instructor can facilitate a debate among the class members regarding whether 26 minutes or 10 minutes is the right estimate.

Students are often quite assertive in their arguments, bolstered by the fact that each side has empirical evidence to offer as support for its claims. However, the sum of the work times in a series of stations will always equal the start-to-finish time, and in Kristen's it is always 26 minutes. After sharing this fact, the instructor can then ask the students who claimed 10 minutes why they argued with such conviction. The point of this section is to introduce potential dangers due to how people misperceive and then use evidence and fact in organizations. This is a great way to foreshadow subsequent questions that illustrate how behavioral issues affect operational decision-making.

Misconception 2: Confusing Effective Capacity and Design Capacity

The instructor can now move on to the second question in the teaching note, "How many orders can you fill in a night, assuming you are open four hours each night?" Usually a few students will answer "eight," having mistakenly taken four hours and divided it by 26 minutes. The teaching note provides an excellent description of how to use a Gantt chart to demonstrate the fact that the mixing of the second dozen ought to start while the first dozen is in the oven. At this point, students will usually settle in on a number around 22 dozen cookies per night as the capacity. This is calculated by some variant of taking 240 minutes per night, subtracting off some of the activities to reflect the system's start-up time, then dividing the remaining minutes by the 10-minute cycle time (the variability in answers derives from which particular activities students choose to subtract off).

After showing the class the correct calculation, the instructor should demonstrate an "easier" way to find capacity by taking the 240 minutes per night and dividing it by the cycle time of 10 minutes to get a capacity of 24 dozen per night. The instructor then asks, "Which one is right?" Inevitably, the class will argue that the first calculation, the one they did, is right. From the perspective of teaching an OM course, this distinction between effective capacity (22 dozen per night) and design capacity (24 units per night) can be used to introduce concepts of waste and variability that will be addressed later in the course as lean and quality management.

From a managerial perspective, one can sharpen the focus on this distinction by asking, "To which of these two numbers should you hold your staff accountable?" The class quickly realizes that the 24 dozen per night is impossible given the current configuration.

From a behavioral perspective, the instructor can now raise questions about variability in human performance specifically due to incentives and motivation. The instructor should describe how both overly difficult and overly easy goals are demotivating, and that the managerial challenge is to set goals and targets in such a way that they are challenging, without being perceived as impossible, in order to maximize performance. For example, the instructor can ask students what would happen if a manager insisted on using 24 dozen per night as a performance metric. The answer is that such a metric is likely to demotivate employees who either know this goal isn't realistic or learn so while attempting to meet it. The probable outcome is much lower performance than could otherwise be achieved without an unrealistic anchor in place. This topic often raises a rich discussion about what might impact workers' perceptions of performance targets, including social considerations and perceptual biases (e.g., like anchors).

Misconception 3: Adding Capacity to a Nonbottleneck Operation

At this point, the instructor should inform the class that it is time to move away from the base case of one dozen per order, and take advantage of the fact that the mixing bowl can hold up to three dozen cookies per batch. To raise this issue, the instructor can ask, "Would you give a discount to provide an incentive for your customers to order two dozen of the same kind of cookie?" The students will offer a variety of reasons why such a discount should or shouldn't be given. This provides the instructor with an opportunity to introduce the concept of capacity analysis by asking the class to calculate capacities and utilizations as the metrics to compare the impact of orders of one dozen versus two dozen cookies. Table 4.1 shows an example of the table that can be used to organize this discussion.

As the instructor completes the analysis on the board, students quickly realize that the oven remains the bottleneck and that total capacity for the system remains 24 dozen per night, even though the capacity for both you and the roommate has gone up. This demonstrates the third misunderstanding. Increasing capacity at a nonbottleneck operation does not increase system throughput.

From a behavioral perspective, the instructor can emphasize the fact that people struggle to connect cause and effect, which leads to a fallacy of "Any action is better than no action." To draw out this lesson, the instructor can tell the story about adding capacity to mixing and traying, using language that resonates with most people with working experience.

> It would be like your boss coming up to you and saying, "We don't have the budget to get another oven right now, but I can give you two more people in the mixing department, and I just need you to get it done for me."

Table 4.1. AN EXAMPLE OF CAPACITY ANALYSIS

One dozen per order scenario			
Resource	**Time per order**	**Capacity**	**Utilization**
You (mix, tray)	6 + 2 = 8	240 / 8 = 30	24 / 30 = .80
Roommate (timer, box, pay)	1 + 2 + 1 = 4	240 / 4 = 60	24 / 60 = .40
Oven	10	240 / 10 = 24	24 / 24 = 1.00
Two dozen per order scenario			
Resource	**Time per order**	**Capacity**	**Utilization**
You (mix, tray, tray)	6 + 2 + 2 = 10	(240 / 10) × 2 = 48	24 / 48 = .50
Roommate (timer, box, timer, box, pay)	1 + 2 + 1 + 2 + 1 = 7	(240 / 7) × 2 = 68	24 / 68 = .35
Oven	10	240 / 10 = 24	24 / 24 = 1.00

Given the analysis the students have completed, they see immediately that this logic is flawed, and that no amount of effort will allow the employee to "get it done." At the same time, students with work experience can hear an instance where a boss has approached them with a variant of the above sentence. This provides an opportune lesson about the importance of asking the right questions and focusing on the most useful data in operational decision-making. A good way to end this portion of the discussion is to ask, "If you really want to increase throughput, what needs to happen?" This question is particularly effective because a number of students will likely have been lobbying for a second oven for a while, and it perfectly sets up the next teaching block.

Misconception 4: Doubling Capacity at a Bottleneck

To move into the final teaching block, the instructor asks the students to re-create their capacity analysis, as presented in table 4.1, for the case where there are two ovens. To highlight the final misconception, the instructor should ask, "With two ovens, what is the system's capacity?" Most students will with great gusto answer 48 dozen per night, twice the capacity of the one-oven case, which is incorrect, as now the roommates have become the bottleneck. This discussion moves very quickly, as students recognize that adding a second oven doesn't change the available capacity for either you or the roommate, but does double the capacity of the oven. From an operations management perspective, the instructor will emphasize the lesson that doubling the capacity of a bottleneck operation does not double system capacity, as in most instances the bottleneck shifts to a different resource.

From a behavioral perspective, the instructor can revisit the impact of anchors on decision-making to help explain why the above misconception is so common. Anchoring is especially powerful when a number, object, or idea of great vividness is in focus. In this case, students focus intently on the impact of installing a second oven and overly emphasize the 48 dozen per night, so much so that most lose sight of all the other analysis they have done to this point.

Concluding the Case Discussion

From here, the instructor has a number of options, depending on how much time can be devoted to this case. For example, if the class has already studied variability in business processes and included variability in the opening simulation, the instructor could explore what happens with Kristen's if the time estimates are not deterministic but are stochastic. This follows nicely from the just-finished conversation about shifting bottlenecks.

For most instructors, this will be a good place to conclude the discussion. The conclusions should focus on drawing out the primary operational learning outcomes, similarly to what is described in the teaching note. The addition of the behavioral dimensions to the analysis gives instructors the opportunity to reemphasize the importance of both the analytics of process analysis and the human elements associated with process analysis.

DISCUSSION AND CONCLUSION

Students' reactions to teaching Kristen's in this way is very interesting. Many are surprised that behavioral issues could have anything to do with such a seemingly straightforward operations exercise. Having introduced students to the overlap between human behavior and operations through this activity, instructors will find students much more open to further discussing this topic throughout the class. Students with work experience very quickly understand how the analytics of process analysis are improved by including behavioral issues. Practitioners tend to ask a variant of the question, "How do I get my boss to understand this?"

When teaching undergraduates, instructors can leverage the fact that less experienced students tend to view human irrationality as random, unpredictable, and unmanageable. By incorporating human bias in the Kristen's exercise, students begin to see how errors in judgment are both predictable and actionable. Improved understanding of why these issues arise and how people tend to act when they do arise positions students to be proactive in consideration of the importance of human behavior in operational contexts.

References

Ariely, D., Loewenstein, G, Prelec, D. 2003. Coherent arbitrariness: Stable demand curves without stable preferences. Quarterly Journal of Economics 118 (1), 73–105.

Bazerman, M. 1986. Judgment in Managerial Decision Making. New York: John Wiley & Sons.

Biggart, N. 1977. The creative destructive process of organizational change: The case of the post office. Administrative Science Quarterly 22, 410–428.

Boudreau, J., Hopp, W., McClain, J. O., Thomas, L. J. 2003. On the interface between operations and human resources management. Manufacturing and Service Operations Management 5 (3), 179–202.

Dutton, J., Worline, M., Frost, P., Lilius, J. 2006. Explaining compassion organizing. Administrative Science Quarterly 51 (1), 59–96.

Granovetter, M. 1985. Economic action and social structure: The problem of embeddedness. American Journal of Sociology 91 (3), 481–510.

Kahneman, D. 1992. Reference points, anchors, norms, and mixed feelings. Organizational Behavior and Human Decision Processes 51 (2), 296–312.

Landsberger, H. 1958. Hawthorne Revisited: Management and the Worker, Its Critics, and Developments in Human Relations in Industry. New York: Cornell University Press.

Pfeffer, J., Sutton, R. I. 2006. Evidence-based management. Harvard Business Review 84 (1), 62–74.

Rynes, S., Bartunek, J., Dutton, J., Margolis, J. 2012. Care and compassion through an organizational lens: Opening up new possibilities. Academy of Management Review 37 (4), 403–423.

Sacks, M. A. 2013. Cognitive biases in decision-making. V. Smith (ed.) in Sociology of Work: An Encyclopedia. Thousand Oaks, CA: Sage Publications.

Selznick, P. 1996. Institutionalism "old" and "new." Administrative Science Quarterly 41 (2), 270–277.

Swinkels, A. 2003. An effective exercise for teaching cognitive heuristics. Teaching of Psychology 30 (2), 120–122.

Tversky, A., Kahneman, D. 1986. Rational choice and the framing of decisions. Journal of Business 59 (4), 251–278.

Uzzi, B. 1996. The sources and consequences of embeddedness for the economic performance of organizations: The network effect. American Sociological Review 61 (4), 674–698.

CHAPTER 5

Outflanking Undecided, Ever-Changing Puzzles

The Role of Human Behavior in Scheduling

WOUT VAN WEZEL, KENNETH N. McKAY, AND TONI WÄFLER ■

OVERVIEW

Scheduling encompasses the allocation of firm resources to various tasks and activities (Leung 2004; Pinedo 2012). This involves decisions about priorities, timing, staff assignment, and allocating machines to manufacturing operations. Most people will recognize the result from a scheduling process, which include, for example, Gantt charts, dispatch lists, and staff schedules. Scheduling is usually classified as a complex problem. Even small scheduling problems have a huge number of alternatives from which to choose. Because computers offer a very good means to evaluate and check many alternatives in a short time, since the 1960s scientific research in scheduling has been dominated by operations research. However, scheduling also is an organizational process where human planners perform a variety of activities such as information gathering and interpretation, communication, puzzle-solving, and negotiation with different stakeholders. In this chapter, we discuss the tasks and activities that human schedulers perform, how they cooperate and coordinate their work, and the role played by computer support in this process.

Schedules specify the timing of activities and determine, for example, which people work in what shift, when raw material is purchased, the moment that production of an order starts and needs to be finished, and how finished goods are transported to customers. Therefore, scheduling has a considerable impact on organizational performance. The combination of being a complex problem and having a large performance impact makes scheduling a popular research topic. Many thousands of articles and dozens of textbooks have been written on scheduling from various disciplines and perspectives. To introduce and anchor the role of humans in scheduling, we briefly describe a number of perspectives using the work of Gupta (2002), who summarizes the history of scheduling research by discussing various scheduling paradigms:

- "Might is right": there is no explicit deliberation on the scheduling problem; the decision-maker relies on organizational power and just tells employees what to do.
- "Don't keep the machine idle": scheduling is solved by accepting orders based on machine capacity, avoiding machine down time. Scheduling is centralized, using Gantt charts to schedule and track progress.
- "Tell them what to do": shop floor supervisors are given aggregate quantities (the "what") and are responsible for scheduling their own department (the "when").
- "Divide and conquer": the application of mathematics to scheduling problems. Because the problems are generally too complex to solve completely, assumptions are made that might not be realistic but that at least lead to scheduling problems that can be solved.
- "Too complex, too expensive": researchers realize that mathematics will not lead to solutions for all scheduling problems. Cases where the worst-case scenario would not be solvable were no longer subject to intense investigation.
- "Something is better than nothing": researchers working in the "too complex, too expensive" paradigms retained focus on analytic solution procedures to find optimal solutions for stylized scheduling problems. Simultaneously, others developed approximate solution procedures, such as heuristics for problems that could not be tackled analytically, working from the idea that some improvement in the objectives is better than nothing at all. This led to solution procedures that were practically applicable, increasing acceptance of scheduling research in practice.
- "Give them something to decide": the advent of enterprise resource planning (ERP) and decision support systems (DSS) gave scheduling algorithms a context. Decision-makers could now provide input to the algorithms and interpret and change the output. This further increased the use of scheduling algorithms in practice.
- "Why bother": Because scheduling problems are too complex to solve, the production system should be designed such that scheduling is not needed. An example is just-in-time production.
- "Let the computer tell us": The complexity of scheduling problems provides a challenging context for approaches in artificial intelligence. Several techniques have been extensively researched for use in

> scheduling. These include, for example, rule-based expert systems, constraint satisfaction, and genetic algorithms. Although successful for some scheduling problems, these techniques have not shown general applicability.

The scheduling paradigms clearly follow scientific developments in management research, respectively management science, operations research, MRP/ERP/DSS, lean production, and artificial intelligence. Each paradigm is vulnerable to criticism. Analytic optimization approaches solve nonexisting problems, heuristics do not solve to optimality, automatic learning algorithms in artificial intelligence are black boxes that can give unpredictable results, and so on. However, I would like to emphasize that the paradigms are not mutually exclusive. Each still exists and each has its own specific context within which it can be employed successfully.

During the past several decades, parallel to these scientific developments, research in behavioral and organizational aspects of scheduling has been a relatively small but stable niche. Interestingly, a recurring theme is the gap between scheduling theory and scheduling practice, including, for example, Pounds (1963), Conway, Maxwell, and Miller (1967), Miller (1987), McKay, Safayeni, and Buzacott (1988), Buxey (1989), Kleinmuntz (1990), Waters (1990), Hofstede (1992), MacCarthy and Lui (1993), Higgins (1996), LaForge and Craighead (2000), Herrmann (2006), and Pinedo (2012). Although the influence of the various research paradigms is clearly present in practice, scheduling theory attends to only a small part of the work of human schedulers. Empirical research focused on scheduling situations—without exception—reveal that scheduling involves much more than merely solving a puzzle. Consequentially, quarreling over the best way to solve this puzzle is of essential, but limited, value to most companies. For example, an early description of the scheduling task explicitly notes that planners have to anticipate future difficulties and discount them (Coburn 1918). Anticipation does not fit well in any of the dominant scheduling paradigms, because it involves difficult-to-model things like imaginative speculation, creativity, weighing risk, and empathy with stakeholders.

Although being in a relative research niche, behavioral research in scheduling has yielded considerable knowledge on how organizational scheduling processes take place in organizations and how human schedulers think and operate in these contexts. This chapter discusses results from a number of methodologies that have been applied, including, for example, longitudinal case studies, surveys, experiments, and cognitive task analyses.

CASE EXAMPLE

In contrast to other chapters in this text I will postpone theoretical discussions until after I've had a chance to set the stage with a short case example. The case exemplifies the activities involved in the creation of a schedule, based on an office furniture manufacturer (De Snoo et al. 2011; De Snoo, Van Wezel, and Wortmann 2011). This case is used in the scheduling game described later in the chapter.

The make-to-order office furniture manufacturer processes about 150 client-specific orders each day. Twenty-five sales agents are responsible for order procurement. Roughly 30,000 product parts are purchased from a large group of suppliers and used in the three manufacturing departments: metalworking, painting, and assembly. The standard lead time of work in progress is five days (figure 5.1): one day for each of the manufacturing departments, one day for testing, and one day for loading and transport. The sixth day is used for delivery (figure 5.1).

Over 200 operators work in the departments in multiple shifts. Each department is managed by a production manager and several foremen. The production manager is not involved in the daily operations, but is responsible for implementing long- and mid-term strategy and developing staff schedules. The foremen act as information hubs between the schedulers and the operators. They work as operators at the various workstations but have the extra responsibility to communicate information to and from the schedulers.

Metalworking consists of 40 workstations. Production orders have different routings, and orders are produced in batches. The batch size depends on order size and available capacity. The products from the metalworking department are painted and powder-coated at painting. Two powder-coating lines are available. One of these lines is highly flexible but not efficient, and one requires long cleanup and setup times but is faster and thus suitable for large batches. The assembly department operates seven assembly lines. Both self-produced components and purchased parts from suppliers are assembled into final products and packaged for delivery to customers.

Each manufacturing department has its own scheduler (figure 5.2). The main task for the schedulers is to cluster orders on certain dates and to assign them to work cells or production lines. Each department has a different preference for the sequence of production. For example, the painting department likes to combine all orders that need to be painted black because they have to clean the whole painting line when they switch colors. However, the metalworking department prefers to combine all orders that have the same material thickness so they have to set up their bending machine only once.

The resulting schedules are released to the shop floor daily. The schedules specify what work needs to be done on what day for each department for several days. In general, the order of activities during the day does not matter so departments can determine an efficient sequence for themselves. This is an example of the "Tell them what to do" paradigm as discussed by Gupta (2002). An exception is rush orders that need to be pushed through several departments on one day. These orders are discussed during a work meeting early in the morning.

In addition to creating schedules, the schedulers are confronted with many requests to change existing schedules because of all kinds of events like rush orders,

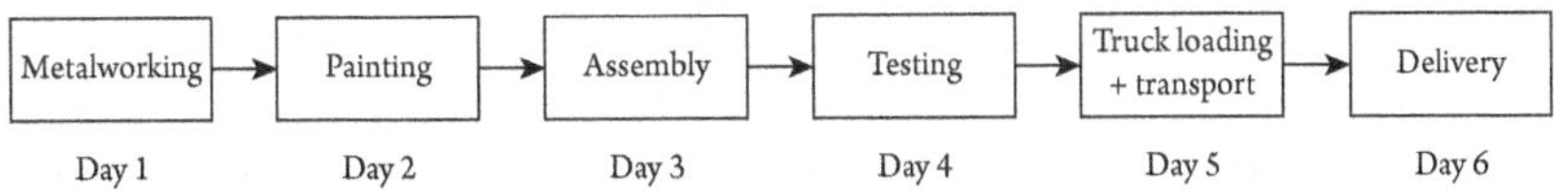

Figure 5.1 Lead Time for Departments

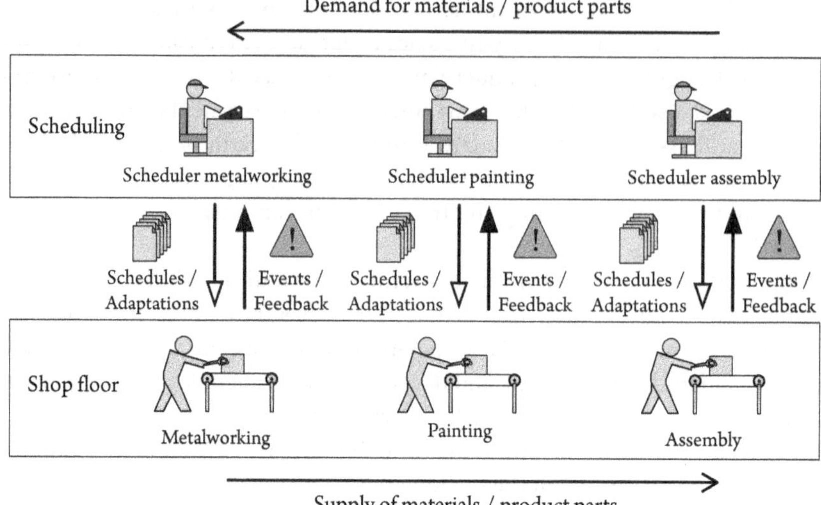

Figure 5.2 Flow of Material and Information

order changes, material supply problems, and machine failures. Based on new information from (among others) salesmen, product developers, suppliers, and foremen, the schedulers modify the schedules and communicate changes to the operators. De Snoo and coauthors (2011) measured all interactions on a typical day in the company and found that 220 interactions took place between schedulers and others, taking from two to four hours per day. Because the schedulers were not located on the production floor, most communications took place by phone. De Snoo, Van Wezel, and Wortmann (2011) reported that relocation to the production floor led to more face-to-face collaborative communication, which improved scheduling effectiveness.

Delivery reliability is the most important performance objective. A special job function, the "troubleshooter" or "order chaser," urges schedulers to schedule and operators to produce products that have to be delivered soon. The firm realizes an average delivery reliability rate of more than 95%.

In our case study, it is possible to have late orders, which is important. For some industries such as the automotive supply chain, it is not acceptable to create a plan that has any late orders, and constraint relaxation techniques are used to ensure that an assembly plant will not be shut down. If lateness is strictly forbidden, the relevance of traditional scheduling heuristics encompassing lateness is questionable.

The company faces various complex scheduling problems. Each of the 150 daily orders includes a multitude of operations. For example, a table needs legs that must be cut, bent, and welded in the metalworking department; cleaned, painted, and varnished in the paining department; and assembled in the assembly department. One order of 50 tables involves hundreds of activities. Multiply by 150 orders and the factory faces thousands of manufacturing activities per day, which is too many to create a detailed schedule for. The scheduling department resolves this limitation by first dividing the scheduling tasks over multiple schedulers. Second, the problem is made smaller by not scheduling every activity.

For example, the schedulers do not specify an exact starting and ending time, but rather specify the day on which a production order needs to be completed. Rather than determining all start and end times for each activity in a department, they only have to specify which orders need to be produced on a given day.

THEORETICAL PERSPECTIVE

Why Scheduling Problems Are Difficult

Since the advent of computers, scheduling research has been dominated by operations research (Muth and Thompson 1963; Pinedo 2012). Computers can compare thousands of alternative schedules per second and can identify constraint violations in schedules that are too large to comprehend by human schedulers. Five basic properties of information make it impossible to investigate all possible scheduling solutions.

- The first is related to *numerical complexity*. Many scheduling problems are "NP-complete." Such problems always need an approximation algorithm to solve in reasonable time (Pinedo 2012). Using approximation means that the solution found is not necessarily the optimum solution. This results in a trade-off between speed and solution quality. The major focus of scheduling research is related to this trade-off.
- The second is *timing disparity of information*. Sometimes, a decision is needed before all required input is available. For example, the lead time of raw material of a manufacturer might be longer than the lead time offered to customers. The result is that supply and demand need to be decoupled.
- The third is *information uncertainty* or inexactness. For example, a recipe in a cookie factory might specify that ingredients need to be mixed for two minutes, but this could be an average. The actual time can depend on the quality of raw material, temperature, humidity, and so on. For scheduling, it is important whether we know the characteristics of uncertainty or not. Scheduling algorithms can take this into account by combining the various uncertainties and by calculating worst-case and best-case scenarios.
- The fourth is the *interpretation of information in its social context*. This subtle and perplexing property is best expressed through example. In one of our visits to a factory, a machine needed an emergency repair at 4:00 p.m. The customer needed to be informed because the order would be shipped late. When we asked the scheduler why he did not immediately inform the customer, he told us that he would wait until 6:00 p.m. His manager would have left for home, and he would call the customer himself. The schedulers at the customer would also have left, and his call would be forwarded to the warehouse. By experience he knew that the warehouse would not have a problem with a late

delivery. If he called his own manager now, the communication with the customer would follow the official route, which would lead to commotion and a dissatisfied customer. These circumstances are very specific to the time of the machine disruption and the specific customer. This kind of information is often time related, dynamic, and based on personal relationships and gut feelings, which makes it impossible to quantify, formalize, and put into formal procedures or use in scheduling algorithms.

- The fifth is information *inaccessibility*: information needed to create a schedule is unavailable at the time that the planning organization and support are designed. Many assumptions need to be made in the face of incomplete information. Decisions are made with best guesses about what is actually where, what the quality is, and how much has been completed.

These five properties underlie scheduling. Roughly, the following mechanisms are used to handle these complexities (figure 5.3).

A first is *task division* of scheduling tasks aligned to the time horizon or cognitive workload. To reduce numerical complexity and to mitigate timing disparity, companies have traditionally used hierarchical decision-making (Anthony 1965). This means that first decisions are made in aggregate for times in the future. This is the planning, scheduling, dispatching hierarchy first documented in the early 1900s and still used today. Within any time horizon, task division can also be related to numerical complexity. The problem can simply be too large for one scheduler to handle for any time period. The second mechanism is *scheduling algorithms*. Algorithms follow prespecified steps to create schedules, can very quickly compare multiple schedules, and can calculate these with compound uncertainties better than humans can. The third is the *human planner*. The first two mechanisms can be designed and formally structured into day-to-day processes. However, using inaccessible or context-sensitive information in a design is by definition impossible. This results in the need for human planners to regulate and handle information flows that cannot be prespecified. The fact human planners play a role in the scheduling process implies that the other mechanisms (hierarchy, task division, algorithms) need to incorporate this role, which is where behavioral operations comes into play.

Table 5.1 describes some examples of each of the complexity factors for different kinds of scheduling.

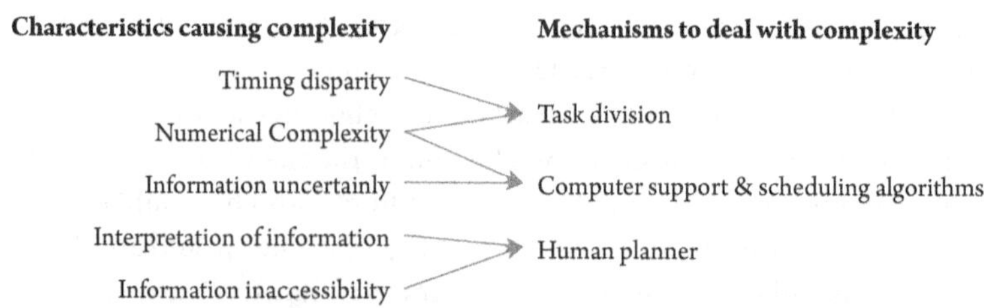

Figure 5.3 Complexity of Scheduling

Table 5.1. Examples

	Manufacturing scheduling	**Transportation scheduling**	**Project planning**
Timing disparity	Lead time of purchasing raw material is longer than lead time of own delivery.	Logistics companies need to hire trucks and drivers before actual transportation orders are known.	People often work in multiple projects simultaneously; they need to reserve capacity before activities start.
Numerical Complexity	N jobs on M machines	What product in which truck? Sequence of stops.	People (being a resource constraint) work in multiple projects simultaneously.
Information uncertainty	Speed and yield of chemical processes	Speed of trucks; traffic jams	Task duration
Interpretation of information	Responsibility for meeting due dates if multiple departments are involved	Delivery time windows	Quality of the outcome of activities
Information inaccessibility	Exact available capacity; maintenance schedules	Flexibility of time windows at customers; options for overutilization of trucks	Possibilities for overtime of employees

Information inaccessibility and interpretation require that human schedulers be included in the scheduling process. The next section describes the results of empirical research on the human role in planning and scheduling.

Behavioral Aspects of Planning and Scheduling

A Comprehensive Model of Scheduling

Despite the advantages of scheduling algorithms, they often are underutilized. Tenhiälä (2011) reported that only 25 of 89 companies in his survey used finite loading techniques, and a survey reported by Jonsson and Mattsson (2003) showed that only 20 of the 54 manufacturing companies used finite capacity scheduling. This theory/practice gap orbits the following (provocatively stated) positions. On the one hand, operations researchers take the position that modeling unsolvable problems is useless. On the other hand, this claim is refuted by organizational scholars who state that it is useless to solve nonexistent problems. To bridge these opposing views, we need to frame scheduling not only as a problem to solve but also an organizational process that needs to be managed.

Scheduling resembles a sociotechnical network (Wäfler 2001), where the social element consists of human planners and others who, while having no formal role in planning, nonetheless have an impact on planning (e.g., shop floor supervisors or warehouse clerks). The technical element consists of IT systems (e.g., ERP and advanced planning systems).

Scheduling encompasses a variety of tasks and activities including information gathering and interpretation, communication and negotiation with different stakeholders, puzzle-solving, decision-making, and problem-solving (Jackson, Wilson, and MacCarthy 2004; Kreipl and Pinedo 2004; MacCarthy and Wilson 2001a; McKay, Safayeni, and Buzacott 1995b; McKay and Wiers 2006; Van Wezel, Van Donk, and Gaalman 2006). In practice, there are no clear-cut design criteria that prescribe how scheduling processes should be organized. To anchor theory that describes scheduling task design, we first describe what the typical week of a human scheduler might look like in the office furniture factory described in the case example.

- On Monday/Tuesday the scheduler starts to collect all the data needed to create a schedule for the following week. Information about goals and constraints the schedule should obey is needed. This includes actual and expected orders, delayed production from the previous week, available inventory, expected deliveries, machine availability, staff availability, and expected results from this week.
- On Wednesday, a preliminary schedule is made. Various departments can set different and often conflicting goals and constraints, regarding production lead times, service costs, and staff workload. Schedulers have to balance these different interests and communicate and negotiate with these stakeholders. Alternative schedules are developed and choices are made. The starting point is the due dates promised to customers; minimizing due date violations is often a primary concern. A hard constraint is that all material must be available. Somewhat softer constraints are the availability of operators, hours of overtime, scheduled maintenance, and so on. Material availability can be a soft constraint if delivery can be expedited by the supplier.
- On Thursday, the preliminary schedule is discussed with the operations manager, the sales manager, and the shop floor foremen. Decisions must be made bearing on what orders will miss the due date, how maintenance will be scheduled, what setups are necessary, and how much time they take.
- On Friday, the schedule is released and the shop floor can start to prepare for the next Monday.

In many factories, there is a stark contrast between tasks as they are described and the activities that are actually performed. In past decades scheduling has been analyzed using various paradigms, including natural decision-making, sociotechnical system design, and cognitive ergonomics. The late 1980s and early 1990s saw a surge of empirical research in planning and scheduling, including Crawford and coauthors (1999), Higgins (1999), McKay (1992), McKay, Safayeni, and Buzacott (1995a; 1995b), Mietus (1994), Nakamura and Salvendi (1994), Stoop and Wiers (1996), Wiers (1996), and Van Wezel (2001). Collections of papers can be found in the edited volumes of MacCarthy and Wilson (2001a) and Fransoo, Wäfler, and Wilson (2011). In this section, we describe a model that encompasses many of these empirical models. The model is based on the framework reported by Jackson, Wilson, and MacCarthy (2004) and has three parts: a categorization of tasks that the scheduler needs to perform, the roles in which these tasks are performed, and the schedulers' external environment.

Jackson, Wilson, and MacCarthy (2004) describe three kinds of tasks:

- Formal tasks: the tasks as formally specified in the job description
- Maintenance tasks: informal activities that the scheduler performs to maintain his or her position, for example, check sources of information
- Compensation tasks: glitches in the formal structure need to be mitigated; for example, wrong information in the information system, people that refuse to work together, and so on

Jackson, Wilson, and MacCarthy (2004) propose that the work of the scheduler also has multiple roles:

- Interpersonal role: This role represents the human scheduler who needs to maintain his or her position in the interpersonal network, for example, exchanging favors or mediating between stakeholders.
- Informational role: The scheduler holds a central position in the information hub; formal and informal information is needed to create a schedule that is accepted by stakeholders. Because of this, organization members know that the scheduler has a clear sense of the state of the factory, the order portfolio, and production progress.
- Decisional role: Three types of decision-making include predicting and solving problems, allocating resources (i.e., creating the actual schedule), and handling disruptive events.

The task categorization does not describe what schedulers actually do. The tasks they describe are collections of related activities that are goal directed. Scheduling activities are usually depicted as problem-solving, and the most basic view is that schedulers follow a Plan-Do-Check-Act problem-solving cycle. Although a scheduling problem is rarely unique, it is also rarely exactly similar to a previously solved problem. Meystel (2006) described a multilayer, multiresolutional recursive "elementary loop of functioning," with a cycle of (1) sensing, (2) sensory processing, (3) building a model based on a combination of the sensory input and both generic and specific knowledge, (4) generating behavior, (5) enacting the behavior, and then (1) sensing the new state again. Hoc (2006) provided a conceptually similar model based on Rasmussen's step ladder (Rasmussen, Pejtersen, and Goodstein 1994), which includes anticipation and abstraction in the reasoning processes during planning.

We follow the activities in the cycle, noting that multiresolutional recursion, anticipation, and abstraction can be part of each activity:

- Problem formulation, opportunity identification, and isolation: why are we planning? An issue, demand, or opportunity to address? (skills in this activity, and the process involved are discussed in Volkema 1983).
- Outcome definition: what are we planning? A company reorganization, a new product launch, or a production run in the factory (e.g., Caves 1980)?
- Quality of outcome (goal) specification: what are the factors that define success? Will it be cost, improved time to market, delivery targets, market share, shareholder value, or quality goals? Will the expected outcomes include nebulous concepts such as innovation (e.g., Mumford, Bedell-Avers, and Hunter 2008)?
- Generation of the plan: the most effective and efficient sequence of actions and activities for organizational resources to follow that will achieve the desired goals, taking risks and uncertainty into account.
- Plan evaluation, approval, and project launch: a particular plan is agreed upon and activities are launched.
- Implementing, monitoring, and maintenance of the plan: as time proceeds, how good is the plan? Does the plan need modifications and, if so, what are the changes? What are the links between plan evaluation and implementation (e.g., Nutt 2007)?
- Closure of the plan: knowing when the outcomes are achieved (or will not be) and understanding the quality of the planning and execution. Knowing what to do next, if there is a "next."

Note that, similar to tasks and roles, the activities do not include any domain specificity. The activities are necessary in all kinds of planning environments (e.g., manufacturing, routing, staff scheduling). Jorna (2006) showed that such an abstraction is viable. His research shows that human schedulers solving scheduling problems in different domains used comparable tactics and activities, for example, counting, checking constraints, relaxing constraints, using visual aids, and so on. Hoc (2006) similarly showed that operators in different domains apply similar strategies (abstraction and anticipation) while rescheduling under time pressure. This is not to say that schedulers can easily transfer from one domain to another, but does indicate that lessons learned in one context can apply to other contexts.

Tasks, roles, and activities are all aspects of the work of individual schedulers. Because no single individual does all of the planning/scheduling in an organization, planning often is not an individual task but is distributed across several human planners that can be organized into a dedicated planning department or distributed throughout various units (e.g., each manufacturing department has its own dedicated planner). There are four important organizational elements in schedulers' tasks: (1) how do schedulers divide their work if there is more than one scheduler, (2) how are their tasks are integrated into the overall organization,

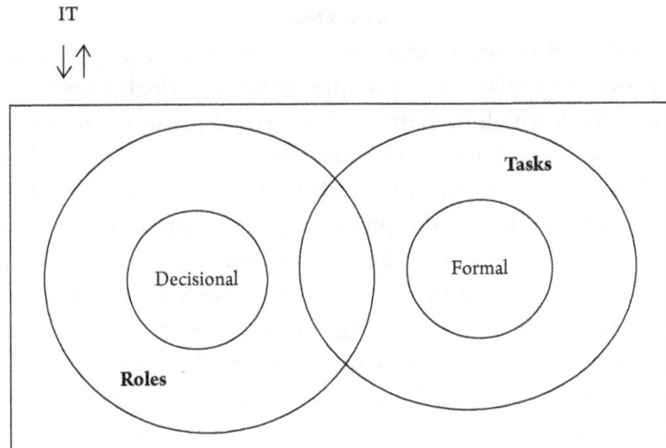

Figure 5.4 Traditional Model of the Scheduling

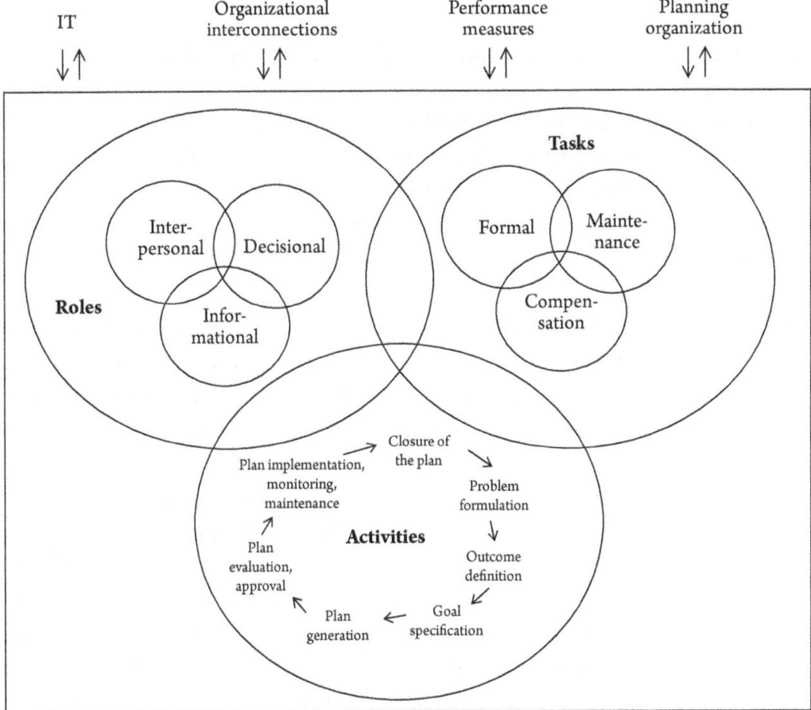

Figure 5.5 Behavioral/Organizational Scheduling
SOURCE: Adapted from Jackson, Wilson, and MacCarthy 2004.

(3) how is the quality of their work measured by management, and (4) how is scheduling supported by decision support systems.

Figure 5.4 depicts the traditional view on scheduling. A scheduler makes and adapts schedules using IT. Figure 5.5 shows the comprehensive scheduling model. Although definitive models cannot be provided, we discuss existing empirical research contributing to the model.

Individual Planning Task Performance

Cognitive models of planning show how problem-solving, planning, and information processing relate. Several approaches in scheduling have been inspired by the way in which humans solve personal planning problems such as making a shopping list, planning a holiday, or playing chess (Van Wezel, Jorna, and Meystel 2006). Das, Karr, and Parrila (1996, 27) stated that "it is the plan that controls human information processing and supplies patterns for essential connections between knowledge, evaluation, and action." This generic description can be extended by the approach reported by Newell and Simon (1972). They described planning as a system of heuristics used by their general problem solver (GPS) "to construct a proposed solution in general terms before working out the details. This procedure acts as an antidote to the limitation of means-ends analysis in seeing only one step ahead" (428). Planning heuristics are used to guide action when a problem is too difficult to solve by means-end analysis. Newell and Simon assume the following steps in planning (1972, 429):

1. Abstracting by omitting certain details of the original objects and operators.
2. Forming the corresponding problem in the abstract problem space.
3. When the abstract problem has been solved, using its solution to provide a plan for solving the original problem.
4. Translating the plan back into the original problem space and executing it.

Complexity is reduced by leaving out details and reasoning by analogy. In this sense, planning is a way to solve problems. Earlier models of planning presume that planning is always a hierarchical process that proceeds according to successive refinement. Sacerdoti (1975) implemented such an approach in his computer program NOAH. In this view, planning is performed by recursively decomposing goals into subgoals until a subgoal can be reached by elementary action. This paradigm is contradicted by Hayes-Roth and Hayes-Roth (1979). They argued "that planning processes operate in a two-dimensional planning space defined on time and abstraction" (312). In these terms successive refinement always works top-down from high to low levels of abstraction and forward in the plan time frame. Thinking aloud protocols from different subjects that perform planning tasks shows that this is not always the case. Hayes-Roth and Hayes-Roth reported what they called "opportunistic planning." Individuals switch in levels of abstraction and move both forward and backward in time in successive reasoning steps. Hayes-Roth and Hayes-Roth (1979) proposed a theoretical framework for cognitive planning that incorporates this behavior. They found that reasoning often takes place heterarchically; plans are created incrementally on multiple hierarchical levels simultaneously where decisions at a detailed level can invalidate plans at a higher hierarchical level. They argued that strict hierarchical planning can rule out good solutions, and that humans compensate for this by opportunistic planning: "the bottom-up component in multi-directional processing provides a potentially important source of innovation in planning. Low-level decisions and related observations can inspire novel higher-level plans" (1979, 306).

Riesbeck and Schank (1989) argued that planning is based on scripts. Instead of conceiving new plans for each problem, humans try to find a plan that was used for previously solved comparable planning problems. Then the basic planning activity is more adaptation than construction. In this paradigm, planning is about memory, indexing, and learning (Hammond 1989), which are interrelated. Plans should be stored in memory so that it becomes easy to find an existing plan from comparisons of new goals with previously handled goals. Here solutions must be remembered so that they can be used for new problems, and a failure to execute the plan suggests that the knowledge the planner has of the execution world may be faulty. Thus, script models can be seen as adding learning to the paradigms already discussed.

To handle complexity, humans apply abstraction hierarchies, heuristics, scripts, and opportunistic planning. Van Wezel, Jorna, and Meystel (2006) described how these mechanisms can also be found in organizational planning by denoting the similarities and differences between planning for yourself versus planning for others. For example, according to Hayes-Roth and Hayes-Roth, the choice of a planning strategy depends on three variables: the problem characteristics, expertise, and individual differences. These can be found in the industrial scheduling literature as well.

First, regarding problem characteristics, Cegarra (2008) discussed a scheduling typology with seven dimensions that shape the scheduling task from a cognitive perspective:

- Uncertainty: the inability to predict future events.
- Process steadiness: disturbances in the scheduled process that can be anticipated.
- Time pressure: whether there is a need to react instantly or can events be processed later.
- Cycle synchronicity: operators, machines, sales, and schedulers themselves can have different preferred cycle times.
- Process continuity: discrete processes such as found in job shops are more difficult to schedule than continuous processes
- Complexity: the numerical complexity of the scheduling task at hand.
- Multiple and contradictory objectives: schedulers might face different objectives from, for example, sales and manufacturing. Even within a manufacturing department, objectives might differ per person, machine, or process.

The dimensions can exist independently of each other and each dimension can lead to different scheduling task characteristics. This implies that in practice many different possible combinations can emerge. Once they occur, however, the dimensions can interact, which further complicates the structure of the scheduling task. Fransoo and Wiers (2006) showed that the complexity of planners' actions increases with the complexity and number of actions conducted. This finding is quite intuitive, but contradicts the reasoning that complexity leads to mental overload and thereby to a reliance on routine decisions. Experiments of Moray and coauthors (1991) showed similar results. Although time pressure resulted in increased perceived workload, operators kept working with a constant level of effort, decreasing the number of scheduled tasks. This effect is demonstrated in our traveling salesman learning activity that can be found at the end of the chapter.

Second, expertise influences task performance. Mietus (1994) and Guerin, Hoc, and Mebarki (2012) showed that planners change their strategies with experience. Experts use a higher level of abstraction and more top-down reasoning than novices.

Third, individual differences lead to differences in task strategies and views on the problem structure; furthermore, these change over time with increased experience. Kiewiet, Jorna, and van Wezel (2005) showed with card-sorting and graph-positioning methods that planners who work in the same company on the same planning task can have very different cognitive maps. Jorna (2006) investigated the problem-solving strategies of 34 planners and found that differences within domains were larger than between domains, and that culture (i.e., Indonesian versus Dutch planners) was an important factor in the differences found.

Performance Metrics of Planning and Scheduling

Traditionally, scheduling research measures performance as the number of constraints that are violated and the extent that scheduling goals are realized. These metrics are related to the projected execution of the schedule. For example, in production scheduling, these can include total completion time, lateness, earliness, tardiness, and machine utilization (Hoogeveen 2005). In workforce scheduling, metrics include total penalty cost due to violating shift balances and total satisfaction of employees' preferences (Cheang et al. 2003), and in patient appointment scheduling, these include doctors' productivity and idle time, total waiting time, and average patient time flow (Cayirli and Veral 2003). Several authors have criticized this approach as being too narrow. For example, MacCarthy and Wilson (2001b) remarked that "objective measurement in planning, scheduling and control must account for the process by which plans are generated and executed, the people who are instrumental in generating them as well as the actual realization of plans and schedules over time" (312). Likewise, Jackson, Wilson, and MacCarthy (2004) noted that the performance measures in their case studies "took the form of contextual expectations generated by other business personnel. Such performance measures represented the way that schedulers were expected, for example, to be good communicators, to share accurate and up-to-date information, to solve problems, and to have a proactive view of requirements" (548). Thus, in addition to typical performance measures, social concepts such as fairness and punctuality also are important. De Snoo, Van Wezel, and Jorna (2011) found three kinds of performance criteria. The first category relates to the effect that executing the schedule will have:

- Number of constraint violations, for example, regarding promises to customers, use of capacity, and labor regulations.
- Costs of schedule execution; for example, batching products of the same family will reduce setup time, and thereby, increase capacity utilization.
- The number of employees' preferences and wishes that are honored.

The second category includes the following:

- Numbers of errors in the schedule, for example, using wrong processing times.
- Robustness and adaptability of the schedule; does it need to be changed after each deviation or can it absorb some unexpected events? If it must be changed, will the changes cascade like a snowball, or will the effects on other parts of the schedule be minimal?
- Understandability of the schedule and of schedule changes: can operators and foremen comprehend the schedule, for example, if their department will have low efficiency due to the schedule, can they understand why?

The third category consists of criteria that are related to the scheduling process:

- Timeliness and reliability of initial release: is it released in time so operators can start to prepare?
- How flexible are schedulers regarding schedule adaptation?
- Accessibility of schedulers and communication and harmonization quality: can the schedulers explain their choices? Can they empathize with operators that must execute the schedule? Can they negotiate without starting conflicts? And so on.
- Cost/efficiency of the scheduling process. Do the planners themselves work efficiently? Do they use their tools correctly?

Organization of the Planning Tasks

Planning is typically distributed across multiple people, and many will not have scheduling as their full-time job (Wäfler 2001). Planning therefore often should be designed as a collaborative task.

The first step in task division is usually driven by timing disparity, numerical complexity, and uncertainty. A clear example is described by Meal (1984), who described the planning organization of a tire manufacturer with multiple divisions developed over the course of decades. Before computers could be used for data processing, planning was decentralized and customer-driven. Each division of the tire manufacturer did its own planning. This led to high stock levels. Noting these stock levels, the company wanted to switch to centralized planning. Although by then this could be facilitated by computers, several disadvantages were found: a complete combined detailed schedule was too large to be reviewed by humans (numerical complexity), the authority of local managers was taken away (inaccessible information could not be accessed anymore), and the forecasts on which the plan was based were not reliable at the item level (timing disparity and uncertainty). The company then decided to segregate the plan in several hierarchical levels. Rather than making a centralized detailed schedule in which all individual customer orders were allocated to production facilities, the company decided to incorporate multiple stages in the scheduling process. At the corporate level, senior management decided which regions would be served by which factory based on aggregated yearly demand by item and by region. At the plant level, the plant manager used monthly demand by product type to determine seasonal patterns. Finally, each shop floor manager determined detailed schedules. This method of hierarchical production planning is now common and facilitated by enterprise resource planning (ERP) systems. For each subplan, different knowledge and expertise is needed. At the corporate level the planners need to know market trends, and on the shop floor the planners know each operator and machine.

The second step in task division is driven by information inaccessibility. Managers often prefer to have a separate scheduler for each department, even if it does not result in full-time jobs. There are cognitive limits to knowing the details and history of each machine and operator. Further, particularly for confidential information, operators need someone that they can trust to represent their interests. Both are facilitated if the department has a dedicated scheduler, especially with someone who has previous experience as an operator.

A third relates to the complexities involved in scheduling and rescheduling. In operations research, these two are like two different worlds, each with own methods, techniques, and tools (Pinedo 2012). In practice the distinction often is not clear. Scheduling and rescheduling overlap and often are done in parallel. During scheduling interdependencies between schedulers can be managed with simple rules and agreements. If issues arise, there is sufficient time available for schedule adaptation, feedback, communication, and coordination. The organizational design of coordination modes can be based upon an analysis of predictable and stable interdependencies. During rescheduling, the situation is quite different. Schedules are released to the operators and are being executed. Events disrupt schedule feasibility and often require an immediate response. Generally, it is uncertain when an event will happen and what its impact will be on one or multiple scheduled operations and resources. Complete rescheduling is usually impossible because of time constraints or is undesirable because it can cause tumult on the shop floor. Therefore, schedules are typically adapted partially (Vieira et al. 2003; Aytug et al. 2005; Subramaniam, Raheja, and Rama Bhupal Reddy 2005). Nevertheless, changing one schedule can easily require modifications to another schedule. For instance, alternative sequencing of operations in one department can be a prerequisite to solving a material shortage problem within someone else's schedule. To find solutions quickly, communication and deliberation between schedulers is necessary (Van Wezel, Van Donk, and Gaalman 2006). Consequently, the design of coordination structures for rescheduling differs from the coordination design for scheduling. Rescheduling poses specific requirements on the task design of the schedulers, especially regarding the design of coordination modes

Figure 5.6 Collaborative Scheduling

to manage task interdependencies. Although scheduling and rescheduling can be done by the same person, and in many organizations this is the case, there are also cases where these tasks are split.

Task division based on hierarchical planning layers, departments, and scheduling/rescheduling can still result in tasks that are too extensive for one person to handle. So a third reason to divide tasks is simply numerical complexity.

Companies tend to distribute planning tasks, but interestingly, De Snoo and Van Wezel (2014) found that collaborative scheduling (i.e., working as a team without task division) can result in better schedules (figure 5.6), suggesting that synergy can improve scheduling when it is done collaboratively.

THE ORGANIZATIONAL INTERCONNECTIVITY OF PLANNING AND SCHEDULING

Extensive research has focused on the organizational design of coordination as an instrument to manage interdependencies between decision-makers (Albino, Pontrandolfo, and Scozzi 2002; Crowston 1997; Molleman and Slomp 2006; Olson, Malone, and Smith 2001; Thompson 1967; Van de Ven, Delbecq, and Koenig 1976). However, the traditional approach of developing coordination structures based on an analysis of predictable and stable interdependencies appears to have limited applicability within organizations operating in high-velocity environments (Crossan et al. 2005; Faraj and Xiao 2006; McPherson and White 2006). Scheduling, and especially rescheduling, provides a clear example of such an environment. The variety and unpredictability of this environment lead to variety in types and criticality of interdependencies. Conditions of high uncertainty and fast decision-making challenge the assumption "that the environment is predictable enough to characterize existing interdependencies and that predefined mechanisms can be designed for various contingencies" (Faraj and Xiao 2006, 1156). The analysis of performance criteria shows that managers and planners who work in dynamic environments consider process criteria (e.g., communication, negotiation, flexibility, understandability of the schedule, and the employees' wishes) more important than a good schedule (De Snoo, Van Wezel, and Jorna 2011a). Interestingly, these are criteria that relate to the interaction of a scheduler with other departments, for example, purchasing, sales, production, quality, finance, human resources, industrial engineering, and IT (McKay and Wiers 2006).

Berglund, Guinery, and Karltun (2011) described the tasks performed at this interface: clarify, negotiate, and joint problem-solving. De Snoo, Van Wezel, and Wortmann (2011) investigated the effects of the relocation of the scheduling department to the center of the shop floor. Their analysis showed that the effectiveness of such interface tasks increased when schedulers and operators were able to communicate more face to face. Concerning performance criteria, Nauta and Sanders (2001) showed that the focus of manufacturing is on efficiency and quality, of planners on delivery performance, and of marketing on customer service. An important conclusion from Nauta and Sanders is that perceived goal differences increase the frequency and seriousness of conflicts between departments.

Berglund and Guinery (2008) investigated the power relations between planning on the one hand and commercial/production departments on the other. They found that planners primarily use informal power versus formal power. Because planners do not have formal power, they must negotiate to find a balance between the goals of sales versus manufacturing. During this process, schedulers tended to work with multiple scenarios in parallel; for example, a political view that is made public, a realistic view that the scheduler think will actually happen, and an optimistic schedule that is communicated in the bartering process (McKay, Safayeni, and Buzacott 1995b).

Nauta and Sanders (2001) explored the relation between personality characteristics and four kinds of planners' negotiation behavior (table 5.2). They concluded that collaborative problem-solving occurs more when individuals are extraverted and agreeable, and when employees perceive high interdepartmental interdependencies. Contending occurs more when individuals are extraverted and disagreeable. Yielding occurs more when individuals perceive a power advantage versus the other department. All kinds of negotiation occur less when organizations have a low-cost strategy.

From an organizational design perspective, McKay and Wiers (2006) described two kinds of connections that planning can have with other departments: structural and functional. Structural interconnections depend on the scheduling task division; what aggregate layers do we distinguish, and how are the corresponding scheduling and rescheduling tasks divided between the schedulers and the

Table 5.2. NEGOTIATION STRATEGIES

Problem-solving	**Negotiation partners consider both their own goals and the others' goals.**
Yielding	The partner adjusts to the demands of the other.
Contending	The partner imposes preferred solutions on the other.
Avoiding	The partner neglects the conflict.

shop floor? Related aspects are information visibility, decision depth, and decision breadth. Functional connections describe the flow of information, which depends on the scope and formalisms used (e.g., the number of participants in the process and how they communicate), and the solution space (i.e., the density and elasticity of constraints). Wiers (2009) offers an example, discussing how autonomy depends on uncertainty (probability and extent of unforeseen events) and human recovery (the ability and latitude of operators to handle the disturbances themselves):

- *Smooth shop*: little uncertainty and little need for human intervention. The scheduler can make the schedule and focus on optimization.
- *Social shop*: little uncertainty, but there is frequent need for human intervention in the production process. Detailed scheduling decisions should therefore be allocated to the operators, which means that the schedule of the scheduling department should allow for some decision latitude.
- *Stress shop*: much uncertainty, but no possibility for the shop floor operators to handle this, because the uncertainty is caused by external factors. The schedulers will handle all rescheduling.
- *Sociotechnical shop*: a high level of uncertainty, but also a local need to be able to handle exceptions. There is little utility in making a detailed schedule as the operators will not be able to execute it anyway.

Due to specific characteristics of scheduling, customized coordination theories need to be developed. The decision latitude of sales, planners, and shop floor operators, and the appropriate coordination mechanisms between these departments, must be determined. However, theory to support these organizational design decisions is limited.

Computer Support for Planning and Scheduling

Scheduling problems have always been an important application area for decision support systems (DSSs) (Eom and Lee 1990; Eom and Kim 2006; Eom et al. 1998). A DSS improves the quality of decisions pertaining to unstructured and large-scale problems by coupling the cognitive resources of individuals with computer capabilities (Keen and Scott-Morton 1978). However, in scheduling systems, while a great deal of emphasis has been placed on large-scale problems, the user has been somewhat neglected. Framinan and Ruiz (2010) proposed a generic architecture for manufacturing scheduling systems and describe the following functionality:

- Scope of the system: the system can support one or more aggregate layers (planning, shop floor control, reactive scheduling, and so on).
- Problem modeling: the system can detect the suitable model (combination of objects, constraints, goals) itself, adapt it to the specific situation, and be able to represent the solutions.

- Problem-solving: creating the actual schedule using algorithms or heuristics, on the appropriate level and within the model chosen.
- Solution evaluation: analysis of the solution, for example, analyzing scenarios with multiple objectives and uncertainty.
- Capacity analysis: the detection of bottlenecks before and during scheduling.
- User interface: entering parameters, representation of the schedule (e.g., a Gantt chart), displaying constraints and goals, and interactions with the user.
- Integration with existing information systems: for example, ERP systems for orders, bills of material, recipes, stock positions, and so on. But also interact with shop floor control systems and systems of customers.

Framinan and Ruiz (2010) essentially mitigate human expertise in their scheduling system. However, scheduling, and especially rescheduling, is subject to extemporized information that is unavailable at the time of the design of the system. Additionally, scheduling decisions need to encompass interpretation of information by stakeholders, which is not necessarily stable. For example, Conway, Maxwell, and Miller (1967, 3) argued that "much of the research literature in sequencing refers to the job-shop scheduling problem and uses the terminology of manufacturing: job, machine, operation, routing, and processing-time. In fact, the work is based on this type of idealized pure-sequence abstraction of such a manufacturing shop and the results are equally applicable to problems in transportation, communication, services, etc. Actually one might say that the results are equally inapplicable, since this idealized model is not an exact representation of any real job-shop." McKay, Pinedo, and Webster (2002) specifically noted that the dynamic nature of scheduling gives the human scheduler an important role in the scheduling process. Therefore, we should explicitly consider the role of the human in the design of scheduling support. Below, we will outline factors that can be used to determine the kinds of interaction between the human and the computer, and when these interactions are appropriate.

Behavioral Effects of Using Scheduling Algorithms

There is general recognition that scheduling algorithms need to support rather than replace the human scheduler because constraints and goals are usually too complex to fully consider in an algorithm or heuristic (Sanderson 1989). However, using an algorithm that contains simplifications like neglecting constraints and optimizing a single goal in a multicriteria scheduling problem results in new tasks for human schedulers such as the need to check the schedule for errors. These changes can have unintended side-effects. For example, the human scheduler might be overloaded with too much information (Baek 1999), system input and output can be difficult to understand (Sanderson 1989; Higgins 1992), and the introduction of a system can result in boredom, demotivation, or complacency (Parasuraman et al. 1993). The success of decision support systems depends not only on the objective quality of system output but also on user-related factors such as the perceived usefulness, ease of use, and job relevance (Sabherwal, Jeyaraj, and Chowa 2006; Venkatesh and Bala 2008). Technology acceptance, postadoptive behavior, and use risks of decision support have seen extensive attention in literature, but are essentially ignored in the design of scheduling algorithms (Chopra et al. 2004; Hoch and Schkade 1996; LaForge and Craighead 2000; Singh and Singh 1997).

Nakamura and Salvendy (1994) argued that the computer "must have models of the human operator so that it can infer the possible actions that the humans might take for any system state" (342). Haider, Moodie, and Buck (1981) showed that an interactive scheduling system can only be effective if a scheduler can relate the objective that is being optimized with the information about the jobs and the shop being displayed. Further Baek (1999) showed that in complex job shop scheduling situations operators "performed significantly better when working with initial solutions that were generated by themselves. This implies that computer aiding that is incoherent to human problem-solving strategies may be less effective than commonly expected." If the goals pursued by the algorithm have no clear link to the objectives of the planner, or algorithms are not understood by the decision-maker, the subsequent inability of the person to gain insight into the problem contributes to information overload (Sharit, Eberts, and Salvendy 1988) and poor performance.

In line with this reasoning, Prietula and coauthors (1994) proposed that the human planner and the scheduling support system should work in "coincident problem spaces." The models themselves need not be similar, but at the points of interaction understandable communication must be possible. Hence, successful use of an algorithm is not only determined by the quality of the solution procedure and the quality of the mapping, but also by the way in which results are communicated in the user interface. This is confirmed by experiments of Cegarra and Hoc (2008), who found that result comprehensibility is necessary for good performance, but that understanding the algorithm itself might lead to lower performance due to higher cognitive costs. Chenoweth, Dowling, and St Louis (2004) showed that cognitive feed-forward (such as instructions or training) and cognitive feedback (i.e., not only feedback on the outcome itself but also on the system and the decision strategy that it used) increase awareness of the improved accuracy that complex models offer. Explanation increases perceived usefulness and acceptance. However, differences in reasoning patterns and cognitive maps between individual schedulers performing the same task (Mietus 1994; Kietwiet et al. 2005; Guerin, Hoc, and Mebarki 2012) complicate representation issues.

The role of the human scheduler is to process extemporary information. Because it is by definition impossible to predict when and where such information will emerge, the scheduler needs to understand the schedule at all times, and must be able to intervene at each decision moment. A mismatch between schedulers' mental models and the reasoning and communication process of the support system can lead to three risks: trust, complacency, and loss of skill and adaptability due to loss of situation awareness.

If schedulers do not trust the system, they will neglect it. Because of the introduction of automation, the role of the human changes from active controller to supervisory controller (Lee and Moray 1992). Arkes, Dawes, and Christensen (1986) and Lee and Moray (1994) showed that operators tend to use automation if trust exceeds self-confidence, and that manual control is used if self-confidence exceeds trust. Dixon, Wickens, and McCarley (2007) showed that reliance on the system decreases with increasing system failures, and that compliance (i.e., response time and accuracy of the operator's reaction if the system indicates a problem) decreases with increasing numbers of false diagnoses. De Vries, Midden, and Bouwhuis (2003) highlighted the importance of error feedback on trust, self-confidence, and whether humans choose to use automatic planning. They concluded that transparency of process feedback can increase initial trust and acceptance of new technology. Riedel and coauthors (2011) showed that while good performance increases trust, performance variability decreases trust, concluding that high performance is more important for trust than low variability.

A second risk is overreliance or complacency. Cegarra and Hoc (2008, 613) defined complacency as "an unjustified assumption of satisfaction in which a human accepts suboptimal performance because of the cognitive cost of evaluating or correcting the machine's proposal." They show that complacency can be avoided by increasing result comprehensibility, but that grasping the internal workings of an algorithm does not reduce complacency. Complacency can also lead to nonvigilance based on an unjustified assumption of a satisfactory system state (Inagaki 2003). If the introduction of an algorithm changes the task of an operator from problem-solving to monitoring, it must be taken into account that humans cannot maintain effective visual attention for more than about half an hour (Bainbridge 1983). Therefore, Kuo and Hwang (1998, 166) proposed to "leave some thinking space to human schedulers" in the design of an interactive scheduling system.

A third risk is loss of skill and adaptability due to reduced situation awareness (Hoc 2000). Introduction of a system can lead to "cognitive starvation," and, as a consequence, human planners cannot deal with exceptions anymore (Wiers and Van der Schaaf 1997). Van Nimwegen and van Oostendorp (2009) reported that performance aided by an interface providing guidance was worse than performance aided by an interface without guidance, which attributed to proactive thinking. When properly designed, however, support can also improve situation awareness and adaptability because it can reduce workload and provide integrated information (Endsley and Kiris 1995).

Involving human expertise in the design of scheduling systems is essential. Support should not replicate human decision-making, but should account for usage effects such as trust, complacency, vigilance, and situation awareness. Therefore, the system design should account for the following design criteria:

1. The scheduling goals of the human scheduler and system need to be aligned. Misalignment of goals and variability in performance decrease trust.

2. The system should communicate the decision strategy and schedule in a comprehensible way, which increases acceptance and trust and decreases complacency.
3. The system should account for human limitations such as short-term memory and attention span, and individual differences.
4. Human schedulers should be provoked to participate in the scheduling process, or risk losing their long-term mental model of system functioning and structure, and their ability to deal with exceptions.

These criteria imply that the requirements specification, which precedes design and development in the software engineering process, needs to be more than a mathematical formulation of a scheduling problem.

Design Methodology for Scheduling Support

Cegarra and Van Wezel (2012) described three properties that scheduling systems should have to address situational oversimplification and utilize cooperation skills, mental flexibility, and human scheduler creativity:

1. Adaptability: "accommodate medium- and long-term changes in the problem-solving environment."
2. Flexibility: "accommodate heterogeneity in the current (short-term) decision-making context."
3. Acceptability: "the ability to take into account the cooperative outlook of the humans who participate in the decision-making process."

Simple but understandable algorithms have low acceptability (Cegarra and Hoc 2008; Green and Appel 1981). Hence, algorithms should be able to solve complex problems. However, such algorithms are usually based on a one-off analysis of the scheduling problem, impeding the adaptability and flexibility needed for sustained user acceptance. Cegarra and Van Wezel (2012) argued that support should link to schedulers' mental models in two ways. First, the interface should use commonly accepted metaphors and make use of human pattern-recognition capabilities. Second, algorithms should capitalize on human abilities. To create adaptable, flexible, and acceptable systems, we need to uncover information on the scheduling problem to find applicable algorithms, but also information on the way the human schedulers work and think. Cegarra and Van Wezel (2011) compared three perspectives to analyze information requirement methods for scheduling:

1. Normative: it prescribes how the tasks should be done, e.g., hierarchical task analysis (Annett 2000; Annet and Duncan 1967).
2. Descriptive: it describes how the task is currently performed. An example is a Cognitive Task Analysis (Schraagen et al. 2000).
3. Formative: it provides an exhaustive description of the scheduled domain, including physical and functional interrelations (Higgins 1999).

Cegarra and Van Wezel (2011) used Vicente (1999) to compare these information requirement approaches. The *device dependency* expresses to what extent the method depends on the currently used "devices" that execute the task (e.g., humans, computer programs, etc.). The *event dependency* specifies whether novel circumstances can be detected. The *psychological relevance* indicates how the schedulers' point of view is considered in the analysis. These aspects can be linked to the adaptability, flexibility, and acceptability of scheduling systems (table 5.3). Traditionally, DSS for scheduling follow a *normative* approach: an existing solution procedure is adapted to specific circumstances, and tasks are assigned to the scheduler. Such an approach is not device independent, event independent, or psychologically relevant. Thus, adaptability and flexibility are low and acceptability has two sides. High performance increases acceptability, but low psychological relevance decreases acceptability. A *descriptive* analysis is device dependent and event dependent, but psychological relevance is high. This decreases adaptability because new circumstances will by definition not be encountered in descriptive analysis. However, flexibility and acceptability are high. Finally, a *formative* analysis is device and event independent, but psychological relevance is low because it analyzes the domain, not task performance.

Table 5.3. EFFECTS OF ANALYSIS APPROACHES

	Adaptability	**Flexibility**	**Acceptability**
Normative analysis	Low	Low	Low/high
Descriptive analysis	Low	High	High
Formative analysis	High	High	Low

Table 5.4. LEVELS OF AUTOMATION

1.	Human completes the job up to the point of turning it over to the computer for implementation.
2.	Computer helps by determining the options.
3.	Computer helps determine which steps human need not follow.
4.	Computer selects action, and human may or may not do it.
5.	Computer selects action and implements it if human approves.
6.	Computer selects action; informs human in plenty of time to stop it.
7.	Computer does whole job and tells human what it did.
8.	Computer does whole job and tells human what it did only if human explicitly asks.
9.	Computer does whole job and tells human what it did, and then the computer decides if the human should be told.
10.	Computer does the whole job if it decides it should be done, and if so tells human, if it decides the human should be told.

SOURCE: Sheridan and Verplank 1978.

This makes adaptability and flexibility high, acceptability low because the current way of working is not considered.

Cegarra and Van Wezel concluded that all three approaches are needed to address the tasks and roles of human schedulers. However, exhaustive normative, descriptive, and formative analyses are likely to be time consuming and costly. Van Wezel, Cegarra, and Hoc (2011) proposed applying function allocation to mitigate these limitations. Per subtask the effects of automation (trust, complacency, loss of adaptability) constitute a risk—the higher the risk and the costlier the possible effects, the more important human involvement. This technique has its origin in cognitive engineering, where it is used to determine appropriate task division between human and computer in dynamic, high-risk situations. Table 5.4 shows an example with various levels of automation.

In function allocation, the level automation that corresponds to the required level of human involvement determines the appropriate task analysis methods. For example, a subtask on level 1 would need no normative analysis, whereas a subtask on level 10 would need no descriptive analysis.

The involvement of humans in computer-supported scheduling orbits information that cannot be specified in advance. The computer model can get out of date or cannot capture the flexibility necessary to real circumstances. The human should always be able to tell the computer what can be done and the computer should accept it. For example, the scheduler can temporarily have one machine do two things at the same time, or assign work to a machine not listed in the computer as being possible.

LEARNING ACTIVITIES

Game 1: Manufacturing Scheduling

Based on de Snoo and van Wezel (2014). (The game can be played physically with Lego bricks.)

The furniture-manufacturing case serves as the inspiration for a scheduling game showing the effects of cooperation in a dynamic scheduling situation. The game can be used to play a stylized simplified scheduling situation in approximately 30 minutes. It shows the effects of collaboration when schedulers need to solve complex problems in which they are simultaneously under time pressure and mutually dependent.

The scheduling situation can be characterized as a flexible job shop. There are three departments, and each has three similar machines (sawing, cutting, milling). The schedules are strongly interconnected. Each order consists of two operations. Processing times differ per operation. Transport times, setup times, and inventory are not taken into account. Participants are confronted with event information at different points in time (see table 5.5). Participants have a range of possibilities in changing a plan: schedule an order earlier or later on the same machine; move an order to another machine; add or remove an order. The schedulers are jointly responsible for the timely delivery of orders and the efficient utilization of machines. Because of the routing of the orders, adaptation of one schedule quickly results in infeasibility in another order.

The game can be played simulating several alternative scheduling situations to demonstrate how communication and collaboration can influence the scheduling process:

1. Players start with an empty schedule. Participants need to create the schedule based on a description of products and their operations.
2. Players start with a complete schedule that will be executed tomorrow. The schedule is purposefully suboptimal so participants can immediately start to optimize. Events (e.g., order cancellations, new rush orders; table 5.5) invalidate the schedule, and participants must coordinate to fix it.
3. Starting with the same schedule as in situation 2, but the schedule is currently being executed. Events invalidate the schedule, but as the game progresses, there are fewer opportunities to make changes. The scheduling decisions for orders that production has already started cannot be changed; preemption is not allowed. Therefore, the number of orders that can be moved decreases as the game progresses. Time

Table 5.5. Events Provided to the Participants

1.	**8:30 a.m.** The sales department has received a request from a potential client to deliver a trial product. If the delivery of this product is achieved on time, the client will likely place substantial orders in the near future. The management has therefore decided to fulfill this request. Order 13 has to be delivered at the latest at 17:00; the product first requires sawing (processing time three hours), and then has to be cut (processing time three hours).
2.	**8:50 a.m.** The distribution department reports product damage during onward delivery. The product has to be remilled. Milling is the only processing activity required for this "rush order" (processing time is two hours). Order 14 has to be ready by 15:00.
3.	**9:40 a.m.** The raw materials for order 12 do not meet quality standards. Therefore, these materials have to be resupplied. Order 12 is therefore postponed; it can be removed from the milling and sawing schedules.
4.	**10:10 a.m.** The shop floor notifies that the cutting department does not have the highly specialized skills required for order 4. Management decides to outsource the cutting activities for order 4. Order 4 only needs input from the sawing department.
5.	**10:40 a.m.** The production manager reports that sawing machine 1 requires attention. Maintenance activities will take place between 14:00 and 15:00. No orders can be scheduled on the machine during this hour.
6.	**11:20 a.m.** A rush order (order 15) is received that has to be delivered by 16:00. The product first requires cutting (processing time is two hours), and then milling (processing time two hours).

pressure is higher when the schedule has already been released since there is less time to react. For example, consider a rush order arriving at 8:50 a.m. (event 2 in table 5.5). If the execution of the schedule has already started, three orders (numbers 6, 9, and 3) can no longer be moved. Moreover, at 11:00 a.m. two further orders are scheduled to start (orders 2 and 12), reducing yet further the number of movable orders. Although in this situation there are more constraints, the number of alternatives that have to be considered also is lower.

To express the organizational design options, collaboration can be organized in three ways (figure 5.7):

1. Individual decision-making: participants are physically separated from each other. They can only view their own schedule and can communicate changes to it by specifying the recipient scheduler's name and the change they propose. Deliberations about alternatives or decisions are not allowed.
2. Collaborative decision-making: participants are placed apart as in the individual setting and, again, each has his or her own schedule that may not be communicated. However, in this mode, the schedulers are allowed to communicate or deliberate with each other in face-to-face conference. Cooperation clearly has some costs: the schedulers have to leave their working places and, after deliberations, have to apply the agreed-on actions to their individual schedules (with a risk of errors due to poor recall).
3. Group decision-making: the three schedules are combined and the participants are physically located around the same table. They are instructed to handle all events jointly and to make all decisions together.

To play the game, the participants are provided with a Lego board with bricks representing scheduled orders, and an order book containing the delivery time and processing time per operation. The interdependencies within and between the initial schedules are the same for each pair of schedules; that is, each schedule contains the same number of orders with equal variance in processing times, the sequence dependencies between two production operations related to a single order are equal, and each schedule contains the same

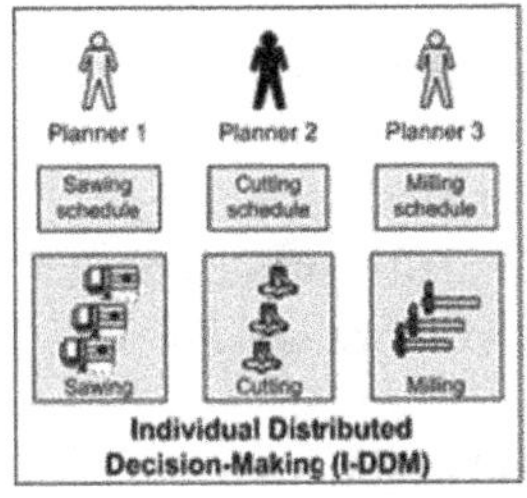

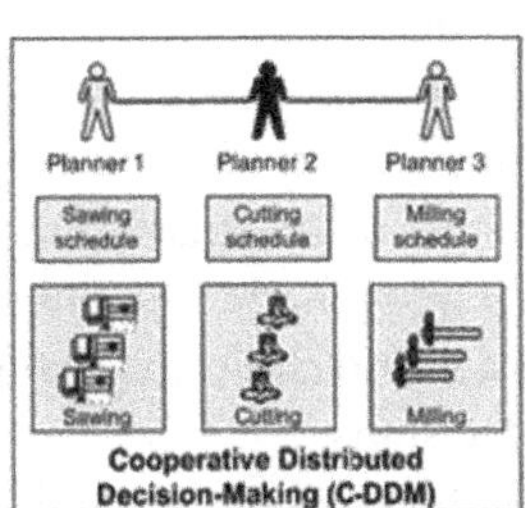

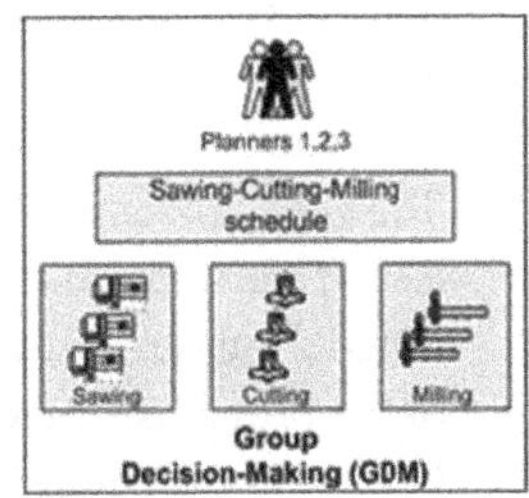

Figure 5.7 Coordination Modes in Scheduling

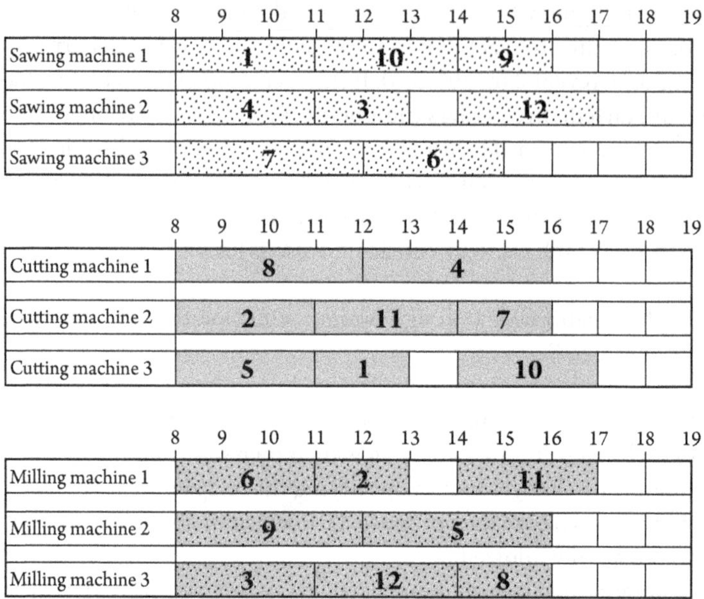

Figure 5.8 Start Schedules

amount of slack and redundancy (figure 5.8). At fixed points in time the groups are confronted with written information concerning an event (table 5.5). Players have 12 minutes to update and improve their schedules. These 12 minutes represent a four-hour period (8:00 a.m. till 12 noon); a digital clock shows the progress of time. In this way, complexities of scheduling reality are simulated. If there is time, participants can play the game a second time under different circumstances.

During the debrief participants can reflect on several of their experiences:

- The difference between starting with an empty schedule and adapting an already complete schedule. When participants start with an existing schedule, they need to first grasp the interconnections, which is difficult when events are piling up. We regularly see that participants first remove everything from the schedule and then build it from scratch. This can be related to the use of scheduling algorithms; if the schedule is created by an algorithm, human schedulers find it more difficult to make changes relative to a schedule they made themselves.
- The effect of time pressure on task performance, and the difference between (offline) scheduling and (online) control.
- The consequences of changes on an already finished schedule. A lesson learned can be that in dynamic situations, detailed centralized scheduling is not always a sound choice, as changes will invalidate most of the previously made decisions.
- Perceived task interdependency, power struggles, and negotiation strategies can be discussed.

- The need for communication and transparency of information. Especially the individual decision-making mode leads to schedule errors, for example, by scheduling operations of the same job on multiple machines simultaneously.
- The task division that appears in the group decision-making mode. Did one of the participants take the lead, or were all decisions made collaboratively?

Note that this game is played in the context of a "naive" or new scheduler, not a scheduler with years of experience. No game will teach all of the things expert schedulers know and do. Experienced schedulers have different tactics, know the other schedulers and politics, and so on, and would work in a collaborative situation differently than novice participants in this game. However, the game teaches some of the key concepts of behavioral operations in scheduling.

Game 2: The Traveling Salesman

Based on Bendoly and Prietula (2008).

Many antecedents to performance have nonmonotonic effects. Such antecedents suffer from the law of diminishing returns, which makes the relation between cause and effect asymptotic. For example, increasing the number of employees for a given task increases the need for coordination, which at some point can offset scale efficiencies. Sometimes the relation can even be curvilinear. Pierce and Aguinis (2013) call this the Too-Much-of-a-Good-Thing Effect. An example is workload of employees. A very low workload will result in boredom and nonvigilance of employees. A very high workload, however, harms performance as well. This inverted-U form of the relationship between workload and performance (or the Yerkes-Dodson Law; Yerkes and Dodson 1908) results from two opposing phenomena. The first, based on goal-setting theory (Locke 1968; Locke and Latham 1990), is that a limited amount of work pressure leads to a rise in motivation compared to no pressure at all. In contrast, too ambitious goals can lead to a decrease in motivation (Karasek 1979), as frustration and stress may cause individuals to exert less effort (Lawler and Suttle 1973; Erez and Zidon 1984; Locke and Latham 1984). Managing nonmonotonic relations is difficult because they differ per individual and can change over time. An example of this latter issue is the effect of skills on individuals' interpretation of a particular workload level. An experienced, highly skilled employee might not be deterred by a high workload as easily as an inexperienced employee.

The game described in this section demonstrates both phenomena: a too high and a too low workload are detrimental for performance, but highly skilled employees are less sensitive to workload than unskilled employees. The game is based on a well-known problem in operations research: the traveling salesman problem (TSP). In its most basic form it is a sequencing problem. A salesman has to visit a set of cities, starting and ending at his home address. He wishes to

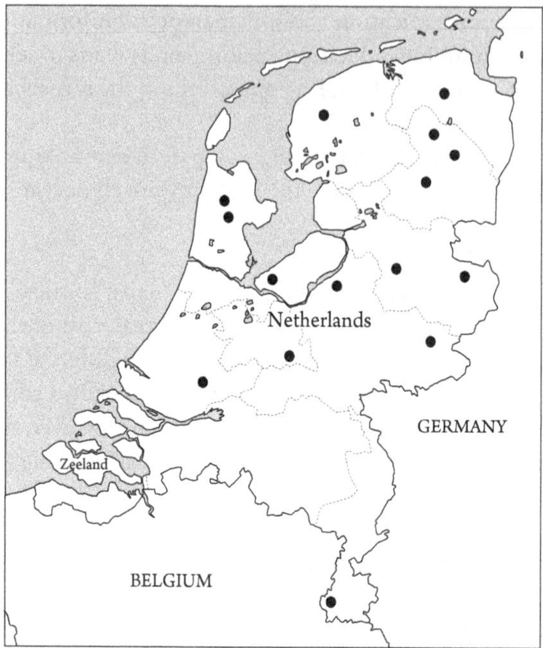

Figure 5.9 Map with Cities to Visit

travel the shortest route possible. Similar to the manufacturing sequencing problem discussed previously in this chapter, this problem is NP hard. The game is played by showing a map with a number of dots that indicate cities to be visited (figure 5.9). The first dot that is clicked indicates the start of the route. Each subsequent dot clicked extends the route to include the corresponding city. There are two performance measures: the distance of the route, and the time participants need to create a route.

Because the goal of the game is to show the effect of workload on performance, first a base speed rate needs to be determined for each individual. The base rate is determined by solving TSP problems until a stable solution speed is achieved. This can be detected by calculating a three-problem moving average reference frame. When the variation in the last five subsequent moving averages does not differ by more than 5%, the moving average of the last three decisions is the base rate.

Once the base rate is determined for all participants, the game itself can be played. There are two parameters that need to be manipulated:

1. The workload is simulated by a queue of TSP problems to solve. A problem that is solved is removed from the queue, and the solution time and travel distance are stored to calculate performance. Problems are added to the queue automatically in one of three speed levels:
   a. Much lower than the base rate. The participant is waiting until a new problem arrives. This is to show that boredom and nonvigilance lead to low performance.

b. A bit higher than the base rate. The participant must make more effort than during the calibration phase but manages to handle the workload.
c. Considerably higher than the base rate. The participant must work much faster than during calibration, and might even be faced with a continuously increasing queue.

2. Expertise is manipulated by teaching participants a heuristic, for example the "nearest-next" heuristic, where the next city in the route is always the city that is closest to the last city in the route. Applying this relatively simple trick often leads to decent routes in a short time, giving the participants the feeling they have mastered the task.

Depending on the teaching goal, the number of participants, and the available time, these settings can be played by each individual or distributed over multiple participants.

The debrief should focus on differences between the speed settings and the effects of skill:

- Figure 5.10 shows typical results that can be found for motivation, speed, and quality under the different workload settings. Increase in skill impacts perceptions of work pressure and shifts the level of workload most conducive to peak performance. Topics of discussion are, for example, how participants trade off quality for speed when workload increases, how this influences their motivation, and whether or not applying the heuristic mitigated the effects of an increased workload.
- Discussion can point out practical settings where workload can be designed. Students can reflect on their own experiences; what happens when deadlines for multiple courses are close together? Examples in manufacturing are assembly lines and project management, and in a service setting one can think of the difference between a central queue compared with a queue for each server.

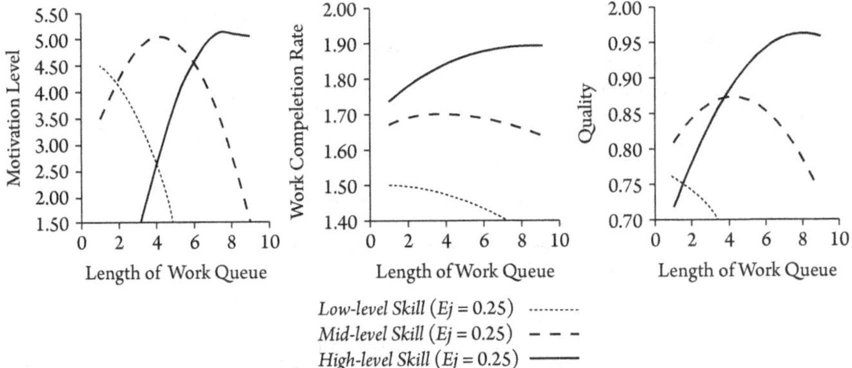

Figure 5.10 Nonmonotonic Relations and the Effect of Skills
SOURCE: Bendoly and Prietula 2008.

Curvilinear relations caused by the Too-Much-of-a-Good-Thing Effect are in general understated. The game can be used as a hands-on example and impetus to discuss other examples. The overview of Pierce and Aguinis (2013) can serve as a starting point.

DISCUSSION

Scheduling problems are traditionally handled by operations management as numerically complex problems that need advanced algorithms and computational power to find near optimal solutions. However, terms like *branch-and-bound* or *simulated annealing* have no meaning for human schedulers that need to solve these problems day to day in actual companies. Scheduling problems are puzzles: the schedulers start with many pieces and need to build a coherent whole. However, the desired end-state of a scheduler's puzzle is not precisely known. During the puzzle-solving process, the pieces of the puzzle change; they might be adapted or altogether disappear and new ones might be added. Additionally, information, goals, and rules can be interpreted differently by various stakeholders. One of the strategies that organizations employ to mitigate the effects of dealing with many detailed decisions simultaneously is to work with larger, more aggregate puzzle pieces. Each larger puzzle piece has one or more smaller puzzles within. For example, if the schedule specifies which orders need to be produced on what day, but not at what moment or in what sequence (as in our case description), small changes during the day can be handled within the departments.

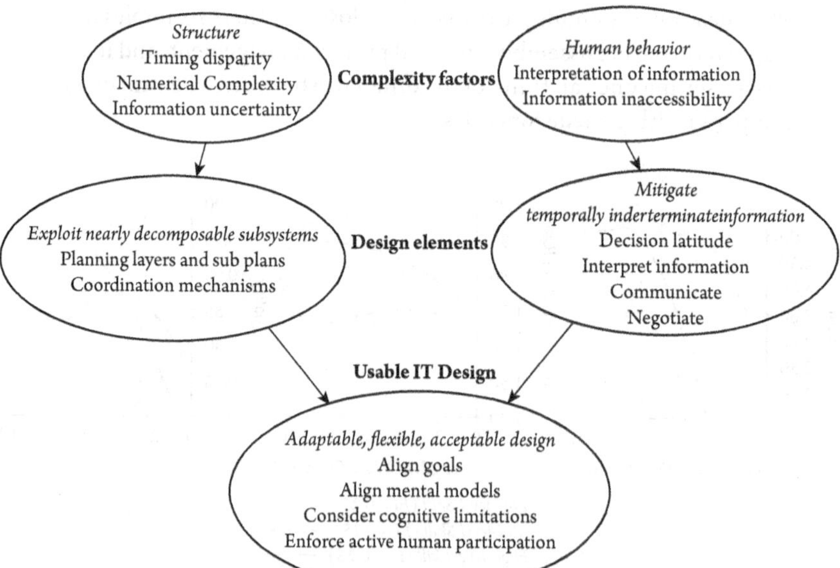

Figure 5.11 Elements of Human Behavior in Scheduling.

This highlights the role of human schedulers. They make the puzzle with the pieces that are available and deal with changes. A task division with nearly decomposable subsystems always needs coordination. Collecting missing information, communication, interpretation, and negotiation are especially prevalent when an event in one department invalidates that department's schedule, and a solution needs a constraint violation in another department. Human schedulers try to develop solutions that keep all stakeholders satisfied by searching for flexibility in established constraints. Often, however, the pain of constraint violations needs to be put somewhere. Since departments are evaluated on their departmental goals, they are not always immediately willing to accept a hit in their performance to solve another department's problems. Here the added value of the human scheduler is clear. Knowing when a department or individual can be pressured, keeping tabs on future compensation, and being convincing to colleagues, managers, and operators are at the core of the skills of human schedulers.

Figure 5.11 summarizes all the elements that are discussed in this chapter.

References

Albino, V., Pontrandolfo, P., Scozzi, B. 2002. Analysis of information flows to enhance the coordination of production processes. International Journal of Production Economics 75 (1), 7–19.

Annet, J. 2000. Theoretical and pragmatic influences on task analysis methods. J. M. Schraagen, S. F. Chipman, V. L. Shalin (eds.) in Cognitive Task Analysis. Mahwah, NJ: Lawrence Erlbaum Associates.

Annett, J., Duncan, K. D. 1967. Task analysis and training design. Occupational Psychology 41, 211–221.

Anthony, R. N. 1965. Planning and Control Systems. Boston: Harvard Business School Press.

Arkes, H. R., Dawes, R. M., Christensen, C. 1986. Factors influencing the use of a decision rule in a probabilistic task. Organizational Behavior and Human Decision Processes 37 (1), 93–110.

Aytug, H., Lawley, M. A., McKay, K., Mohan, S., Uzsoy, R. 2005. Executing production schedules in the face of uncertainties: A review and some future directions. European Journal of Operational Research 161 (1), 86–110.

Baek, D. H. 1999. A visualized human-computer interactive approach to job shop scheduling. International Journal of Computer Integrated Manufacturing 12 (1), 75–83.

Bainbridge, L. 1983. Ironies of automation. Automatica 19, 775–779.

Bendoly, E., Prietula, M. 2008. In "the zone": The role of evolving skill and transitional workload on motivation and realized performance in operational tasks. International Journal of Operations and Production Management 28 (12), 1130–1152.

Berglund, M., Guinery, J. 2008. The influence of production planners and schedulers at manufacturing and commercial interfaces. Human Factors and Ergonomics in Manufacturing and Service Industries 18 (5), 548–564.

Berglund, M., Guinery, J., Karltun, J. 2011. The unsung contribution of production planners and schedulers at production and sales interfaces. J. C. Fransoo, T. Wäfler, J. Wilson (eds.) in Behavioral Operations in Planning and Scheduling. Berlin: Springer.

Buxey, G. 1989. Production Scheduling: Practice and Theory. European Journal of Operational Research 39, 17–31.

Caves, R. E. 1980. Industrial organization, corporate strategy and structure. Journal of Economic Literature 18, 64–92.

Cayirli, T., Veral, E. 2003. Outpatient scheduling in health care: A review of literature. Production and Operations Management 12 (4), 519–549.

Cegarra, J. 2008. A cognitive typology of scheduling situations: A contribution to laboratory and field studies. Theoretical Issues in Ergonomics Science 9 (3), 201–222.

Cegarra, J., Hoc, J. M. 2008. The role of algorithm and result comprehensibility of automated scheduling on complacency. Human Factors and Ergonomics in Manufacturing and Service Industries 28 (6), 603–620.

Cegarra, J., van Wezel, W. 2011. A comparison of task analysis methods for planning and scheduling. J. C. Fransoo, T. Wäfler, J. Wilson (eds.) in Behavioral Operations in Planning and Scheduling. Berlin: Springer.

Cegarra, J., van Wezel, W. 2012. Revisiting decision support systems for cognitive readiness: A contribution to unstructured and complex scheduling situations. Journal of Cognitive Engineering and Decision Making 6, 299–324.

Cheang, B., Li, H., Lim, A., Rodrigues, B. 2003. Nurse rostering problems: A bibliographic survey. European Journal of Operational Research 151 (3), 447–460.

Chenoweth, T., Dowling, K. L., St Louis, R. D. 2004. Convincing DSS users that complex models are worth the effort. Decision Support Systems 37 (1), 71–82.

Chopra, S., Lovejoy, W., Yano, C. 2004. Five decades of operations management and the prospects ahead. Management Science 50 (1), 8–14.

Coburn, F. G. 1981. Scheduling: The coordination of effort. I. Mayer (ed.) in Organizing for Production and Other Papers on Management, 1912–1924. Easton: Hive Publishing.

Conway, W., Maxwell, W. L., Miller, L. W. 1967. The Theory of Scheduling. Reading, MA: Addison-Wesley.

Crawford, S., MacCarthy, B. L., Wilson, J. R., Vernon, C. 1999. Investigating the work of industrial schedulers through field study. Cognition, Technology and Work 1 (2), 63–77.

Crossan, M., Cunha, M. P. E., Vera, D., Cunha, J. 2005. Time and organizational improvisation. Academy of Management Review 30 (1), 129–145.

Crowston, K. 1997. A coordination theory approach to organizational process design. Organization Science 8 (2), 157–175.

Das, J. P., Karr, B. C., Parrila, R. K., 1996. Cognitive Planning. New Delhi: Sage.

De Snoo, C., van Wezel, W. 2014. Coordination and task interdependence during schedule adaptation. Human Factors and Ergonomics in Manufacturing and Service Industries 24, 139–151.

De Snoo, C., Van Wezel, W., Jorna, R. J. 2011. An empirical investigation of scheduling performance criteria. Journal of Operations Management 29 (3), 181–193.

De Snoo, C., Van Wezel, W., Wortmann, J. C. 2011. Does location matter for a scheduling department? A longitudinal case study on the effects of relocating the schedulers. International Journal of Operations and Production Management 31 (12), 1332–1358.

De Snoo, C., Van Wezel, W., Wortmann, J. C., Gaalman, G. J. 2011. Coordination activities of human planners during rescheduling: Case analysis and event handling procedure. International Journal of Production Research 49 (7), 2101–2122.

de Vries, P., Midden, C., Bouwhuis, D. 2003. The effects of errors on system trust, self-confidence, and the allocation of control in route planning. International Journal of Human-Computer Studies 58 (6), 719–735.

Dixon, S., Wickens, C. D., McCarley, J. M. 2007. On the independence of reliance and compliance: Are false alarms worse than misses? Human Factors 49, 564–572.

Endsley, M. R., Kiris, E. O. 1995. The out-of-the-loop performance problem and level of control in automation. Human Factors 37 (1), 381–394.

Eom, S. B., Kim, E. 2006. A survey of decision support system applications (1995–2001). Journal of the Operational Research Society 57 (11), 1264–1278.

Eom, S. B., Lee, S. M. 1990. A survey of decision support system applications (1971–April 1988). Interfaces 20 (3), 65–79.

Eom, S. B., Lee, S. M., Kim, E. B., Somarajan, C. 1998. A survey of decision support system applications (1988–1994). Journal of the Operational Research Society 49, 109–120.

Erez, M., Zidon, I. 1984. Effect of goal acceptance on the relationship of goal difficulty to performance. Journal of Applied Psychology 69 (1), 69–78.

Faraj, S., Xiao, Y. 2006. Coordination in fast-response organizations. Management Science 52 (8), 1155–1169.

Framinan, J. M., Ruiz, R. 2010. Architecture of manufacturing scheduling systems: Literature review and an integrated proposal. European Journal of Operational Research 205 (2), 237–246.

Fransoo, J. C., Wäfler, T., Wilson, J. R., eds. 2011. Behavioral Operations in Planning and Scheduling. New York: Springer.

Fransoo, J. C., Wiers, V. 2006. Action variety of planners: Cognitive load and requisite variety. Journal of Operations Management 24 (6), 813–821.

Green, G. I., Appel, L. B. 1981. An empirical analysis of job shop dispatch rule selection. Journal of Operations Management 1 (4), 197–203.

Guerin, C., Hoc, J. M., Mebarki, N. 2012. The nature of expertise in industrial scheduling: Strategic and tactical processes, constraint and object management. International Journal of Industrial Ergonomics 42 (5), 457–468.

Gupta, J. N. 2002. An excursion in scheduling theory: An overview of scheduling research in the twentieth century. Production Planning and Control 13 (2), 105–116.

Haider, S. W., Moodie, C. L., Buck, J. R. 1981. An investigation of the advantages of using a man-computer interactive scheduling methodology for job shops. International Journal of Production Research 19 (4), 381–392.

Hammond, K. J. 1989. Chef. C. K. Riesbeck, R. C. Schank (eds.) in Inside Case-Based Reasoning. Hillsdale, NJ: Lawrence Erlbaum Associates.

Hayes-Roth, B., Hayes-Roth, F. 1979. A cognitive model of planning. Cognitive Science 3, 275–310.

Herrmann, J. W. 2006. Rescheduling strategies, policies, and methods. J. W. Herrmann (ed.) in Handbook of Production Scheduling. New York: Springer.

Higgins, P. G. 1992. Human-computer production scheduling: Contribution to the hybrid automation paradigm. P. Brodner, W. Karwoski (eds.) in Ergonomics of Hybrid Automated Systems-III: Proceedings of the Third International Conference on Human Aspects of Advanced Manufacturing and Hybrid Automation, Gelsenkirchen, August 26–28, 1992, Germany. New York: Elsevier.

Higgins, P. G. 1996. Interaction in hybrid intelligent scheduling. International Journal of Human Factors in Manufacturing 6 (3), 185–203.

Higgins, P. G. 1999. Job shop scheduling: Hybrid intelligent human-computer paradigm. University of Melbourne, Department of Mechanical and Manufacturing Engineering.

Hoc, J. M. 2000. From human-machine interaction to human-machine cooperation. Ergonomics 43, 833–843.

Hoc, J. M. 2006. Planning in dynamic situations: Some findings in complex supervisory control. W. Van Wezel, R. J. Jorna, A. M. Meystel (eds.) in Planning in Intelligent Systems: Aspects, Motivations, and Methods. Hoboken, NJ: Wiley-Interscience.

Hoch, S. J., Schkade, D. A. 1996. A psychological approach to decision support systems. Management Science 42 (1), 51–64.

Hofstede, G. J. 1992. Modesty in modeling: On the applicability of interactive planning systems, with a case study in pot plant cultivation. University of Wageningen, the Netherlands.

Hoogeveen, H. 2005. Multicriteria scheduling. European Journal of Operational Research 167 (3), 592–623.

Inagaki, T. 2003. Adaptive automation: Sharing and trading of control. E. Hollnagel (ed.) in Handbook of Cognitive Task Design. Mahwah, NJ: Lawrence Erlbaum.

Jackson, S., Wilson, J. R., MacCarthy, B. L. 2004. A new model of scheduling in manufacturing: Tasks, roles, and monitoring. Human Factors 46 (3), 533–550.

Jonsson, P., Mattsson, S. 2003. The implications of fit between environments and manufacturing planning and control methods. International Journal of Operations and Production Management 23(8), 872–900.

Jorna, R. 2006. Cognition, planning and domains: An empirical study into the planning processes of planners. W. Van Wezel, R. J. Jorna, A. M. Meystel (eds.) in Planning in Intelligent Systems: Aspects, Motivations, and Methods. Hoboken, NJ: Wiley-Interscience.

Karasek, R. A. 1979. Job demands, job decision latitude and mental strain: Implications for job redesign. Administrative Science Quarterly 24, 285–311.

Keen, P. G. W., Morton, M. S. S. 1978. Decision Support Systems: An Organizational Perspective. Reading, MA: Addison-Wesley.

Kiewiet, D. J., Jorna, R. J., van Wezel, W. 2005. Planners and their cognitive maps: An analysis of domain representations using multi dimensional scaling. Applied Ergonomics 36, 695–708.

Kleinmuntz, B. 1990. Why we still use our heads instead of formulas: Toward an integrative approach. Psychological Bulletin 107 (3), 296–310.

Kreipl, S., Pinedo, M. 2004. Planning and scheduling in supply chains: An overview of issues in practice. Production and Operations Management 13 (1), 77–92.

Kuo, W. H., Hwang, S. L. 1998. A prototype of a real-time support system in the scheduling of production systems. International Journal of Industrial Ergonomics 21 (2), 133–143.

LaForge, R. L., Craighead, C. W. 2000. Computer-based scheduling in manufacturing firms: Some indicators of successful practice. Production and Inventory Management Journal 41 (1), 29–34.

Lawler, E. E., Suttle, J. L. 1973. Expectancy theory and job behavior. Organizational Behavior and Human Performance 9, 482–503.

Lee, J., Moray, N. 1992. Trust, control strategies and allocation of function in human-machine systems. Ergonomics 35 (10), 1243–1270.

Lee, J., Moray, N. 1994. Trust, self-confidence, and operators adaptation to automation. International Journal of Human-Computer Studies 40 (1), 153–184.

Leung, J. Y., ed. 2004. Handbook of Scheduling: Algorithms, Models, and Performance Analysis. Boca Raton, FL: Chapman and Hall/CRC Press.

Locke, E. A. 1968. Towards a theory of task motivation and incentives. Organizational Behavior and Human Performance 3, 157–189.

Locke, E. A., Latham, G. P. 1984. Goal Setting: A Motivational Technique That Works. Englewood Cliffs, NJ: Prentice-Hall.

Locke, E. A., Latham, G. P. 1990. A Theory of Goal Setting and Task Performance. Englewood Cliffs, NJ: Prentice-Hall.

MacCarthy, B. L., Liu, J. 1993. Addressing the gap in scheduling research: A review of optimization and heuristic methods in production scheduling. International Journal of Production Research 31 (1), 59–79.

MacCarthy, B. L., Wilson, J. R., eds. 2001a. Human Performance in Planning and Scheduling. New York: Taylor and Francis.

MacCarthy, B., Wilson, J. 2001b. The human contribution to planning, scheduling and control in manufacturing industry: Background and context. B. L. MacCarthy, J. R. Wilson (eds.) in Human Performance in Planning and Scheduling. New York: Taylor and Francis.

McKay, K. N. 1992. A model for manufacturing decisions requiring judgement. PhD diss., University of Waterloo.

McKay, K. N., Black, G. W. 2007. The evolution of a production planning system: A 10-year case study. Computers in Industry 58 (8), 756–771.

McKay, K., Pinedo, M., Webster, S. 2002. Practice-focused research issues for scheduling systems. Production and Operations Management 11 (2), 249–258.

McKay, K. N., Safayeni, F. R., Buzacott, J. A. 1988. Job-shop scheduling theory: What is relevant? Interfaces 18 (4), 84–90.

McKay, K. N., Safayeni, F. R., Buzacott, J. A. 1995a. Schedulers and planners: What and how can we learn from them? D. E. Brown, W. T. Scherer (eds.) in Intelligent Scheduling Systems. Boston: Kluwer Publishers.

McKay, K. N., Safayeni, F. R., Buzacott, J. A. 1995b. "Common sense" realities of planning and scheduling in printed circuit board production. International Journal of Production Research 33 (6), 1587–1603.

McKay, K. N., Wiers, V. 2006. The organizational interconnectivity of planning and scheduling. W. Van Wezel, R. J. Jorna, A. M. Meystel (eds.), Planning in Intelligent Systems: Aspects, Motivations, and Methods. Hoboken, NJ: Wiley-Interscience.

McPherson, R. F., White, K. P. 2006. A framework for developing intelligent real-time scheduling systems. Human Factors and Ergonomics in Manufacturing and Service Industries 16 (4), 385–408.

Meal, H. C. 1984. Putting production decisions where they belong. Business Review 62 (2), 102–111.

Meystel, A. 2006. Multiresolutional representation and behavior generation: How does it affect the performance of and planning for intelligent systems? W. Van Wezel, R. J. Jorna, A. M. Meystel (eds.) in Planning in Intelligent Systems: Aspects, Motivations, and Methods. Hoboken, NJ: Wiley-Interscience.

Mietus, D. M. 1994. Understanding planning for effective decision support. PhD diss., University of Groningen, the Netherlands.

Miller, D. M. 1987. An interactive, computer-aided ship scheduling system. European Journal of Operational Research 32 (3), 363–379.

Molleman, E., Slomp, J. 2006. The impact of team and work characteristics on team functioning. Human Factors and Ergonomics in Manufacturing and Service Industries 16 (1), 1–15.

Moray, N., Dessouky, M. I., Kijowski, B. A., Adapathya, R. 1991. Strategic behavior, workload, and performance in task scheduling. Human Factors 33, 607–629.

Mumford, M. D., Bedell-Avers, K. E., Hunter, S. T. 2008. Planning for innovation: A multi-level perspective. M. D. Mumford, S. T. Hunter, K. E. Bedell-Avers (eds.) in Multi-level Issues in Creativity and Innovation. Amsterdam: Elsevier.

Muth, J. F., Thompson, G. L. 1963. Industrial Scheduling. Englewood Cliffs, NJ: Prentice-Hall.

Nakamura, N., Salvendy, G. 1994. Human planner and scheduler. G. Salvendy, W. Karwoski (eds.) in Design of Work and Development of Personnel in Advanced Manufacturing. New York: Wiley.

Nauta, A., Sanders, K. 2001. Causes and consequences of perceived goal differences between departments within manufacturing organizations. Journal of Occupational and Organizational Psychology 74 (3), 321–342.

Newell, A., Simon, H. A. 1972. Human Problem Solving. Englewood Cliffs, NJ: Prentice-Hall.

Nutt, P. C. 2007. Examining the link between plan evaluation and implementation. Technological Forecasting and Social Change 74, 1252–1271.

Olson, G. M., Malone, T. W., Smith, J. B., eds. 2001. Coordination Theory and Collaboration Technology. Mahwah, NJ: Lawrence Erlbaum.

Parasuraman, R., Molloy, R., Singh, I. L. 1993. Performance consequences of automation-induced "complacency." International Journal of Aviation Psychology 3, 1–23.

Pierce, J. R., Aguinis, H. 2013. The too-much-of-a-good-thing effect in management. Journal of Management 39 (2), 313–338.

Pinedo, M. L. 2012. Scheduling: Theory, Algorithms, and Systems. 4th ed. New York: Springer.

Pounds, W. F. 1963. The Scheduling Environment. J. F. Muth, G. L. Thompson (eds.) in Industrial Scheduling. Englewood Cliffs, NJ: Prentice-Hall.

Prietula, M. J., Hsu, W.-L., Ow, P. S., Thompson, G. L. 1994. MacMerl: Mixed-initiative scheduling with coincident problem spaces. M. Zweben, M. S. Fox (eds.) in Intelligent Scheduling. San Francisco: Morgan Kaufmann Publishers.

Rasmussen, J., Pejtersen, A. M., Goodstein, L. P. 1994. Cognitive Systems Engineering. New York: John Wiley & Sons.

Riedel, R., Fransoo, J., Wiers, V., Fischer, K., Cegarra, J., Jentsch, D. 2011. Building decision support systems for acceptance. J. C. Fransoo, T. Wäfler, J. Wilson (eds.) in Behavioral Operations in Planning and Scheduling. Berlin: Springer.

Riesbeck, C. K., Schank, R. C. 1989. Inside Case-Based Reasoning. Hillsdale, NJ: Lawrence Earlbaum.

Sabherwal, R., Jeyaraj, A., Chowa, C. 2006. Information system success: Individual and organizational determinants. Management Science 52 (12), 1849–1864.

Sacerdoti, E. D. 1975. The nonlinear nature of plans. Proceedings of the Fourth International Joint Conference on Artificial Intelligence. San Francisco: Morgan Kaufmann.

Sanderson, P. M. 1989. The human planning and scheduling role in advanced manufacturing systems: An emerging human factors domain. Human Factors 31, 635–666.

Schraagen, J. M., Chipman, S. F., Shute, V. J. 2000. Cognitive Task Analysis. Mahwah, NJ: Lawrence Erlbaum Associates.

Sharit, J., Eberts, R., Salvendy, G. 1988. A proposed theoretical framework for design of decision support systems in computer-integrated manufacturing systems: A cognitive engineering approach. International Journal of Production Research 26 (6), 1037–1063.

Sheridan, T. B., Verplank, W. L. 1978. Human and computer control of undersea teleoperators. Cambridge, MA, MIT Man-Machine Systems Laboratory Report.

Singh, D. T., Singh, P. P. 1997. Aiding DSS users in the use of complex OR models. Annals of Operations Research 72, 5–27.

Stoop, P. P., Wiers, V. C. 1996. The complexity of scheduling in practice. International Journal of Operations and Production Management 16 (10), 37–53.

Subramaniam, V., Raheja, A. S., Rama Bhupal Reddy, K. 2005. Reactive repair tool for job shop schedules. International Journal of Production Research 43 (1), 1–23.

Tenhiälä, A. 2011. Contingency theory of capacity planning: The link between process types and planning methods. Journal of Operations Management 29 (1), 65–77.

Thompson, J. 1967. Organizations in Action: Social Science Bases of Administrative Theory. New York: McGraw-Hill.

Van de Ven, A. H., Delbecq, A. L., Koenig, R., Jr. 1976. Determinants of coordination modes within organizations. American Sociological Review 41, 322–338.

van Nimwegen, C., van Oostendorp, H. 2009. The questionable impact of an assisting interface on performance in transfer situations. International Journal of Industrial Ergonomics 39 (3), 501–508.

Van Wezel, W. 2001. Tasks, hierarchies, and flexibility: Planning in food processing industries. PhD diss., University of Groningen, the Netherlands.

Van Wezel, W., Cegarra, J., Hoc, J. M. 2011. Allocating functions to human and algorithm in scheduling. J. C. Fransoo, T. Wäfler, J. Wilson (eds.) in Behavioral operations in planning and scheduling. Berlin: Springer.

Van Wezel, W., Jorna, R. J., Meystel, A. M., eds. 2006. Planning in Intelligent Systems: Aspects, Motivations, and Methods. Hoboken, NJ: Wiley-Interscience.

Van Wezel, W., Van Donk, D. P., Gaalman, G. 2006. The planning flexibility bottleneck in food processing industries. Journal of Operations Management 24 (3), 287–300.

Venkatesh, V., Bala, H. 2008. Technology acceptance model 3 and a research agenda on interventions. Decision Sciences 39 (2), 273–315.

Vicente, K. J. 1999. Wanted: Psychologically relevant, device- and event-independent work analysis techniques. Interacting with Computers 11, 237–254.

Vieira, G. E., Herrmann, J. W., Lin, E. 2003. Rescheduling manufacturing systems: A framework of strategies, policies, and methods. Journal of Scheduling 6 (1), 39–62.

Volkema, R. J. 1983. Problem formulation in planning and design. Management Science 29, 639–652.

Wäfler, T. 2001. Planning and scheduling in secondary work systems. B. L. MacCarthy, J. R. Wilson (eds.) in Human Performance in Planning and Scheduling. London: Taylor and Francis.

Waters, C. 1990. Expert systems for vehicle scheduling. Journal of the Operational Research Society 41 (6), 505–515.

Wiers, V. C. S. 1996. A quantitative field study of the decision behaviour of four shopfloor schedulers. Production Planning and Control 7 (4), 383–392.

Wiers, V. C. S. 2009. The relationship between shop floor autonomy and APS implementation success: Evidence from two cases. Production Planning and Control 20 (7), 576–585.

Wiers, V. C. S., Van Der Schaaf, T. W. 1997. A framework for decision support in production scheduling tasks. Production Planning and Control 8 (6), 533–544.

Yerkes, R. M., Dodson, J. D. 1908. The relation of strength of stimulus to rapidity of habit-formation. Journal of Comparative Neurology and Psychology 18 (5), 459–482.

CHAPTER 6

Hitting the Target

Process Control, Experimentation, and Improvement in a Catapult Competition

GEORGE EASTON

OVERVIEW

This chapter describes a team-based student project used as a capstone in an operations course taught on process analysis and Six Sigma at the Goizueta Business School at Emory University. The project involves the accuracy of shooting a catapult by teams consisting of four or five students. The project culminates in a Catapult Competition, which is generally held during the final exam period. The results of this competition form a major portion of the students' grade on the project. There is an additional written part of the assignment that constitutes the remaining portion of the project grade. The student teams are given the catapult they will shoot during the competition about a month in advance. Most student teams prepare fairly intensely for the competition over a two- to three-week period. Because the students are not given the target distances in advance, they must build a statistical model of the catapult's performance in order to determine what settings to use to shoot the target distances during the competition.

The Catapult Competition demonstrates a number of key concepts central to quality management systems and to Six Sigma in particular. Some of the concepts include the ideas of process, statistical control, common cause variation, special cause variation, and process capability (see, for example, Montgomery 2012 or Pyzdek and Keller 2010). Many of these concepts relate specifically to behaviors or perceptions typical among managers and, therefore, within organizations. Understanding these concepts should lead to different behaviors that help managers avoid common misconceptions and tactical mistakes. The Catapult Competition also sheds some light on randomness and performance evaluation, the tendency for people to believe in advance that they have more control over random outcomes than they do (Langer 1982), to assign causes to random outcomes after the fact (Fischhoff 1982; Tversky and Kahneman 1982), and to accept performance evaluation based on outcomes affected by a substantial degree of random variation.

THEORETICAL PERSPECTIVES

In many ways, the primary purpose of implementing a quality management system, such as Six Sigma, is to change the behavior of an organization's leaders, managers, and employees, from the top of the organization to the front line. It is true that part of the implementation of quality management systems involves changing various aspects of the infrastructure. But the majority of the effort associated with implementing quality initiatives, and certainly the most challenging parts, focuses on changing employee behavior, perceptions, thought processes, and ultimately organizational culture. Thus, behavior-related ideas are central to Six Sigma, total quality management (TQM), and other quality management systems.

One of the most fundamental aspects of quality management is a focus on "process." To a great extent "process" is the "atom" (or perhaps the "molecule") in quality management systems, in that it is viewed as a fundamental organizational building block. Quality management systems thus focus to a large extent on creating, controlling, and improving processes.

The idea of process is, at once, both very simple and surprisingly complex. It seems so simple that it is often given very little thought. But, in practice, things are not so simple. For example, if processes are important, then it is essential to have an operational definition of what a process is so that it is clear whether a work activity can be considered to be a process or not. Beyond whether or not there actually is a "process," it is also important to be able to determine if the process is appropriately defined for the tasks it addresses. Processes look very different for different kinds of work. A process on the factory floor of a manufacturing plant is different in character from a planning process or a problem-solving process. Such processes are defined at different levels of detail and in different ways (Easton 1993).

It is not possible to completely address the notion of process here, or differences in how processes are appropriately defined for different types of work. But, fundamentally, the idea of "process" is about structuring work. One of the great lessons that can be taken from the quality management movement over the last 30 years is that world-class levels of performance require more structure and rigor (that is, more "process") than naturally occurs within organizations. This is essentially a behavioral observation. The required level of structure and rigor do not tend to occur naturally.

Building on the idea of "process," another fundamental idea in quality management is of a process being in a state of (statistical) "control." To understand the concept of "control" in the quality management sense, it is first necessary to understand and accept the idea that almost all processes produce variation; and that a substantial part of this variation is, essentially, random (Pyzdek and Keller 2010). That is, the process's output is not identical every time, and the differences cannot be deterministically predicted. This idea is surprisingly hard for people to accept, and even harder for them to internalize. Managers commonly behave as though process performance is entirely deterministic or that any random variation is negligible. This often tacit assumption has many consequences, including leading managers to assign blame when processes produce defects or things otherwise go wrong. Such attributions of blame often emerge without any consideration of the possibility that the defect was entirely a result of the random variation. That is, there is no specific "cause" associated with the defect. Nevertheless, managers often tend to assign blame in such circumstances, operating as though it is obvious that there is a cause and someone is at fault. The idea that a process is in a state of "control" means that the variation that the process produces is stable and predictable (in a statistical sense). This stable variation is called the *common cause* or *intrinsic* variation (Pyzdek and Keller 2010; Deming 1986a; 1986b; Montgomery 2012). It is the variation that is inherent in the process, the variation that occurs when the process is functioning well.

Variation that occurs because of some kind of disruption to the process is called *special cause* variation (Pyzdek and Keller 2010; Deming 1986a; 1986b; Montgomery 2012). The incidents or factors underlying this variation are called special or assignable causes. This kind of variation *does* have specific causes that potentially can be identified (or assigned) and, ideally, prevented. Identification of special causes ranges from easy to difficult, with more difficult situations (which are not uncommon) requiring significant problem-solving effort (including, for example, experimentation). But the basic idea is that special cause variation is due to a disruption of the process and, consequently, a cause of the disruption can be uncovered—and potentially avoided in the future.

The methods of statistical process control (SPC) provide technical tools, based on statistical theory, that quantify process variation and offer criteria for assessing whether or not special cause variation has occurred (Montgomery 2012). That is, SPC provides tools and criteria to determine whether or not a process is "in control." When the process goes out of control (that is, special cause variation is detected), there is reason to believe that the "normal" functioning of the process has been disrupted and that a specific cause or causes can be found.

Related to the ideas of common and special cause variation is the idea of whether or not process variation can be controlled by process operators. Operator controllable variation is variation that the operator can control (which in most cases also means that the operator must be able to measure it). Non- or uncontrollable variation is variation that cannot be controlled by the process operator. Common cause variation is *not* controllable by the process operator. It is intrinsic to the process. It may be possible to reduce it, but this is typically difficult and requires some kind of fundamental change to the process. On a day-to-day basis, it is simply not controllable by the process operators. Special cause variation, in contrast, is often, but not always, controllable by the process operator, depending on the circumstances and the nature of the cause.

Note that the above discussion has focused on the intrinsic (common cause) variation in the process and whether or not the process is being disrupted by special cause variation. These are ideas that relate to whether or not the process is stable. Stability is a distinct idea, and a distinct characteristic of a process, that is different from whether or not the process produces product that is within specifications. It is perfectly possible for a process to be completely stable and yet have common cause variation that is sufficiently large that the process cannot reliably produce within specifications. Note that when a product's characteristics fall outside of the specifications, it is a defect.

The concept of process capability captures the idea that a process can reliably produce product within specifications. Thus, capability connects the ideas of control and intrinsic variation to the specifications (i.e., required performance). Note that the idea that a process is capable has, as a prerequisite, the requirement that the process is in control. A process that is not in control is not stable, and a process that is not stable cannot be counted on to reliably produce within specification limits. A capable process is one that is in control and has intrinsic variation small enough to remain entirely contained within the specification limits. Technical methods, generally called process capability indices, exist that quantify whether or not a process is capable (Pyzdek and Keller 2010).

These ideas relate to behavior, perception, and cognition in some very important ways. First, as mentioned above, managers, and other employees as well, often appear to expect that processes have either no or negligible random variation. This expectation that processes are essentially deterministic manifests in both behavior and design of the company systems. Careful examination of both individual behavior and company systems often reveals a tacit assumption that random variation is negligible (because such variation is not taken into account) or that any variation that does occur must have an identifiable and controllable cause. These assumptions are implicit and pervasive. For example, companies frequently do not take into account random variation when developing budgets. Consider the budget for producing a month's production of a manufactured product. There is often substantial random variation in such a cost because the defects, waste, downtime, energy, and labor are all random even when everything is working well. Yet almost everyone will talk about the "cost" of the product as though it is deterministic.

Because of the tendency to assume all variation has a specific cause, process operators (and their managers) tend to want to tamper with the processes (Krehbiel 1994; Deming 1986a; Pyzdek and Keller 2010). Process tampering refers to making adjustments to processes when they are in a state of statistical control, that is, in response to common cause variation. Because common cause variation is random process variation, it generally makes no sense to make adjustments to the process to try to "fix" or "correct" such variation. One of the behavioral impacts of implementing SPC is that process tampering is usually reduced because SPC gives clear criteria for identifying special cause variation (Pyzdek and Keller 2010).

Approaches to improving performance that tacitly trivialize the impact of random variation are used in many companies, often as primary improvement strategies. For example, if incentives are the primary strategy for improving performance, the tacit implication is that common cause variation is not one of the most important factors impacting performance. For all practical purposes, incentives cannot reduce common cause variation. Recognition of this is one of the ideas that underlies Deming's famous quote, "Best efforts are not sufficient" (Deming 1986a; 1986b). Best efforts in operating the process generally will not reduce common cause variation—what is required is a fundamental change in the system. If best efforts are not enough, then it is not reasonable to expect incentives to drive process improvement to the required performance levels. The most incentives can do is to focus attention and increase effort. Attention and effort are, of course, important, but just not enough.

Even when managers do recognize that processes produce variation, there is a general tendency for managers to behave as if all processes are both in control and capable. Most processes, even those well managed from a quality point of view, go out of control on occasion. In many organizations, a substantial fraction of the processes are out of control at any given time and some (sometimes many) processes are out of control more often than not. For processes that are not measured (and many are not), the vast majority are likely out of control.

Further, many managers (and employees) not only believe that processes are in control but are capable as well. When things are going wrong (e.g., when customers complain), many managers never seem to ask whether the process is in control or, if it is, whether it is capable. Instead, they seek to hold someone "accountable." This is 21st-century vernacular for finding who is at fault, who is to blame. But in many cases, processes are not sufficiently capable to meet customer requirements or are subject to special causes (i.e., are not in control) that are not due to any of the employees involved directly with the process. Rather, the problem stems from characteristics of the system. Deming (1986b, 142) claims that "the system that people work in and the interactions with [other] people may account for 90 to 95 percent of performance."

These ideas are what motivate Deming's point number 8 of his famous 14 points: "Drive out fear" (Deming 1986a; 1986b). Here the idea is that, fundamentally, the results belong to the system far more than to front-line employees. "Drive out fear" means that managers need to stop seeking people to "hold accountable" for poor performance, but should instead look primarily to system design, including the design and implementation of the quality management systems.

A great deal of research in psychology has focused on human perception of probabilities, variation, and randomness (Pious 1993; Kahneman et al. 1982; Nickerson 2004). Several key concepts from psychology appear to have critical implications for understanding various aspects of quality management. One of the most important is the "fundamental attribution error," which appears to be a basic human trait (Ross 1977; Ross and Anderson 1982; Pious 1993). The fundamental attribution error refers to the apparently human tendency to attribute poor outcomes to people's character, abilities, and so on (i.e., to their personal qualities) rather than to recognize external drivers as a potential cause. As a classic example, the driver that cuts us off on the highway is a "jerk" or an "idiot."

People tend not to attribute this action to an honest mistake or consider that the other driver is possibly impatient because he is going to the hospital. Rather we humans tend to assign blame. As another example, people tend to blame victims for the misfortune they experience. So the victim of a theft wasn't careful, the victim of heart disease ate too much bacon, and so on.

Thus, psychological research on attribution suggests that it may be a natural human characteristic for managers (and others) to "drive in fear" by seeking to assign blame when things do not go well. There is no similar natural tendency for managers to seek explanations in characteristics of system. The natural impulse is to jump to the conclusion that problems results because front-line employees are careless or lazy or stupid. This would certainly explain the phenomena observed by Deming that led him to include "Drive out fear" in his 14 points (Deming 1986a; 1986b).

The results from informal polling over the last several years indicate that very few of the MBA students entering the elective course Process Analysis and Six Sigma have ever heard of the fundamental attribution error. But it seems very important to know that blaming people for bad outcomes, especially blaming people that you do not know well personally, is a part of human nature. To counter such a natural tendency, leaders and managers need to first have this understanding and then carefully monitor their own reactions and behaviors. Knowing about the fundamental attribution error is more likely to help managers understand why self-monitoring, a key aspect of "emotional intelligence" (Goleman 1995), is important than would mere exposure to Deming's admonishment to "drive out fear."

In summary the following behavioral issues are important in the context of quality management:

1. More structure (more "process") is generally needed than occurs naturally in organizations.
2. Managers tend to (subconsciously) ignore or downplay the important of random variation.
3. Managers and other employees tend to behave as though all variation has an identifiable cause.
4. Employees tend to tamper with processes that are in control.
5. Managers and other employees tend to believe that all process are in control and capable, and thus often fail to consider these issues when things go wrong (such as customer complaints).
6. Managers have a strong tendency to assign blame. This tendency may stem from the fundamental attribution error together with the belief that all variation has a specific cause.
7. Many managers tend to believe that more effort is the solution to problems and the route to improvement. Thus, they fail to appreciate Deming's statement that "best efforts are not sufficient."

All of these behaviors relate to the Catapult Competition project described in the remainder of this chapter.

LEARNING ACTIVITY

The Catapult Competition that is described in this section is a team-based exercise I developed in 2001. It has been used a capstone project in various courses taught on operations management and quality management over the last 13 years. Most recently, this activity has served as the capstone project in an elective course, Process Analysis and Six Sigma, over the last five years at the Goizueta Business School and Emory University. The course is primarily taught to MBA students, but there also have been undergraduate students and master's-level students from Emory's Rollins School of Public Health.

As the name implies, the Catapult Competition involves firing a catapult. The catapult used is the "Statapult" (Air Academy Associates 2014), a training device that has achieved some level of renown among Six Sigma practitioners. I first encountered the Statapult while observing training conducted as a part of a Six Sigma–related initiative at Delta Airlines around 2000. I jokingly tell my students that they are not a part of the Six Sigma "club" if they have not had experience with the Statapult. The stature of this device in Six Sigma lore is the reason that I use this particular catapult. There is no reason why some other similar catapult would not be suitable for this exercise as well.

The most common use of the Statapult in Six Sigma training is to teach SPC. In typical SPC training, the catapult is fired using prescribed settings, and the data generated by measuring where the ball lands are used to construct control charts, identify special causes, and so on. More advanced uses of the catapult include teaching experimental design and analysis of the resulting experimental data. The Statapult can also be used to teach advanced methods such as robust design (Taguchi et al. 2004). The catapult has a number of control parameters and settings that affect both the distance it shoots and the variability.

The Catapult Competition is intended to reinforce process concepts, the idea of experimentation, the problem-solving process (referred to as DMAIC in Six Sigma: Define-Measure-Analyze-Improve-Control; see, for example, Pyzdek and Keller 2010, chapter 5), and regression analysis. But the approach taken in the Catapult Competition is quite different from the way that the Statapult is typically used in Six Sigma training. A number of factors came together to suggest the kind of exercise reported here.

First, simply having students shoot the catapult at a particular distance or target was too simple for a major course project and would only illustrate the ideas of process control and process capability to the students. When I was originally developing this exercise, I was planning to use it in a basic operations management course. Since such an introductory operations course does not cover experimental design, making the exercise more advanced by using the Statapult to illustrate design of experiments (DOE) was not really an option. On the other hand, all of the students in this elective have had statistical methods courses through regression. In fact, their knowledge of regression should be much more advanced than one would typically encounter in Six Sigma training in industry.

I thought it was also important to illustrate certain principles about randomness and random variation. At the time, I was teaching the core operations management course in the executive MBA program, so my students were typically in their mid-30s and had a great deal of business experience. Because of my experience with total quality management and Six Sigma, I knew there were important concepts and principles that are a part of the quality disciplines that were not (and still are not) widely understood among US managers. As the beginning of an effort to expand and change the students' thinking, very early in the course I surveyed the executive MBA students about what they believed were the characteristics of great C-level leaders (CEO, COO, CIO, CFO, etc.). I generally got what I consider to be the "usual" set of responses. These include statements like "Hold people accountable," "Create the right incentives," "Reward performance," "Make the tough decisions," "Create a vision," and so on.

It is interesting to consider these kinds of statements, all of which seem both simple and sensible enough on their face, in the light of the implications of Deming's point 8 in the 14 points ("Drive out fear"), Deming's quote "Best efforts are not sufficient," and Deming's famous bead experiment (Turner 1998; Latzko and Saunders 1995). Deming's bead experiment is a quality training exercise that simulates a production process that is fundamentally not capable (and therefore produces defects), even though it is in control. When the bead experiment is run, "workers" are "held accountable" based on their "performance." But their performance is entirely random. Holding people "accountable" for random outcomes is virtually certain to drive in fear over time.

The ideas of "holding people accountable" and "pay for performance" in contrast to "Best efforts are not sufficient" and "Drive out fear" led me to frame the exercise as an objective competition based on the student team's performance in accurately shooting the catapult. Shooting accuracy is objective performance that can be measured and rewarded using points that affect the students' grades (pay for performance). The "twist" in the competition I have developed in comparison to typical training exercises is that I do not have the students shoot the catapult at one fixed target or at one fixed specification of the catapult's settings. Rather, the students are presented with random target distances.

The distances that the student teams are to shoot are not given to them in advance, although the range of distances is. The students are told that they will have to shoot at three randomly selected target distances between 80 and 130 inches from the base of the catapult. During the actual competition, the random distances are given to each of the shooting teams one at a time. Thus, the student team's primary task is to figure out how to accurately shoot the catapult at any specified distance between 80 and 130 inches.

The student teams consist of four to five students. While the catapult can be fired with three students, it is much better to have at least four students on a team. The students are given a "kit" that includes the following (see figure 6.1):

1. The catapult (including the rubber band that propels the catapult's arm)
2. The ball that will be shot
3. A tape measure
4. Two pieces of poster board, preferably of a dark color, that will serve as the landing area for the shots (the "landing pad")
5. Masking tape
6. Baby powder
7. A plastic cup

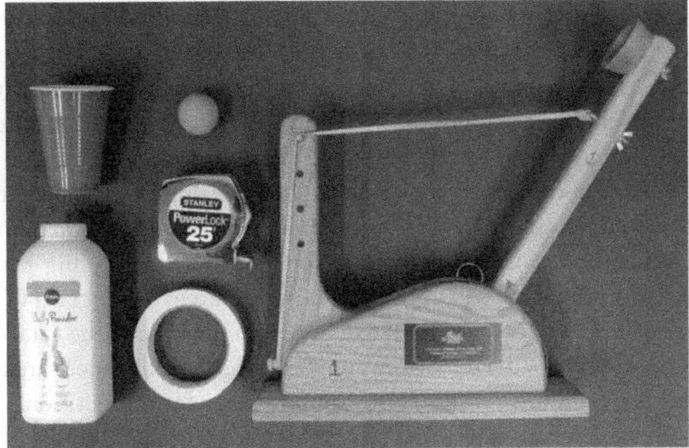

Figure 6.1 The Catapult Competition Kit

The student teams are given these kits approximately one month before the actual competition.

Figure 6.2 shows the catapult and the adjustments that students can make. Specifically, the students are allowed to adjust three factors: (1) the location of the pin on the front vertical arm (the "front pin") of the catapult, which has four possible positions; (2) the location of the pin that stops the forward travel of the catapult arm (the "stop pin"), which has six possible positions; and (3) the pull-back angle of the arm, a continuous variable, which ranges from wherever the stop pin stops the forward travel to 180 degrees. There are two other factors that can be adjusted

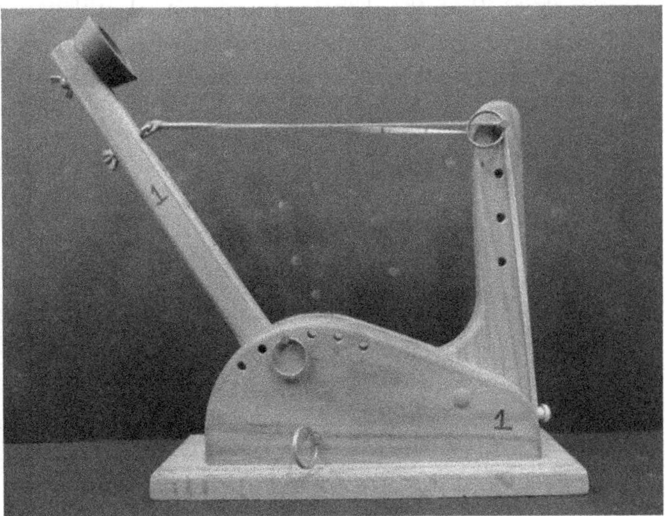

Figure 6.2 The Catapult
There are three factors that can be adjusted for the Catapult Competition. The factors are (1) the location of the pin on the front vertical arm (four positions); (2) the location of the pin at the top edge of the base that limits the motion of the arm (the "stop pin"—six positions); and (3) how far back the arm is pulled (maximum is 180 degrees).

on the catapult, the position of the cup that holds the ball and where on the arm the rubber band connects. But in order to simplify the competition, I require that the students hold these two factors constant using the settings I prescribe.

The actual Catapult Competition is conducted in two rounds. The student teams are randomly divided into two groups of equal size, with the first group shooting during the first round and the second group shooting during the second round.

Prior to the first round, all teams set up and are permitted to practice for about 20 minutes. Setup involves placing the catapult and the landing pad (poster board) so that the landing pad covers the range of target distances (80″ to 130″). The tape measure is placed so that it extends from the base of the catapult to the far end of the landing pad. During the competition, firing distances are read from the tape measure. Figure 6.3 shows the catapult setup for competition.

Randomly assigned to each shooting team are two of the nonshooting teams, each of which supplies one student whose role is to measure and record shot distances. The two recorders are tasked with independently measuring the distance that each shot travels to the nearest eight of an inch (the finest graduation on the tape measures is a sixteenth of an inch). The shooting distances are given to one of these two recorders on a folded piece of paper with instructions that they are to reveal the distances to the shooting team one at a time as they are required, keeping them secret until the next distance is required. These shooting distances are randomly selected for each team (using a process described in more detail below) and rounded to the nearest inch.

When the competition begins, the recorder with the "secret" distances gives the first distance to the shooting team. The shooting team then needs to quickly determine the settings they will use for the catapult in order to shoot the required distance. The team is allowed to use a notebook computer for this, but they cannot take any practice shots. Thus, the shooting team must select their settings and shoot based on whatever "model" of the catapult they have developed, and the result of every shot taken counts in the competition. The shooting team then fires

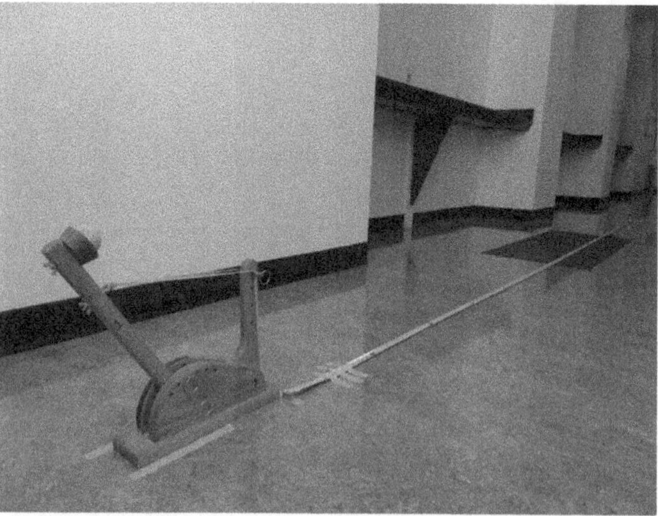

Figure 6.3 The Catapult Setup for Competition

10 shots, trying to hit as close to the target distance as possible. They can make whatever adjustments they want to during these 10 shots, but every shot counts.

Before each shot, the ball fired by the catapult is dusted with baby powder so that it leaves a mark on the landing pad in order to aid the measurement of the distance traveled by the two recorders. The two distances should be measured independently by the two recorders, and these are then averaged. Accuracy of the shots is assessed using the squared deviation from the target distance. To simplify and streamline the process, the competition does not involve any sort of angular accuracy, only the perpendicular distance from the base of the catapult to where the ball lands. The job of the recorders is to look at the location of the ball, make a "visual" orthogonal projection onto the tape measure, and report the distance. Figure 6.4 shows the mark left by a shot together with the tape measure that is used to determine the distance.

Once the shooting team has fired 10 shots at the first distance, the recorder with the "secret" distances gives the team the second distance. The shooting team then determines what settings will be used for this distance. They then fire 10 shots trying to hit the second distance. This process is repeated one more time so that the team will ultimately have fired 10 shots at each of three randomly selected distances, for a total of 30 shots. Performance is assessed using the mean-squared error; that is, the squared distance from the target is computed for each shot and these are then added up and divided by 30.

Originally, the Catapult Competition assignment only involved the competition and the grades were entirely based on the accuracy of the shooting (100% pay for performance). Over the last few year, however, I have made about 60% of the grade based on the shooting performance, with the other 40% based on a written report (in the DMAIC format) that describes how the team developed their model for determining catapult settings, the process they use for shooting the catapult, how they brought it into control, and so on. I only give general instructions

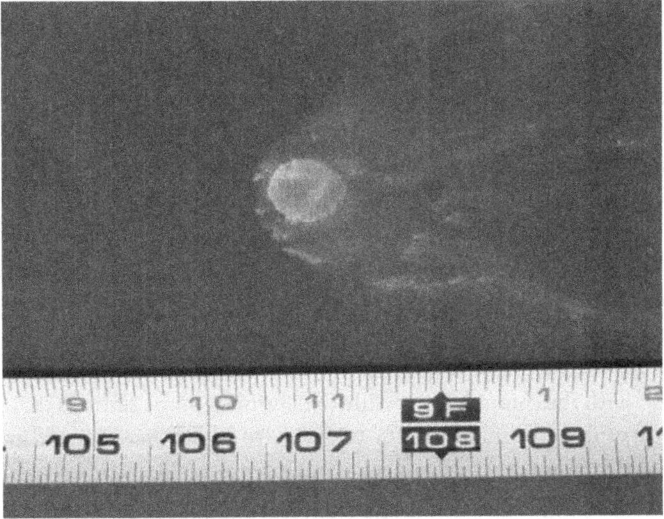

Figure 6.4 The Mark Left by the Ball

with respect to the written report, except for two requirements. The report must use the DMAIC format and it must present control charts that demonstrate that the team can shoot the catapult in an "in control" manner. The entire competition is usually worth about 20% of the overall course grade.

How Teams Should Prepare for the Competition

If students have deeply understood the course material (which may or may not be the case), the strategy for executing the project is fairly straightforward. First, a team needs to figure out how to shoot the catapult in an "in control" fashion. In this step, the student team should "pick any low-hanging fruit" with respect to preventing special cause variation and reducing common cause variation. The team should also develop an understanding of how much intrinsic variation there is in the shooting process. They should develop a clear and well-specified shooting procedure, including clear roles for the team members. As mentioned above, one of the requirements of the written part of the assignment is that students demonstrate that the shooting process is in control by providing the relevant control charts.

The next thing the teams need to do is develop a model to predict the distance the catapult will shoot based on the settings. This is one of the few areas where I give students some guidance. Specifically, I suggest (but do not require) that teams each build a regression model to predict the expected distance the catapult will shoot based on the settings. The teams are not permitted to communicate with each other about the project, so each team must create its own approach based on its own data. During the competition, student teams are given a target distance, a Y-value in the regression equation. They then have to solve the regression model "backward" to determine a corresponding set of X-values (the catapult settings). Note that the solution is usually not unique, so when multiple settings (multiple X-values) can be used to shoot a given distance, students will have to decide which of the possibilities to use.

One of the three factors students are allowed to change is a continuous variable (how far back the shooting arm is pulled). The other two factors correspond to holes drilled in the catapult for inserting pins, so these are ordered categorical variables. These ordered categorical variables can be modeled via dummy variables (reinforcing what the students should know from their previous regression course). I specifically suggest to students that they consider using dummy variables for these settings, although I do not tell them exactly how to do this unless they ask. Some teams use the pin hole numbers as the corresponding X-variable instead of dummy variables (which is permitted but not recommended).

So an efficient approach to the project might go along the following lines:

1. "Play" with the catapult for a while to determine some settings that shoot the catapult in the middle of the target range and at the short end and long end of the target range and to get a rough sense of the accuracy (variation).
2. While "playing" with the catapult, start identifying what the shooting "process" will need to be (such as roles for each person) and what the

major sources of variation are (such as the catapult not being held down in a stable fashion). There is a great opportunity to use some of the quality tools here such as the cause-and-effect diagram.

3. Pick settings that shoot in the middle of the range, and work the process out until the catapult can be shot in an in-control fashion. Define and document the shooting process, including the roles of each team member. It is generally not too difficult for students to figure out how to shoot the catapult so that the distances are in reasonable statistical control when they are not changing the settings. To satisfy the requirements of the assignment, control charts demonstrating statistical control also should be produced.
4. The team should then demonstrate that the catapult can be shot in an in-control manner at the settings identified during the informal "playing" stage that result in a longer distance and a shorter distance. This step is optional, but it does not take a great deal of time to do and it is useful to be reasonably sure that the shooting process developed will work well over the full range of distances required.
5. Once the catapult can be shot in a stable and in-control fashion, the next step is to run a designed experiment in order to develop a statistical model that predicts the shooting distances. It is natural to consider a factorial experiment. There are three settings (factors) on the catapult that students are allowed to change: the front pin location with four settings, the stop pin location with six settings, and the pull-back of the shooting arm. Thus, if one were to use three different pull-back distances, there are $4 \times 6 \times 3 = 72$ combinations of the levels of the factors. You probably want at least five shots at each of the settings, so this means a total of 360 shots. While this could be done (once they get going, a team can easily shoot 100 shots per hour), this is a practical exercise, not a theoretical one, and some simplification makes a great deal of sense. In addition, the "playing" stage above (step 1) should have clearly shown students that not all of the settings make sense. A very reasonable experiment to end up conducting might involve two levels for the front pin, two levels, for the stop pin, and three or four levels for the arm pull-back. With four pull-back levels and five replicates, such an experiment would involve $2 \times 2 \times 4 \times 5 = 80$ observations. The number of replicates could easily be increased to 10, which would mean a total of 160 observations.
6. Regression can then be used to build a model for the expected shooting distance based on the pin setting and the arm pull-back. For each of the four combinations of the front pin and the stop pin, the model can then be back-solved for the pull-back distance required to shoot the distance. When there are multiple feasible solutions, a decision must be made about which one to choose. Estimating the standard deviation corresponding to the settings is one way to choose between multiple settings that shoot the same distance.
7. The final step is to validate the model in a future session.

All of the above can be completed in about three two- to three-hour sessions *if* the team knows what they are doing and has a clear plan.

How Teams Actually Prepare for the Competition

What actually happens when the typical team tries to prepare for the competition is quite different. Most teams experience several false starts and a good deal of "groping" around. This is probably foreseeable as the "how to" part of the project is unstructured and unspecified. This vagueness and ambiguity, however, is probably also one of the key reasons that students learn so much from the project. Students, of course, have a hard time truly understanding and internalizing answers to questions or ways to approach particular issues until the question or issue is their own. There is nothing like struggling with an unstructured problem to make various issues real to students.

Many teams, perhaps most teams, seem to expect to meet for one afternoon and conduct a factorial experiment to collect the data they need to create the model they will use in the competition. They often begin the experiment without having "played around" with the catapult, so they do not have a good idea of what kinds of settings hit the target range. Some settings shoot completely outside of the target range (either much too far or much too short) and create missing values because the ball does not land in the range covered by the tape measure. Such settings should not even be a part of the experiment used to create the model. Thus, simplification of the experiment based on the knowledge gained by playing around with the catapult early on to get a feel for its performance is both appropriate and generally a great benefit.

Students often begin their experiment without giving much thought, in advance, to process control (in spite of the fact that this is probably the leading topic in the course). Usually, in the process of trying to conduct this experiment, students uncover, and try to address, a number of process control issues. Two issues that almost every student team uncovers are stability of the catapult (it must be firmly held down, and it is very hard for one person to both shoot the catapult and hold it down firmly) and operator-to-operator variation.

A casual examination of the catapult may lead one to believe that it is trivial to shoot. While it is not difficult to shoot the catapult, it is not trivial to shoot the catapult accurately. It really takes a team of three to five people to conduct the data collection necessary to assess process control and to conduct the experiment to develop the shooting distance model. Here are the typical roles students assume:

- One person must hold down and stabilize the catapult. This is extremely important and is done by either standing on the edges of the base of the catapult or by holding the body down with one hand anterior to the location of the pin that stops the forward motion of the catapult arm.
- One person will actually shoot the catapult. Usually this person's functions are to dust the ball with baby powder, load it into the cup, draw

back the catapult arm the required amount (there is a scale in degrees), and release it to complete the shot.
- At least one person must observe where the ball lands and measure the shot distance, retrieve the ball, and return it to the shooter. When the data collection really ramps up, these are too many tasks for one person, so most teams use two people—one retrieve the ball and return it to the shooter, and one to spot the ball's landing location, measure the distance, and record it.

Teams sometimes have people in other roles. For example, in the list above, I have not discussed who will input the target distances into the spreadsheet model on a notebook computer to obtain the required catapult settings. Since this is done only three times during the competition between the sets of 10 shots, this role can be performed by either the person stabilizing the catapult or the shooter. There is also a parallax issue in reading the angle scale that measures the degree of arm pull-back. Some teams dedicate a separate person to reading the scale who does so from a fixed position next to the scale (usually by the student lying on his or her stomach, sighting carefully between the marks on the scale and the arrow on the arm).

Teams that just jump right in and try to conduct the experiment immediately without "playing" with the catapult first (and beginning to develop a systematic approach) generally begin to figure out that this was a mistake as the experiment unfolds. They "discover" some of the process control issues (like holding down the catapult base) as they get into the experiment. Since they make changes in their procedures during the experiment, they know that their "process" was not consistent during the experiment's data collection, and they have a sense that this might contaminate their results. Sometimes, they discover that this first experiment was ineffective when they realize that they really do not know how to analyze the data because they have missing data due to settings that shoot the catapult wildly outside of the target range.

Teams often come to me with questions after their first data collection. Teams that have jumped right in (without playing around with shooting the catapult, addressing process control issues, or thinking about analyzing the results) have often tried to do a massive factorial experiment using all possible settings. As discussed above, these teams almost always have missing data that they do not know how to handle. In most cases, they have only one replicate at each setting because of the large number of combinations they are considering. Many of these teams begin to realize, during their conversation with me, that they have major problems with the data from their first experiment. I generally ask them about whether their shooting process was consistent during the experiment, suggest simplification of the design, and emphasize the importance of replicates. Quite a few teams at this stage realize that they should probably conduct their experiment again. Other teams, however, do not realize that their initial data collection is essentially unusable until they try to validate their model on a subsequent shooting session.

DISCUSSION

The Catapult Competition project is very beneficial to the students. It forces them to confront many of the issues faced in controlling real processes in companies. It demonstrates common cause variation and special cause variation. It also requires experimentation and reinforces students' understanding and use of regression analysis, thereby building on previous courses.

The competition also illustrates concepts like process standardization. Essentially all teams understand that they should try to reduce variation affecting the process even before they have objective evidence that such variation matters. This is made most obvious by the fact that virtually every team selects only one person to actually shoot the catapult, a person who does not change between the data collection and the competition. That is, they recognize the issue of operator-to-operator variation and realize that they should eliminate it without actually conducting an experiment to confirm that it is there. In the course of working through the project, students internalize why processes must be well defined.

Many teams go far beyond the recognition that it is a good idea to eliminate operator-to-operator variation, standardizing many other aspects of the shooting process as well. Such aspects include how the catapult arm is held (e.g., between thumb and index finger or pulled down with the thumb), how sighting of the angle scale is done to measure the degree of pull-back, how the ball is placed in the cup, or how quickly the catapult arm is pulled back, and so on. In short, the Catapult Competition causes students to think hard about sources of variation.

The project also illustrates some issues relating to measurement precision. The competition instructions clearly indicate that the distances should be measured to the nearest eighth of an inch. This is essentially impossible to do using only a visual read of the distance the ball travels, even when the ball is dusted with baby powder and leaves a mark (see figure 6.4, a photograph of the mark left by the ball together with the tape measure). Even with instructions that the distance should be measured to the center of the mark, it is difficult or impossible to measure the distance to the nearest eighth of an inch. For example, in figure 6.4, it would be very reasonable to measure the distance the ball traveled as either 106¾ or 106⅞ inches. In the process of trying to measure where the ball lands to the nearest eighth of an inch, it becomes clear to most students that there is a significant amount of random measurement variation and that the "real" distance can easily vary from a student's best estimate (which should be to the nearest eighth of an inch) by at least two- or three-eighths. This understanding is enhanced by the fact that the two measurers usually do not end up with exactly the same measurement. Measurement error is, of course, an important feature of real measurement systems.

The structure of the competition, while demonstrating issues of measurement error by demanding that students measure to a precision not realistic with the unaided eye, is designed to reduce this measurement error by averaging measurements made by two independent assessors. It is also interesting to note that it is very difficult, psychologically, for the two observer students to actually make their measurements independently. This is another interesting behavioral feature of the exercise. The students' instincts are not to just make their own independent measurements, report them, and then rely on the average to reduce variability. Rather they appear to have a strong urge to discuss the measurement with the other assessor in order to reach consensus. This urge is so strong (i.e., it appears to be so natural) that it is very difficult to keep the two assessors from discussing their measurements even after repeated, forceful reminders that they should make their own best assessment and report it. Further, intellectually, students understand why independent measurements are important and that averaging reduces variability. But they nevertheless have a very hard time adhering to the procedure.

I use one other technique both to reduce measurement error and to increase the shooting team's confidence in the measurement process. When the two recorder's measurements differ by more than three-quarters of an inch, the distance used for the shot is taken to be the closest distance to the target of the recorders' two distances and their average. Thus, when the recorders disagree, the shooting team gets the benefit of the doubt and the best number for the team of the three numbers is used. So disagreement between the recorders generally benefits the shooting team. This means that the shooting team is not particularly distressed when the recorders' measurements do not agree.

There are some more advanced issues in the catapult project that few teams address. In particular, the elastic properties of the rubber band are quite complex. For example, how the rubber band is pulled back does matter. If the rubber band is pulled back quickly, it has more power than if it is pulled back slowly. Related to this, one thing that matters a lot is the "dwell," the length of time that the rubber band is held with the catapult arm pulled back to the intended shooting angle. To get the most accurate shooting, it is most effective to pull the rubber band back and let it stabilize. Occasionally, I will have a team that discovers this, and will use a technique such as pulling the arm back to the desired angle and then counting to three before releasing the arm. In addition, the rubber bands are most likely affected by temperature, and their properties most likely change over time.

It would not be hard to have a quite a few follow-on exercises that would drive home many of these concepts that the students have begun to appreciate as a result of the catapult project. For example, it would be interesting to have students run experiments to demonstrate the effects of dwell, or determine if there is detectable operator-to-operator variation. There is also the issue of selecting among the settings when multiple settings are predicted by the regression model to shoot the same distance. The setting that has the smallest standard deviation is the one that should be used. It would be interesting to lead students through conducting the experiments necessary to determine which among the competing settings is best. This could be taken as far as conducting formal Taguchi-methods analysis (Taguchi et al. 2004).

It would also be interesting to experimentally address the stability of the shooting performance, and thus the statistical model, over time. It is quite likely that the rubber band's characteristics do change over time, and thus from shooting session to session. One approach for addressing these kinds of changes might be to calibrate the shooting model for each session. This could be done by setting the catapult to shoot at a standard distance (e.g., 100″, about in the middle of the range of distances), and then use the deviation from the expected distance to adjust the model. For example, if a team shot 20 shots at settings supposed to yield a distance of 100″ but the average came out to 95″, this would suggest that all distances should be scaled by a factor of 100 / 95 = 1.053 before being entered into the model to determine the settings to be used. Or perhaps the adjustment should be additive rather than multiplicative (i.e., add 100 − 95 = 5″ to each distance before putting it into the model). I believe that I have had only one team make any attempt at a formal method for calibrating their model for each session (and thus for the actual competition).

While many interesting follow-on exercises could be done, this could only work in the context of a one-semester course if the competition could be conducted in the first half of the semester. I don't think that the students know enough about the concepts of process and process early on in the course for this to be feasible.

Some "Quick and Dirty" Statistical Analysis

I now turn attention to one of the motivations for the original design of the Catapult Competition, namely the idea of "pay for performance" and how it relates to concepts like common cause variation. Specifically, I would like to determine the extent to which the differences in performance between the teams may be explained by random variation rather than differences in effectiveness of the teams' shooting methods and models (the team's shooting ability). Figure 6.5 shows the mean-squared error for the 16 teams in the competition that occurred in December 2013 plotted in order from the best performance to the worst. This plot suggests that there is a dramatic difference between the performance of the best teams and the worst teams. For example, the best team had an MSE of 3.08, while the worst team had an MSE of 48.79, a factor of almost 16.

The distribution of the MSE, however, is very skewed. Because of this, I have remade the plot using the natural log of team MSEs (figure 6.6). This plot creates a substantially different impression, with the performance of the worst team now only a factor of about 3.5 times the performance of the best team.

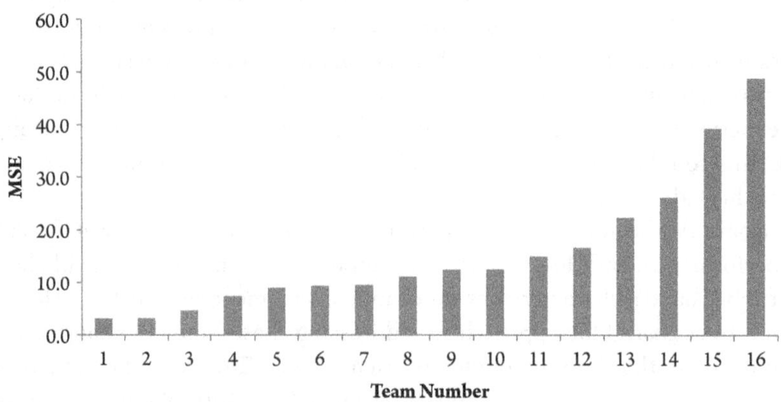

Figure 6.5 Team Mean-Squared Errors

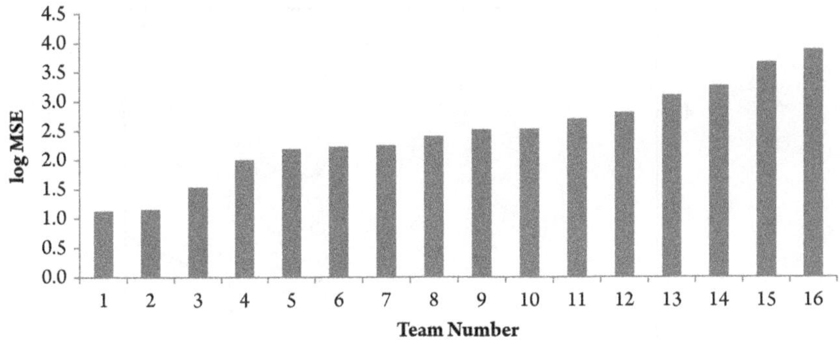

Figure 6.6 Team Mean-Square Errors (Log Scale)

Some "quick and dirty" statistical analysis can be used to try to assess whether there is evidence that there are real differences in teams' shooting ability. First, I use a quantile-quantile plot (also called a probability plot), a standard graphical method for examining distribution shape. If there are no differences between the teams, the MSEs should look like 16 random draws from the same distribution. Such plots are often used in analysis of variance (ANOVA) to examine main effects and interactions to see if they appear to deviate from what would be expected if the main effects and interactions were 0.

If the distances of the shots taken are normally distributed with constant variance, and if the statistical models that the teams used are "accurate" so that the shots are unbiased, then the MSEs are estimating the variance of the distribution of the shooting error. Sample variances are proportional to χ^2 random variables with n–1 degrees of freedom. This suggests that a χ^2 quantile-quantile plot (χ^2 probability plot) might be informative. In a sample standard deviation, the sample mean is used to estimate the true mean. This is the reason that the degrees of freedom are n–1, not n. But in this case, the sample mean is not used to estimate the true mean because the target distances are given. If the shooting models are unbiased, the deviations from the target distances will have expectation 0. As a result, we sum up the squared deviations, and the appropriate degrees of freedom is n. Here $n = 30$. Whether one uses 29 or 30 degrees of freedom will make no practical difference in the plots. Figure 6.7 shows the χ^2 quantile-quantile plot base on 30 degrees of freedom.

If the MSEs really did follow a χ^2_{30} distribution, then the points in the figure would fall on approximately a straight line. To aid in interpretation of the plot, I have plotted a line fit to the middle 50% of the points. This plot suggests that the two worst teams, and perhaps the four worst teams, have mean-squared error higher than they should have if the differences in the MSE performance of the teams were due to chance. That is, the figure suggests that the worst two teams, and perhaps the worst four teams, really are different from the rest. The MSE performance of the other teams, however, looks like they could be random draws from the χ^2_{30} distribution.

I explore this a bit further by running a one-way ANOVA. I base the dependent Y-variable on the squared deviations from the target. Because I do not want

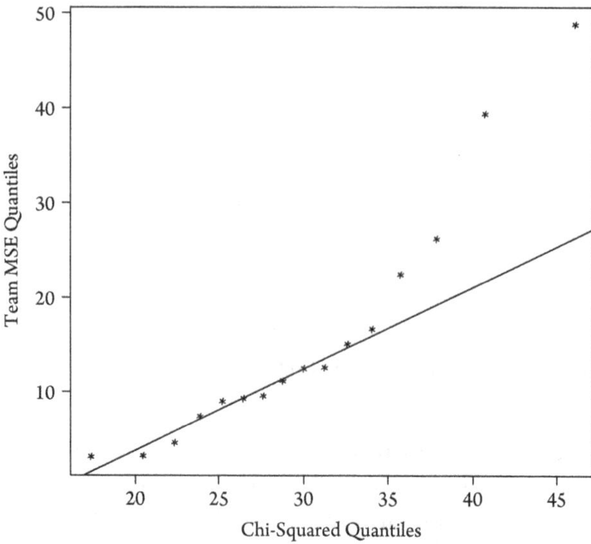

Figure 6.7 Chi-Squared Quantile-Quantile Plot

this analysis to be influenced unduly by a few outliers, I have removed the largest positive (the longest long shot) and largest negative (the shortest short shot) from each teams data, leaving 28 observations for each team. Thus this one-way ANOVA has 16 levels (one for each of the 16 teams) and 28 replicates (for the 30 shots each team takes minus the two trimmed shots). Finally, because these squared deviations are highly skewed and because a few of the deviations are 0, I use the log of the squared deviations after adding 0.25 to each deviation. Adding a small number to the data to allow for logs to be taken when there are zeros is a technique referred to in Tukey (1977) as "starting" the data. Thus, I end up with 28 logged deviations for each team.

The results of the ANOVA are highly significant, with the *p*-value of the F-test for the equality of the means being less than 0.0001 (the analysis was performed with the JMP statistical software; JMP 2013). Examination of the residuals does not show any important deviations from the assumptions of normality and equal variance. This means that the ANOVA should be reasonably valid, and there is extremely strong statistical evidence that not all of the teams are the same with respect to their ability.

Although the teams are not all the same, to identify which teams actually differ from each other, I used JMP to run Tukey's HSD test, which is a multiple comparison test of whether or not the differences between each pair of tests is significant. Table 6.1 shows the output in the form of JMP's "Connecting Letters" report. In this table, teams are statistically different if they do not have the same letter in any of their letter columns. Conversely, any teams that do have the same letter in one of their letter columns are not statistically different. The overall significance level for all the tests combined is 5%.

From the table, there is evidence that the team with the best performance in the competition is better than the six worst teams (since the A letter spans the first

Table 6.1. JMP "Connecting Letters" Output

Team	Letter A column	Letter B column	Letter C column	Letter D column	Team mean (smaller is better)
1	A				0.0032
2	A	B			0.4760
3	A	B			0.6111
4	A	B			0.7601
5	A	B	C		1.0286
6	A	B	C	D	1.1247
7	A	B	C	D	1.1475
8	A	B	C	D	1.2176
9	A	B	C	D	1.2391
10	A	B	C	D	1.2938
11		B	C	D	1.4050
12		B	C	D	1.4065
13		B	C	D	1.5285
14		B	C	D	1.6128
15			C	D	2.2617
16				D	2.3852

Note: The table shows the results of Tukey's HSD multiple comparisons test for the team means.

10 teams but not teams 11 to 16). But this also means that there is no statistical evidence that the best-performing team differs in ability from teams ranking 2 to 10. Similarly, the second best team is significantly better than the worst two teams (see the letter B column). The worst team is significantly worse than the top five teams (see the letter D column), but not statistically different from the teams ranking 6 to 15. Finally, the teams ranking 6 to 10 are not statistically different from any of the other teams since each of these teams has all four of the letters A–D.

Thus, the statistical evidence indicates that the best-performing teams are really better than the worst-performing teams. But a great deal of the variation in performance may be due to random variation. This conclusion is consistent with what would be expected in advance. It also is consistent with ideas put forward by a number of quality management "gurus" that performance evaluation really should only give greater rewards to the few best for whom there is really evidence of better performance than the vast majority of employees. Similarly, rewards or compensation should only be withheld from the few worst performers for whom there is evidence of performance really worse than the vast majority. Everyone else should be rewarded roughly the same. For a discussion of performance appraisal from this point of view, see Deming (1986a) and Scholtes (1997).

When I first began using the Catapult Competition, it certainly occurred to me that students might complain that the grade for the catapult competition was determined, to a large extent, by random variation. Had such complaints occurred, I was prepared to justify the competition by pointing to the class's own advocacy of "pay for performance" and "holding people accountable." I would also point out that the Catapult Competition is entirely fair in that everyone is treated in an identical manner, the results are objective, all of the teams have the same opportunity to excel or not at the time of the competition, and that the best/worst teams really are different (so the team's approach is important). But in all of the times I have run the competition, no student has ever objected that shooting performance in the Catapult Competition has a large random component, and that grading based on the outcome of the competition therefore also has a large random component. In fact, students appear to be very comfortable with the fact that the competition results are entirely objective and they accept the results without argument, or even much discussion. What the students do discuss is what their team did or did not do, what errors were made, and what mishaps occurred that resulted in their team's performance. Such discussion is generally very causal and deterministic and lacking in mention of random variation.

The idea that the results of the Catapult Competition have a large random component is certainly not unique. In fact, the vast majority of situations where grades are assigned contain large random components. This also is true in most athletic competitions. It also is true whether or not "grading" is based on rank (order of finish in many athletic competitions) or on an absolute scale. Grades for the Catapult Competition are based on rank, but could instead be based on an absolute scale determined by predefined ranges of the shooting MSEs. Such ranges could be chosen by considering quantile ranges of the distribution of MSEs based on the performance of the teams in past competitions. But this would still involve the same kind of randomness in the resulting final grades, unless the performance categories were large in comparison to the variation. Even then, there would be similar issues of randomness for performance results that are close to the cutoff boundaries. So we constantly face situations, in academic classrooms as well as firm performance contexts, where outcomes and corresponding rewards are, at least to a substantial extent, random.

It would seem then that we are all conditioned to accept assessment based on results that contain large random components. "Conditioned" may be the wrong word here, because this tendency may well be inherent or tacit and not really present at a conscious level of awareness. We seem to believe in advance that we have substantial control over random outcomes. After the fact, we find causes so that the random outcomes tend to not seem that random at all.

References

Air Academy Associates. 2014. Statapult. http://www.sixsigmaproductsgroup.com/Products/tabid/111/ProdID/29/Language/en-US/CatID/3/Statapult_Catapult.aspx, downloaded March 26, 2014.

Deming, W. E. 1986a. Out of the Crisis. Cambridge, MA: Massachusetts Institute of Technology Center for Advanced Engineering Study.

Deming, W. E. 1986b. Quality Productivity and Competitive Position. Cambridge, MA: Massachusetts Institute of Technology Center for Advanced Engineering Study.

Easton, G. 1993. The 1993 state of U.S. total quality management: A Baldrige examiner's perspective. California Management Review 35 (3), 32–54.

Fischhoff, B. 1982. For those condemned to study the past: Heuristics and biases in hindsight. D. Kahneman, P. Slovic, A. Tversky (eds.) in Judgment under Uncertainty: Heuristics and Biases. Cambridge: Cambridge University Press.

Goleman, D. 1995. Emotional Intelligence. New York: Bantam.

JMP. 2013. Version 11.0. SAS Institute Inc., Cary, NC.

Kahneman, D., Slovic, P., Tversky, A. eds. 1982. Judgment under Uncertainty: Heuristics and Biases. Cambridge: Cambridge University Press.

Krehbiel, T. C. 1994. Tampering with a stable process. Teaching Statistics 16, 75–79.

Langer, E. 1982. The illusion of control. D. Kahneman, P. Slovic, A. Tversky (eds.) in Judgment under Uncertainty: Heuristics and Biases. Cambridge: Cambridge University Press.

Latzko, W. J., Saunders, D. M. 1995. Four Days with Dr. Deming: A Strategy for Modern Methods of Management. Reading, PA: Addison-Wesley.

Montgomery, D. C. 2012. Statistical Quality Control. New York: Wiley.

Nickerson, R. S. 2004. Cognition and Chance: The Psychology of Probabilistic Reasoning. Mahwah, NJ: Lawrence Erlbaum Associates.

Pious, S. 1993. The Psychology of Judgment and Decision Making. New York: McGraw-Hill.

Pyzdek, T., Keller, P. 2010. The Six Sigma Handbook: A Complete Guide for Green Belts, Black Belts, and Managers at All Levels. 3rd ed. New York: McGraw-Hill.

Ross, L. 1977. The intuitive psychologist and his shortcomings: Distortions in the attribution process. L. Berkowitz (ed.) in Advances in Experimental Social Psychology, vol. 10. New York: Academic Press.

Ross, L., Anderson, C. A. 1982. Shortcomings in the attribution process: On the origins and maintenance of erroneous social assessments. D. Kahneman, P. Slovic, A. Tversky (eds.) in Judgment under Uncertainty: Heuristics and Biases. Cambridge: Cambridge University Press.

Scholtes, P. 1997. The Leader's Handbook: Making Things Happen, Getting Things Done. New York: McGraw Hill.

Taguchi, G., Chowdhury, S., Wu, Y. 2004. Taguchi's Quality Engineering Handbook. New York: Wiley-Interscience.

Tukey, J. W. 1977. Exploratory Data Analysis. New York: Pearson.

Turner, R. 1998. The red bead experiment for educators. Quality Progress 31 (6), 69–74.

Tversky, A., Kahneman, D. 1982. Causal schemas in judgments under uncertainty. D. Kahneman, P. Slovic, A. Tversky (eds.) in Judgment under Uncertainty: Heuristics and Biases. Cambridge: Cambridge University Press.

CHAPTER 7

The Wait or Buy Game

How to Game the System That's Designed to Game You Back

ANTON OVCHINNIKOV

OVERVIEW

The Wait or Buy game introduces students to strategic consumer behavior within the context of dynamic pricing and revenue management (RM). Dynamic pricing and revenue management refer to the practice of changing prices over time, for example, airlines' pricing strategies or retail markdowns. Strategic consumers anticipate future prices and time their purchases to maximize utility. For example, in October a consumer may see a desirable scarf selling for $60, but anticipating that by January the scarf may be discounted down to $30, he or she may delay purchasing it until January. Likewise, a consumer who sees an advertised airfare of $475 for travel from Miami to New York may be tempted to wait with the hope that fares will drop.

This pattern of behavior introduces two critical questions: (1) How do consumers make the wait-or-buy decision? (2) How should firms dynamically price goods/services to maximize profits in the face of strategic consumer behavior?

Current managerial practice does not effectively address either of these questions. With regard to the firm question, strategic consumer behavior is typically addressed in a logical, yet ad hoc way. For example, an airline may institute a rule closing certain low fare-classes a predetermined number of days prior to departure so that prices generally increase, incentivizing consumers to buy as soon as their travel needs emerge. Retail firms reduce inventory and practice inventory cross-shipping between stores to diminish the probability of consumers finding an item in stock at a discounted price—which discourages waiting. With regard to the consumer question, "big data" made it possible to predict future prices. A service originally called FareCast (which is now part of Bing Travel) provides such predictions for airfares.

Both of these questions are subject to active research attention. Although answers remain elusive (as discussed below), higher-level insight is beginning to emerge. The Wait or Buy game immerses students in a situation highlighting these questions so that they develop answers for themselves. There are three versions of the game. In the first version, students adopt the role of buyers who must decide whether to buy early or wait for a lower price. Explicit in this role is acknowledgment of the risk of not acquiring the product, or acquiring it at a higher price. The buyer competes with multiple computer-generated buyers and with a computer-generated seller. In the second version, students adopt the role of the seller, who faces strategic, computer-generated buyers and must determine the number of discounted units to offer. The third version of the game is live, pitting students in the roles of buyers and seller against one another.

Below, I frame a theoretical approach to help understand these two questions, briefly describe the design of the game, and then present examples of its classroom application. A demonstration version of the game is available at http://waitorbuy.darden.virginia.edu/demo. For the full version of the game, please contact Darden Business Publishing. DBP will provide qualified instructors with a login and password, teaching notes that describe the game, sample analysis, and a detailed discussion of the game pedagogy.

THEORETICAL PERSPECTIVE

Revenue management models traditionally assume that consumers are myopic and buy immediately upon seeing a price below their valuation (see Talluri and van Ryzin 2004). Revenue management with strategic consumers is a relatively newer topic in operations management, which started with assumptions about how strategic consumers behave and derived analytical predictions bearing on firm response. The topic has seen increasing research attention. For example, Aviv and Pazgal (2008) showed that the benefits of changing prices contingent on earlier sales are small when dealing with strategic consumers. Liu and van Ryzin (2008) showed that sellers may benefit by strategically rationing inventory (i.e., understocking) to induce consumers to buy early. Ovchinnikov and Milner, J. M. (2012) showed that when consumers begin to learn discount patterns, sellers should intermix periods when discounted items are available with periods when some inventory is strategically perished—although this no means a complete list; Levin, Sahin, Su, Swinney, Zhang, and many others also have made valuable contributions (for a review see Shen and Su 2007).

Behavioral research focused on revenue management decision-making also has typically framed seller decision-making in situations when consumers are myopic. Bearden, Murphy, and Rapoport (2008) reported the results of an experiment testing decision biases in a traditional revenue management context (i.e., without strategic consumers), and Bendoly (2011) extended their work to multiple classes of capacity. The results from both these studies suggest that sellers may be overly demanding when they have a lot of time and inventory (i.e., priced their "scarf" too high in "October"), but are insufficiently demanding toward the end of the selling period (i.e., priced too low in "January").

The article by Kremer, Maintin, and Ovchinnikov (2013) is perhaps the only operations management article that considers sellers' behavior when some consumers are strategic. Interestingly, their results suggest the opposite pattern. Sellers acted myopically when faced with strategic consumers. They priced too low early in the selling season, thus selling more and obtaining a larger-than-optimal profit in the primary selling season (in "October"), but by doing so diminished their ability to generate revenue in the markdown period ("January").

Studies of buyers' behavior are also very scarce. Li, Granados, and Netessine (2013) used empirical data from the travel industry to estimate the proportion of strategic consumers. They found that over 35% of consumers exhibit elements of strategic behavior. The results from Mak and coauthors' (2013) lab experiments indicated that only 6% of consumers exhibit completely myopic behaviors. The majority—even though they sometimes either buy when should have waited or wait when should have bought early—in the aggregate, look as if they are all strategic. The "mistakes" of those who wait instead of buying cancel out the mistakes of those who buy instead of waiting, so that a given consumer could safely assume that all other consumers are fully strategic. The seller, however, can benefit by exploiting the fact that in every selling season a not-insignificant proportion (up to 40% in their study) acts somewhat myopically. Osadchiy and Bendoly (2010) offer an alternative view on whether consumers are strategic, but generally also find that many of them are.

Dynamic pricing with strategic consumers is somewhat similar to the problem of selling a durable good, which has attracted significant attention in economics literature (see Coarse 1972; Lazear 1986; and Besanko and Winston 1990 for the fundamental analytical treatments of the firm's question—assuming, again, that buyers are fully rational, and Reynolds 2000; Cason and Reynolds 2005, and Cason and Mago 2010 for the experimental treatments). While conceptually similar to the operations research referenced above, this research evaluates settings not in focus in operations research; for example, the case when a single seller interacts with a single buyer over a single unit of the good—clearly not a setting observed in retail markdowns.

CASE EXAMPLE

The Wait or Buy game is wrapped around a stylized instantiation of a circumstance I encountered when helping a midsize online florist optimize its logistics. In this situation, flower growers (buyers) ship roses every Friday to a regional distributor using an air-carrier firm (seller). Each week buyers have a fixed shipping budget and want to save as much as possible by shipping at a low price. Prices are constant Monday through Wednesday, but on Thursday the seller may offer several units of capacity at a discount and then raise the price on Friday on any unsold units. This situation is then repeated over a number of weeks.

Although some buyers purchased early during the Monday through Wednesday window, some tried to "game the system," waiting until Thursday. They were competing with other growers for the limited discounted capacity. Further, the Thursday price was typically low enough to attract other kinds of shippers (not necessarily flower growers), who would otherwise not use air transportation for their goods. Thus the growers who waited until Thursday were competing for capacity attractive to additional nonflower shippers as well.

The seller generally limited the number of units of capacity available at the discounted price on Thursday. It knew that some of the waiting growers, who did not receive a unit of discounted capacity, would still be willing to ship their flowers at a price higher than was available during the Monday–Wednesday window. The Friday price and the Thursday units of capacity were selected so as to, ideally, capture the leftover demand from growers who waited for a discount by did not get a unit of capacity.

In rare situations when a grower was left out of capacity, there remained the outside option to ship flowers with a general courier carrier. This option was viewed as inferior by the growers, for both price and nonprice reasons. Although the price was somewhat (but not much) higher than a typical "Friday" price, the real issue was that the extra transportation legs, loading/unloading, and short-term storage at the courier warehouse had negatively affected flowers' quality by the time they arrived at the distributor.

It is tempting to ask why the growers and the air carrier hadn't established a long-term contractual relationship rather than relying on the spot-market interaction and "gaming" each other. This failure is primarily related to a lack of trust between the growers and the air carrier: in the past there had been long-term contracts, but because growers occupied only a fraction of carrier's capacity, it had always had an incentive to discount the remaining capacity, which in turn incentivized the growers to abjure from the existing contract. Neither growers nor carrier were interested in exploring the long-term contract option.

LEARNING ACTIVITY

Teaching Objectives

The Wait or Buy game is designed for a class in which the instructor wants to discuss strategic consumer behavior in a dynamic pricing and revenue management context. Version 1 serves as a common "platform" that creates a common point of reference for strategic consumer behavior. Although many students will have personal real-life experiences, these are likely to be quite diverse, making it hard for instructors to start the discussion from scratch. After developing a common understanding of these behaviors, students then manage the revenues of the air-carrier firm in version 2 and compete against each other in version 3.

By playing the game and discussing their strategies, students will be able to accomplish the following learning objectives:

- Understand what "strategic consumer behavior" means in the revenue management and dynamic pricing context, and how it is linked to other areas of management and pricing
- Describe what kinds of behaviors are implied and what drives these behaviors
- Explain and demonstrate why strategic consumer behavior is a problem for a revenue management system that ignores it; illustrate the phenomenon of "spiral down"
- Analyze a firm's revenue management strategy with respect to its ability to deal with strategic consumers; criticize several popular strategies
- Suggest improvements to firm revenue management strategy to increase the efficiency with which it is able both to prevent and to exploit strategic consumer behavior

In a course where the underlying revenue management concept is in less direct focus (e.g., in a general decision models/quantitative analysis/management science class), the objectives could be modified as follows:

- Understand the dynamics of buyer-seller competition
- Be able to model these dynamics and provide insight into buyers' and sellers' strategies
- Reinforce the use of decision trees, probabilities, and expected outcomes (expected utility) in decision-making under uncertainty
- Reinforce the use of dynamic decision-making (downstream decisions)
- Illustrate the use of dynamic programming; build and solve dynamic programming models

Variants of the Game

Version 1 puts students into the familiar role of consumers (buyers) who behave strategically and decide whether to:(1) buy early when the product is guaranteed to be available, or (2) wait for a lower price but risk not acquiring the product or acquiring it at a higher price. Each game round (one week) students are asked to make a seemingly simple decision: Buy now or wait until Thursday?

Version 2 puts students into the role of the air carrier (seller). Each game round (one week) students are asked to decide how much of the unsold capacity as of Thursday should be offered at a discount. Historical information about students' past decisions as well as a variety of other data is available to facilitate decision-making. Version 3 combines versions 1 and 2 and sets students in competition against one another. Some students play the role of buyers (as in version 1), and one student plays the role of the seller (as in version 2).

In version 1, a single student plays as a buyer (flower grower) against a computer generating the actions of the seller and other buyers. While some of these other buyers are also strategic (i.e., they may decide to wait or buy according to some algorithm), others are bargain hunters (i.e., they attempt to purchase anytime a discount is offered). In version 2, a single student plays the role of seller (air carrier) against a computer that generates all buyers' actions. As with version 1, some buyers are strategic, while some are bargain hunters. Version 3 is the general version of the game where the seller and buyers are played by students.

Instructions

Buyer's Instructions

Imagine yourself as a flower grower. You grow beautiful roses and ship them to a flower distributor who then sells them to retailers. Each week, on Friday evening, you ship a new batch of fresh roses using an air-freight carrier, MoonQuest.

You have a budget of $2,999 per week to make the shipment. MoonQuest charges $2,999 per shipment, but it offers a lower early-week price of $2,500—if you place an order for the shipment any time before Wednesday evening, you are guaranteed to ship at $2,500. You will then make $499 in saved shipping costs.

Lately, however, you have noticed that when MoonQuest has some empty capacity it has not sold by Thursday, it may drop the price to $1,500 per shipment. Thus, waiting until Thursday could result in $1,499 in net savings on shipping.

Such a drop in price, however, could attract shippers that otherwise would not be using MoonQuest's services at all. You estimate that there are three such shippers, in addition to MoonQuest's four regular shippers including you. MoonQuest's total capacity is six shipments or "units," which are of approximately equal size and weight.

It is not clear how much of the unsold capacity MoonQuest is willing to discount. MoonQuest may not discount all the capacity it has: For example, if it has three unsold units on Thursday morning, it may put only two units on sale at $1,500 each; then, once those two units are sold, MoonQuest may raise the price for the remaining unit above the initial $2,500 early-week price. Your experience suggests that this remaining unit could go for as high as $2,999, the full price.

Your experience also suggests that other regular price shippers may also (like you) be thinking of waiting until Thursday in order to take advantage of the discount. Thus, if you wait, there is no guarantee that you will ship your roses at all—you may not get the shipping at a discount, and you may not get it at the full price. In that case, you would be forced to use the general overnight courier to ship the roses. This costs $4,000.

In the simulation, you will be playing for 40 weeks (periods), and each week, you will make a decision to either place an order now or wait until Thursday. If you don't make any choice, then your order will be automatically placed on Thursday. Each week (period) you may have access to the data on the number of units of MoonQuest's capacity sold at regular price during this week, and the number of units put on sale the previous week. Hopefully, this will help you make a better decision.

Objective: Save money by ending with the highest-possible net savings
Decision: Each period, place order now (M–W) or wait until Thursday
Link to the game: http://waitorbuy.darden.virginia.edu
Logins, passwords, and game ID are provided by your instructor.

Seller's Instructions

Imagine yourself as a pricing and revenue management analyst for an air-freight carrier called MoonQuest. Among other flights, you are managing a weekly flight departing on Friday evening from Miami, Florida, to a New York city. This flight is historically used to take fresh flowers to the city's floral retailers.

Given customs, logistics, and other factors, the aircraft can carry up to six standardized cargo containers. The full fare you charge per container is $2,999.

The demand consists of two segments. In the first segment, there are four major flower growers. To ensure their demand, you are giving these growers a discounted fare of $2,500 on orders placed Monday through Wednesday (M–W). You also guarantee capacity for the orders placed on those days. In exchange, the growers guarantee they have enough volume that a shipment is necessary every week. The second segment consists of several local manufacturers. These manufacturers typically do not use air freight because of the high cost, but you estimate that if the price per shipment decreased to $1,500, three manufacturers would be willing to ship each week.

Given these considerations, your pricing is as follows: $2,500 per unit is charged M–W for the four flower growers. On Thursday the remaining (two) units of capacity are allocated first-come, first-served to other shippers, which obviously cannot guarantee that any capacity will be available.

Lately you have noticed, however, that the growers have started to game your pricing. Some growers appear to be willing to risk the capacity guarantee and have been waiting until Thursday to place their orders, even though they are aware of their need for shipping earlier in the week. As a result, you believe MoonQuest is missing some revenue-generating opportunities. In an effort to improve the situation, you decide to limit the number of units of capacity available at a discounted price on Thursday, and offer all remaining capacity as of Friday morning at the full fare ($2,999). You hope that by dynamically adjusting the number of units available at a discount, you can discourage growers from waiting for discounts, while still selling your remaining capacity in most cases. That might, of course, disappoint the growers, who as a result may not be able to ship with MoonQuest at all. But in your opinion their inability to ship would be their own fault. Had the growers bought early, they would have been able to ship their flowers. In the worst case, a third-party shipping option, which would cost $4,000, also was available for growers.

In the simulation, you will play for 40 weeks (periods). In each period, you will make a decision about how many units of inventory to offer at a discounted price of $1,500 on Thursday. You can access various pieces of information, such as sales in the current or past weeks, your historical decisions, and the number of shipments purchased at different prices, among other things. Hopefully, this will help you make a better decision.

Objective: Make more money by ending with the highest-possible revenue
Decision: How many units to put on sale each Thursday
Link to the game: http://waitorbuy.darden.virginia.edu
Logins, passwords, and game ID are provided by your instructor.

Game Interface

This is an online game. The instructor provides a URL, login, password, and game ID, and the student logs in as he or she would on a regular website. On the back end, the game is tied into a database with game parameters and results. The visual interface is done in Adobe Flash. System requirements are checked at the first login. At each login, the player is asked to agree to an informed consent. Below I review the students' interface; the instructor interface is discussed in the teaching note available from the Darden Business Publishing.

Game 1: Buyer's Interface

Figure 7.1 depicts a typical student interface. A calendar is presented at the top of the window, together with a time clock measuring the time left to make a decision for a current week. Below the calendar is a message line that reports the progression of the week (e.g., if the player had been able to get discounted carrier space or not).

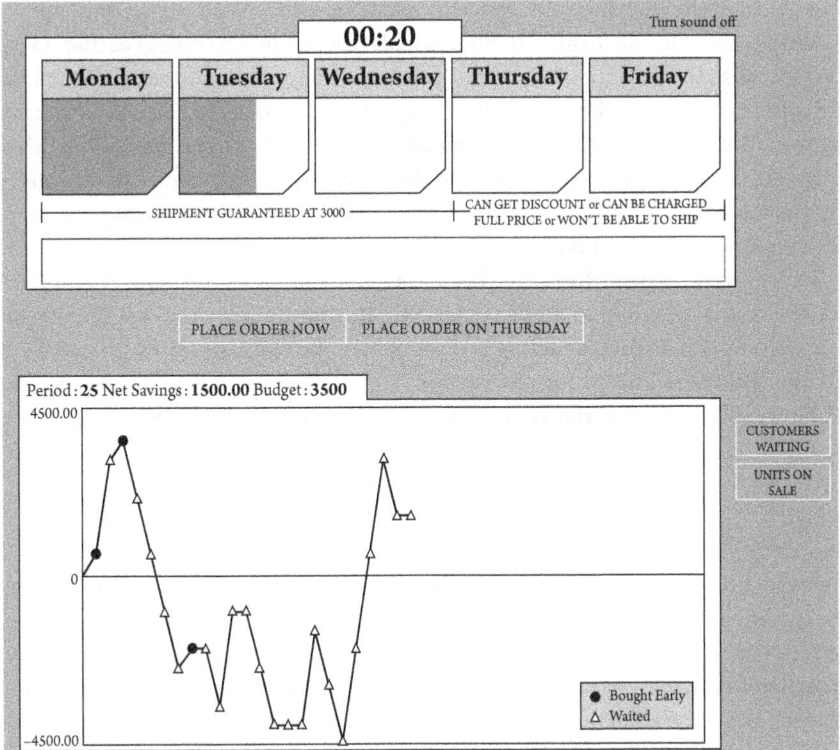

Figure 7.1 Student Interface, Game 1

Two buttons—"Place Order Now" and "Wait Until Thursday"—are in the center of the window. Immediately below the decision buttons is the chart depicting the net savings from the beginning of the game, as well as the set of decisions made so far (a yellow triangle is pictured for the weeks when a Wait choice was made, and a green circle is depicted for the periods with a Buy decision).

Available information (e.g., the number of customers who waited in previous periods; a full list is given in the Instructor's Interface section) can be displayed either as buttons or as a table—per the instructor's choice. If the information is displayed as buttons, the player has to click on a button to obtain the information, and then close the pop-up window to proceed (figure 7.2a). If the information is displayed as a table, the player sees all the information fields simultaneously (figure 7.2b).

Once started, the game cannot be paused; a player can, however, close the browser completely, and then log back in later to start from the round that was interrupted. At the end of the game, once the final decision round has been completed, the game stops and reports players' final net savings. The player with the highest level of savings wins.

Game 2: Seller's Interface

Overall, the seller's game interface is very similar to the buyer's interface in version 1 (figure 7.3), with two specific differences: (1) human players are given some extra time between Wednesday and Thursday to finalize their capacity decision, and (2) all of the information needed to make an optimal decision is available.

With respect to the former distinction, players can make choices earlier. However, because the amount of capacity that can be offered at a discount (the *remaining capacity*) changes, the initial choice may become infeasible; hence extra time is given. With respect to the remaining capacity, the data can be displayed both as a separate table (same as in version 1, to the right of the charts) and directly on the charts. Clicking on the colored boxes next to the information description turns the corresponding chart on and off.

However, the bigger difference between versions 1 and 2 is found "behind the scenes" and is invisible to student players—it is in the way strategic buyers' behavior is modeled. This modeling is discussed in the teaching note available from Darden Business Publishing. In version 3, where some players are buyers and some are sellers, the interfaces on each side are identical to those described above.

Instructor's Interface

Below is a brief review of the instructor's interface; a full description is available for qualified instructors via the Darden Business Publishing. The instructor's interface is designed to give instructors flexibility in their deployment of the game. Instructors can add, modify, and delete games, test-play games, add and remove players, and access a database with game results.

Within a game there are five areas of instructor control: (1) pricing, demand, and capacity parameters, (2) timing of the game rounds, (3) data pertaining to the

(a)

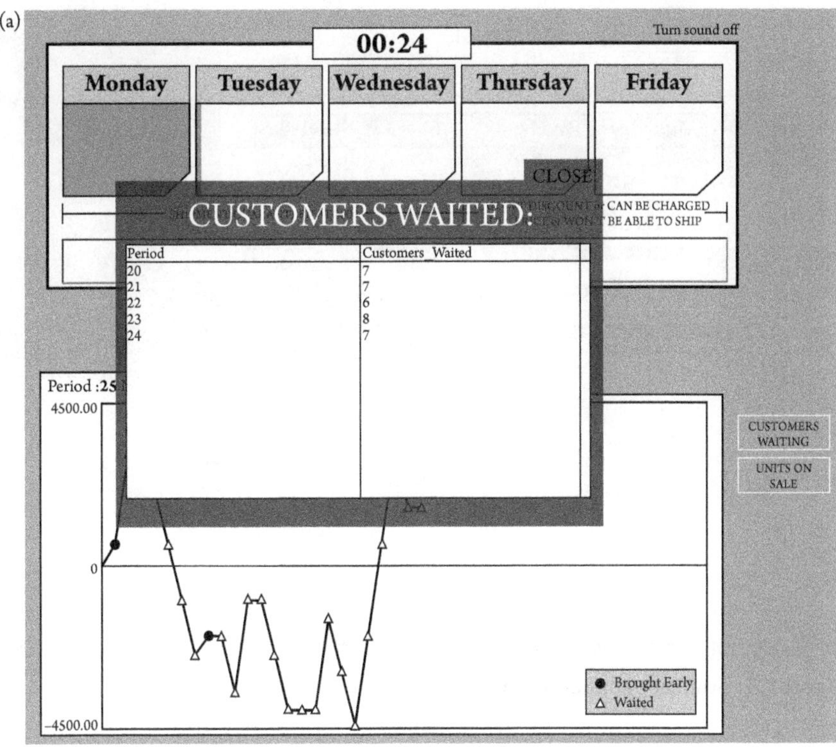

(b)

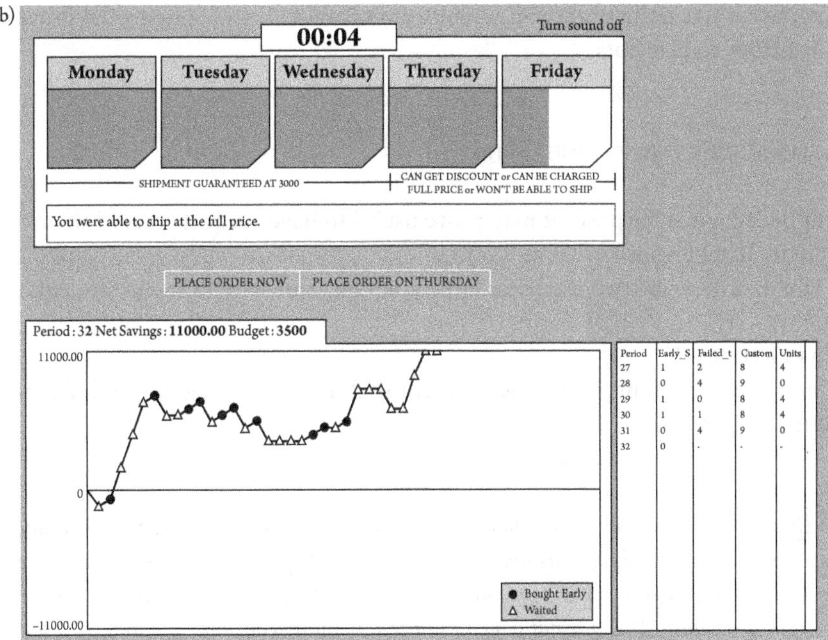

Period	Early_S	Failed_t	Custom	Units
27	1	2	8	4
28	0	4	9	0
29	1	0	8	4
30	1	1	8	4
31	0	4	9	0
32	0	-	-	-

Figure 7.2 Two Options for Viewing Available Information
a. Buttons
b. Table

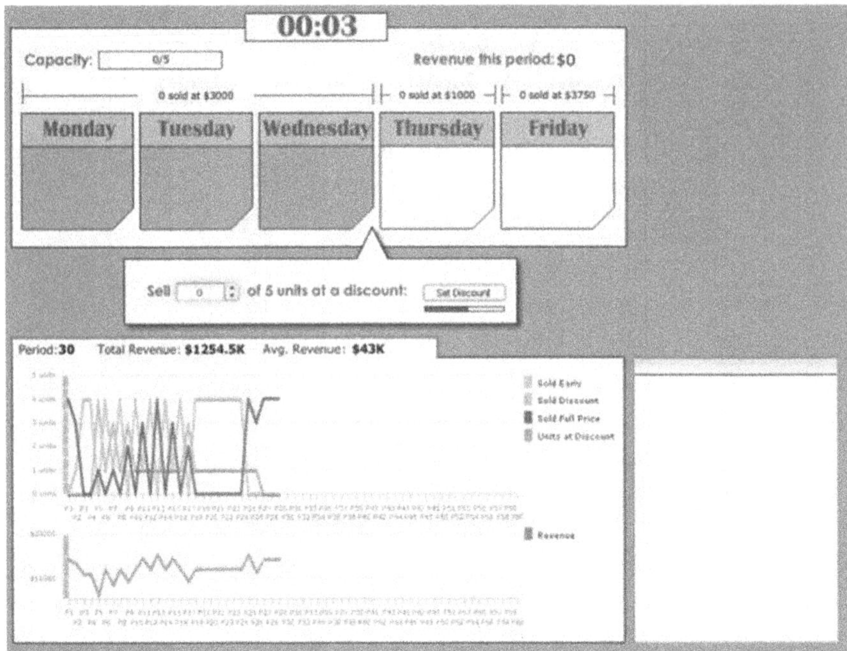

Figure 7.3 Student interface, Game 2

behavior of both sellers (in version 1 only) and buyers (both versions 1 and 2), (4) available information and its display, and (5) input/output of players' data. The interface is naturally slightly different for versions 1, 2, and 3; figure 7.4 provides illustrative screenshots.

Experiences Playing the Game

For pedagogical purposes it may prove useful to have students record their own activity in tables such as 7.1 and 7.2.

Below I describe two experiences playing the game with different students.

Experience 1

Course: A 2.5-hour MBA elective entitled Dynamic Pricing and Revenue Management

Before-class assignment:

> *By now you probably know that dynamic pricing revenue management is about changing prices and capacity availability over time. In particular, it sometimes leads to situations where a certain product's price could be significantly lower in the future than it is today. This has not gone unnoticed by many consumers, and as a result, even those consumers who would otherwise purchase a product at today's price may choose to wait for a better deal in the future. Such waiting is called strategic consumer behavior and is a relatively new, yet important challenge in revenue management.*

In this class, we will discuss the issues and challenges of strategic consumer behavior in dynamic pricing revenue management. To do so we will play a computer-based pricing simulation game. In this game some of you will adopt the role of seller, and others will adopt the roles of buyers. We will play this game in class and discuss the different strategies you come up with. As a result of this discussion, you will have a better understanding of the role of consumer behavior in dynamic pricing and revenue management, and the ways a firm's pricing strategy can be used to prevent and also to take advantage of such behavior.

In order to help you prepare for the in-class experience, you should play two games at home. In game 1, you will adopt the buyer's role of, and the seller will be played by the computer. In game 2, you will adopt the seller's role, and buyers will be played by the computer. The instructions for these games and the passwords/logins are attached. Please think about how to play before logging on. The best-performing buyers and sellers in these home games will be awarded memorable prizes.

Note that before coming to class students have played as both buyers and sellers and have thought about how they should play.

During class, we started with a quick (five- to 10-minute) review of what they have learned in the course to this point—a format rather typical for the courses I teach. Then for another five to 10 minutes, we reviewed the fundamentals of the underlying business problem and the game: what prices are charged and when,

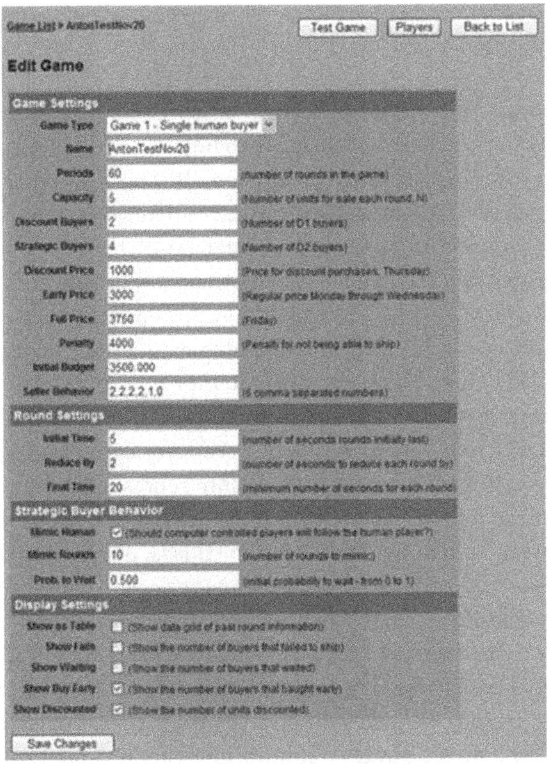

Figure 7.4a Instructor's Interface for Game 1

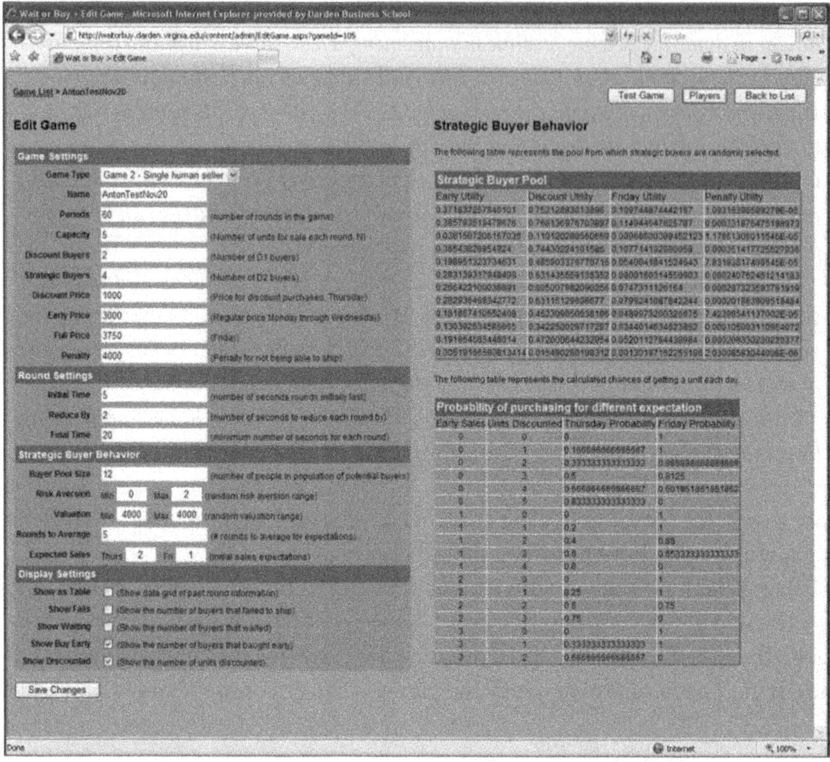

Figure 7.4b Instructor's interface for Game 2

what the demands and capacities are, how discounted units are allocated, and what the implications of that allocation are to buyers and the seller.

We then start discussing the buyer's problem. It is interesting to note that even though this was a rather quantitative elective, students were not naturally thinking about the buyer's problem as a problem of maximizing expected value or utility. Rather, they are thinking in terms of ("optimally") intermixing the periods in which they wait with the periods in which they buy early.

Students will typically talk about their strategies as either conservative or risky. Some will intermix these strategies and attempt to explain what makes them change their tack. This discussion often resembles the "hot hand" logic seen in "one-armed bandit" machine experiments. Another common logic is breaking even: for example, if waiting and failing to ship represents a loss of $1,500, and buying early represents a gain of $500, then students might argue that they would buy early three times after one failure to ship (this is, of course, not quite correct since it ignores the opportunity cost of not buying early the first time).

This discussion leads nicely to the mixed strategy equilibrium concept. Without much problem, students realize that if it makes total sense for a buyer to pursue any pure strategy (i.e., always buy early or always wait), then the same is true for other buyers, which in turn makes the strategy clearly inferior. At this point, one could discuss how a mixed strategy equilibrium can be analyzed and recognize that to employ this approach requires that buyers understand how the seller is making decisions. While discussing the buyer's problem, it is useful to bring up an alternative approach to making the wait-or-buy decision using a decision tree and maximizing expected value (or utility, depending on how comfortable students are with the concept of utility). Once you have put the tree on the board, start computing the probabilities. Students will immediately realize that one needs yet again to know how many units the seller will put on sale.

At this point (ideally 35 to 45 minutes into the class), acknowledge that any reasonable approach to the buyer's problem requires understanding the behavior of the seller and transition to the seller's problem. Start by asking how students made decisions when they were playing the seller's game, and solicit their strategies. Expect to hear the following observation: if the seller puts lots of inventory on sale, then more buyers wait. If the seller puts little or nothing on sale, then buyers purchase early. For students, that implies the seller should try to "game" the buyers. Again, interestingly, students will not typically think about maximizing the seller's expected revenue. Rather, they will be preoccupied with the psychological aspects of how buyers react to the seller's actions.

Here it is important to avoid getting deep into such discussion. Instead, point to the difference in the time of making the decision between buyers and sellers and to differences in the information they have. In particular, you should expect some students to observe that unlike buyers, at the time the seller makes a decision, the seller knows the number of buyers who purchased early and, correspondingly, the number who wait. Inform the students that the current state of the art in RM (e.g., see Talluri and van Ryzin 2004) is in fact to optimize revenue for each origin-destination pair independently. Such statically optimal strategy can be developed for the game as follows.

Ask, "Suppose the seller learns that all four units were sold M–W. How many of the available six units should be put on sale on Thursday?" This leads to a simple decision tree; the answer is two. Then ask, "Now can you speculate as to what the seller's strategy might look like?" Look for the response that seller's strategy is a lookup table that determines the number of units at a discount for each value of early sales. Move down the table by asking, "Now if three units were sold M–W, how many of the remaining three should be put on sale on Thursday?" Spend more time on this part because the decision tree is more difficult. A discounted unit can be sold to one waiting strategic buyer, in which case nothing is sold on Friday, or to a bargain-hunting buyer, in which case the firm can sell one unit on Friday if it put two or fewer units on sale on Thursday.

With some help from the instructor, in computing hypergeometric probabilities, the students can evaluate the expected outcome in each case and arrive at a result similar to what's shown in the teaching note. This can take from 15 to 25 minutes. As the total time consumed to this point is approaching 60 to 70 minutes, the class is ready for a break. Before the break, however, summarize the analysis of buyer and seller, and invite the students to log in and start playing version 3 of the game once they are ready.

Game 3 takes about 20 minutes. I have found that it is critical to ensure that all students return from the break promptly because all team members must log in for the game to proceed.

The remainder of the class time can be dedicated to discussing game 3 and its takeaways. That part of the discussion should begin by asking how sellers chose to play. While some sellers simply follow the static optimal strategy developed above, some may adjust strategy to dynamically "teach" buyers. Identify the buyer teams whose seller followed the static optimal strategy and discuss their strategies. In particular, ask whether the seller encouraged or discouraged buyers from waiting. The goal of this discussion is to make clear that a static optimal strategy applied in a dynamic setting does in fact control buyers' waiting because it puts fewer units on sale if many buyers wait, and conversely it puts more units on sale if few buyers wait.

Once this point is raised, switch to those sellers who dynamically managed waiting and ask what they did differently. The explanations you hear are not likely to be particularly persuasive and are more likely to be along the buyer *psychology* line ("I was trying to teach the buyers to do *X*"). Here it might be worthwhile to consider asking, "So, are you in the business of education or of managing your company's revenue?"

Now switch to buyers. Ask if buyers would play better if they had some information. Then ask what information they would like to have. Expect to hear that early sales information would be helpful. Ask how buyers would use this information. Ask if the seller would be willing to share it, and expect to hear a resounding *no*. Some students might point out that certain websites (e.g., Expedia) do in fact show how many seats are available at a given price. My current work-in-progress research shows that, in this game, buyers in fact cannot use similar information to take a benefit. In a controlled experiment, for example, on average buyers who had access to information paid a higher price per shipment than those who did not have information. This was likely because of buyers' overconfidence in their ability to process information and incorrectly anticipating sellers' reaction.

To conclude the class, go over the main takeaways by restating the questions developed above:

- What is strategic consumer behavior and why it is a problem for RM?
- What should the firm know about buyer behavior?
- What should the firm's strategy be?
- What should buyers take into consideration when deciding to wait or buy early?

Finally, point out that RM with strategic consumers is still an emerging area of research and practice.

Experience 2

Course: A 90-minute executive MBA core in decision analysis.

This simulation is assigned on the second to last day of a comprehensive decision analysis course that covers probability, decision trees, Monte Carlo simulations, and matrix games (best response, pure and mixed strategy equilibrium, value and information asymmetry, signaling, and single- and multiple-period prisoner's dilemma).

The before-class assignment is as follows:

In this penultimate class, we will work on a revenue management problem where the seller dynamically changes prices for its product to increase revenues, and buyers try to game the seller in order to purchase the products at lower prices. Such situations are quite common, for example, in airline ticket pricing.

You will receive an e-mail with links and instructions. You will need to analyze the buyers' and the seller's strategy, as well as play two interactive simulations. In one you play the role of buyer, and a second where you will play the role of seller—in which you will play against the computer.

In class we will play the same game again. But in class you will play against each other. (Some students will play as buyers and some as sellers.) We will then discuss the strategies you used, the analysis you performed, and the intuition you developed. Through this process, we will summarize and review the material you learned in decision analysis.

And, it will be fun! The best-performing buyer and seller in the home games will be awarded memorable prizes. Think before you play . . .

In class, we use the first few minutes (five to 10) to remind students about the structure of the game and the sequence of events. We then use another 15 to 20 minutes to play game 3. Live, in class, some students are assigned the role of seller and are randomly matched with three to four buyers. In the teams with three buyers, the fourth buyer is played by a computer.

At about 30 minutes into the class, we start the game analysis by asking buyers, "How are you deciding whether to buy early or wait?" Because the simulation is being played in an otherwise analytical course, a common response is that buyers look at a decision tree of some kind. Draw the tree, point out the outcomes, and ask about the probabilities. Wait to hear that the probabilities depend on what the seller will do.

At this point, some 40 minutes in, turn attention to the seller's decision by asking sellers: "How are you decide on the number of units to discount on Thursday?" Expect three issues to emerge:

Naturally (after seeing a decision tree for the buyers), sellers also will try to explain their strategies using a tree.

Expect sellers to point out that by the time they make a decision, they already know buyers' decisions (sales M–W). Ask sellers to elaborate on this information asymmetry and its value. Ask sellers to comment on how their strategies would be different if they saw, for example, zero sales M–W (meaning all buyers are waiting), as opposed to observing a case in which no one is waiting. If the group is struggling, ask what is the most desirable outcome for the seller, what is the least desirable, and why.

Do not limit this discussion only to the game 3 sellers—all students played sellers in their out-of-class assignment. The goal of discussion with sellers is to come up with the idea of best response. After seeing the M–W sales in the current period there *is* a certain strategy that maximizes sellers expected revenue, and finding such a strategy is the goal (see the "Brief Analysis" section in the teaching note). Expect someone to have the best response strategy (from his or her assignment).

Someone might challenge the idea of playing the best response, arguing that the seller should strategically "teach" buyers to behave in a certain way. Open up this idea for broader discussion. Consider asking: "Is the best response strategy to teach buyers to do something?" Expect to hear that, in fact, it is. That strategy discourages buyers from always waiting. Likewise, it discourages buyers from never waiting. Expect to hear a reference to the role of information (cases such as "Maxco, Inc. and the Gambit Company" could be used to cover that topic) (Wallace and Hammond 1994).

As an epilogue to the discussion about "teaching," ask if any seller practiced that, and specifically ask about that seller's revenue. Point out that if in fact buyers behaved in a perfectly rational way, the seller could do better by teaching them and by alternating periods with many and few units on sale. Even so, buyers have all kinds of biases, and thus a seller's best response is a very robust and practical strategy. It capitalizes on the downstream nature of the seller's decision and exploits the value of the seller's information. The entire sellers' discussion can easily take 30 minutes.

To conclude, turn back to the buyers and ask, "Now, knowing how the seller behaves, should you wait or buy early?" Look for a student who will refer to mixed equilibrium—indeed, if a buyer knew all the other buyers were waiting, then it is certainly beneficial for him or her to buy early, and so on. Thus, the only possible equilibrium is when some buyers wait and some buy early. Because that is likely to be the case within the class, just listing the reasons could be sufficient. Some will argue they are risk-averse; others will argue that they wanted to break even (or the reverse, lock in the savings they got earlier); a third subgroup will argue that they were alternating. All of those are reasonable strategies that buyers follow in practice, and thus knowing about them is helpful for sellers. The discussion should last at least 15 minutes.

In the remaining five minutes, summarize the class by stating all or some of the following:

- As in *any* competitive situation, it is critical to think through not one's own problem, but also consider the problem from the other side.
- Downstream decisions add information and value if one is able to react to that information.
- The best response strategy is single-period revenue maximization for the seller. This strategy recognizes strategic consumer behavior and therefore discourages excessive consumer waiting.
- Mixed strategy equilibrium is best for buyers—wait sometimes, buy early other times. Assuming all buyers have the same probability to wait, that probability can be optimized using a Monte Carlo simulation.
- Theoretically, the seller can do better by using a dynamic strategy that incorporates a buyer's response into a seller's strategy, which can involve periodic discounts (i.e., intermixing the periods of some inventory at a

discount with periods of zero units at a discount). Interestingly, while under such a strategy some customers pay higher prices than others, it is hardly unethical. Without dynamic pricing, both the average price will be higher (i.e., those who purchase will pay more on average) and the quantity sold will be lower (i.e., some consumers will not be able to purchase at all).

- For such a strategy to be successful, buyers should be able to read sellers' signals, and the seller should be able to read buyers' signals.
- In the simulation, however, we see that buyers react partly irrationally. It is not clear whether signaling in such situations really works. In practice, therefore, sellers that play the best response are likely to do very well.

DISCUSSION

Dynamic pricing and revenue management with strategic consumers is still an emerging area of research and practice. The algorithms for managing such situations are rarely developed and even less so embedded in RM systems. Thus it is crucial for RM managers to understand higher-level insights and intuition on how to price dynamically when facing strategic consumers, how to deal with the

Table 7.1. BUYER FORM

Week	Your decision (B or W)	Rationale: Why you made the decision you made?

challenges that strategic consumers present, and how to capitalize on potential opportunities. The Wait or Buy game is a teaching tool for developing such intuition that can be successfully used in an MBA classroom.

In addition to developing the needed intuition, the game also is a valuable tool to illustrate (and reinforce) the behavioral aspects of the story. In a competitive situation it is crucial to understand how the opponent will behave, and given that the opponent is human, what are the predictable irrationalities that are likely to emerge, and how to capitalize on them. Both buyer and seller behaviors are of interest for further investigation, and a number of operations management scholars are undertaking such research (e.g., Mak et al. 2013 for buyers and Kremer, Maintin, and Ovchinnikov 2013 for sellers). The data collected through the game also are of particular interest as they bear on the question of how consumers make the decision to wait or to buy. A comprehensive analysis of this question, rooted in behavioral theories and observations from data, would be of a fundamental importance to the theory and practice of dynamic pricing and revenue management and the many industries where they are practiced.

Table 7.2. Seller form

Week	**Your decision (# of units)**	**Rationale: Why you made the decision you made?**

REFERENCES

Aviv, Y., Pazgal, A. 2008. Optimal pricing of seasonal products in the presence of forward-looking consumers. Manufacturing and Service Operations Management 10 (3), 339–359.

Bearden, N., Murphy, R., Rapoport, A. 2008. Decision biases in revenue management: Some behavioral evidence. Manufacturing and Service Operations Management 10 (4), 625–636.

Bendoly, E. 2011. Linking task conditions to physiology and judgment errors in RM systems. Production and Operations Management 20 (6), 860–876.

Besanko, D., Winston, W. L. 1990. Optimal price skimming by a monopolist facing rational consumers. Management Science 36 (5), 555–567.

Cason, T. N., Mago, S. D. 2010. A laboratory study of duopoly price competition with patient buyers. Economic Inquiry 51 (2), 1123–1141.

Cason, T. N., Reynolds, S. S. 2005. Bounded rationality in laboratory bargaining with asymmetric information. Economic Theory 25 (3), 553–574.

Coase, R. 1972. Durability and Monopoly. Journal of Law and Economics 15 (1), 143–149.

Kremer M., Maintin B., Ovchinnikov, A. 2013. Strategic consumers, myopic retailers. Working paper.

Lazear, E. P. 1986. Retail pricing and clearance sales. American Economic Review 76 (1), 14–32.

Li, J., Granados, N., Netessine, S. 2013. Are consumers strategic? Structural estimation from the air-travel industry. Working paper.

Liu, Q., van Ryzin, G. 2008. Strategic capacity rationing to induce early purchases. Management Science 54, 1115–1131.

Mak, V., Rapoport A., Gisches E. J., Han, J. 2013. Purchasing scarce products under dynamic pricing: An experimental investigation. Working paper.

Osadchiy, N., Bendoly, E. 2010. Are consumers really strategic? Implications from an experimental study. Working paper.

Ovchinnikov, A., Milner, J. M. 2012. Revenue management with end-of-period discounts in the presence of customer learning. Production and Operations Management 21 (1), 69–84.

Reynolds, S. S. 2000. Durable-goods monopoly: Laboratory market and bargaining experiments. Rand Journal of Economics 31 (2), 375–394.

Shen, Z.-J. M., Su, X. 2007. Customer behavior modeling in revenue management and auctions: A review and new research opportunities. Production and Operations Management 16 (6), 713–728.

Talluri K. T., van Ryzin, G. J. 2004. Theory and Practice of Revenue Management. New York: Springer Science + Business Media.

Wallace, D. L., Hammond, J. S. 1994. Maxco, Inc. and the Gambit Company. Case no. 9-174-091. Cambridge, MA: Harvard Business Publishing.

CHAPTER 8

Seeing the Forest (and Your Tree)

Envisioning Motivation and Performance in Work Design

KAREN EBOCH ■

OVERVIEW

The learning activity in focus in this chapter is designed to help develop an understanding of job design and process improvements by drawing from personal experience and observation. Concepts related to work and process flows are integrated across a range of areas within operations management (OM), including quality, lean systems, capacity, inventory management, and facility layouts. However, understanding the nuances of process flow and design can be difficult for the typical operations student.

With traditional OM content focused on manufacturing jobs, examples offered to students often fall within mass production or assembly line contexts. In light of both limited experience and industrial opportunities, asking students to prepare and translate these diagrams and charts is often an extremely abstract exercise—akin to asking them to plan a trip to the moon. However, most students begin working in minimum wage service sector jobs. In addition, they also often compare roles and responsibilities, and share stories with peers as they begin to explore various occupations, leading to the development of intuitive preferences for job design. These shared stories and relatively universal exposure to food and retail venues allow for the demonstration of operational tools and techniques.

In this exercise, students begin by completing an observation worksheet dealing with typical jobs in retail or food service. Once a set of basic duties is determined, groups are formed to develop flow charts for processes, such as serving customers at a restaurant. Process improvements are then addressed from both an operational perspective and with regard to motivation potential and job performance.

State of Management Practice

Operations management (OM) has a strong research foundation in manufacturing organizations emphasizing improved efficiency and effectiveness. Within the context of capacity and facility layouts, OM research often focuses on flow charts and assembly line balance to track process steps in light of ongoing demand (Battaia and Dolgui 2013; Becker and Scholl 2006). Value stream mapping (VSM) takes the process analysis a step further, focusing on the valued added by each step, and is recognized as a critical driver of process improvements in lean manufacturing (Bertolini et al. 2013). As the service sector has grown, the focus of OM has transitioned toward more structurally labor-intensive environments, with an effort to adapt theory and principles to these settings (Schmenner 1986; 2004). Service blueprinting has emerged as a pragmatic approach to trace customer interactions within the service process, and also to distinguish front- and back-room activities from organizational structures (Bitner, Ostrom, and Morgan 2008).

While flow charts offer critical insight into drivers of quality and productivity (Nebl and Schroeder 2011), job design encompasses more than scheduling tasks or balancing assembly line work. Designing jobs to enhance workers' motivation and engagement requires additional considerations (Bendoly et al. 2010). Unfortunately, the motivation, team, and human aspects of job design often are treated in isolation from OM strategy in management and organizational behavior (OB) courses and research (Kinicki and Williams 2013; Kreitner and Kinicki 2013; Robbins and Judge 2014; Schermerhorn 2012). Drawing heavily on economics, psychology, sociology, and organizational theory, typical OB texts present behavioral research regarding individual, team, and organizational dynamics linked to productivity as a critical dependent variable, but the operational flows and pressures are not typically well developed.

In order to facilitate this conceptual integration, it is essential to develop deeper understandings of the interrelations between operational objectives and the people working assigned roles. Behavioral operations (BeOps) research provides this foundation by developing connections between cognitive psychology, social psychology, group dynamics, and systems dynamics to OM (Bendoly et al. 2010). Gino and Pisano (2008) defined this emerging field of behavioral operations as "the study of human behavior and cognition and their impacts on operating systems and processes" (679). Development of this connection within the context of minimum wage retail and food services jobs reinforces the critical importance of an interdisciplinary focus across market sectors—not merely on manufacturing and operations management.

THEORETICAL PERSPECTIVE

Traditional OM

Both OM and OB have roots in Frederick Taylor's scientific management (Zuffo 2011). Worker selection and evaluation are central to his principles, as reflected by the fabled "Schmidt," who improved both speed and pig-iron processing time with proper tools and techniques. Taylor linked wages to productivity, showing the potential of compensation to induce workers to accept direction and improve performance (Taylor 1911). Following Henry Ford's adaption of Taylor's principles for his assembly line, other industrialists followed, streamlining jobs to specialized tasks for improved efficiency. When Elton Mayo applied Taylor's scientific research methods in the Hawthorne studies, additional human factors emerged that often seemed to conflict with operational expectations (Mayo 1933). It was at this juncture that OB branched off to focus on the application of behavioral sciences to the workplace, while OM focused on the exploration of process improvements (Kreitner and Kinicki 2013).

On the OM side, work to establish optimal line flows leveraged emerging linear programming and simulation technologies designed to balance assembly line tasks. As production became more complicated, the models grew in complexity to develop more realistic methods (Becker and Scholl 2006). Hayes and Wheelwright (1984) refocused research on process strategies with alignment to product and human resource strategies. While their discussion of worker participation and skill building has not been as broadly disseminated as the product-process matrix, acknowledgment of behavioral influence in job design has persisted in OM research. As total quality management (TQM) and lean manufacturing redefined production standard practices, the use of teams and empowered employees further reinforced the importance of concentrating on worker impact (Womack, Jones, and Roos 1990).

Growth in the service sector further expanded the focus of OM research beyond traditional manufacturing settings. Schmenner (1986) proposed a service matrix to align resources, much like Hayes and Wheelwright's (1984) manufacturing product-process matrix. Schmenner (2004) continued to investigate service firms and the Theory of Swift, Even Flow. As a consequence of the observation that process productivity increases with flow speed and not necessarily with the speed that value is added, steps should be taken to reduce wait time and delay-inducing variability. Through the use of process flow charts and service blueprinting to diagram current methods, organizations can identify ways to improve efficiency and innovation (Bitner et al. 2008).

Anchoring in OB

The divide insulating Taylor's financial motivation from Mayo's social pressures not only split management along operational and behavioral lines, it also necessitated the development of social models to reconcile emergent discrepancies

(Kreitner and Kinicki 2013). Maslow's (1943) hierarchy provides that individuals are motivated by different drivers, depending on their upward progression through five levels of need. Beginning with physiological needs (i.e., basic human needs including food, clothing, and shelter), individuals progress through safety/security, belongingness, and self-esteem needs, eventually to arrive at the highest level need, self-actualization. Alderfer's (1972) ERG (existence, relatedness, growth) theory—paralleling Maslow's hierarchy—refined conceptualization of the movement between needs levels to allow for upward and downward progressions. Relatedness is a corollary to Maslow's belongingness needs, with existence overlapping the lower-level physiological/safety and security needs and growth the upper-level self-esteem and self-actualization needs. Alderfer allowed for downward movement, or frustration-regression, as the result of change in circumstance or an inability to reach a higher-level need. By recognizing individual workers' dominant need, leaders are positioned to customize motivational rewards in an effort to fulfill a needs deficit and thereby improve performance.

While early motivation theories relied on external rewards including money, social recognition, and praise, Hackman and Oldham (1980) proposed the job characteristics model, which introduced motivational aspects of the design of jobs themselves. These authors postulated that five core job characteristics (i.e., skill variety, task identity, task significance, autonomy, and performance feedback) influenced three critical psychological states (i.e., experienced meaningfulness of work, experienced responsibility for work outcomes, and knowledge of work results), which in turn affected work outcomes (i.e., internal work motivation, growth satisfaction, job satisfaction, work effectiveness, and absenteeism). More specifically, the first three job characteristics of skill variety (amount of different abilities required to complete the various tasks of a role), task identity (extent to which the job requires a whole or recognizable piece of work), and task significance (magnitude of impact the job has on the lives of others) combine to determine the perceived meaningfulness of the work. Autonomy (extent the job enables the individual to experience freedom, independence, and discretion in completing tasks) elicits the worker's experience of responsibility for the work outcomes. Performance feedback the worker receives directly regarding the effectiveness of the work by the job itself provides knowledge of work results, the third critical psychological state. By designing jobs with higher levels of these core characteristics, enhanced psychological states could be reached, resulting in improved work outcomes. The ability of the psychological states to result in the desired work outcomes (increased levels of intrinsic work motivation, satisfaction with personal growth/development, satisfaction with the job itself, and work effectiveness, as well as reduced absenteeism) is moderated by three factors—knowledge and skill growth (did the worker increase abilities), need strength (did the worker desire challenging work), and work context satisfaction (did the worker look for personal satisfaction from the job or outside the organization).

In order to use the job characteristics model to design more motivating jobs, Hackman and Oldham (1980) proposed that the core job characteristics could be combined to create a "Motivating Potential Score" (MPS). The Job Diagnostic

Survey measures the five core job characteristics using a seven-point scale ranging from least (1) to most (7) motivating. The MPS is calculated by taking the average of the skill variety, task identity, and task significance scores, which is then multiplied by the feedback and autonomy scores. Lower scores indicate poor motivating potential, and a higher priority for redesign to improve the position's motivational properties. Low scores tend to prevail in typical assembly line work. Worker empowerment and task enlargement/rotation gained traction as methods to increase MPS and worker motivation just as TQM reinforced the same concepts from a quality and lean perspective (Fried and Ferris 1987).

Initiating organization-level job changes, even when done to address workers' needs or motivation, can result in resistance and frustration (Connor, Lake, and Stackman 2003). Leadership skills are critical in the direction of change, and the impact of leadership underscores the bearing managers have on an organization's performance and employee motivation (Piccolo and Colquitt 2006). Perceptions of fairness, equity, and organizational justice also can override the motivational design of a job or reward system (Bing and Burroughs 2001; Bowen, Gilliland, and Folger 1999; Colquitt et al. 2001). Thus, it is essential to take care in the design and implementation of worker roles and process improvements.

CASE EXAMPLE

Employing over 2.2 million workers worldwide and 1.3 million in the United States, Wal-Mart is the largest retailer and the largest private employer in the world (Wal-Mart Stores 2013). As a discount retailer, Wal-Mart constantly seeks efficiencies to lower costs and offers greater customer value. Much of the savings comes from strategic supply chain management, which includes the development of leading-edge distribution networks and inventory management technologies with strategic sourcing partnerships. Wal-Mart also is known for its workforce policies and huge numbers of minimum wage, part-time employees. Currently more than 70% of the firm's managers begin their career as sales associates. This affords them insight into the nature of the front-line interactions employees have with customers on the sales floor.

With a focus on the delivery of quality customer service, a stocked sales floor, and a motivated workforce, Wal-Mart management is assessed based on the percentage of operational expense to sales (Fishman 2006). Pressure to lower expenses often results in efforts to minimize employee costs and innovative approaches to increase efficiency. For example, inventory tracking advances, such as barcoding and electronic data interchange (EDI) systems, have decreased required store-line tasks such as pricing individual units or stock counts for reordering. Self-scanning registers and rotating bagging wheels also have increased efficiencies in checkout areas. By regularly analyzing and reanalyzing the roles and duties of store-line employees, Wal-Mart continues to seek cost reductions and savings to increase customer value.

Because of Wal-Mart's size and global penetration, there is a great deal of broad industry familiarity with its business model and methods. This allows for

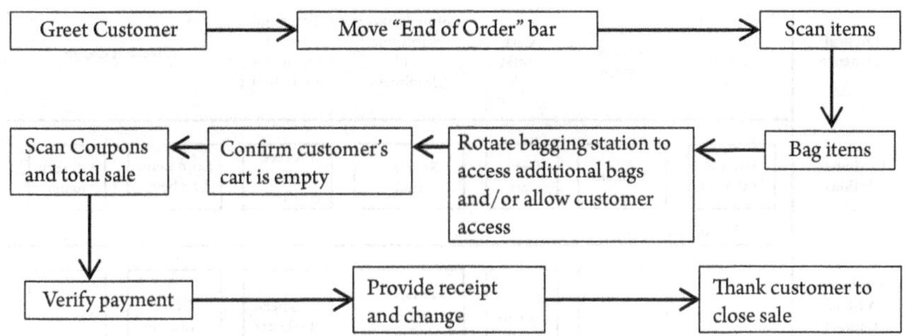

Figure 8.1 Wal-Mart Cashier Primary Function

discussion of its processes as an illustration of OM concepts impacting process improvements in the service sector. With the front cashier as an example, a simple flow chart of the key aspects of the role can be created (figure 8.1).

While the simple flow chart in figure 8.1 captures the repetitive nature of the cashier role, it does not provide detail bearing on specific skills needed or other tasks employees may be required to perform. For example, register supplies, such as register tape, bags, and change, have to be replenished periodically. However, this baseline process can be used to discuss the role and elaborate on the additional OM-relevant details.

At Wal-Mart, for example, if customer traffic is low cashiers may be dispersed to the sales floor to stock or to perform housekeeping duties. When traffic is high, management also may call employees hired within departments to assist at the front registers. When viewed through an OM lens, this cross-training and usage allows for productivity flexibility and improved efficiencies without resource duplication. In consideration of the motivating potential of the role, the skill variety involved in the position, and therefore the position's motivating potential, increases as employees are asked to engage in a wider range of tasks. However, motivation can be weakened if employees feel that the rotation is executed in an unequitable way, and that they are being asked to do more than their fair share of the work.

The rotation between the cashier and sales floor task sets also can be approached from the perspective of delivering overall customer value. Using service blueprinting, a simple flow of customer shopping experiences can be mapped, from parking in the lot to browsing the sales departments and eventually leading to completing the transactions with a cashier or self-scanning (figure 8.2).

This more holistic view of store operation facilitates exploration of the interactions and dependencies between cashiers with employees in the various departments. For example, customers consider store appearance, stock availability, and the overall shopping experience when determining where to shop. If those elements fail to meet customer expectations, the decision to shop elsewhere is likely (Fishman 2006). Additionally, support processes for inventory management and tracking can be tracked further upstream beyond organizational boundaries to suppliers and their relationships as desired to illustrate the interconnectivity of all aspects of the supply chain in providing a quality experience to the customer.

Physical Evidence	Wal-Mart Exterior Parking Lot	Entry way Interior design	Cart corral	Store layout, selection, and cleanliness	Front end layout Open lane indicators	Checkout design		
Customer Actions	Arrive at Wal-Mart	Walk in	Get a cart	Shop for goods	Proceed to checkout	Load items on belt	or	Self scan items
	line of interaction							
Onstage/ Visible Contact Employee Actions		Greet Customer	Provide a cart	Restocking goods Straightening Cleaning	Cashiers at register stations	Greet customer Scan items		Monitor registers
	line of visibility							
Backstage/ Invisible Contact Employee Actions		Security monitoring for potential threats		Receiving of inventory Disposal of waste		Verifying signage for pricing and promotions		
	line of internal interaction							
Support Processes		Database of shoplifters		EDI inventory tracking		Programming of UPC codes, pricing, promotions		

Figure 8.2 Wal-Mart Service Blueprint (simplistic)

When operations flows are viewed with flow charts or service blueprints, opportunities for employee disruptions and potential bottlenecks can be identified. This also can help to demonstrate the dependence of Wal-Mart store operation on employees performing their assigned tasks. Failure to correctly complete role-critical activities can result in a diminished customer experience and lost sales. Maintaining employee motivation to execute assigned duties effectively and also ensuring all relevant duties are assigned are key management functions.

LEARNING ACTIVITY

Although this is a team-based activity, it is recommended that each student begin by completing an observation worksheet for a typical job and focal duties in retail or food service. Once the basic duties are determined by individual members, teams are formed to develop process flow charts. These might include serving a customer at a restaurant or helping a customer find a product. Process improvements are then addressed from an operational perspective, but also with a focus on the motivational aspects of job design. Depending on the "in class" versus "out of class" work and level of detail desired by the instructor, this activity can be managed in a 50-minute class or over a week.

The activity begins with asking each student to reflect on a particular minimum wage service sector job with which he or she is most familiar. Accesses to official job descriptions are not necessary. Rather, based on personal experiences, observations, and discussions with peers, students will attempt to list all of the tasks and duties required in the position (see appendix A, "Student Handout: Phase 1"). Once the initial role has been analyzed and the tasks and duties associated with the role identified, the student's focus is expanded to include other workers the position relies on or interacts with to accomplish encompassed tasks/duties to provide customer value. With a focus on customer value, students are asked to consider how many workers are required to deliver service to customers, how tasks are divided among those workers, and how the tasks interrelate. Once students have carefully considered the various components necessary for service delivery, they are then asked to draw a process flow chart of the steps necessary to complete a typical "transaction."

As each student has different experiences and perceptions of service, the results from this first assignment will vary. However, using this nominal group technique, each student will come prepared to engage in phase 2 of the activity. Phase 2 focuses on the combination of team members' perceptions to create a more accurate picture of the dominant flow of customer value in various service settings (see appendix B, "Class Group Handout: Phase 2"). Teams of between four and five students should be formed based on the commonality of roles analyzed to compare duties and process flow charts. Depending on the number of students and roles selected, teams may be formed based on specific organizations (i.e., McDonald's versus Taco Bell, Macy's versus Wal-Mart) or industries (i.e., fast food versus slow food/sit-down restaurants, discount versus specialty retailers). Teams are asked to compare their lists of tasks and duties and flow charts, and to select one job title for further analysis. Once a specific role is selected, students should then combine their lists and brainstorm any missing tasks or duties overlooked in the first phase of the activity. A flow chart for delivery of customer value should be created specifically reflecting the task responsibility of the targeted role versus those of other employees on which the focal role "depends."

Using the flow chart as a current state definition, student teams are then asked to identify and to determine how volume and productivity are linked to the division of tasks within/between roles identified, as well as how the interdependent processes identified can be improved. Finally, as improvements are suggested, teams are asked to consider the individual worker motivation changes that emerge with task changes and productivity expectations.

Creating a service blueprint can be substituted for or instituted in addition to the flow chart, depending on the learning objectives in focus. The service blueprint may be a more tractable starting point for students to consider in light of customer service experiences. This approach also can encourage students to consider both job-dependent backstage and support processes that must occur for the visible transactions to transpire.

Once all the teams have completed the required diagrams and analysis, results should be shared in the class as a whole. Allow each team to present its conclusions. Doing so can highlight perceptual differences in job task importance, as well as varying degrees of familiarity with operations. Attention should be paid to the completeness of the steps the teams develop. The language used in the descriptions also should be challenged against the possibility of value judgments of those crafting the diagrams toward minimum wage workers or various levels of management. Personal experiences may influence perceptions. "Horror stories" of jobs or shopping/dining experiences also can enhance understanding of how people impact the delivery of goods and services—through process design and execution.

DISCUSSION

By drawing on students' personal experiences and applying OM and BeOps concepts, this exercise offers a method to promote higher-level thinking through active, problem-based learning. Students are placed in the position of managers determining solutions to real-world workflows and productivity issues. Understanding how to evaluate, synthesis, analyze, and apply concepts has been acknowledged as a goal of education since the publication of Bloom's (1956) taxonomy. L. Dee Fink (2003) expanded Bloom's application and integration to include development of a human dimension, through deepened understanding of oneself and others. Daniel Pink (2005) argued for right- and left-brain integration as a holistic and creative approach to succeed in today's business climate. Howard Gardner (2007) defined the cognitive abilities needed for success in terms of a disciplined, synthesizing, creating, respectful, and ethical mind.

As students list all the tasks employees contribute toward the delivery of customer value, an awareness of what must be properly executed to accomplish a simple transaction emerges. Students will begin to see and understand some of the complexities involved in tracking and designing workflows for a basic operation such as taking and processing orders at McDonald's. Through the discussion, student examples also may demonstrate the following:

- Confusion of the workflows beyond an individual role, as the interaction of jobs requires attention be paid to the big picture and delivery of customer value.
- Missed steps that seem too obvious to list but significantly impact customer value. An easy way to demonstrate the need to capture every task is to ask students to list all the steps in a simple routine action, such as making a peanut butter and jelly sandwich or tying their shoes, and then demonstrate trying to accomplish the action using only the steps provided.
- Distinctions between front- and back-room operations. While organizations may intentionally place tasks in or out of customer view, the visibility impacts how the job is completed, employee motivation, and perceptions of customer perceptions of value. A discussion can be led comparing perceptions regarding the food quality when dining in restaurants that prepare menu items in front of customers versus those with closed kitchens.
- Coordination of efforts required to produce desired goods/services. Handoffs between workers may appear seamless to customers when

done correctly. But attributions of responsibility for a failed execution may be misdirected, and lead to misdirected consequences such as a poor server tip for errors made by the chef.
- Places that allow for lower levels of performance. Some roles and tasks allow for additional slack time, or may represent buffers needed to ensure recovery from heavy flow. In other cases, dependency relationships among actions may temporarily distort the sense of urgency associated with task execution.
- How incentives can be used to encourage better productivity. Suggestive selling contests among workers is a common method to increase transaction magnitude, while moving from hourly to commission pay systems may increase compensation variability.
- Places jobs could be "traded" or changed to make jobs more motivating. A useful discussion of process improvement can follow an analysis of the absence or degree of each of the five key dimensions of skill variety, task identity, task significance, autonomy, and feedback from the job.
- Distinctions within the flow charts between value- and non-value-added steps. While students are accustomed to viewing service transactions from the customer's perspective, analyzing roles through an operational and motivational lens can help explain why tasks are accomplished one way and how non-value-added steps become embedded in work methods

When process flows fail to deliver desired outcomes, the fault may be reflective of a combination of operational and behavioral factors. Behavioral impact on the delivery of customer value should also be separated from the work designed to deliver it. As workers get bored with routine tasks, error likelihood increases, resulting in quality declines and safety issues. Unmotivated workers also are more frequently absent and are more likely to turn over. Understanding how to design processes to increase both motivation and productivity can generate synergies to improve organizational efficiency.

Planning workflow requires more than balancing an assembly line or scheduling a shop floor. Understanding how the tasks individual workers are assigned impact motivation and performance can provide the critical link to quality and productivity in both manufacturing and service contexts. While students reflect on their own frustrations from minimum wage jobs in food service and retail, methods to improve these jobs are explored. Points of intersection between operational efficiency and motivation may be leveraged to develop win-win work design solutions.

Appendix A. Student Handout: Phase 1

By this stage in your life, you have probably had a minimum wage job in the service sector or know somebody who has. For this assignment you are to consider the typical job in a food service or retail establishment.

Pick a job that you feel most familiar with to list and describe all the tasks and roles required. Consider how many different tasks you would be expected to complete and how those tasks are related to ultimately delivering customer value. For example, if you worked the late-night shift on weekends at Taco Bell, what would your job entail?

Once you have exhausted your knowledge of a role (whether based on your personal work experience, stories from friends, or observation as a customer), consider the other workers that must coordinate their work in order to complete a transaction with the customer and actually deliver the value.

How many workers are needed to produce the meal or deliver the service?

What are the duties assigned to each?

How do the tasks relate to each other?

Finally, draw a process flow chart of the steps to complete the transformation. Be sure to label your focused role versus the roles of others that must be coordinated, as well as distinguish between those tasks accomplished in the front (visible) versus the back of house (unseen by the customer). Bring your descriptions and flow chart to class for further discussions!

Appendix B. Class Group Handout: Phase 2

Based on the roles you analyzed, gather into groups to compare duty lists and process flow charts. As a group, select one job title and combine your lists along with additional brainstorming to identify as many duties that are expected as possible.

Create a flow chart of the dominant flow of customer value that includes this role. Indicate which aspects are done by this individual and which are done by others. If you know the position titles associated with the other roles, include that information, especially if the role reoccurs in your analysis.

How could the process be improved?

How does the volume impact the division of tasks?

How motivating are the jobs?

Does motivation impact the productivity and quality delivered?

What can be done to improve the productivity of the role? Would those changes impact the motivating potential of the role?

References

Alderfer, C. P. 1972. Existence, Relatedness, and Growth: Human Needs in Organizational Settings. New York: Free Press.

Battaia, O., Dolgui, A. 2013. A taxonomy of line balancing problems and their solution approaches. International Journal of Production Economics 142 (2), 259–277.

Becker, C., Scholl, A. 2006. A survey on problems and methods in generalized assembly line balancing. European Journal of Operational Research 168 (3), 694–715.

Bendoly, E., Croson, R., Gonçalves, P., Schultz, K. 2010. Bodies of knowledge for research in behavioral operations. Production and Operations Management 19 (4), 434–452.

Bertolini, M., Braglia, M., Romagnoli, G., Zammori, F. 2013. Extending value stream mapping: The synchro-MRP case. International Journal of Production Research 51 (18), 5499–5519.

Bing, M. N., Burroughs, S. M. 2001. The predictive and interactive effects of equity sensitivity in teamwork-oriented organizations. Journal of Organizational Behavior 22 (3), 271–290.

Bitner, M. J., Ostrom, A. L., Morgan, F. 2008. Service blueprinting: A practical technique for service innovation. California Management Review 50 (3), 66–94.

Bloom, B. S., ed. 1956. Taxonomy of Educational Objectives: The Classification of Educational Goals. New York: Susan Fauer.

Bowen, D. E., Gilliland, S. W., Folger, R. 1999. HRM service fairness: How being fair with employees spills over to customers. Organizational Dynamics 27 (3), 7–23.

Colquitt, J. A., Conlon, D. E., Wesson, M. J., Porter, C. O., Ng, K. Y. 2001. Justice at the Millennium: A meta-analytic review of 25 years of organizational justice research. Journal of Applied Psychology 86 (3), 425–445.

Connor, P. E., Lake, L. L., Stackman, R. W. 2003. Managing Organizational Change. 3rd ed. Westport, CT: Praeger.

Fink, L. D. 2003. Creating Significant Learning Experiences: An Integrated Approach to Designing College Courses. San Francisco: John Wiley & Sons.

Fishman, C. 2006. The Wal-Mart Effect: How the World's Most Powerful Company Really Works—and How It's Transforming the American Economy. New York: Penguin.

Fried, Y., Ferris, G. R. 1987. The validity of the job characteristics model: A review and meta-analysis. Personnel Psychology 40 (2), 287–322.

Gardner, H. 2007. Five Minds for the Future. Boston: Harvard Business School Press.

Gino, F., Pisano, G. 2008. Toward a theory of behavioral operations. Manufacturing and Service Operations Management 10 (4), 676–691.

Hackman, J. R., Oldham, G. R. 1980. Work Redesign. Reading, MA: Addison-Wesley.

Hayes, R., Wheelwright, S. 1984. Restoring Our Competitive Edge: Competing through Manufacturing. New York: John Wiley & Sons.

Kinicki, A., Williams, B. K. 2013. Management: A Practical Introduction. New York: McGraw-Hill/Irwin.

Kreitner, R., Kinicki, A. 2013. Organizational Behavior. 10th ed. New York: McGraw-Hill.

Maslow, A. H. 1943. A theory of human motivation. Psychological Review 50, 370–396.

Mayo, E. 1933. The Human Problems of an Industrial Civilization. New York: Macmillan.

Nebl, T., Schroeder, A. 2011. Understanding the interdependencies of quality problems and productivity. TQM Journal 23 (5), 480–495.

Piccolo, R. F., Colquitt, J. A. 2006. Transformational leadership and job behaviors: The mediating role of core job characteristics. Academy of Management Journal 49 (2), 327–340.

Pink, D. H. 2005. A Whole New Mind: Moving from the Information Age to the Conceptual Age. New York: Penguin.

Robbins, S. P., Judge, T. A. 2014. Essentials of Organizational Behavior. 12th ed. Upper Saddle River, NJ: Prentice-Hall.

Schermerhorn, J. R. 2012. Exploring Management. Hoboken, NJ: John Wiley & Sons.

Schmenner, R. W. 1986. How can service business survive and prosper? Sloan Management Review 27 (3), 21–33.

Schmenner, R. W. 2004. Service business and productivity. Decision Sciences 35 (3), 333–347.

Taylor, F. W. 1911. The Principles of Scientific Management. New York: Dover Publications.

Wal-Mart Stores, Inc. 2013. Walmart Annual Report. Bentonville: Wal-Mart Stores, Inc.

Womack, J. P., Jones, D. T., Roos, D. 1990. The Machine That Changed the World. New York: Macmillan.

Zuffo, R. G. 2011. Taylor is dead, hurray Taylor! The "human factor" in scientific management: Between ethics, scientific psychology and common sense. Journal of Business and Management 17 (1), 23–41.

CHAPTER 9

Satisfaction Architect

Service Design and Its Behavioral Implications

LOUIS ST. PETER, WALTER L. WALLACE, AND YUSEN XIA ■

OVERVIEW

Today, the service sector is a significant contributor to the economic life of virtually every major mature economy. It is clearly growing in importance even in less mature economies. In the United States, for example, services account for 64% of the gross domestic product (IMF 2012), employ 80% of the workforce (Henderson 2012), generate exports exceeding $600 billon, and create a trade surplus of more than $179 billion. Over the past 30 years, the service sector has enabled the US economy to absorb the increasing need for employment fueled by several factors: a decline in manufacturing employment, an increase in families with multiple wage earners, and an aging population. Combined, these and other related trends have contributed to a growing demand for a wide range of services, particularly those related to healthcare, child care, hospitality, and education.

Even in China, a country that has historically generated economic development and prosperity through basic manufacturing, there is an increasing awareness of the importance of consumer demand as an engine of continued growth (S.C. 2013). Based on experiences elsewhere, this demand, although focused initially on the acquisition of goods, will gradually shift toward an appetite for valued services.

A service, as simply but apply described by Fitzsimmons (2011, 18), "is a time-perishable, intangible experience performed for a customer acting in the role of co-producer." His definition highlights two common aspects inherent in most service offerings: "intangibility" and a "simultaneous process of delivery and consumption." Thus, service managers sometimes have difficulty fully describing their service offering. This reflects both the intangible nature of services and the interactive involvement of customers as cocreators in the unfolding of the service experience.

Services in Manufacturing Environments

Service is a critical strategic element not only for firms focused on the delivery of traditional services such as healthcare, hospitality, and education, but also, increasingly, for firms whose core business is the manufacture and sale of physical products. In most cases manufacturers' incentive for exploring the services option is strategic and is intended to offset growing competitive pressures.

While many of these firms periodically experiment supplementing their product sales with associated service support packages, the "services paradox" impedes most of these efforts. As described by Gebauer, Fleisch, and Friedli (2005), the services paradox occurs when a "substantial investment in extending the services business leads to increased service offerings and higher costs, but does not generate the expected correspondingly higher returns."

Interestingly, Gebauer and colleagues advance an intriguing set of behavioral or organizational factors to explain why the *services paradox* is so ubiquitous. Delving into the firm's imperative to maximize returns, they begin with Vroom's *expectancy theory* as a framework for explaining individual managers' motivation to extend the services business (1964). Three factors drive motivation: valence, expectancy, and instrumentality. *Valence* refers to the intrinsic attractiveness or unattractiveness of potential personal outcomes. For example, if I value potential future personal outcome (*valence*), believe that my efforts will lead to successful organizational outcomes (*expectancy*), believe there is a direct correlation between the outcomes achieved and personal outcomes I value (*instrumentality*), I will extend effort toward achievement of those organizational outcomes.

As applied to the context of services in manufacturing environments, Gebauer, Fleisch, and Friedli suggest that the dynamics surrounding expectancy theory can be complicated by the presence of two human cognitive limitations. The first is the human penchant to overfocus on the obvious and the tangible (Gebauer, Fleisch, and Friedli 2005). The second is the human tendency to stay within the bounds of one's personal "comfort zones" (cf. Bendoly and Prietula 2008; Bendoly et al. 2010). An important, well-documented aspect of our comfort zones (Kahneman et al. 1982) is a strong desire to avoid risk. Manufacturers perceive investments in product development as relatively low in risk and as a more comfortable strategic approach for expanding their businesses. In contrast, manufacturers perceive investment in the development or expansion of service offerings as having significantly higher risk, placing this strategic option outside their comfort zone and range of viable offerings.

Success versus Failure: Some Examples

From the perspective of Johnston and Clark (2008) the criteria for judging the success of a service offering should, at a minimum, include the following:

- The degree it provides customer value
- The degree that it delivers brand value
- The degree it makes a contribution to firm success

One of the more interesting aspects of service-offering success is its paradoxical dependence on both how well the offering meets initial customer expectations and how effectively the organization responds when service failures occur. Nordstrom, Zappos, the Ritz-Carlton are all great illustrations of companies that have mastered this paradoxical dependence, even when a service failure is the result of factors outside of their control. These firms listen attentively to every customer interaction, seeing each as an opportunity to demonstrate their commitment to customer service. They also have achieved continuing financial success. As an illustration, consider the following two examples (Conradt 2011):

> *Nordstrom: Last year a member of the security staff noticed a woman crawling around on her hands and knees on the sales floor. When he discovered she was looking for a diamond that had fallen out of her wedding ring while she was trying on clothes, he got down and searched with her. He also recruited a small team of people to help comb the floors. Eventually, the crew painstakingly picked through the dirt and debris of the store vacuum cleaners before coming up with the woman's diamond.*
>
> *Zappos: A customer's mother had recently had some medical treatment that left her feet numb and sensitive to pressure, rendering most of her shoes totally useless. She ordered her mother six pairs of shoes from Zappos, hoping that at least one of them would work. After receiving the shoes the mother called Zappos to return the shoes that didn't work, explaining why she was returning so many shoes. Two days later, she received a large bouquet of flowers from Zappos, wishing her well and hoping that she recovered soon. Two days later, the customer, her mother, and her sister were all upgraded to "Zappos VIP Members" which gives them free expedited shipping on all orders.*

Unfortunately, there also is no shortage of organizations notorious for their service failures, often contributing to their eventual demise. Sometimes, as in the case of a small local manufacturer of custom-built closets, the issue is designing a service offering that both delivers excellent customer service and also contributes to the financial success of the firm. In this particular case, the manufacturer was the recipient of several service excellence awards but was unable to convert this service excellence into enough additional revenue to sustain its viability as an ongoing business. After filing for bankruptcy, it was eventually purchased by a larger manufacturer. In other cases the failure to remain viable is the direct result of ill-conceived service offerings that reflect, among other factors, the marginalization of customer service, the hubris of believing that "customers are wrong," or even a customer-hostile model. This last factor is fully illustrated by Blockbuster, which not only ignored changing customer preferences but also used punitive measures to discourage their behavior.

THEORETICAL PERSPECTIVE

The "Service Quality" Model: Integrating the Two Aspects of Service Excellence, Design and Delivery

Broadly, we can think about services management as having two major elements: design and delivery. While the primary focus of the chapter is the design process and its behavioral implications, it is important to reflect on the interconnection between these two elements, depicted in figure 9.1.

The two connecting arrows in the figure illustrate the purpose of the design process—to specify the intent and details of the delivery process. In return, feedback from the delivery process provides valuable information on delivery execution and is thus a valuable source of data for refining service offerings.

In general, customer service reflects a balance between organization capability to provide the service, the effectiveness of the delivery process, and the empathy of those delivering the process. When any of these factors are out of balance, service failures are likely. These failures can have multiple sources: the process, the systems and equipment that support the process, customer expectations, the actions or inaction of staff delivering the service, and even customers' actions. This framing is characteristic of systems models and alludes to the value of managers' systems thinking (Bendoly 2014).

The SERVQUAL model, developed by Zeithaml, Parasuraman, and Berry (1990), provides an applicable approach for diagnosing service quality by measuring five dimensions of service quality (i.e., reliability, responsiveness, assurance, empathy, and tangibles). A comparison is first made between customer service expectations and the experience with the service actually delivered. Discrepancies between expectations and experiences reveal a gap in service quality. These gaps are typically measured along two dimensions. The first is whether the discrepancy falls above or below the zone of tolerance surrounding customers' expectations. The zone of tolerance reflects the degree that customers accept as reasonable some variation in the quality of the service they experience. The second is the magnitude of the experienced gap. Figure 9.2 illustrates five common potential gaps.

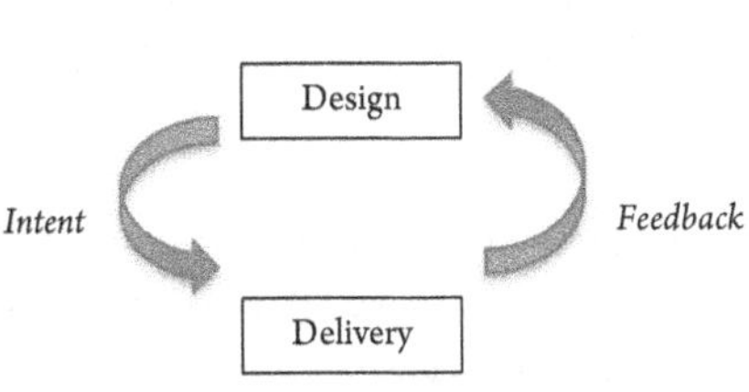

Figure 9.1 Interconnection in the Design and Delivery Service System

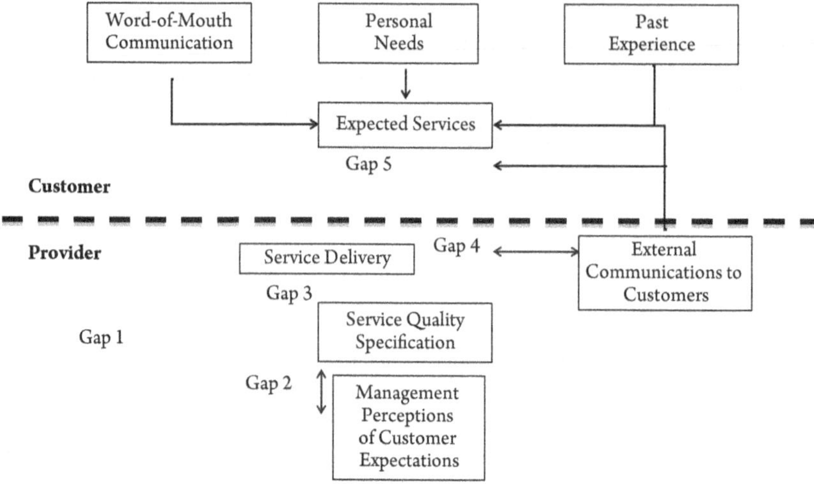

Figure 9.2 Five Common Service Gap Risks

Gap 1 is the difference between customer expectations and management's perceptions of those expectations. Typical causes include inadequate market research, a management disconnect from what actually happens at the point of contact with customers, or untested assumptions about what is important to customers.

Gap 2 is the difference between management's perception of customer needs and service quality design specifications. Typical causes include constrained resources, management indifference, unclear or ambiguous service design, or haphazard service development processes.

Gap 3 is the gap between service quality design specifications and the delivered service. Typical causes include the inadequate training, inability/unwillingness of service deliverers to meet design specifications, and ad hoc modifications they may introduce to deal with variations in the expectations of customers being served.

Gap 4 is the gap between service delivery and external communication. Here, company statements or advertisements have generated customer expectations that are inconsistent with what is being delivered. Typical causes include marketing messages that overpromise or exaggerate, or failure to carefully manage customer expectations.

Gap 5 is the gap between the service that customers expect and the service they actually experience. Typical causes reflect all the factors that potentially generate the above gaps, encompassing the total effect of all the other gaps.

Central to assessment of this overall gap are five dimensions of service quality: reliability, assurance, tangibles, empathy, and responsiveness (Berry 1995). In the supporting SERVQUAL measurement instrument, these five dimensions are reflected by a total of 22 specific items: four for "tangibles," five for "reliability," four for "responsiveness," five for "assurance," and five for "empathy." Customers

EXPECTATIONS	PERCEPTIONS
This survey deals with your opinions of banks. Please show the extent to which you think banks should possess the following features. What we are interested in here is the number that best shows your expectations about institutions offering banking services.	The following statements relate to your feelings about the particular bank XYZ you chose. Please show the extent to which you believe XYZ has the feature described in the statement. Here we are interested in a number that shows your perceptions about XYZ bank.
Strongly Disagree *Strongly Agree*	*Strongly Disagree* *Strongly Agree*
1 2 3 4 6 7	*1 2 3 4 6 7*
(E)	**(P)** **Gap Score P-E**
Tangibles	**Tangibles**
E1. Banking companies will have up-to-date equipment. ____	**E1.** XYZ bank has up-to-date equipment. ____ ________
E2. The physical facilities at banks will be visually appealing. ____	**E2.** XYZ bank's facilities are visually appealing. ____ ________
E3. Employees at banks will be well dressed and appear neat. ____	**E3.** XYZ's reception desk employees are well dressed and appear neat. ____ ________
E4. The appearance of the physical facilities of banks will be in keeping with the type of services provided. ____	**E4.** The appearance of the physical facilities of XYZ bank is in keeping with the type of services provided. ____ ________

Figure 9.3 Sample SERVQUAL Form for the "Tangibles" Dimension

are asked to rate their expectations and perceptions for each of these using a seven-point scale. Figure 9.3 shows a sample form of the section measuring the "tangibles" service dimension.

Once customers have completed the instrument, the average of each dimension's expectation rating is subtracted from its average perception rating, and becomes the basis for assessing possible root causes and remedial approaches.

Traditional Service Design

When the delivery process is seen only as a *transaction*, a provider's focus on the ability to deliver a high-quality total-service experience reflects a reasonable standard of excellence. Viewed as an "operation" that transforms inputs into outputs, these transactions encompass a combination of labor, material, and technology into a viable, valued service. In this context customer-induced variability is viewed as a problem to be solved: how much should providers accommodate the variation that customers introduce into the process? The standard approach treats this decision as a trade-off between cost and quality, as measured by customer satisfaction. More accommodation means increased costs, less accommodation means less-satisfied customers.

In contrast, if providers are able to move beyond a transactional view of the service and frame it as an *experienced-based relationship*, new possibilities emerge. When service providers have an understanding of customer behavior, as well as the technical features of the service process, the coproduction and interaction of the customer and the service provider creates an opportunity for enhanced encounters and outcomes.

More recently, there has been a growing recognition that these *experienced-based relationships* are likely to become a dominant economic force in the services sector. The primary drivers of this trend are twofold: major developments in proprietary software and data analytics that enable an unprecedented level of individual customization of services. For example, the Nordstrom *experience* is a personalized service based on the development of a face-to-face relationship between an individual salesperson and the customer (Spector and McCarthy 2012). In contrast, the Ritz-Carlton *experience* is highly scripted and supported by an information database that tracks guests' personal preferences (Gallo 2011). If a customer has a propensity for exotic travel and lavish accommodations, the Ritz-Carlton might customize a special offer around its Phulay Bay Reserve.

Given the increasing importance of services as a driver of economic success, it is critical to rethink, in fundamental ways, the traditional service delivery process. What we know about the effective delivery of services has grown significantly over the last two decades and has had a positive impact on the quality of the delivery process. Yet there is growing evidence of persistent consumer dissatisfaction with many service transactions. Here we explore both some of the lessons of the past two decades and some of the intriguing insights from studies in behavioral operations and associated fields. Such findings have the potential to take the current level of effective service delivery to even greater heights.

State of Management Practice: The Six Elements of Service Design

The traditional design process includes six key elements. When these are integrated into a comprehensive service system, the service will meet the following evaluative criteria: it will (1) be efficiently implemented, (2) be robust enough to handle variations in demand and resources, (3) be easy to use, (4) result in consistent performance, (5) consistently create customer value, and (6) ensure full delivery by tightly linking front- and back-office operations.

1. Developing a ***service concept*** defines a *target market* and *desired customer service experiences.* It typically describes how proposed services will compete in the marketplace and differ from competitive offerings.

Example: Lending Tree.com, using its Internet-based software, simplifies the loan application process through a single application to generate several mortgage offers from competing lending institutions.

Example: Zappos, building on its core value to "deliver wow through service," provides customers free delivery and a full-year return policy.

Example: The Orient Express rail service between London and Venice offers a unique travel and dining experience, reminiscent of the luxurious life of 19th-century leisure classes.

2. Creating a ***service package*** describes the combination of *physical items, sensual experiences, and psychological elements* intended to fulfill customer-defined needs. For a restaurant *physical items* might include the design of the facility and other touchable commodities such as tableware and napkins; the *sensual experiences,* the taste and aroma of the food and surrounding sights and sounds; and the *psychological elements,* a relaxed or comfortable environment, a feeling of importance or status, or a sense of well-being. Each of these elements should be consistent with and reinforce the service concept.

Example: To create this unique experience, the Orient Express uses luxury compartments and vintage dining cars, well-uniformed employees offering impeccable service, gourmet meals, a top-notch wine selection, and travel across some of Europe's most beautiful landscapes.

3. Based on the service package, the ***performance specifications*** outline the *expectations* and *requirements* of targeted customers and broadly state how customers' needs will be met. These specifications also may include the expectations and requirements of specific, high-valued segments, thus forming an established basis for customized services. These expectations and requirements form the basis of the next two steps in the design process, the design and delivery specifications.
4. ***Design specifications*** describe services in sufficient detail to facilitate the replication of the service experience from individual to individual and from location to location. It describes core activities to be performed, skills required by those delivering the service, and execution guidelines. These guidelines may include cost and time targets, the degree of discretionary authority, and the major design elements of the facility: size, layout, equipment, and location.
5. The ***delivery specifications*** describe the work processes required to deliver the service. This may include a general step-by-step workflow, a

work schedule, results to be delivered, and the location where the work is to be performed.

6. The ***service recovery plan*** provides a training program and specifies the degree to which front-line employees are empowered to take corrective actions in response to service failure. It recognizes that service failures are learning events. It is more than a defensive strategy against customer defection. It is an opportunity to enhance the overall service experience, to establish customer loyalty, and to build customer advocates. This happens when the recovery process is fast and easy, seen as fair by customers, and handled in a professional manner, and when employees are empowered and rewarded for their recovery efforts. In fact, heroic service recovery frequently becomes legendary, establishing the firm's reputation for best-in-class service.

Beyond the Limits of the Traditional: Five New Principles

As noted earlier, the traditional focus on the elements of service design deals with the issue of customer variability as a problem and focuses on finding the best trade-off between the costs of variability and the benefits of satisfied customers. A common solution is to supplement a broad general service offering with a limited number of customized offerings targeted at smaller segments, this customized offerings having significantly greater profit potential than the general offering. While this is a viable approach for many types of services, it has some significant limits.

In contrast, adopting a more expansive view, it is possible to frame variability not as a problem but as an opportunity. This opportunity emerges with recognition that the effective management of variability requires a service provider to accept customer behavior as a normal and expected part of the service delivery process.

The rental of DVDs offers an illustration. From their inception Netflix and Blockbuster had very different approaches to variation in DVD rental periods. Blockbuster's revenue model was based on per movie rental fee and structure, much like checking a book out from a library. Under this model, rapid video return maximized revenue. Thus rental periods were limited, and failure to return "on time" was "punished" as an "undesirable" behavior. Using the classic problem-reduction approach, Blockbuster charged fees for late returns. While this reduced the percentage of late returns, it also created a great deal of customer dissatisfaction.

As other models evolved, Blockbuster experienced a large number of defections to other providers, particularly Netflix, which offered a dramatically different approach. The Netflix subscription model charged a monthly fee, based on the number of videos customers could hold at one time. As each video was returned, a new video from the customer's queue was received. This accommodated customers' viewing patterns, accepting variability as normal and simultaneously ensuring a continuous revenue stream.

This and other behavioral sciences aspects of service encounters are just beginning to be considered by service providers (Bendoly et al. 2010). The effective management of service encounters requires an understanding of both the technical features of the service process and also the underlying psychological dynamics of customer behaviors and perceptions. The example of video rentals demonstrates how acceptance of behavioral patterns as normal makes available new, more effective ways of enhancing service offerings. These approaches defy accepted notions of variation as an ever-changing compromise between costs and customer satisfaction.

Acceptance of variation in customers' behavioral patterns is only a first step. The next is recognition that customer satisfaction depends not on an objectively experienced reality, but on the experience as it is remembered. To better understand this idea, it is useful to explore the idea of *experienced utility* (Kahneman 2000). In general we expect experienced utility to reflect the impact of two factors: the duration and intensity of the pain or pleasure derived from an experience. Thus if it were possible to measure the minute-by-minute pleasure or pain experienced and then plot the resulting curve, the area under the curve would reflect the totality of the experience (Kahneman 2013).

One interesting attempt to do this is reported in a study by Redelmeier and Kahneman (1996), who studied patients undergoing colonoscopy. The patients were asked once every 60 seconds to rate their pain on a 10-point scale. The variation in the duration of the procedures was from four to 69 minutes, and their experienced pain as reported varied significantly throughout the procedure. Figure 9.4 shows an example of the pain reported by two typical patients.

Graphically the results of *experienced utility* are exactly as expected: patient B's area under the curve is far greater than patient A's, reflecting a similar peak level of pain but a far longer period of duration or time to complete the procedure: 24 minutes, compared to 8 minutes for patient A.

After the completion of the procedure, patients were asked to rate their "total amount" of pain on a 1 to 10 scale. The expectation was that the recall of the experience would yield results consistent with the above graphs. Contrary to their anticipated results, two surprising patterns were observed.

1. The duration of the procedure had no effect whatsoever on postprocedure ratings.
2. The best predictor of postprocedure ratings was the average of two specific points: the highest level of pain experienced at any point during the procedure and the level of pain reported at the very end of the experience.

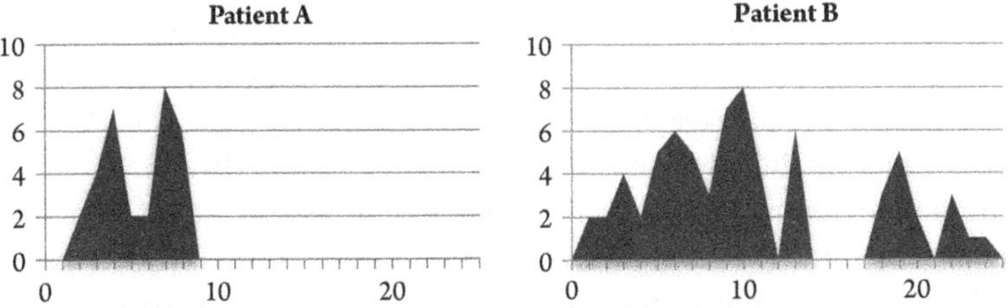

Figure 9.4 Pain Levels Reported by Patients

Kahneman argued that this apparent conflict reflects, in effect, "two selves": an *experiencing self* that reports what we are experiencing in the present and a *remembering self* that reports how we felt overall about the experience (for an interesting biometric study of managerial stress and arousal in the OM context, see Bendoly 2011).

Thus if we understand the factors that impact how an experience is likely to be remembered, a third facet can be added to the service design process. The third facet encompasses how we remember and evaluate the experience after the fact. Below we explore three aspects of service encounters that significantly impact how the experience is remembered (Chase and Dasu 2001):

- *The flow of the service experience or* what is happening at each step of the process
- *The flow time* or how long it seems to take at each step of the process
- *Judging of the encounter performance* or how the encounter is remembered

Flow of the Service Experience

The summary assessment of a service experience impacts whether or not a service provider is likely to be reused. As Ariely and Carmon (2000), among others (Baumgartner, Sujan, and Padgett 1997; Redelmeier and Kahneman 1996; Loewenstein and Pelec 1993) have noted, our summaries of our previous experiences reflect three aspects of what happened:

- The trend in the sequence of pain or pleasure
- The high or low points of the experience
- How the experience ended

In general the research reveals that people attend to the rate of improvement in the experience as it progresses and prefer experiences that improve. As previously noted, the level of pain or pleasure experienced at the end point has a huge impact on how the experience is remembered.

Flow of Time

As Friedman (1990) has noted, our view of time often is distorted by its situational context. Specifically, four well-confirmed observations stand out: (1) when we are deeply engaged in what we are doing we lose track of time, (2) when we actively attend to the passage of time we overestimate its duration, (3) when the number of events included in an experience increases, our after-the-fact estimate of its duration increases independent of the actual time spent, and (4) we pay little attention to the duration of an experience unless it is significantly shorter or significantly longer than our expectations established by similar past experiences (Cook et al. 2002).

Judging the Encounter Performance

When our service experiences go unexpectedly well or unexpectedly astray, we often have a strong urge to seek a single, clear driver of the experience. We are likely to reject the frequent reality that a combination of minor events could have been the underlying cause. This means that we tend to focus on discrete events and reject the possibility that the process was flawed, look for specific deviations from normal routines as likely discrete causes, and most often see the last event that occurred as the primary cause.

Translating the Behavioral Factors into Five New Principles for Designing Service Experiences

Chase and Dasu (2001) argued that these general behavioral rules can be translated into five new service design principles. The intent of these principles is not to replace the six standard design elements, but to provide additional elements that dramatically increase the likelihood of maximizing service effectiveness criteria: service will (1) be efficiently implemented, (2) be robust enough to handle variations in demand and resources, (3) be easy to use, (4) result in consistent performance, (5) consistently create customer value, and (6) ensure full delivery by tightly linking front- and back-office operations.

Principle 1: Finish Strong

Last impressions, not first ones, stay in customer memories.

> ***Example:*** Malaysian Airlines helps travelers with baggage collection and ground transportation—the last stage of travel. This intensive service makes passengers feel lavishly cared for. One loyal customer still describes the experience to fellow travelers—nine years later.

Traditional approaches to services management stress the importance of a well-designed process from beginning to end, noting in particular the importance of the service "bookends," the beginning and the end of the service encounter. This reflects conventional wisdom about the importance of our first and last impressions. In a perfectly rational, planned world, it is difficult to argue with the importance of a well-honed process that works well at each stage of the process. In reality, however, the best-designed processes don't always work as intended. To begin with, there are many factors outside of the control of the process. For example, airlines often experience flight delays due to weather or other external events. Even among those events under control, conflicting demands often result in less than desirable outcomes for some customers. For example, coach accommodations are by design limited, reflecting the economics of the low price paid. On long flights these small coach class accommodations often become cramped and uncomfortable. It is also critical to recognize that the interactions between humans rarely follow ideal patterns or scripts. Humans are self-directed and capable of deciding their own paths, not necessarily the ones prescribed for them.

Chase and Dasu argued, given these realities, that it is far more important to ensure a strong ending than a great beginning. Underlying their claim are two basic observations from behavioral science:

- The ending of an event stands out more clearly in memory than its beginning.
- People are more favorably disposed toward processes that show improvement as they progress than processes that are even in performance or deteriorate.

Principle 2: Get Bad Experiences out of the Way Early

Bad experiences include unpleasant news, discomfort, and long lines. This prevents these experiences from dominating customers' memory of the entire process.

> ***Example:*** Many doctors recognize the anxiety that patients often have about painful or unpleasant procedures. In the best practices, these unpleasant procedures are scheduled at the beginning of the visit. In most practices they are typically scheduled at the end of the visit.

It is understandable that people are reluctant to deliver bad news to others. We feel great anxiety about their reaction and thus we prefer to postpone the delivery of bad news as long as possible. Unfortunately, it is likely to have just the opposite implications for customers:

- Since there is substantial anxiety associated with potentially unpleasant events, we prefer to get them out of the way quickly and as soon as possible.
- In contrast, we prefer to have desirable events occur at the end of a sequence of events so we can enjoy the pleasure of savoring them.

Principle 3: Segment the Pleasure, Combine the Pain

Break pleasant experiences into multiple stages; blend unpleasant experiences into a single stage.

> ***Example:*** The Internet World trade show segments pleasure by spreading plenty of product demos (attendees' favorite activity) throughout the show.

> It combines—and reduces—pain by minimizing boring paperwork. Attendees preregister on the Internet and gather information at any booth with a single swipe of preprogrammed badges.

Chase and Dasu reflect on "asymmetric" reactions to loses and gains. On the pleasure or gain side a great deal of research indicates that multiple small or short-duration outcomes are perceived as more desirable than larger or longer events that are equal in amount or duration. As some theme parks have discovered, most people view two 90-second rides as lasting longer than one three-minute ride.

Unfortunately, when it comes to the loss or pain side, many businesses ignore this principle, particularly the idea of combining instances of pain. Two flagrant examples stand out: the use of multiple waiting lines and both the use and number of prompt levels required to successfully navigate most automated telephone routing systems. Renewing your driver's license often requires successful negotiation of three lines: one to check that you have all the required documentation, one to present the documentation, take an eye test, and have an updated photo taken, and a third line to pick up a temporary license. After all that your permanent license is mailed to you within a week or so.

Most private physician offices also spread the pain across multiple process phases. Typically, you sign in and present your insurance card when you arrive, wait to be called to be seated in an examination room, wait for a physician's assistant to arrive, take your vital signs and update your medical history, wait to actually be examined by the attending physician, wait to undergo blood tests and other testing procedures, and then finally "check out" and pay whatever copay is required.

Regarding telephone routing systems, multiple examples are available. On one recent personal experience, I successfully negotiated four levels of prompts just to have the opportunity to wait 20 minutes to talk to a live representative. The problem is so pervasive that a number of websites were created to instruct consumers how to shortcut the prompt process.

Principle 4: Build Commitment through Choice

People feel happier and more comfortable when they believe they have some control over an uncomfortable process.

> ***Example*:** When customers complained about slow repair of their Xerox machines, the repair company let them request faster service for urgent problems, slower service for less urgent ones. Customers' satisfaction rose—they wanted choice more than immediate service.

Studies of motivation have consistently demonstrated that people exert more effort, feel more responsible for results, and are more satisfied with their work when they have some degree of control over how the work is performed. This same principle applies to service encounters. As Chase and Dasu noted, allowing donors to decide which arm from which blood is drawn significantly decreases their reported discomfort with the procedure.

Even with more serious procedures, the medical community has recognized the importance of allowing patients to make "informed decisions" about their treatment options. One local medical facility dealing with the treatment of cancer uses this principle to promote their services. Their television commercial features one of their patients extolling the "virtues" of having options and not being restricted to a "cookie-cutter" approach to their treatment.

One last word of caution: choices are good, but too many choices can be overwhelming. The key is to give people choices, but not too many choices.

Principle 5: Give People Rituals and Stick to Them

Perform repetitive, familiar actions—especially during long-term, professional service encounters: kickoff dinners, final celebrations, handwritten thank-you notes, and so on.

Example: Most cruise lines offer a captain's dinner and a midnight buffet.

With just a little reflection it is not difficult for us to understand the important role rites of passage and their associated rituals play in our lives. They mark most of the important events in our lives: births, baptisms, graduations, marriages, promotions, retirements, deaths, among others. What may not be as obvious is the important role that they play in the smaller part of our lives as well. These can be as small as a verbal thank you, an expression of appreciation, or even simple body language confirming we truly heard what someone said.

These small rituals, it turns out, can play a significant role in service encounters as well, particularly when the encounters have unsatisfactory endings. The typical approach with service failures is to offer customers material compensation in response of a service failure. If the lapse in service is actually the result of a task failure or results in a material loss, this is, in fact, an appropriate approach. But often service failures are the result of "mistreatment," for example, rudeness or being ignored. In these instances, ironically, material compensation may actual backfire. What is far more effective is the simple ritual of acknowledging what happened and offering a sincere apology.

CASE EXAMPLE

The best way to understand the interplay between the "elements of service design" and the "the new behavioral principles" is within the context of a consolidated case example using Carnival Cruise Lines.

Illustrating the Six Elements of Service Design

Step 1: Defining the Service Concept

Carnival has had an established service concept in the marketplace since its inaugural voyage in 1972. This service concept defines both the target market and the breath of customer service experiences:

> *Popular, mass-market cruise line with sailings to the Caribbean, Mexico, Europe and Alaska. Six world-class cruise lines, each a leader in a particular style of cruise vacationing. From simple pleasures to exotic adventures, we make it easy to choose the vacation that fits your lifestyle.* (www.worldsleadingcruiselines.com)

Step 2: Developing the Service Package

The service package is a combination of physical, sensual, and psychological items. For Carnival these components are broken down into the suite accommodations on board (open to the water or open to the interior), dining options, daily entertainment (poolside, rock climbing, or table tennis), nightly entertainment, and the onshore destinations for sightseeing. Each component ensures that the service concept is reinforced. A multitude of onboard amenities provide endless opportunities to stimulate the senses and appeal to customers' interests.

Step 3: Establishing Performance Specifications

The performance specifications outline the expectations and requirements of targeted customers. Here Carnival must distinguish between customer requirements and customer expectations. Customer requirements include a safe, enjoyable cruise experience punctuated by varying levels of entertainment on and off the cruise line. These requirements might be designated as general in nature and establish the minimal performance standard for all of the cruise experiences. The customer expectations are more targeted and customized depending on the audience. For example, a party seeking the highest "5 Star" service on a cruise line would book with Cunard Cruise Line and sail on the *Queen Mary 2*, which has a reputation for elegance and excellence. In this best-of-the-best environment, the performance standard goes beyond the essential customer requirements to ensure all the customer's targeted expectations are met.

Step 4: Outlining the Design Specifications

Carnival has six distinctive cruise lines that feature different offerings, each of which affords activities that may not be found on other Carnival cruise lines. A casino on board would require a different set of provider skills from a cruise line focused on deckside or dockside activities. Certain facilities and activities targeted at a family-oriented cruise would not be found on Cunard's *Queen Mary 2*, where opulence and style are the focus.

Step 5: Setting the Delivery Specifications

The delivery specifications for the many processes on board are spelled out. Schedules for departures, dinning offerings, entertainment, cabin services, and other service amenities are developed. All physical deliverables are inventoried and staged prior to departure, such as food and bar items, towels, and bed linens. All below-deck locations are prepped and checked to ensure that all the service deliverables are on board.

Step 6: Establishing a Service Recovery Plan

In this final step, policies and procedures are established for "service recovery" if a service delivery failure occurs. It is an opportunity to enhance the overall service experience, to establish customer loyalty, and to build customer advocates. In 1972, on its inaugural voyage, Carnival's *Mardi Gras* cruise liner hit a sandbar outside the port of Miami. In response, Carnival executives invited all their stranded guests to join them on deck to enjoy an open bar, turning the stalled ship into a floating party and an advertisement for their "fun ship" brand (Bloomberg 2013). Of course, recovery from some service failures can be far more difficult. After the *Costa Concordia* ran aground off the coast of Italy in 2012, killing 32 people, Carnival dramatically cut cruise prices to its best customers to encourage their continued loyalty.

Illustrating the Behavioral Principles

Principle 1: Finish Strong

Last impressions, not first ones, stay in customers' memories. Carnival's various cruise lines utilize this basic principle, typically focusing on the dining and entertainment experience during the last night at sea. However, by extending the perspective to what happens during and after disembarkation, there are potential additional opportunities for services that build on this principle. In effect, customers' last impressions can sometimes extend beyond what is normally viewed as the end of the service experience. For example, sometimes those departing a cruise suffer from a mild form of "motion sickness" known as "disembarkment syndrome." Typically, the best remedies for this condition are walking and jogging. Carnival could offer a special "Back to Land" service that included extra days at a hotel with a physical exercise program to treat the "motion sickness."

Principle 2: Get Bad Experiences out of the Way Early

Bad experiences include unpleasant news, discomfort, and long lines. This prevents these experiences from dominating customers' memory of the entire process. As an illustration, the worst part of the trip, getting on board and having your luggage delivered to your cabin, occurs at the very start of the cruise. Clearly getting this process completed as rapidly as possible is the most desirable outcome, but understandably, given the large capacity of today's modern vessels, this is a logistical challenge under the best of circumstances. A less obvious application centers on the occurrence of unplanned events (weather, mechanical failures, etc.) that have a negative impact on cruisers' experience. The key here is to provide needed information to passengers in a timely way. For example, letting passengers know immediately of arrival delays gives them time to make changes to their land arrangements and avoid unpleasant delays once they have departed.

Principle 3: Segment the Pleasure, Combine the Pain

Break pleasant experiences into multiple stages; blend unpleasant ones into a single stage. Principle 3, particularly the notion of segmenting pleasure, is the backbone of most cruises. Carnival offers its passengers an ongoing array of short, but varied activities to keep them engaged in the cruise experience.

Principle 4: Build Commitment through Choice

The relationship between choice and satisfaction is well established in a wide range of contexts, including service encounters. One way Carnival has adopted this principle is by offering customers a wide range of dinning and activity options. A new possibility might include changes to Carnival's "Fly Aweigh Program," which includes, as part of the cruise price, airfare to and from your home and your port of embarkation. The attractions of this "package" program are twofold: savings on the total cost of the trip and the "insurance" offered if the flight is canceled or delayed. Unfortunately, in return, you give up your choice of the carrier, seat selection, departure and arrival times, and number of stopovers. Using principle 4, Carnival could offer an alternative "package" for those who would like more choice in their travel arrangements. This would allow travelers to make their own arrangements to and from the port of embarkation and offer them an onboard "credit" that would approximately match Carnival's cost for the block booking included with the "Fly Aweigh Program."

Principle 5: Give People Rituals and Stick to Them

Again, most cruise lines have mastered the use of principle 5. Examples utilized by Carnival and others include midnight buffets, special dinners at the end of the cruise, and nightly entertainment.

LEARNING ACTIVITY

The following brainstorming activities can be used as either individual or team-based exercises. Based on their work or personal experience, each participant or participating team is asked to select one specific service context to apply to all of the three activities.

1. **Applying the traditional design steps (table 9.1)**
2. **Applying the behavioral principles (table 9.2)**
3. **Modifying the Service Quality Model**

Above we described the SERVQUAL model and pointed out that gap 5 asks customers to assess the gap between the service they expected and the service they experienced. We also noted that there is in effect a sixth or hidden gap between what customers actually experienced and how the experience is remembered. In this exercise, participants are asked to expand their thought process about assessing service quality and suggest how they might modify their gap assessment process to deal with this "hidden gap."

Table 9.1. Applying the Traditional Design Steps

Select a service context you have worked in or experienced as a customer. Using the template provided, design a service offering that includes each of the design elements as appropriate.

Service context:
Service Concept: *Target segment desired customer services*
Service package: *—Physical items:*
—Sensual experiences:
—Psychological elements:
Performance specifications: *—Required:* *Target segment expectations:*
Design specifications: *—Activities to be performed:* *—Skills required by providers:* *—Execution guidelines (cost & time targets, degree of discretionary authority):*
Delivery specifications (workflows, schedules, & results to be delivered):
Recovery plan: *Actions / Who is authorized*

Table 9.2. Applying the Behavioral Principles

In this exercise participants extend the service design elements created using the Traditional Design step (Table 9.1) by specifically incorporating Chase and Dasu's five principles into their service offering.

Description of how service offering incorporates . . .
Principle 1:
Principle 2:
Principle 3:
Principle 4:
Principle 5:

DISCUSSION

The science of designing "great" service encounters has progressed significantly. Many of the basic design principles have withstood the test of time. We hope the exercises and discussion in this chapter will have helped readers develop an appreciation of their value and gain some practical experience in their application to real-life service encounters. The behavioral principles are not intended to replace the traditional design element, but to increase understanding of how the design elements can be better applied to human interactions.

Implications for Practitioners

Traditionally, the role of the customer as "coproducer" introduces an unpredictable element into any service offering that is difficult to deal with in the design process. Visualizing this element from a behavioral sciences perspective opens up new strategies for understanding coproduction and more effectively incorporating the ramifications of coproduction into service offerings.

First, the link between expectations and experience is never straightforward. Positioning, marketing, and physical elements are intended to shape the customer experience, to help build a customer story. However, no matter how meticulous the intended story, humans are self-directed entities that interpret the "story" from their own perspective, impacting both their expectations and experiences. At best the intended story can only point them in a general direction.

Second, there is always a hidden gap between what was actually experienced in real or present time and what is remembered about both those experiences and our underlying expectations in future reflections. In effect customers create their own stories about what they expected and what they experienced. Customer recall of both is almost by definition imperfect. The most effective designs will focus as much attention on what is likely to be remembered as on what will be experienced.

Implications for Operations Management and the Behavioral Sciences

To date what is available is a set of interesting conceptual ideas, supported by solid basic research in behavioral operations that borrows largely from the economics literature. Unfortunately, the applicability of these intriguing findings to services management is mostly supported only by anecdotal data. For the operations management community, there is a growing need to determine how the findings from the behavioral sciences can be systematically incorporated into the design and delivery process. This includes working to develop and test new potential design elements. For the behavioral sciences, the growing importance of services to the world economy opens up a significant opportunity for applied research. The work to date as applied to the services context, though thought provoking, is still in its infancy.

References

Ariely, D., Carmon, Z. 2000. Gestalt characteristics of experiences: the defining features of summarized events. Journal of Behavioral Decision Making 13, 191–201.

Baumgartner, H., Sujan, H., Padgett, D. 1997. Patterns of affective reactions to advertisements: the integration of moment-to-moment responses to overall judgments. Journal of Marketing Research 34, 219–232.

Bendoly, E. 2011. Linking task conditions to physiology and judgment errors in RM systems. Production and Operations Management 20 (6), 860–876.

Bendoly, E. 2014. Systems dynamics understanding in project execution: information sharing quality and psychological safety. Production and Operations Management 23 (8), 1352–1369.

Bendoly, E., Croson, R., Gonçalves, P., Schultz, K. 2010. Bodies of knowledge for research in behavioral operations. Production and Operations Management 19 (4), 434–452.

Bendoly, E., Prietula, M. 2008. In "The Zone": The role of evolving skill and transitional workload on motivation and realized performance in operational tasks. International Journal of Operations and Production Management 28 (12), 1130–1152.

Berry, L. L. 1995. Relationship marketing of services—growing interest, merging perspectives. Journal of the Academy of Marketing Science 23 (4), 236–245.

Bloomberg BusinessWeek. 2013. Will Carnival Party On? February 25–March 3, 16–17.

Chase, R. B., Dasu, S. 2001. Want to perfect your company's service? Use behavioral science. Harvard Business Review 72 (6), 78–84.

Conradt, S. 2011. 11 of the best customer service stories ever. http://mentalfloss.com/article/30198/11-best-customer-service-stories-ever.

Cook, L. S., Bowen, D. E., Chase, R. B., Dasu, S., Stewart, D. M., Tansik, D. A. 2002. Human issues in service design. Journal of Operations Management 20, 159–174.

Fitzsimmons, J. 2011. Service Management: Operations, Strategy, Information Technology. 7th ed. New York: Irwin/McGraw-Hill.

Friedman, W. J. 1990. About Time: Inventing the Fourth Dimension. Cambridge, MA: MIT Press.

Gallo, C. 2011. Wow your customers the Ritz-Carlton way. Forbes. www.coporate.ritzcarlton.com/en/About/Goldstandards.htm.

Gebauer, H. Fleisch, E., Friedli, T. 2005. Overcoming the services paradox in manufacturing companies. European Management Journal 23 (1), 14–26.

Henderson, R. 2012. Employment outlook: 2010–2020. Industry employment and output projections to 2020. Monthly Labor Review 2 (1), 65–83.

International Monetary Fund (IMF). 2012. Nominal GDP data for 2012. World Economic Outlook Database, April.

Johnston, R., Clark, G. 2008. Service Operations Management: Improving Delivery. 3rd ed. Harlow: Pearson Education.

Kahneman, D. 2000. Experienced utility and objective happiness: A moment-based approach. D. Kahneman, A. Tversky (eds.) in Choices, Values, and Frames. Cambridge: Cambridge University Press.

Kahneman, D. 2013. Thinking, Fast and Slow. New York: Farrar, Straus and Giroux.

Kahneman, D., Slovic, D., Tversky, A. 1982. Judgment under Uncertainty: Heuristics and Biases. Cambridge: Cambridge University Press.

Loewenstein, G., Pelec, D. 1993. Preferences for sequences of outcomes. Psychological Review 100, 91–108.

Redelmeier, D. A., Kahneman, D. 1996. Patient's memories of painful treatments: Real-time and retrospective evaluations of two minimally invasive procedures. Pain 66, 3–8.

S.C. 2013. The post-industrial future is nigh. Economist, February 19. www.economist.com/blogs/analects/2013/02/services-sector.

Spector, R., McCarthy, P. D. 2012. The Nordstrom Way to Customer Service Excellence. 2nd ed. Hoboken, NJ: John Wiley & Sons.
Vroom, V. 1964. Work and Motivation. New York: John Wiley & Sons.
Zeithaml, V. A., Parasuraman, A., Berry, L. L. 1990. Delivering Quality Service: Balancing Customer Perceptions and Expectations. New York: Free Press.

CHAPTER 10

Sharing the Load

Group Behavior and Insights into Simulating Real-World Dynamics

DIEGO CRESPO PEREIRA AND DAVID DEL RIO VILAS

OVERVIEW

In industrial engineering as well as management practice, Modeling and Simulation (M&S) methodology is a powerful tool for the design and improvement of manufacturing systems and services. Despite its many applications (Bangsow 2012) and its many advantages over other analysis methodologies (Banks et al. 2010) a currently open issue is the appropriateness of modeling human performance and behavioral effects (Baines et al. 2004).

Research has established that often-unanticipated human behavior can have a critical impact on production system performance (Bendoly and Prietula 2008; Powell and Schultz 2004). Factors such as motivation, tiredness, and group behavior are examples of behavioral factors that potentially influence the throughput of a production facility. However, simulation models do not typically incorporate these effects. For instance, classic texts (Banks et al. 2010; Robinson 2004) hardly mention the topic of human behavior modeling. Human factors often are treated in a rather "mechanistic" way, that is, they are dealt with in the same way as other resources, such as machines.

The common practice in M&S application is to introduce human variability by means of a statistic distribution accounting for variations in task times. The only other individual effects that may be accounted for are learning curve variations (Baines et al. 2005). This assumption implies that human task times are independent from the manufacturing system state, which is an assumption challenged by other research (Schultz et al. 1998; Schultz, Juran, and Boudreau 1999).

The teaching activity described in this chapter was designed to demonstrate how behavioral effects can lead to inaccuracies in the results from simulation models when applied to labor-intensive processes. The case study was inspired based on a real manufacturing plant from the mining industry that heavily relies on human work. Differences between "classic" simulation models and the real system can be attributed to behavioral effects (e.g., Bendoly et al. 2010):

1. **Feedback effects,** in relation to how laborers adjust their work pace depending on working conditions
2. **Interdependence effects,** in relation to how laborers interact when work share is enabled

The next section provides a review of how human factors are dealt with in simulation models, and behavioral effects that should be accounted for. The real manufacturing case that inspired this teaching activity is described in the following section. The section after that presents the teaching activity along with teaching materials. Finally, the last two sections discuss the results that ought to be obtained and conclusions.

THEORETICAL PERSPECTIVE

The primary goals for the teaching activity we describe are to illustrate differences obtained between simulation models in which human resources are modeled in a mechanistic way, and a real manufacturing line in which behavioral phenomena are present, and to evaluate simulation result bias. The classic approach to modeling variation in human performance is to consider a statistical distribution for task times.

The biggest problem modeling a manufacturing line is to estimate how variation in task durations and arrival processes affects queues generation and line throughput. Queuing theory models are not suitable for "real" cases because they require adoption of exponential time distributions seldom reflecting real task durations. Simulation is required to deal with general distributions. In the common approach assumes the nth repetition of a task will follow a random distribution that might be its empirical distribution, a theoretical distribution, or a nonparametric distribution. Task times also are often assumed to be independent and identically distributed. The simulation literature provides several techniques for fitting theoretical distributions to real data. Some methods for dealing with autocorrelated task times and nonstationary time series also are provided. However, these techniques cannot be applied when task times depend on the state of the system. In this case, regression models could be applied to relate task times to other system variables.

The question that has been addressed by previous authors is whether omitting behavioral effects has a relevant impact in simulation results, and what effects should be introduced to refine classic "mechanistic" models.

Two primary classes of models can be considered in this regard:

- Nonstationary models account for variations in task time distributions. They are suitable for representing variability in human performance due to time of day or learning. (Baines et al. 2004; Baines and Kay 2002; Fletcher, Baines, and Harrison 2006 offer a theoretical framework for modeling these effects in simulation models.)
- State-dependent models are suitable for modeling behavioral phenomena because they relate worker performance to systems variables. An example of such a model is offered by Powell and Schultz (2004) in which worker cycle times are generated as a function of queues lengths in the line.

Knowledge from the field of behavioral science can improve the accuracy of simulation models. In spite of intensive research, points of intersection with operations research have received limited attention, despite calls for integration (Bendoly, Donohue, and Schultz 2006; Bendoly et al. 2010).

The majority of the research in the area has focused on the integration of models from behavioral science in discrete events simulation models. For instance, Neumann and Medbo (2009) incorporated factors such as operator autonomy in choosing when to rest, individual difference characteristics such as mean and standard deviation of cycle times or learning rates, and operators' specific capacity in discrete events simulation experiments. Results from this research reveal significant effects on throughput based on different variability levels among workers' characteristics. Elkosantini and Gien (2009), among others, incorporated cognitive models for workers' decision-making in simulation models. These authors conducted feasibility studies and provided guidelines for how to implement them. However, they pointed out the importance of both studying the effective actual application of their approaches to real cases, and the proper model validation.

Another approach discussed in the literature focuses on the execution of experiments in laboratory manufacturing settings. Laboratory experimentation is a common research tool in behavioral science, although few researchers have adopted this approach for studying interactions between technical and behavioral elements in manufacturing.

Schultz and coauthors (Schultz et al. 1998; Schultz, Juran, and Boudreau 1999; Schultz 2003) executed experiments on human performance effects in low inventory systems and work-sharing. They arranged a laboratory flow line consisting of three serial operations. The tasks consisted of introducing codes in a software application representing customer orders, and participants in the research were high school students. The primary conclusions derived from their work can be summarized as follows:

- Individuals' work pace depends on inventory levels. This phenomenon provides insight into why low inventory lines show a higher throughput than expected by classical mechanistic models.
- Work-sharing in a serial line may yield lower than expected throughput due to negative interpersonal interactions.

These authors later analyzed by means of simulation the performance of a serial line with state-dependent effects (Powell and Schultz 2004). In this case task times were assumed to be inversely proportional to workload. This assumption explained observed differences between the throughput of a serial line with low buffers and a classic simulation model.

Bendoly and Prietula (2008) present the results from another experiment. In this case the process consisted of a single operation in which subjects had to solve TSP (traveling salesman problem) instances by means of a software application. Business school students participated and thus had a different functional background than participants the Schultz's experiment. Bendoly and colleagues further explored relations between motivation and task times as well as their interaction with worker skills.

- Their conclusions support the assumption that higher workload increases performance among skilled workers.
- In the case of medium-skilled workers, an inverse U-shaped relation emerges between workload and work pace.
- In the case of low-skill workers, a negative association is observed between workload and performance.

These results imply that learning may play an important role in behavior.

This research suggests that although typically ignored in practice, behavior can influence the accuracy of simulation models. This teaching activity is intended to demonstrate the difficulties of analyzing manufacturing lines with human tasks, and casts doubt on the validity of the conclusions of simulation models.

Three behavioral effects are in focus:

- The relation between motivation and performance
- The relation between workload and performance
- The effect of work-sharing on performance

Motivation is a driver of human performance, although it is not a factor that can be precisely controlled in the experiment. Motivation can be influenced by various means, including incentives.

The relation between workload and performance is governed by two disparate laws. When workload is low, the Yerkes-Dodson law provides that increases in workload enhance performance. In contrast, according to Parkinson's Law, when workload is already high, further increases can harm performance. However, workload perceptions may greatly affect this relationship, and thus great care must be taken as to activity design conditions. Further, variables such as skill can influence workload perceptions (Bendoly and Prietula 2008), which suggests that learning also must be reckoned. Thus, in the experimental design, learning effects might take place and they should be accounted for.

Finally, work share is a condition that may produce divergent performance outcomes. Sharing work means that idle times can be reduced. However, interdependences among workers may lead to a range of outcomes. Fast workers may reduce their pace so they don't end up spending inordinate time helping others, while slow workers may either increase their speed to match others or reduce their speed, since they expect other's help. Schultz's experiment (2003) reveals an instance in which work share yielded negative performance effects.

- Simulation results may be inaccurate if behavioral phenomena are not accounted for and therefore lead to underspecified conclusions.
- The performance of a manufacturing line with low-capacity buffers can be higher than expected and the gains from work share lower than expected.

CASE EXAMPLE

Our operational setting and activities are based directly on the case of a Spanish medium-sized manufacturing company that provides natural roofing slate for institutional and residential buildings. This sector has benefited very little from technological transference from other industries. The level of automation is low as is the application of lean manufacturing principles. Arguably, the reason for the firm's failure to benefit from available modernization is relative geographic isolation of slate production areas, which are primarily located in the northwest mountainous region of Spain. This work is labor intensive, and workers are exposed to hard environmental and ergonomic conditions. It is difficult to find skilled workers, so salaries are high. As a result, labor and operating expenses account for one-third each of the firm's total setup costs. Several actions have been taken to improve production, quality, health and safety, and environmental issues (del Rio Villas et al. 2009; Rego Monteil et al. 2010), with the goal of achieving more efficient and productive processes.

Process Description

Irregular and heavy blocks of slate extracted from a quarry are transported to the manufacturing plant, where they are cut into strips using circular saws. The strips are then cut into slabs, which are carried to splitters on an automated conveyor belt. An operator on an electric rail-mounted vehicle receives and distributes slabs among the splitters according to the specified format and their stock level. Slabs are taken by the splitters one by one and cut in several pieces using a special type of chisel so they can be handled and their quality determined through visual inspection. A smaller chisel is then used to cut these smaller pieces into plates. The chisel is placed in position against the edge of the block and tapped lightly with a mallet, generating a crack in the direction of cleavage. Slight leverage with the chisel serves to split the block into two pieces with smooth and even surfaces.

This process is repeated until the original block is converted into a variable number of pieces, depending primarily on the quality of the slate rock from the quarry, as well as the experience and skill of the splitters. A second operator collects the slates lots on an electric trolley and takes them to a third distribution point from which they are distributed among the cutting machines. The split stone is then mechanically cut according to commercial shape and size. Finally, every slate tile is inspected by trained classifiers prior to being loaded into crate pallets (figure 10.1).

Figure 10.1 The Processing of Slate
From quarry to crate pallets, the slate is extracted (1), cut (2), split (3), shaped (4), classified (5), and packed (6)

Slates are available in different sizes and grades. Quality is assessed based on roughness, color homogeneity, thickness, and presence and position of imperfections (primarily quartzite lines and waving). Accordingly, the company offers three grades for every commercial size: Superior, First, and Standard. Slate that does not meet with quality requirements is set aside and recycled to be cut again into another shape until it complies with standards, or in the event this is not possible, rejected. An operator transports the recycled plates to their corresponding machines. A third task assigned to this transporter is stocking material in buffers previously located near cutting machines when their utilization is full. Thus, a triple flow is shared by one transportation system connecting a push system (lots coming from splitters) and a pull system (lots required by cutting machines). Further, the assignation rules that operators follow is sui generis, resulting in a quite complex system to be modeled.

Identifying Sources of Variability: The PPR (Product-Process-Resources) Approach

The natural roofing slate manufacturing process is commonly perceived by both managers and workers as being highly variable, presenting the following features:

1. The properties of the input slabs to the process are inconstant across time. Some days "good" material enters the process that can be easily split into the target formats and shows good quality in the classification. Other days, when the material is bad, there is more waste in the splitting process.
2. The process bottleneck dynamically moves between the splitters and the classification and packing steps.
3. Large-capacity connection buffers are needed because of the high variability in the raw materials characteristics. Sometimes there is a large

> accumulation of work in process, and space is needed in which to allocate stocks. Sometimes queues disappear and material is quickly consumed, causing starvation in the last steps of the process. This perceived need has led to a layout configured to provide the maximum possible capacity for the connection buffers.

The most relevant source of variability in this process is the variability of the natural slate in both mineral composition and morphology. This falls within the category of "Product" variability. Uncertainty about quality has traditionally led to a relative configuration of the whole manufacturing process with no previously determined schedule and the assignment of operations to machines or workers. This is done in real time based on the state of the system (Alfaro and Sepulveda 2006). A foreman decides the formats to be cut as well as the number and identity of splitters, classifiers, and machines assigned to each format according to his perceptions of process performance. The foreman dynamically adjusts splitters' working hours, adds splitters from a nearby plant, and reassigns workers to classification and packing. The foreman also may change the target format specifications or the thickness goal for the splitters. Thus, this individual introduces another relevant component of variability related to the process rules and resources capacity, that is, "Process" variability.

The labor-intensive nature of this process involves another source of variation. Splitting is a task that requires highly skilled workers among which important differences can be observed in performance. Each splitter has his own technique for splitting slabs, leading to heterogeneous working paces and material utilization. Classification and packing are two additional examples of manual tasks in which a variety of criteria and working procedures are present. In spite of putatively homogeneous quality standards, different classifiers adopt more or less conservative criteria, leading to decision variation. The detailed tasks associated with packing also performed slightly differently by different workers. Even the filling sequence associated with tile piles in the pallets and the characteristics of the pallets themselves are subject to different behaviors. These factors represent "Resources" variability (figure 10.2).

Traditionally, analysis of production systems has primarily focused on technical aspects such as machines, buffers, or transportation elements (Baines and Kay 2002). Human resources are introduced in the same way as machines, and sources of variation related to ergonomics or behavior are essentially ignored (Neuman and Medvo 2009). However, evidence suggests that human performance variability differs from that of machines in several important ways (Powell and Shultz 2004). Humans behave as state-dependent resources with the capability to readjust their work-pace depending on circumstances. Dynamic changes in working rate are related to factors such as experience, aging, time of day, and other external, individual difference factors (Baines and Kay 2002). Although processing rates of machines can be satisfactorily modeled by their cycle time and failures distributions, a detailed model of human performance should include both dynamic and state-dependent factors. Baines et al. (2004) show how simulation results change once certain dynamic effects are taken into account.

Figure 10.2 Actual Classification and Packing Operations and Area

Powell, S. G. and Schultz, K. L. (2004) demonstrate how flow line performance depends on the presence of self-regulated behavior.

LEARNING ACTIVITY

This is a project-based learning activity in process simulation and optimization. The game consists of the design and development of a production line based on the slate process case. Students in teams of four play the roles of both workers and process engineers responsible for the system simulation and improvement. The game involves arranging an experimental manufacturing setting in which product- and process-related variability are controlled. Thus, human resources variability can be isolated and its impact studied in depth (figure 10.3).

Teams are assessed according to the quality of their simulation project, their optimized configuration performance, and their simulation model forecasting capability. Unlike other learning and experimental activities in operations research, the proposed tasks have both a high physical workload and a moderate mental workload, replicating conditions in many manufacturing environments.

The simulation project involves analysis of data gathered in the experimental setting, developing a model in the simulation software ExtendSim, validating the model, optimizing process parameters according to a given reward function, and implementing this solution in the experimental setting. Each group summarizes its results in a technical report that is rated on five criteria: data analysis phase, model implementation, model validation, experimentation and optimization, and technical report presentation and redaction. Evaluation of these aspects of team's performance accounts for 60% of the simulation project score. The remaining 40% is assigned in competition between teams based on their performance in the experimental setting and the precision of their results.

The competitive element is intended to avoid intergroup cooperation, enhancing teams' commitment to achieve good team results. This approach also sets a realistic reward scenario in which scores are not obtained merely by carrying out the work, but also by surpassing competitors and measuring the actual

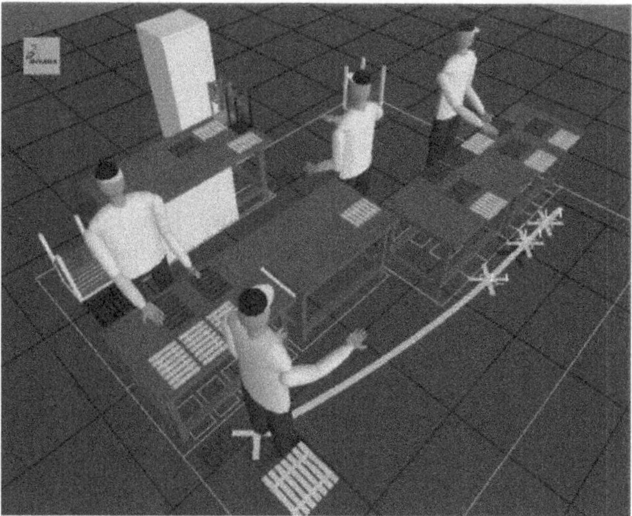

Figure 10.3 Experimental Setting (top) and screenshot of the simulation model implemented in Delmia Quest (bottom)

impact of improvements on processes regardless of how theoretical knowledge was used. Costly projects, in terms of the time devoted to the work, that fail at improving results are penalized relative to those that achieve better results with less effort.

Experimental Setup

The designed process was been inspired by the roofing slates manufacturing plant. This labor-intensive process is characterized by high levels of product, process, and resources variability. Previous research reveals important individual differences in performance that depend on ergonomic conditions (Rego Monteil et al. 2010).

The experimental manufacturing process consists of five tasks arranged in a closed loop. Four of these constitute the analyzed process, and the fifth is disposed in order to close the loop, preventing recirculating starvation or blocking events. The fifth task is converted into an events horizon by means of a security stock of input parts, which are consumed in the event that production output is temporarily incapable of providing enough input.

Process input and output products are the same, that is, piles of a fixed amount of slates. As actual slates may be difficult to obtain, fake slates can be employed instead. The preference and rationale behind providing students with actual material is that they gain some understanding of the conditions within manufacturing environments. Slate tiles are heavy, brittle, and have sharp edges. Special care has to be paid to handling them.

The size of these lots is noted as N_E. Slates are grouped into three types according to two attributes. A fraction p_R of the slates are printed with a red mark on and the rest (fraction $p_G = 1 - p_R$) with a green mark. Green slates are divided into two sizes, large with dimensions 32 × 22 mm and small with dimensions 30 × 20 mm and 27 × 18 mm. These formats correspond to the primary commercial formats in the actual case. The fraction of large slates within the green type is noted as p_L, and the fraction of small slates by p_S. Green slates also display an alphanumeric code printed on their surface made up by two letters and one number that can be generated randomly. Input lots contain a sequence of slate types randomly generated according to the slates proportions (figure 10.4).

The first task is the classification of slates according to their color. This is performed in workstation 1 (WS1). Classified items are batched into lots of size N_R for red slates and N_G for green slates. Every time a lot is passed to the next station the operator registers it in a software application called WS1_Register by pressing either the corresponding red or green lot key.

The second task is performed in workstation 2 (WS2). Here the green slates are measured and classified according to their size. One by one, slates are measured either by means of a reference mark printed at the workplace or based on operator experience. The slate code is then typed on a computer and logged by the application WS2_Register. The slate is then piled in the corresponding lot based on size.

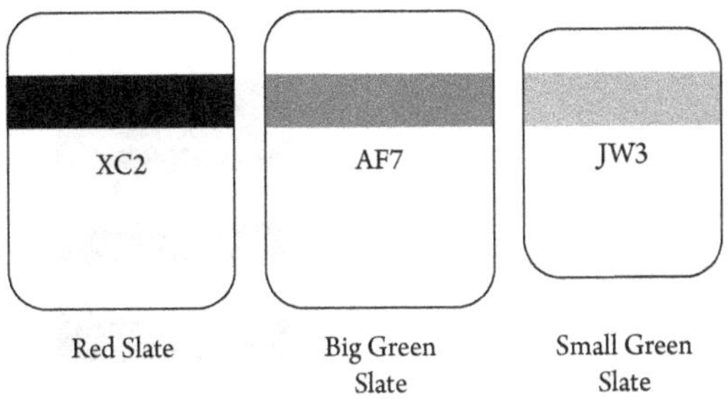

Figure 10.4 Example of Slate Types
Alphanumeric codes are generated randomly.

Errors in either typing or classification are penalized, so that demands on worker's attention are highest within the process.

The third task in the process focuses on transportation. Classified lots from WS1 and WS2 are carried to workstation 3 (WS3). A default parking location is established at an intermediate point between WS1 and WS2 and is marked on the floor.

The function of the fourth task is regeneration of the input lots for the process. A random sequence of N_R slate types is generated and printed in a monitor by the WS3_Register application. Once completed, lots are pushed to a recirculation conveyor, which serves as both the source and the sink for the rest of the process. Each time a lot is pushed, it is registered in the application by pressing a key.

The fifth task focuses on ensuring that the WS1 arrival process is independent from the WS3 state. The closed loop setting results do not differ from those of an open process. The workplace is functionally equivalent to a conveyor belt in which input lots are moved from WS3 back into the source slot. An auxiliary reserve of input lots is placed beside this station for use in cases of lack of output lots from WS3. This is a supervisory/control stage that facilitates the process standardization and helps to restricts process variability. Lot arrivals to WS1 are registered in a control application called Source_Register that also provides functions for managing runs, such as time control or workers assignments to workplaces (figure 10.5).

A process variant is designed by enabling work-sharing between the transporter and WS2. When this collaborative mode is enabled, the transporter assists WS2 workers by entering registries on the computer. The computer has to be easily accessible both to the transporter and to WS2 operator. Whenever the transporter

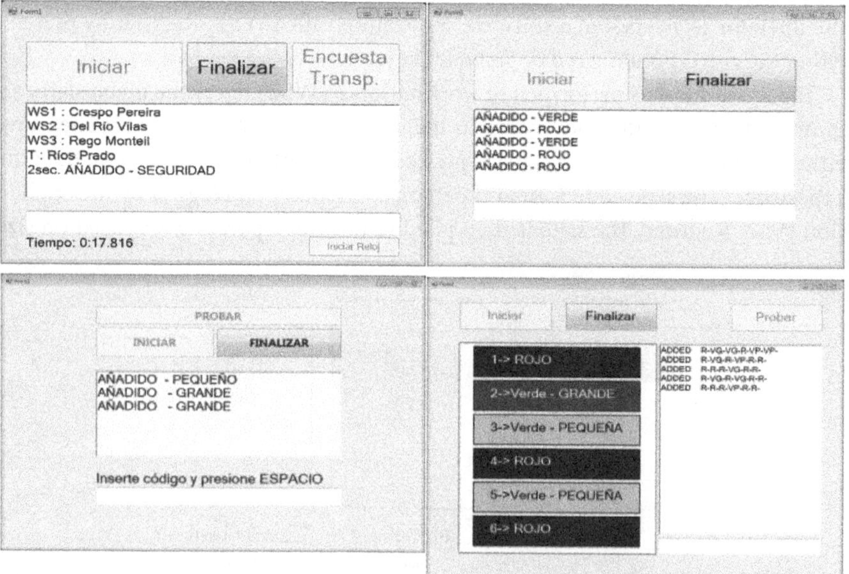

Figure 10.5 Source_Register, WS1_Register, WS2_Register, and WS3_Register applications screenshots (clockwise, and indications in Spanish)

Table 10.1. Tasks Characterization

Task	Physical workload	Mental workload
WS1	Moderate	Moderate
WS2	Moderate	High
T	High	Low
WS3	Moderate	Low

undertakes this support operation, permission has to be granted by the WS2 operator. A simple verbal formula can be employed for asking permission, for example, "Want Help?" "Yes" or "No." Then the WS2 operator focuses only on classifying and moving slates while dictating alphanumeric code to teammates, shortening cycle time. While work-sharing is ongoing, transporters cannot attend to transportation orders from WS1 to WS3, creating a trade-off between these two operations.

The task design is intended to result in different types of processes, based on the degree of physical and mental workload. Table 10.1 shows a characterization of these relationships performed by the research team members.

To build the production line, four tables should be arranged in line, while a fifth is placed nearby as a security buffer of input lots. Slots should be printed on the tables to establish fixed locations for working and buffering. Each workstation counts with a computer, connected to a LAN, running the corresponding application, and connected to a database server—for example, MySQL server—for storing the registered data. Figure 10.6 shows a floor plan of the setting. Table 10.2 shows the function of each slot. The number of parts is constrained to simulate capacitated buffers.

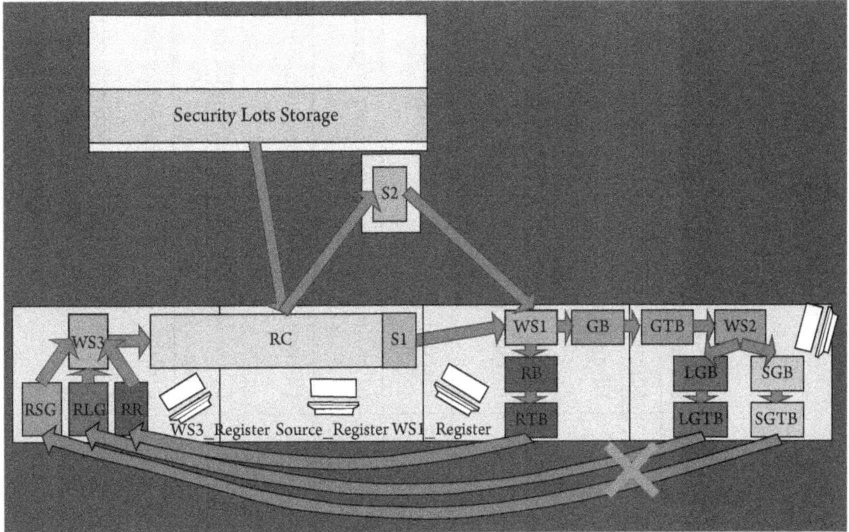

Figure 10.6 Experimental Setting Layout

Table 10.2. Slots in Layout

Slot code	Parts Capacity	Function	Slot code	Parts capacity	Function
S1	1 Input Lot	Pickup point for input lots	***LGB***	1 Large Greens Lot	Batching of large green slates
S2	1 Input Lot	Input lots pickup point for operating under bad ergonomic conditions	***SGB***	1 Small Greens Lot	Batching of small green slates
WS1	1 Input Lot	Working slot for WS1	***RTB***	1 or 2 Reds Lot	Reds lots input buffer to transporter
RB	1 Reds Lot	Batching of red slates	***LGTB***	1 or 2 Large Greens Lot	Large greens lots input buffer to transporter
GB	1 Greens Lot	Batching of green slates	***SGTB***	1 or 2 Small Greens Lot	Small greens lots input buffer to transporter
GTB	1 Greens Lot	Connection buffer of greens lots	***RR***	Unrestricted Red Slates	Buffer of red slates waiting to be recirculated
WS2	1 or unrestricted Greens Lot	Working slot for WS2	***RLG***	Unrestricted Large Green Slates	Buffer of large green slates waiting to be recirculated
WS3	1 Input Lot	Working slot for WS3	***RSG***	Unrestricted Small Green Slates	Buffer of small green slates waiting to be recirculated

Table 10.3. Template for WS1 Form

Time (min:sec)	Type (mark an X)	
	Red Lot	Green Lot
:		
:		

This activity can be carried out without computers. In this case standard forms can be used for registering events. A common clock or synchronized clocks must be arranged for registering consistent times. Three forms are required:

- **WS1 form**, for registering when lots of classified red or green slates are sent to the RTB or GTB positions. Students should write the time in which the lot was sent as well as lot type. Table 10.3 offers a template.
- **WS2 form**, for registering the slate code, size, and the time when it is classified. Table 10.4 provides a template.
- **WS3 form**, for indicating the sequence of slate types that must be followed and the time when the lot is dispatched. Figure 10.7 shows an example of how this form can be designed. The sequence of slates should be generated randomly, although the same sequence can be used for different teams to control variability.

Sources of Variability and Experimental Conditions

Process variability is limited by defining standardized task procedures encompassing the sequence of steps to be performed, permitted actions, and priorities. Penalties in rewards function together with supervision by the activity tutors ensure that operators cannot be benefited by deviating from these permitted actions. Three exceptions to this rule are the following:

1. The transporter is given freedom to choose what lots to prioritize. This is allowed to encompass the different prioritization rules intuitively developed by participants.
2. WS2 operators are given freedom regarding what subtasks to perform first: classifying a slate or typing its code on the computer. Although this degree of freedom may increase the effect of individual differences on performance, it is representative of the variability encountered in real settings. It also allows participants to work most comfortably.
3. When work-sharing is enabled, transporters are given freedom to choose when to offer support to the WS2 operators and when to desist. WS2 operators can refuse assistance.

However, because these sources of variation are human-driven, they are treated together with the other human forms of variability.

Product variability is intentionally introduced by means of the random composition of input lots. Depending on their color, slates flow directly from WS1

Table 10.4. TEMPLATE FOR WS2 FORM

Time (min:sec)	Code	Size (mark an X)	
		Big Slate	Small Slate
:			
:			

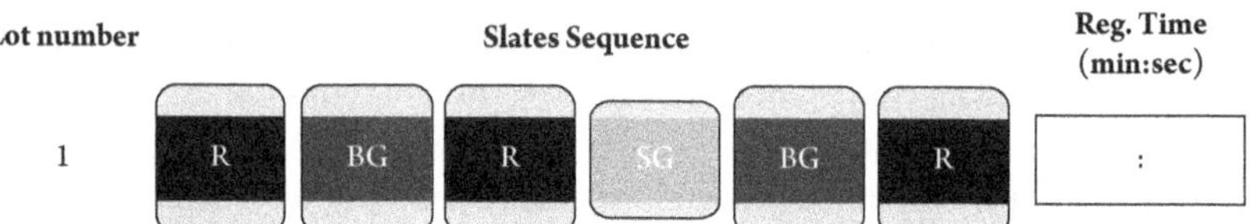

Figure 10.7 WS3 Template

to the transporter, or they go through WS2. This sort of variability is present in many real systems that combine the production of products with different processing steps. This kind of product variability affects line balancing. The WS2 task is slower than WS1 in terms of processing time per slate. When p_R is high, WS1 is the most congested workstation, and the low arrival rate of parts to WS2 leads to idle times. In contrast, when p_R is low there are plenty of green slates to be processed in WS2. Since this is a slower task, this blocks WS1. Thus, the system bottleneck location depends on p_R, and it can be altered by simply modifying values. Further, random temporary variations of average p_R will cause the bottleneck to dynamically change from WS1 to WS2 and vice versa. Although this behavior increases throughput variability—which may obscure human-driven variability—it can be controlled by assigning the same random sequence to all teams.

The red slates probability p_R must be set within the range 0.50–0.65. The preferred value for the activity is 0.6. WS1 and WS2 have a balanced workload when $p_R \approx 0.66$. An unbalanced line is most desirable for this activity, as explained below.

Two working conditions are defined by constraining the capacity of the intermediate buffers between WS1 and WS2.

- In the first arrangement, corresponding to "low inventory conditions," the maximum number of lots that can be stored in the WS2 slot is 1. Only two intermediate lots can be stored between WS1 and WS2. Because WS2 is the bottleneck under this condition, it will cause blocking in WS1.
- In the second arrangement, "high inventory conditions," an unlimited number of slates can be staked in the WS2 slot. Thus both WS1 and WS2 are the source of bottleneck because both stations can operate at maximum pace.

When analyzing the system mechanistically, the results from a simulation model yield higher throughput for the high inventory conditions. This is because both stations can operate at full capacity, and working rates are assumed to be independent of workload conditions and buffers contents.

However, different worker behavior can be expected in these two arrangements. According to results reported in the literature (Powell and Schultz 2004; Schultz et al. 1998) low-inventory systems typically display better-than-expected performance. In addition, the inverse-U relation between workload and performance observed in previous research (e.g., Bendoly and Prietula 2008) leads to lower-than-expected performance for the high-inventory conditions than would be expected from classic simulation models. Under high-inventory conditions, because the system is not balanced, WS2 buffer content will grow across time without reaching stationary conditions. Hence, the WS2 workload will eventually reach levels where Parkinson's Law predicts that performance will decline. Figure 10.8 depicts a typical system situation.

The other experimental factor considered in this activity is work-sharing. Two options are available. The first is to not allow work-sharing. The second is to allow transporters to assist at WS2. Under these circumstances, the task times for WS2 would be expected to shorten with a mechanistic model and overall throughput to rise because it is the system's bottleneck. However, interdependence among workers may favorably or unfavorably affect performance. For instance, fairness issues arising from unequal distribution of workload might lead to lower performance. Cooperation also requires a decision process and setup times that can be perceived negatively by busy workers.

Activity Outline

The experiment is conducted in four phases.

The first phase introduces participants to the process and task procedures. It incorporates a single session of four production runs, each of five minutes duration. No information regarding the process should be given to participants beforehand. Operators are randomly assigned to workplaces and rotated at each run. Thus all participants will have an opportunity to try every task, and reference cycle times can be computed.

The second phase comprises a number of runs that must be kept equal to the number of experimental conditions (treatments). The number of runs ranges from

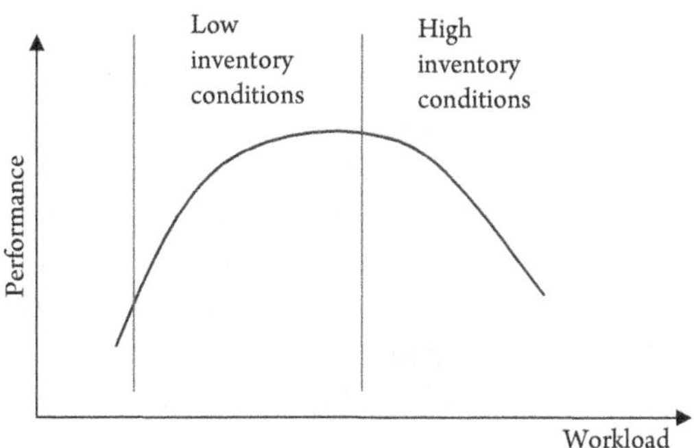

Figure 10.8 Expected Motivational Effects under Two Working Conditions

Table 10.5. Template for WS2 Form

Recommended priority for including it in the experiment	Treatment	Description
1st	O	Low inventory, no work-sharing
1st	A	High inventory, no work-sharing
2nd	B	Low inventory, work-sharing
3rd	AB	High inventory, work-sharing

two up to four. Each run is 12 minutes long. The number of teams should ideally be a multiple of the number of treatments so that the experimental design is more robust.

The treatments are presented in table 10.5.

The assignment of treatments to teams must follow the following rules:

- For a given run, the number of times that a treatment is assigned to a team must be the same for all treatments. For example, if there are eight teams and the number of treatments is set to four, each treatment will be assigned twice in each run.
- Each team can only be assigned with each treatment once.
- Treatment assignment must be randomized.
- The assignment of participants to workstations must be random. Once established, assignment must be equal for all the treatments.
- The sequence of slate types within a lot generated by WS3 must be randomized, but kept constant for all the treatments and teams.

In order to ensure that the subjects commit themselves to the activity, a weak incentives mechanism can be established. The results-based qualification of phase 2 is calculated as follows. A 100% score is given to teams that obtain an average throughput rate higher that the 80% of the maximum observed in a single production run. Teams that do not achieve this goal lose the proportional part of the reward score.

The third phase consists of the simulation of the system by participants. The simulation model must be constructed in a mechanistic way for comparison with real settings, so task times are introduced by means of independent and identical distributions. Alternative classical modeling methodologies can also be used. The goal is to evaluate biases in results estimation due to a failure to model behavioral effects.

For model building, data can be collected from software applications and videos. Applications records provide lists of events occurring in the system. They span entries of lots in the system, exits from WS1, processed items in WS2, and exits in WS3. Thus it is possible to build a basic list of events within WS1, WS2, and the system as a whole. This can be used to plot a graph of buffer contents and to calculate average residence times—similar to how results are obtained from simulation software models.

Figure 10.9 displays the plot of slates in WS1 as a function of time. It includes the contents of buffers WS1, GB, and RB plus the slates processed by operator 1.

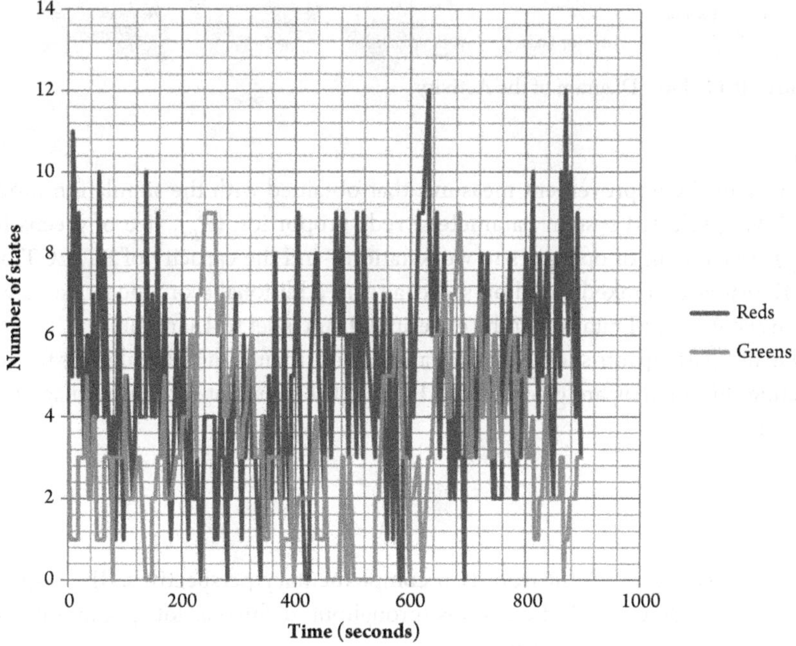

Figure 10.9 Slates Contents in WS1

Figure 10.10 displays a plot of the total residence time in the system as a function of the number of lots exiting from WS3. The two observed leaps in residence times correspond to lots that suffered a delay in WS3 due to starvation.

In the fourth phase students are evaluated by means of a reward function dependent on throughput rates, work-in-process levels, and errors. In this phase, students

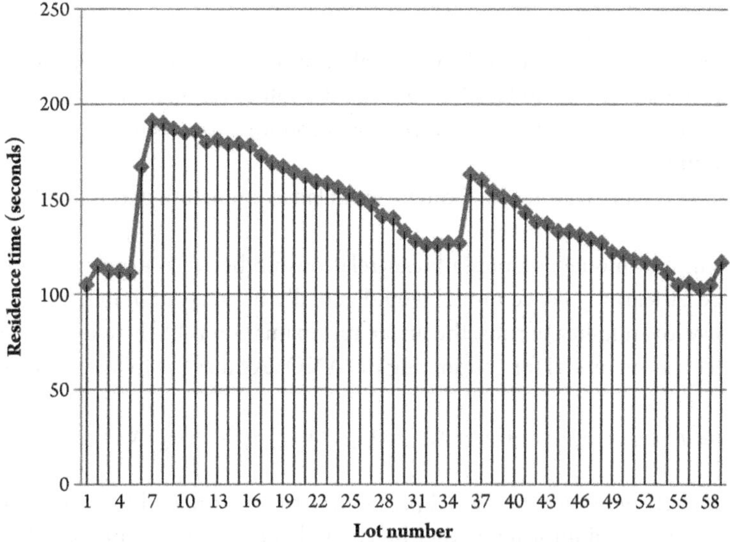

Figure 10.10 Total residence time of output lots in WS3

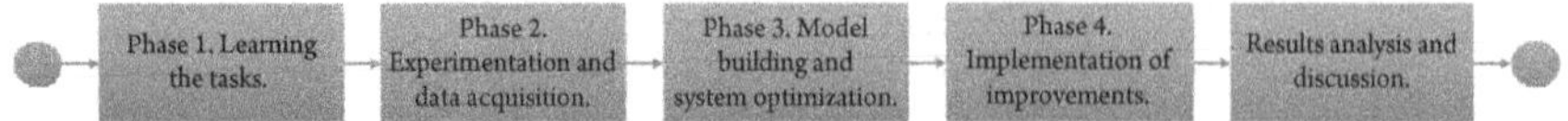

Figure 10.11 Flow Diagram of the Activity

implement the improvement measures that obtained with the simulation model, modifying selected system parameters: reds proportion (P_R), size of greens lots (N_G), assignment of operators to workstations, and the capacity of RT, LGT, and SGT. Teams are ranked based on score, and an additional score incentive may be given accordingly. Duration of the experiment run is set to 15 minutes.

Finally, participants should analyze and discuss their results. Guidelines for conducting this analysis are given below. Figure 10.11 illustrates the flow diagram of the activity.

DISCUSSION

The analysis is carried out from two complementary perspectives. The response variable considered in all the cases is throughput, defined as lots per unit of time produced by WS1 + WS2 or by WS3.

The first perspective is to compare results across the different treatments to assess the significance of behavioral effects. In this case results must be compared to those from a general simulation model in which behavior is not modeled. This simulation model should be developed by the instructors and should take the average individual differences in task times that can be estimated from the first phase. The model behavior must be compared to that of the real system.

To do so, an analysis of variance, with the treatment conditions as the independent variable, can be performed. The variables to introduce in the model are the following:

- The inventory level factor (low or high, 0 and 1 values respectively) x_I
- The work-sharing mode (off or on, 0 and 1 values respectively) x_{WS}
- A group effect variable, introduced for accounting for group induced variability x_G
- An experience factor, which can be modeled as a function of run number n

The simplest model assumes a linear relationship between experience and performance. A learning curve model would actually be most desirable, but because of the very low number of runs, the linear approximation is likely to be sufficient.

The regression model for conducting the ANOVA takes the following form:

$$\mathit{Throughput} = \beta_0 + \beta_I \cdot x_I + \beta_{WS} \cdot x_{WS} + \beta_{L\cdot WS} \cdot x_{L\cdot WS} + \sum_{G} \beta_G \cdot x_G + \beta_n \cdot n.$$

The β coefficients are the model parameters to be estimated by regression. Hypothesis testing will inform whether behavioral effects are present. G is the set of teams, excluding one referent team.

The interpretation of the β parameters hypothesis tests will yield various conclusions, as shown in table 10.6.

As an example of the results that were obtained designing this teaching activity, table 10.7 displays regression model estimates along with parameters significance levels. These results are provided for WS2, which is the bottleneck and thus constrains throughput. As can be seen here, learning effects were clearly present. However, although higher inventory would be expected to reduce starvation events and thus enhance throughput, no significant effects were observed. The *p*-value for the one-sided T-test with null hypothesis $\beta_I > 0$ was .2. It clearly contradicts the expected increase in performance, suggesting that behavioral phenomena are at work. The result is consistent with previous research (Powell and Schultz 2004; Schultz et al. 1998), and it can be explained by phenomena described by Bendoly and Prietula (2008).

The previous results can be compared to those from a simulation model. Learning effects are not accounted for. As it can be seen in table 10.8, simulation results do show the expected increase in throughput because of higher inventory conditions.

The second approach compares the results from the simulation models developed by participants to the results achieved in the last run. Another important factor that must be considered in this comparison is that motivation is likely to be much higher because of the high incentive that the results-based score represents. Thus, motivation effects on performance can be tested by comparing results from a simulation model developed from data in which motivation was normal to a case where motivation is higher.

The solutions obtained by participants are provided in table 10.9. It can be seen that most teams adopted configurations in which the reds fraction was close to the balanced line value of 0.66 (figure 10.12). It can also be seen that more teams opted for low inventory settings. A remarkable observation is that no team opted to enable work-sharing in the final run. This suggests that the students did not perceive any gain from work-sharing, which contrasts with the results expected in a mechanistic model and supports previous observations (Schultz 2003).

Table 10.10 shows the expected scores obtained by teams with the scores that they achieved in the final run.

Great differences were observed between the forecast scores and real scores. This is primarily due to the higher work rate in this run. The average throughput was 20% higher than in the previous runs. This difference alone cannot be explained by learning effects.

Concluding Remarks

Results from this educational activity allow for tests of the effect of three behavioral phenomena on the throughput of a manufacturing line. Motivational effects in performance, the complex relation between workload and performance, and workers' interdependence effects account for observed differences between a classical model

Table 10.6. Interpretation of Experiment Results

β coefficient	Significant negative value	Not significant	Significant positive value
β_I	The result contrasts the expected increase in performance from a mechanistic model. Behavioral effects might explain this divergence.	Two possible conclusions cannot be distinguished. The behavioral effects could counteract the benefits from increased buffer capacity, or they may be caused by lack of testing power. Comparison of percentage variations to the simulation model is required.	The result matches what is expected in a mechanistic model. However, comparison to the simulated increases in performance may uncover behavioral effects.
β_{WS}	The result contrasts expected increase in performance from a mechanistic model. Negative interdependence effects can explain this divergence.	Two possible conclusions cannot be distinguished. The behavioral effects could counteract the benefits from work-sharing, or they may be caused by lack of testing power. Comparison of percentage variations to simulation models is required.	The result matches what is expected in a mechanistic model. However, comparison to the simulated increases in performance may reveal positive or negative behavioral effects.
$\beta_{I\cdot WS}$ (Interaction between factors, previous literature provides no clear results of what to expect in this regard.)	Interaction between high inventory level and work-sharing is negative, indicating that work-sharing in high-inventory systems reduce performance less than in low-inventory systems.	The interaction is not significant, indicating that a linear effect of performance from these two factors can be assumed.	Interaction between high inventory level and work-sharing is positive, indicating that work-sharing in high-inventory systems increases performance more than in low-inventory systems.
β_G	Differences among teams are present if they are significant. This factor is not of interest.		
β_n	Forgetting-like effects are at play. This result suggests problems in the experiment because there is no theoretical foundation for this.	No learning effects detected.	Learning effects are present.

Table 10.7. Regression Model for WS2 Output

Factor	Parameter estimate	*p*-value (two-sided T-test)
(Intercept)	0.130	.000
Experience	0.004	.003
High Inventory	−0.006	.395
Work-sharing On	−0.001	.937
R squared		.4312
F-statistic		5.179
F-test *p*-value		4.823E−4

Table 10.8. Simulation Results for Inventory Effect on WS2 and Z-Test for Differences in Means

WS2 Simulation (230 runs)		
Setting	**Mean throughput**	**Std. deviation**
Low inventory	31.00	1.18
High inventory	31.44	1.29
Z-statistic		3.039
p-value		.02983

Table 10.9. Configuration Parameters for the Experiment

Group	Configuration Parameters			
	Reds Fraction	*Transfer Lot Size*	*Work share*	*Inventory*
1	.66	3	No	Low
2	.74	3	Yes	High
3	.674	4	No	Low
4	.6162	2	No	High
5	.6	3	No	High
6	.75	3	No	Low
7	.65	3	No	Low
8	.8	3	No	Low

and observed line results. These phenomena are influenced by three experimental factors: incentives, buffer capacities, and work-sharing.

No significant effects were observed from changes in buffers capacity, work-sharing, process state perception, or approach. This result contrasts with those obtained from a simulation model in which human resources were introduced in a mechanistic way. Buffer capacity increases and work-sharing were expected to

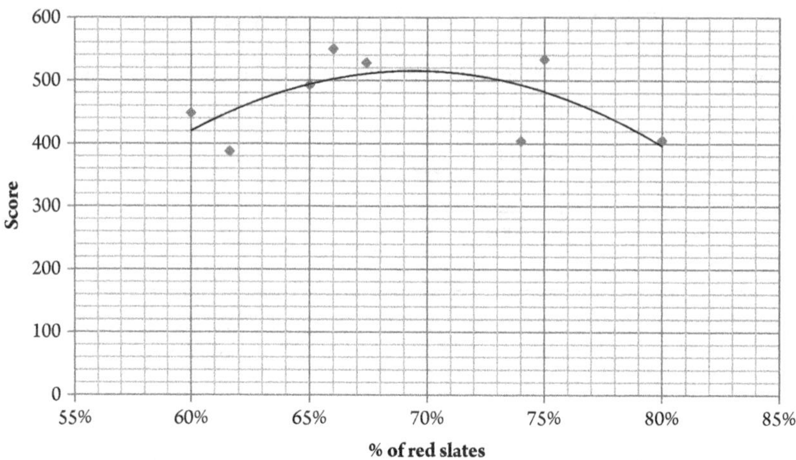

Figure 10.12 Relation between the Percentage of Red Slates and the Score

Table 10.10. RESULTS OBTAINED IN THE LAST SESSION

Group	Result in the final session			
	Obtained score	*Forecast score*	*Error*	*Mark*
1	550	202.0	172.28%	66.7%
2	404	221.7	82.17%	19.0%
3	528	423.0	24.78%	76.2%
4	387	297.8	30.07%	23.8%
5	448	390.4	14.77%	61.9%
6	533	200.0	166.68%	61.9%
7	493	305.9	60.97%	52.4%
8	405	294.2	37.70%	38.1%

lead to a significant increase in throughput. Although several limitations have been identified when extending these results to real manufacturing environments, they are consistent with those obtained by Schultz and coauthors (Schultz, Juran, and Boudreau 1999; Schultz 2003). Human behavior effects appear to counteract the expected benefits of increasing buffer capacities and work-sharing.

These results have several practical implications for manufacturing process managers. Great care must be taken when undertaking changes that may affect workers' motivation and their workload levels. Experimental results suggest that expected gains from work-sharing or increasing inventories may not be realized in practice. For simulation practitioners, these results indicate that omitting behavioral effects can lead to inaccurate models and the implementation of ineffective measures.

It will be critical for further research to assess the validity of these findings and to deepen the explanation of the drivers underlying the patterns of effects we observe.

Practical approaches for calibrating and introducing behavioral models in simulation should be developed and analyzed so that more accurate results can be obtained when dealing with the simulation of labor-intensive processes.

References

Alfaro, M., Sepulveda, J. 2006. Chaotic behavior in manufacturing systems. International Journal of Production Economics 101 (1), 150–158.

Baines, T. S., Asch, R., Hadfield, L., Mason, J. P., Fletcher, S., Kay, J. M. 2005. Towards a theoretical framework for human performance modelling within manufacturing systems design. Simulation Modelling Practice and Theory 13 (6), 486–504.

Baines, T. S., Kay, J. M. 2002. Human performance modelling as an aid in the process of manufacturing system design: A pilot study. International Journal of Production Research 40 (10), 2321–2334.

Baines, T. S., Mason, S., Siebers, P.-O., Ladbrook, J. 2004. Humans: The missing link in manufacturing simulation? Simulation Modelling Practice and Theory 12 (7–8), 515–526.

Bangsow, S., ed. 2012. Use Cases of Discrete Event Simulation. Berlin: Springer.

Banks, J., Carson, J. S., Nelson, B. L., Nicol, D. M. 2010. Discrete-Event System Simulation. Upper Saddle River, NJ: Prentice-Hall.

Bendoly, E., Croson, R., Gonçalves, P., Schultz, K. 2010. Bodies of knowledge for research in behavioral operations. Production and Operations Management 19 (4), 434–452.

Bendoly, E., Donohue, K., and Schultz, K. 2006. Behavior in operations management: Assessing recent findings and revisiting old assumptions. Journal of Operations Management 24 (6), 737–752.

Bendoly, E., Prietula, M. 2008. In "the zone": The role of evolving skill and transitional workload on motivation and realized performance in operational tasks. International Journal of Operations and Production Management 28 (12), 1130–1152.

del Rio Vilas, D., Crespo Pereira, D., Crespo Mariño, J. L., Garcia del Valle, A. 2009. Modelling and simulation of a natural roofing slates manufacturing plant. Proceedings of the International Workshop on Modelling and Applied Simulation, no. c., EMSS.

Elkosantini, S., Gien, D. 2009. Integration of human behavioural aspects in a dynamic model for a manufacturing system. International Journal of Production Research 47 (10), 2601–2623.

Fletcher, S. R., Baines, T. S., Harrison, D. K. 2006. An investigation of production workers' performance variations and the potential impact of attitudes. International Journal of Advanced Manufacturing Technology 35 (11–12), 1113–1123.

Neumann, W. P., Medbo, P. 2009. Integrating human factors into discrete event simulations of parallel flow strategies. Production Planning and Control 20 (1), 3–16.

Powell, S. G., Schultz, K. L. 2004. Throughput in serial lines with state-dependent behavior. Management Science 50 (8), 1095–1105.

Rego Monteil, N., del Rio Vilas, D., Crespo Pereira, D., Rios Prado, R. 2010. A simulation-based ergonomic evaluation for the operational improvement of the slate splitters work. Proceedings of the 22nd European Modeling and Simulation Symposium, no. c., EMSS.

Robinson, S. 2004. Simulation: The Practice of Model Development and Use. Hoboken, NJ: Wiley.

Schultz, K. L. 2003. Overcoming the dark side of worker flexibility. Journal of Operations Management 21 (1), 81–92.

Schultz, K. L., Juran, D. C., Boudreau, J. W. 1999. The effects of low inventory on the development of productivity norms. Management Science 45 (12), 1664–1678.

Schultz, K. L., Juran, D. C., Boudreau, J. W., McClain, J. O., Thomas, L. J. 1998. Modeling and worker motivation in JIT production systems. Management Science 44 (12, Part 1), 1595–1607.

PART THREE

Lessons in Supply Chains and Integrative/Enabling Technology

CHAPTER 11

Booms, Busts, and Beer

Understanding the Dynamics of Supply Chains

JOHN STERMAN

OVERVIEW

> The central core of many industrial companies is the process of production and distribution. A recurring problem is to match the production rate to the rate of final consumer sales. It is well known that factory production rate often fluctuates more widely than does the actual consumer purchase rate. It has often been observed that a distribution system of cascaded inventories and ordering procedures seems to amplify small disturbances that occur at the retail level. . . . How does the system create amplification of small retail sales changes? . . . [W]e shall see that typical manufacturing and distribution practices can generate the types of business disturbances which are often blamed on conditions outside the company.
>
> —Jay W. Forrester (1961, 22)

The purpose of a supply chain is to provide the right product at the right time. As customer requirements change, supply chain managers respond by adjusting the rate at which resources are ordered and used. Supply chains are thus governed primarily by negative feedback. Because supply chains typically involve substantial time delays, they are prone to oscillation—production and inventories chronically overshoot and undershoot appropriate levels. Figure 11.1 shows industrial production in the United States for consumer goods and materials since 1950.

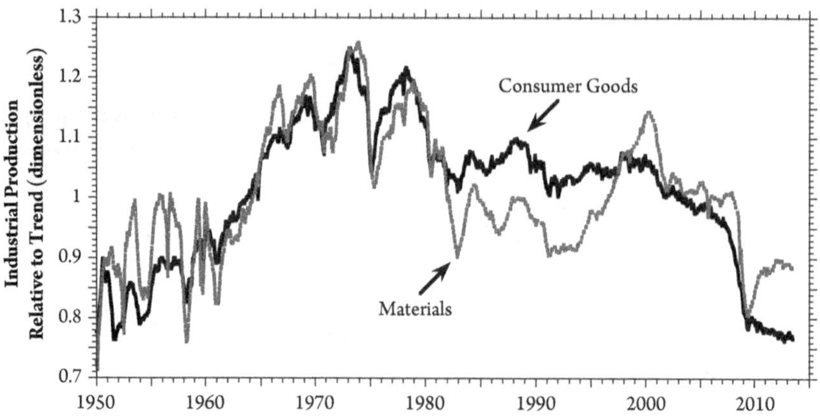

Figure 11.1 Oscillation, Amplification, and Phase Lag in the Aggregate Supply Chain

SOURCE: US Federal Reserve, series B51000 and B53000, January 1950–August 2013. The trend is the best exponential growth fit to each series.

The data are detrended (the long-run growth rate of manufacturing output since 1950 is about 3.2%/year). The data reveal three important features:

1. *Oscillation*: Production fluctuates significantly around the growth trend. The dominant periodicity is the business cycle, a cycle of prosperity and recession averaging about 4.5 years in duration, but exhibiting considerable variability.[1]
2. *Amplification*: The amplitude of the fluctuations in materials production (upstream in the supply chain compared to consumer goods) is significantly greater than that in consumer goods production. For example, the standard deviation of the fractional rate of change in monthly output is 11.7% per year for consumer goods, but 17.6% per year for materials, some 150% of the consumer goods figure.[2]
3. *Phase lag*: The peaks and troughs of the cycle in materials production tend to lag behind those in production of consumer goods.

These three features, *oscillation*, *amplification*, and *phase lag*, are pervasive in supply chains. Typically, the amplitude of fluctuations increases as they propagate from the customer to the supplier, with each upstream stage tending to lag behind its immediate customer.

The amplification of fluctuations from consumption to production is even greater in specific industries. The top panel in figure 11.2 shows the petroleum

1. The NBER, official arbiter of business cycle timing in the United States, reports an average peak-to-peak cycle duration of 56.4 months over 33 cycles from 1854 through 2009, with a standard deviation of 28.5 months and a range from 17 to 128 months (http://www.nber.org/cycles.html).

2. Standard deviation in annualized rate of change in the seasonally adjusted monthly data.

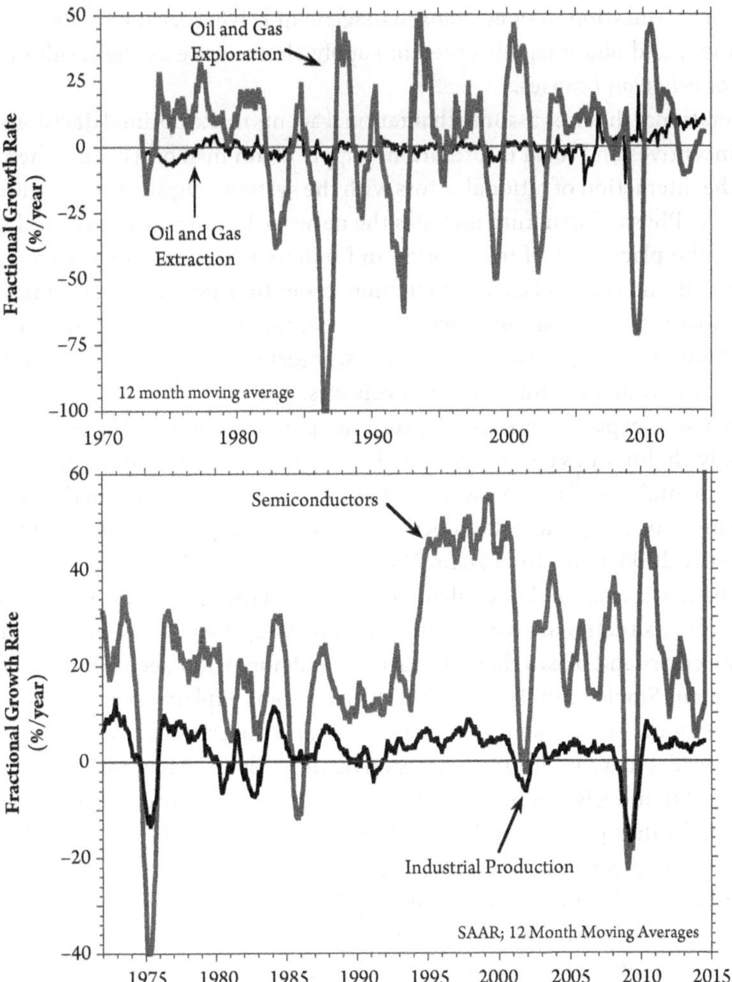

Figure 11.2 Amplification in Supply Chains
Top: Oil and gas production and drilling activity, United States.
Bottom: Semiconductor production compared to industrial production, United States
Graphs show 12-month centered moving averages of the annualized fractional growth rates calculated from the seasonally adjusted monthly data.

supply chain (the figure shows the annualized growth rate; the graph shows 12-month centered moving averages to filter out the high-frequency month-to-month noise).

The amplification is substantial: drilling activity fluctuates about three times more than production, imposing large boom-and-bust cycles on the suppliers of drill rigs and equipment. The bottom panel shows the semiconductor industry. Semiconductor production is at the upstream end of the supply chain for electronic equipment and fluctuates far more than industrial production as a whole. Other industries show similar amplification, including machine tools (Anderson, Fine, and Parker 2000; Sterman 2000).

A central question in operations management is whether the oscillations, amplification, and phase lag observed in supply chains arise as the result of *operational* or *behavioral* causes.

Operational theories assume that rational agents make optimal decisions given their incentives and local information. Supply chain instability must then result from the interaction of rational actors with the system's physical and institutional structure. Physical structure includes the network linking customers and suppliers and the placement of inventories and buffers within it, along with capacity constraints and time delays in production, order fulfillment, transportation, and so on. Institutional structure includes the degree of horizontal and vertical coordination and competition among firms, information availability within each organization, and decision-makers' incentives.

Behavioral explanations also capture the physical and institutional structure of supply chains, but view decision-makers as boundedly rational actors with imperfect mental models, who use heuristics to make ordering, production, capacity acquisition, pricing, and other decisions (Morecroft 1985; Sterman 2000; Boudreau et al. 2003; Gino and Pisano 2008; Bendoly et al. 2010; Croson et al. 2013). These heuristics may yield excellent or suboptimal results depending on how well they capture situational complexities (Simon 1982). Behavioral theories encompass the errors and biases that often arise in judgment and decision-making (e.g., Kahneman, Slovic, and Tversky 1982). Behavioral explanations also recognize that situational factors such as time pressure and poverty consume scarce cognitive resources that can diminish decision quality (Shah, Mullainathan, and Shafir 2012) and that decisions made under stress can be strongly conditioned by fear, anger, and other psychophysiological reactions (Lo and Repin 2002; Rudolph and Repenning 2002).

To illustrate the difference between operational and behavioral theories, consider a simple supply chain with a single producer servicing two competing retailers. If there is an unexpected increase in final demand, both retailers will place additional orders. If those orders exceed capacity, then the product will be placed on allocation—each retailer receiving only a fraction of what it desires. In that case, rational retailers might respond strategically by ordering more than they actually want in hopes of gaining a larger share of the total available shipments from the supplier, leading to what Sterman (2000) calls "phantom orders." The result would be amplification of the change in final demand, or even a demand bubble (Lee, Padmanabhan, and Whang 1997; Cachon and Lariviere 1999; Armony and Plambeck 2005). Alternatively, retailers might use behavioral decision rules such as "Order more whenever there is scarcity" or even suffer from emotional overreactions leading to hoarding inventory as deliveries fall. Such heuristics and emotional reactions would also lead to amplification of final demand (e.g., Sterman and Dogan 2014).

The difference matters. If supply chain instability arises from operational factors and rational behavior, then policies must be directed at changing the system's physical and institutional structure, including incentives. If instability arises from bounded rationality and emotional arousal, such policies may not be sufficient. To illustrate, gasoline shortages have sometimes caused service stations to run out, leading to "Sorry—No Gas" signs. Notable episodes include the 1979 gas crisis in the United States, transport strikes in Europe in 2000, and the aftermath of Superstorm Sandy in 2012 on the east coast of the United States. In each case, gas shortages led to long lines as people queued, often for hours, in an attempt to top off their tanks. For example, after Superstorm Sandy,

> Drivers waited in lines that ran hundreds of vehicles deep, requiring state troopers and local police to protect against exploding tempers.
>
> . . . The lines themselves only exacerbated the problem; reports in the local media provoked drivers to buy gasoline before stations ran out. Some spent what fuel they had searching for more and could be seen pushing vehicles toward relief.
>
> "I just want to have it, because you don't know how long this is going to last," said Richard Bianchi, waiting in the half-mile line at the Sunoco in Union [New Jersey] with a tank that was three-quarters full.
>
> "People are panicking," said Jimmy Qawasmi, the owner of a Mobil in the Westchester County town of Mamaroneck.[3]

If such behavior is rational, then policies that alter the institutional structure and incentives such as maximum purchases or odd-even rules (limiting people to purchases every other day based on license plate last digit) should reduce demand and ease shortages. If hoarding is a behavioral and emotional response to scarcity, then these actions may worsen the situation by reinforcing people's belief that there really is a shortage and increasing the number of people who queue even when their tanks are nearly full. Of course any situation may involve a mix of strategic, rational action and behavioral, emotional response.

In this chapter I show how supply chain instability, including oscillation, amplification, and phase lag, arises from the interaction of supply chain physics with behavioral decision processes. Amplification and phase lag arise from the presence of basic physical structures, including stocks of inventory and delays in adjusting production to changes in incoming orders. Oscillations, however, are not inevitable. They arise from boundedly rational, behavioral decision processes. Experimental studies show that supply chain instability, including oscillation, amplification, and phase lag, along with demand bubbles, hoarding, and phantom ordering, arises even in experimental settings in which there are no operational factors that might make such behavior rational.

I also present two learning activities that can be used to teach principles of supply chains. The Manufacturing Case (Booth Sweeney and Sterman 2000) is a simple paper-and-pencil exercise that tests participants' understanding of accumulation and time delays in a simple inventory management setting, and explores the origin of amplification and phase lag. The Beer Distribution Game (Sterman 1989a) is a role-play simulation of a simple supply chain widely used to teach principles of operations management, system dynamics, and systems thinking.

3. *New York Times*, November 2, 2012, http://www.nytimes.com/2012/11/02/nyregion/gasoline-shortages-disrupting-recovery-from-hurricane.html.

THEORETICAL PERSPECTIVE

Supply chains consist of cascades of firms, each receiving orders and adjusting production and production capacity to meet changes in demand. Each link in a supply chain maintains and controls inventories of materials and finished product. To understand the behavior of a supply chain and the causes of oscillation, amplification, and phase lag, it is first necessary to understand the structure and dynamics of a single link; that is, how individual firms manage inventories and resources as they attempt to balance production with orders. Such balancing processes always involve negative feedback.

The Stock Management Problem: Structure

All negative feedback processes require comparing the state of a system to the desired state, then initiating corrective actions to eliminate discrepancies. In such a *stock management* task, managers seek to maintain a stock (the state of the system) at a particular target level, or at least within an acceptable range. Stocks are altered only by changes in their inflows and outflows. Typically, managers must set the inflow to compensate for losses and usage, and to counteract disturbances that push the stock away from its desired value. Often there are lags between the initiation of a control action and its effect and between a change in the stock and the perception of that change by decision-makers. The duration of these lags may vary and may be influenced by the manager's own actions.

Stock management problems occur at many levels of aggregation. At the level of a firm, managers must order parts and raw materials to maintain inventories sufficient for production to proceed at the desired rate. They must adjust for variations in the usage of these materials and for changes in delivery delays. At the individual level, you regulate the temperature of the water in your morning shower, guide your car down the highway, and manage your checking account balance. At the macroeconomic level, central banks like the US Federal Reserve seek to manage the stock of money to stimulate economic growth and avoid inflation, while compensating for variations in credit demand, budget deficits, and international capital flows.

The stock management control problem can be divided into two parts: (1) the stock and flow structure of the system and (2) the decision rules managers use to order and produce new units (figure 11.3).

The stock to be controlled, S, accumulates at the acquisition rate AR less the loss rate LR:

$$S_t = \int_{t_0}^{t} (AR - LR)ds + S_{t_0}. \tag{11.1}$$

Losses include any outflow from the stock. Losses may arise from usage (as in a raw material inventory) or decay (as in the depreciation of plant and equipment or spoilage of fresh produce). The loss rate must depend on the stock itself—losses

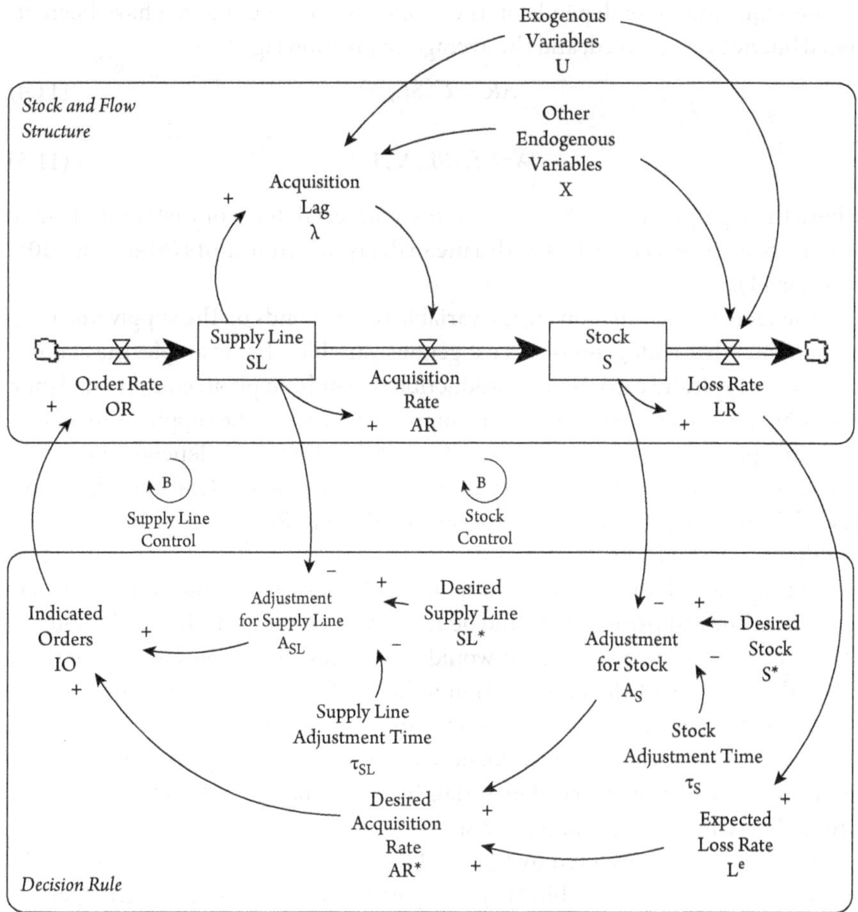

Figure 11.3 The Generic Stock Management Structure
The determinants of the desired supply line are not shown (see text).

must approach zero as the stock is depleted—and also may depend on other endogenous variables, **X**, and exogenous variables, **U**. Losses may be nonlinear and may depend on the age distribution of the stock, captured by a loss rate function:

$$LR = f_{LR}(S, \mathbf{X}, \mathbf{U}). \tag{11.2}$$

In general, managers cannot add new units to a stock simply because they wish to do so. Typically there are delays in acquiring new units, creating a *supply line* of orders that have been placed but not yet received: A firm seeking to increase its capital stock cannot acquire new units immediately and must await construction or delivery. New workers cannot be hired and trained instantly. It takes time for your car to stop after you step on the brakes, and it takes time for the economy to respond after the Federal Reserve changes interest rates. The supply line accumulates orders less the rate at which units are completed and enter the stock:

$$SL_t = \int_{t_0}^{t} (OR - AR)\,ds + SL_{t_0}. \tag{11.3}$$

The acquisition rate depends on the supply line SL of units that have been ordered but not yet received, and the average acquisition lag, λ:

$$AR = \mathcal{L}(SL, \lambda) \tag{11.4}$$

$$\lambda = f_{\lambda}(SL, \mathbf{X}, \mathbf{U}), \tag{11.5}$$

where the lag operator $\mathcal{L}(SL, \lambda)$ denotes a material delay or distributed lag in which acquisitions lag orders with a mean delay of λ time units (Sterman 2000, chapter 11).

In general, the acquisition lag is a variable that depends on the supply line itself and on the other endogenous and exogenous variables. For example, the acquisition rate is typically capacitated: production depends on plant, equipment, labor, and other resources; deliveries from a supplier depend on the supplier's inventory and transportation capacity; construction of new buildings depends on the capacity of the construction industry in the region, and so on. Consider the recovery of the housing industry from the so-called Great Recession of 2007. During the downturn, housing starts and the supply line of homes under construction were very small. Homes could be built quickly because labor and equipment were abundant. The acquisition lag would be at or even below normal levels. As housing starts recover, the acquisition lag would remain low until construction activity nears the capacity of the construction industry. Once capacity is fully utilized, the acquisition lag increases as the supply line rises relative to the acquisition rate. The acquisition lag can also be influenced by managerial decisions, as when a firm chooses to expedite delivery of materials by paying premium freight or speeding production with overtime and extra shifts.

The structure represented by figure 11.3 is quite general. The system may be nonlinear. There may be arbitrarily complex feedbacks among the endogenous variables, and the system may be influenced by a number of exogenous forces, both systematic and stochastic. The delay in acquiring new units often is variable and may be constrained by supplier capacity. Table 11.1 maps common examples into the generic form. In each case, the manager must choose the order rate over time to keep the stock close to its target level. Note that most of these systems tend to generate oscillation and instability. The structure can be applied to systems from management to medicine and beyond. As an example, McCarthy and coauthors (2014) developed a system dynamics model to improve treatment of long-term hemodialysis patients suffering from anemia. The model captures the time delays between treatments with erythropoiesis-stimulating agents and changes in hemoglobin levels, showing how a new treatment protocol stabilizes hemoglobin levels, leading to better patient outcomes and lower treatment costs.

Turning to the decision rule, the formulation for orders captures managers' decision-making process. Following the principles outlined by Sterman (2000, chapter 13), such formulations must be based only on information actually available to decision-makers, must be robust under extreme conditions, and must be consistent with knowledge of the actual decision-making process, even if the way people actually make decisions is not optimal. In most stock management

Table 11.1. Examples of the Stock Management Structure

System	Stock	Supply line	Loss rate	Acquisition rate	Order rate	Typical behavior
Inventory management	Inventory	Goods on order	Shipments to customers	Arrivals from supplier	Orders for goods	Business cycles
Capital investment	Capital plant	Plant under construction	Depreciation	Construction completion	New contracts	Construction cycles
Equipment	Equipment	Equipment on order	Depreciation	Equipment delivery	New equipment orders	Business cycles
Human resources	Employees	Vacancies and trainees	Layoffs and quits	Hiring rate	Vacancy creation	Business cycles
Cash management	Cash balance	Accounts receivable	Expenditures	Payments received from customers	Bills issues to customers	Fluctuations in cash flow and account balances
Marketing	Customer base	Prospective customers	Defections to competitors	Recruitment of new customers	New customer contacts	Boom and bust in customer base
Hog farming	Hog stock	Immature and gestating hogs	Slaughter rate	Maturation rate	Breeding rate	The "hog cycle"
Agricultural commodities	Inventory	Crops in the field	Consumption	Harvest rate	Planting rate	Commodity cycles

Table 11.1. (Continued)

System	Stock	Supply line	Loss rate	Acquisition rate	Order rate	Typical behavior
Commercial real estate	Building stock	Buildings under development	Depreciation	Completion rate	Development rate	Real estate booms and busts
Cooking on electric range	Temperature of pot	Heat in coils of range	Diffusion to air	Diffusion from coils to pot	Setting of burner	Overcooked dinner
Driving	Distance to next car	Momentum of car	Friction/drag	Velocity	Gas and brake pedals	Stop-and-go traffic
Showering	Water temperature	Water temperature in pipes	Drain rate	Flow from shower head	Faucet settings	Freeze-then-burn
Blood sugar regulation	Glucose in bloodstream	Sugar and starch in GI tract	Metabolism	Digestion	Food consumption	Cycles of energy level
Social drinking	Alcohol in blood	Alcohol in stomach	Metabolism of alcohol	Diffusion from stomach to blood	Alcohol consumption rate	Drunkenness

situations, the complexity of the feedbacks among the variables makes it impossible to determine the optimal strategy. Instead, people use heuristics or rules of thumb to determine the order rate. The ordering decision rule proposed here assumes that managers, unable to optimize, instead exercise control through locally rational heuristics. The model thus falls firmly in the tradition of bounded rationality and the behavioral theory of the firm pioneered by Simon (1982) and Cyert and March (1963).

Three considerations are fundamental to any decision rule for orders. First, managers should replace expected losses from the stock. Second, managers should reduce the discrepancy between the desired and actual stock by ordering more than expected losses when the stock is less than desired, and less than expected losses when there is a surplus. Third, managers should pay attention to the supply line of unfilled orders and adjust orders to eliminate any discrepancies between the desired and actual supply line.

To formalize this intuition, first note that the order rate in most real-life situations must be nonnegative:

$$OR = MAX(0, IO), \tag{11.6}$$

where IO is the indicated order rate, the rate indicated by other pressures. Order cancellations are sometimes possible and may sometimes exceed new orders. The costs of and administrative procedures for cancellations are likely to differ from those for new orders. Cancellations, if possible, should therefore be modeled as a distinct outflow from the supply line, governed by a separate decision rule, rather than as negative orders (Sterman 2000, chapter 19 provides a suitable formulation).

The indicated order rate is formulated as an anchoring and adjustment process (Tversky and Kahneman 1974). Managers are assumed to base orders on the desired acquisition rate, AR^*, which is the rate at which they would like to add items to the stock. Managers then adjust orders above or below the desired acquisition rate by an amount designed to bring the supply line of unfilled orders in line with its goal (the Adjustment for the Supply Line, A_{SL}):

$$IO = AR^* + A_{SL}. \tag{11.7}$$

The desired acquisition rate is similarly formulated as an anchoring and adjustment process. Managers seek to replace expected losses, L^e, modified by an amount designed to bring the stock in line with its goal (the Adjustment for the Stock, A_S):

$$AR^* = L^e + A_S \tag{11.8}$$

Why does the desired acquisition rate depend on expected losses rather than the actual loss rate? The current value of a flow represents the instantaneous rate of change. Actual instruments and information systems, however, cannot measure instantaneous rates of change but only average rates over some finite interval. The velocity of an object is calculated by measuring how far it moves over some period of time and taking the ratio of the distance covered to the time interval. The result is the average speed over the interval. The actual speed throughout the interval can vary, and the velocity at the finish line may differ from the average. Similarly, the sales rate of a company *right now* cannot be measured. Instead sales rates are estimated by accumulating total sales over some interval of time such as an hour, day, week, month, or quarter. The reported sales rate is the average over the reporting interval, and sales at the end of the period may differ from the average over the interval. No matter how accurate the instruments, the rate of change measured and reported to an observer always differs from the instantaneous rate of change.

While in principle all flows are measured and reported with a delay, in practice the delay is sometimes so short relative to the dynamics of interest that it can be omitted. If the loss rate is directly observable by the decision-maker with essentially no delay or measurement error, it can be acceptable to assume L^e is the actual loss rate. Most often, however, the loss rate is not directly observable and must be estimated, introducing measurement, reporting, and perception delays. Further, even if losses are reported frequently, with little lag, it may be necessary or desirable to filter and smooth those data. For example, most manufacturing firms do not use raw order or shipment data as direct inputs to orders for materials or the production start rate. Orders and shipments are typically quite noisy, while it is costly to change production. Firms deliberately filter out high-frequency noise in shipments or customer orders so as to avoid overreacting to temporary variations. Such filtering is often accomplished with exponential smoothing or other forms of moving averages. Finally, expected losses might also include knowledge of seasonal variations or other factors.

The feedback structure of the ordering heuristic is shown in the bottom part of figure 11.3. The adjustment for the stock A_S creates the balancing (negative) Stock Control feedback loop. The simplest formulation is to assume the adjustment is linear in the discrepancy between the desired stock S^* and the actual stock:

$$A_S = \left(S^* - S\right)/\tau_S, \tag{11.9}$$

where S^* is the desired stock and τ_S is the stock adjustment time (equivalently, $1/\tau_S$ is the fraction of the discrepancy between desired and actual inventory ordered per time unit). The desired stock may be a constant or a variable.

The adjustment for the supply line is formulated analogously to the adjustment for the stock:

$$A_{SL} = \left(SL^* - SL\right)/\tau_{SL}, \tag{11.10}$$

where SL^* is the desired supply line and τ_{SL} is the supply line adjustment time. The supply line adjustment forms the negative Supply Line Control loop.

Figure 11.3 does not show the feedback structure for the desired supply line. In some cases the desired supply line is constant. More often, however, decision-makers seek to maintain a sufficient number of units on order to achieve the acquisition rate they desire. By Little's Law the supply line must, in equilibrium, contain λ time units worth of desired throughput. Several measures for desired throughput are common. The desired supply line may be set to yield the desired acquisition rate, AR^*:

$$SL^* = \lambda^e * AR^*, \tag{11.11a}$$

where λ^e, the expected acquisition lag, represents the decision-makers' current beliefs about the length of the acquisition delay (which, in general, may differ from the actual acquisition delay).

Equation (11.11a) assumes a rather high degree of decision rationality. Decision-makers are assumed to adjust the supply line to achieve the desired acquisition rate, which includes replacement of expected losses and correction of temporary gaps between desired and actual inventory. As described below, experimental evidence shows decision-makers often are less sophisticated. Managers frequently do not adjust the supply line in response to temporary imbalances in the stock but base the desired supply line on estimated long-run throughput requirements—the expected loss rate L^e:

$$SL^* = \lambda^e * L^e. \tag{11.11b}$$

The formulation for the desired supply li+ne should be based on empirical investigation of the actual decision-making process (e.g., Senge 1980; Croson et al. 2013; Sterman and Dogan 2014).

Whichever formulation for the desired supply line is used, the longer the expected delay in acquiring goods or the larger the desired throughput rate, the larger the supply line must be. If a retailer wishes to receive 1,000 widgets per week from the supplier and delivery requires six weeks, the retailer must have 6,000 widgets on order to ensure an uninterrupted flow of deliveries. The adjustment for the supply line creates a negative feedback loop that adjusts orders to maintain the acquisition rate at the desired value given the (expected) delay between orders and delivery. Without supply line feedback, orders would be placed even after the supply line contained sufficient units to correct shortfalls in on-hand stocks, producing overshoot and instability. The supply line adjustment also compensates for changes in the acquisition lag. If the acquisition lag doubled, for example, the supply line adjustment would induce sufficient additional orders to restore acquisitions to the desired rate.

There are many possible ways managers may form the expected acquisition lag λ^e, ranging from constants through guesstimates to sophisticated forecasts. Usually, it takes time to detect changes in delivery times. Customers often do not know that goods they ordered will be late until after the promised delivery time has passed. The expected acquisition lag can then be modeled by a perception delay representing the time required to observe and respond to changes in the actual delay. For example, Senge (1980) found expected delivery times for capital plant and equipment lagged actual delivery times by 1.3 years for firms in the US economy.

The formulation for the order rate conforms to core principles for behavioral models (Sterman 2000, chapter 13). First, the formulation is robust: Orders remain nonnegative no matter how large a surplus stock there may be, and the supply line and stock therefore never fall below zero. Second, information not available to real decision-makers is not utilized, such as the instantaneous value of the loss rate, or the solution to the dynamic programming problem determining the optimal order rate. Finally, the ordering decision rule is grounded in well-established knowledge of decision-making behavior, such as the anchoring and adjustment heuristic. Expected losses form an easily anticipated and relatively stable starting point for the determination of orders. Loss rate information is typically locally available and salient to decision-makers. Replacing losses will keep the stock constant at its current level. Adjustments are then made in response to the adequacy of the stock and supply line. No assumption is made that these adjustments are optimal. Rather, pressures arising from discrepancies between desired and actual quantities cause managers to adjust the order rate above or below the level that would maintain the status quo.

The Stock Management Problem: Dynamics

To illustrate the behavior of the stock management structure, consider how a manufacturing firm manages its product inventory. Figure 11.4 adapts the generic stock management structure to the case of inventory and production control. The firm maintains a stock of finished inventory and fills orders as they arrive. In this simple illustration, assume that customers are delivery sensitive—orders the company cannot fill immediately are lost as customers seek other suppliers

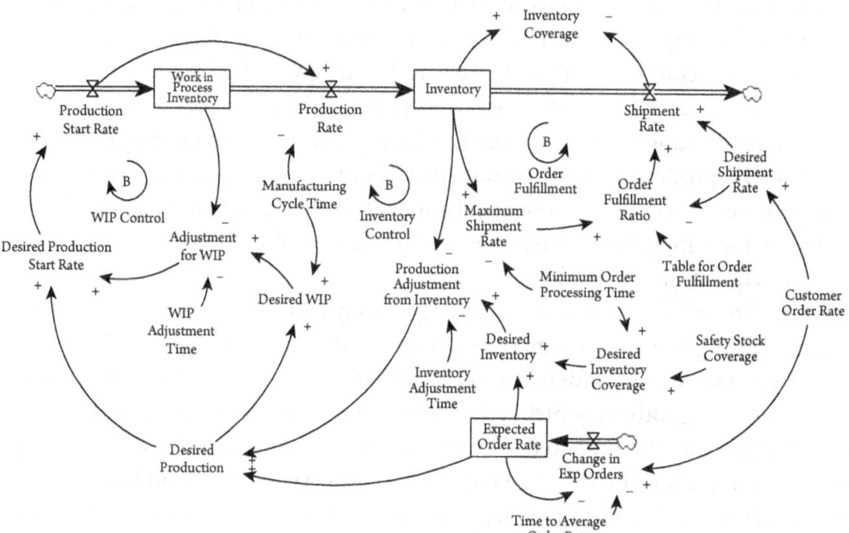

Figure 11.4 The Stock Management Structure Adapted for a Manufacturing Firm

(Sterman 2000, chapter 18, extends the model to add an explicit backlog of unfilled orders). Production takes time. The supply line is the stock of work in process inventory (WIP), which is increased by production starts and decreased by production.

The key production control and inventory management decisions are order fulfillment (determining the ability to fill customer orders based on inventory adequacy) and production scheduling (determining the rate of production starts based on the demand forecast and the firm's inventory position, including WIP inventory). The model includes three important negative feedbacks. The Stockout loop regulates shipments as inventory varies: If inventory is inadequate, some items will be out of stock and shipments fall below orders. In the extreme, shipments must fall to zero when there is no inventory. The Inventory Control and WIP Control loops adjust production starts to move inventory and WIP toward desired levels. In this initial model there are no stocks of materials and no capacity constraints (either from labor or capital). These extensions are treated in Sterman 2000, chapter 18.

For purposes of illustration, we assume there are no capacity constraints or materials shortages that might limit production starts, so the actual production start rate is equal to the desired production start rate. Following the standard stock management structure, desired production starts are anchored on desired production and adjusted to bring the stock of WIP in line with the desired WIP level. Desired production, in turn, is anchored on the Expected Order Rate, then adjusted to bring the stock of finished goods inventory in line with the desired level. Because incoming customer orders are typically noisy, the firm, as is common, uses first-order exponential smoothing to filter out high-frequency random variation in customer orders. The firm seeks to maintain enough finished goods inventory to provide excellent customer service and so seeks to maintain a certain desired number of weeks of inventory coverage. Desired inventory coverage consists of the minimum time required to process and ship orders plus safety stock coverage large enough to provide excellent customer service. The model is fully documented in Sterman 2000, chapter 18.[4]

Note that the model deliberately omits the primary operational factors that can make amplification a rational outcome (Lee, Padmanabhan, and Whang 1997). There are no quantity discounts, so order batching is never rational. Prices are constant, so there is never any incentive to order more (or less) in anticipation of

4. The parameters in the simulation in figure 11.5 are given below:

Parameter	Base Case Value (Weeks)
Minimum Order Processing Time	2
Safety Stock Coverage	2
Manufacturing Cycle Time	8
Inventory Adjustment Time	8
WIP Adjustment Time	2
Time to Average Order Rate	8

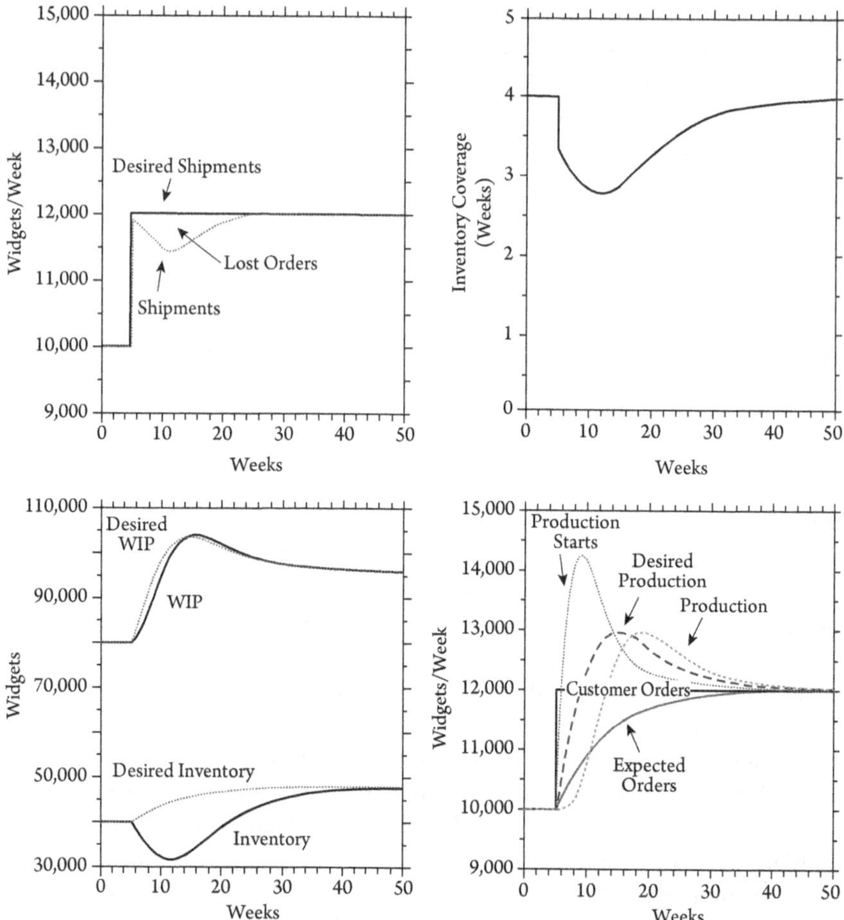

Figure 11.5 Response of the Manufacturing Model to a 20% Step Increase in Orders

rising (falling) prices. Each customer has only one supplier and each supplier only one customer, so there is no incentive to place phantom orders.

Now consider the impact of an unanticipated 20% increase in customer orders, from an initial equilibrium with throughput of 10,000 units/week (figure 11.5). The desired shipment rate rises immediately after the step increase in demand. Inventory coverage immediately drops from its initial value of four weeks to 3.33 weeks. Immediately after the customer order rate jumps, inventory has not yet changed, and the firm is initially able to fill nearly all the incoming orders, despite the increase. However, because production continues at the initial rate of 10,000 widgets/week, inventory falls. As inventory falls, so too does the firm's ability to ship. A maximum of about 5% of orders go unfilled and are lost (along, most likely, with the firm's reputation as a reliable supplier).

The growing gap between desired and actual inventory forces desired production to rise above expected orders. As it does the quantity of work in process required to meet the higher production goal also grows, opening a gap between the desired and actual level of WIP. Thus the desired production start rate rises further above the desired production rate.

As time passes the firm recognizes that the initial increase in demand is not a mere random blip and gradually raises its demand forecast. As expected orders rise, so too does desired inventory, further increasing the gap between desired and actual inventory and desired production. Production starts reach a peak more than 42% above the initial level approximately four weeks after the shock, 210% more than the change in customer orders.

The rapid increase in production starts soon fills the supply line of WIP, but production lags behind because of the eight-week manufacturing delay. Production does not surpass shipments until more than six weeks have passed; throughout this period inventory continues to fall even as the desired inventory level rises. Inventory stops falling when production first equals shipments. The system is not yet in equilibrium, however, because of the large gap between desired and actual inventory and between orders and expected orders. Production eventually rises above shipments, causing inventory to rise until it eventually reaches the new, higher desired level. Note that the peak of production comes about one-quarter year after the change in orders, much longer than the eight-week production delay suggests.

The consequences of the stock management structure for supply chain management are profound:

1. **The process of stock adjustment creates significant amplification**. The initial response to an unanticipated demand increase is a decline in inventory. The production delay means an initial drop in inventory is inevitable—it is a fundamental consequence of the physical structure of the system. The reduction in inventory contrasts sharply with the firm's desire to hold more inventory when demand increases to maintain acceptable inventory coverage and customer service.
2. **Amplification of the demand shock is unavoidable**. Because inventory must initially fall, the only way to return it to its initial level and then raise it to the new, higher desired level is for production to exceed shipments. Production must overshoot the shipment rate long enough and by a large enough margin to build inventory up to the new desired level. Production starts must overshoot orders even more, so that the level of WIP can be built up to a level consistent with the higher throughput rate.
3. **The peak production start rate must lag the change in customer orders**. The adjustment to production from the inventory gap reaches its maximum at about the point inventory reaches its minimum. Inventory bottoms out only after production has finally risen enough to equal shipments, an event that must lag the change in orders. Like amplification, phase lag is a fundamental and inevitable consequence of the physical stock and flow structure.
4. **Amplification is temporary**. In the long run, a 20% increase in customer orders leads to a 20% increase in production starts. But during

> the disequilibrium adjustment to the new equilibrium, production starts must temporarily rise above orders because that is the only way inventory can be rebuilt to initial levels, and the only way inventory and WIP stocks can rise to the new, higher equilibrium levels consistent with higher customer demand.

The firm's suppliers therefore face much larger changes in demand than the firm itself, and much of that surge in demand is temporary. Upstream firms, such as those supplying plant, equipment, and materials, will not face a single, permanent change in orders but a much larger, and temporary, surge in demand. Each supplier will, for the same reasons, necessarily amplify and delay the change in orders they receive. As that signal is passed up the supply chain to their suppliers, and theirs, the result is the characteristic amplification and phase lag observed in commodities, construction, and so many other industries.

The stock management structure thus explains why supply chains generate amplification and phase lag. Given the structure of the system, specifically, production delays and forecast adjustment delays, production and production starts must overshoot, amplify, and lag changes in demand, no matter how smart the managers of the firm may be. Amplification and phase lag arise even though there is no order batching, no price variations, and no horizontal competition among customers for limited supply. Although those factors may indeed contribute to amplification in supply chains, they are not necessary.

Though amplification and phase lag are inevitable, oscillation is not. Even though the actors use boundedly rational and not optimal decision rules, the response to the demand shock shown in figure 11.5 is smooth and stable (given the base case parameters).

CASE EXAMPLE

The simulation above shows how a single link in a supply chain creates amplification and phase lag in response to changes in customer demand. Do people understand why? Unfortunately, the answer is no. To illustrate, figure 11.6 shows a simple exercise, the Manufacturing Case (MC), which assesses people's understanding of the stock management structure in an extremely simple context (Booth Sweeney and Sterman 2000).

The Manufacturing Case is an example of a simple stock management task. Here a firm seeks to control its inventory in the face of an unanticipated step increase in customer demand and a lag between a change in the production schedule and the actual production rate, analogous to the stock management structure in figure 11.4.

There is no unique correct answer to the MC task. However, the trajectories of production and inventory must satisfy certain constraints, and their shapes can be determined without any quantitative analysis. The unanticipated step increase in customer orders means shipments increase, while the production delay means production remains, for a time, constant at the original rate. Inventory therefore

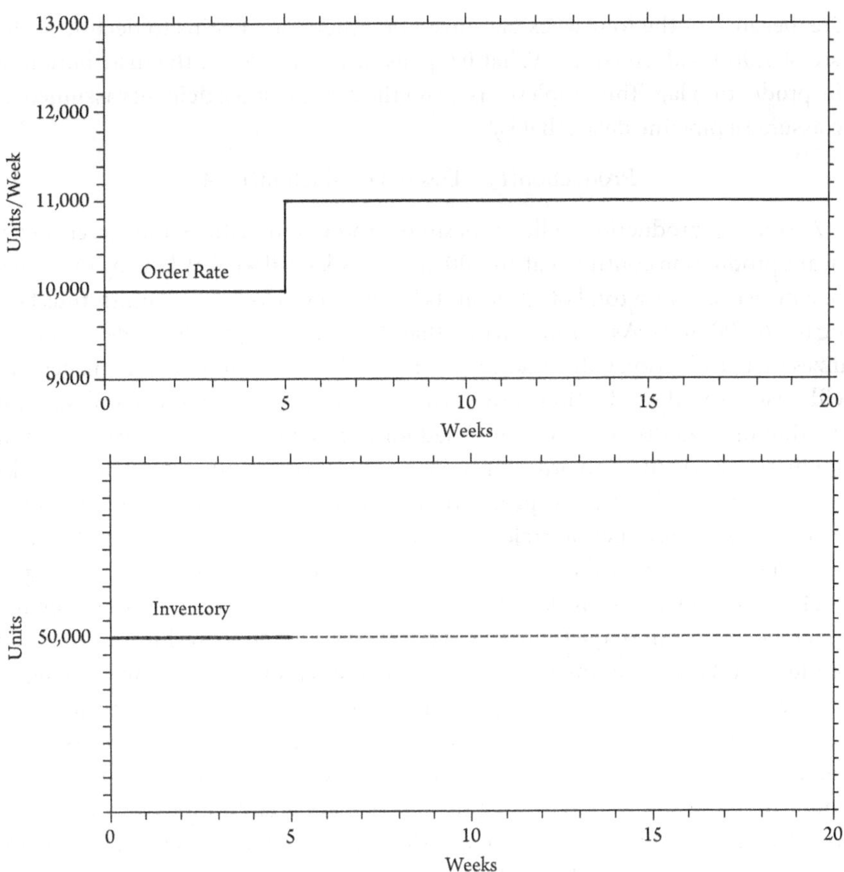

Figure 11.6 The Manufacturing Case
SOURCE: Booth Sweeney and Sterman 2000.

declines. The firm must not only boost output to the new rate of orders, but also rebuild its inventory to the desired level. Production must therefore overshoot orders and remain above shipments until inventory reaches the desired level, at which point production can drop back to equilibrium at the customer order rate.[5]

Further, since the task specifies that the desired inventory level is constant, the area bounded by the production overshoot must equal the quantity of inventory lost during the period when orders exceed production, which in turn is the area between orders and production between week 5 and the point where production rises to the order rate. A few modest assumptions allow the trajectories of production and inventory to be completely specified. When customer orders increase from 10,000 to 11,000 widgets/week, production remains constant at the initial

5. In real supply chains desired inventory would likely rise. For the purpose of the exercise, we assume desired inventory remains constant. This is made clear in the instructions. Assuming "constant desired inventory" makes the task far simpler and makes it easier to interpret the results and determine whether participants sketch pathways for production starts that are consistent with conservation laws.

rate, because of the four-week lag. Inventory, therefore, begins to decline at the rate of 1,000 widgets/week. What happens next depends on the distribution of the production lag. The simplest case, and the case most participants assumed, is to assume a pipeline delay, that is,[6]

$$\text{Production}(t) = \text{Desired Production}(t-4).$$

Assuming production follows desired production with a four-week delay means production continues at 10,000 units/week until week 9. During this time, inventory drops by a total of 1,000 units/week × 4 weeks = 4,000 units, thus falling to 46,000 units. Assuming further that the firm understands the delay and realizes that production will remain at its original level for four weeks, management will raise desired production above orders at week 5, keep it above orders until an additional 4,000 units are scheduled for production, and then bring desired production back down to orders. Production then traces this pattern four weeks later. Assuming, finally, that production remains constant during the period of overshoot gives production trajectories such as those shown in figures 11.7 and 11.8. Figure 11.7, typical of many correct responses, shows production rising in week 9 to 12,000 units/week and remaining there for the next four weeks, giving a rectangle equal in shape to that for the period $5 < t \leq 9$ when shipments exceed production. Of course, the production overshoot can have any shape as long as the area equals 4,000 widgets. Figure 11.8 shows an unusual correct response in which the participant shows production rising in week 9 to 13,000 widgets/week and remaining there for two weeks. This response clearly shows the participant understood the task well. However, that participant was the only one, out of 225, who drew a pattern with the duration of the overshoot ≠ 4 weeks while also maintaining the correct area relationship.

It is possible that production and inventory could fluctuate around their equilibrium values, but while such fluctuation is not inevitable, the overshoot of production is: the only way inventory can rise is for production to exceed orders, in exactly the same way that the only way the level of water in a bathtub can rise is for the flow in from the tap to exceed the flow out through the drain.

The MC is quite simple, involving only one stock, one time delay, and one negative feedback loop. Nevertheless, in a group consisting of MBA students, executive MBA students, and other graduate students at the MIT Sloan School of Management ($N = 225$), performance was poor. Only 44% of the participants showed production overshooting orders. Instead, most showed production adjusting with a lag to the new customer order rate but not overshooting: they failed to understand that building inventory back up to its desired level requires production to exceed orders.

Figure 11.9 shows typical erroneous responses. The top panel shows the most common error. The participant shows production responding with a lag, but rising up only to the new level of orders. There is no production overshoot. Further, the trajectory of inventory is inconsistent with the production path.

6. Other patterns for the delay are possible, such as some adjustment before week nine and some after, and were coded as correct as long as production did not begin to increase until after the step increase in orders.

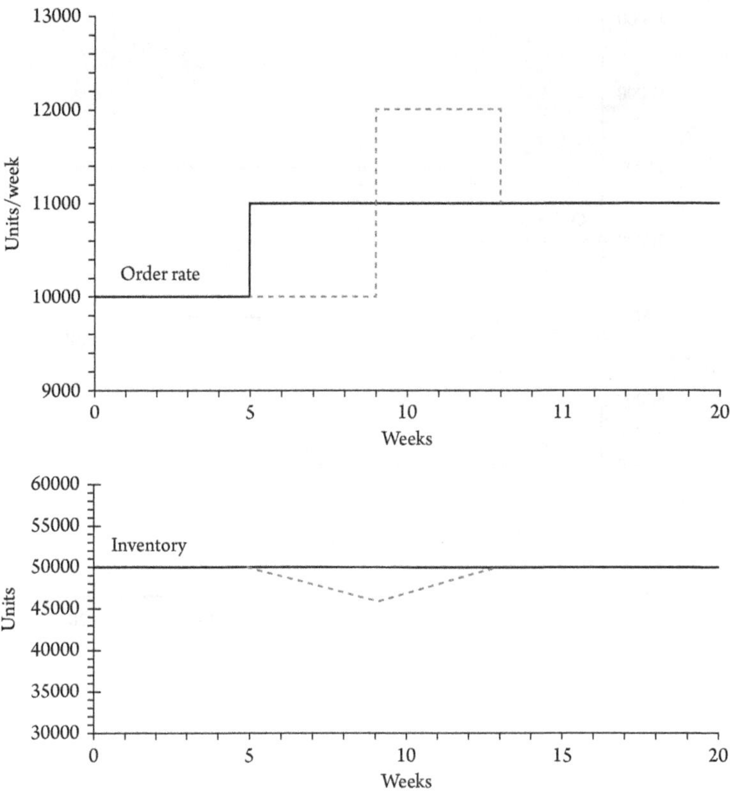

Figure 11.7 A Correct Response to the Manufacturing Case.
Note that the path of inventory is consistent with the path of production.

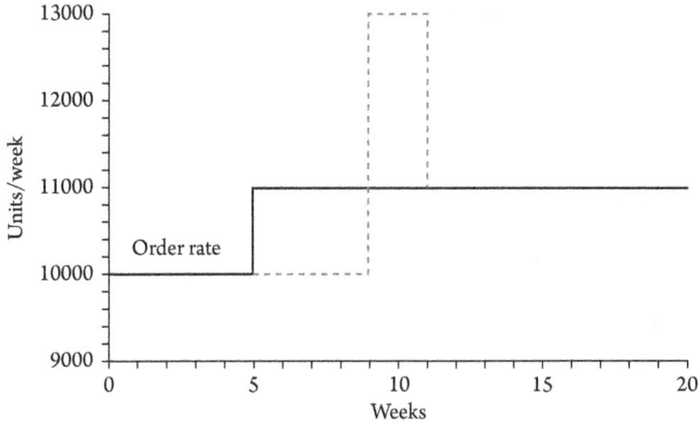

Figure 11.8 An Unusual Correct Response to the Manufacturing Case

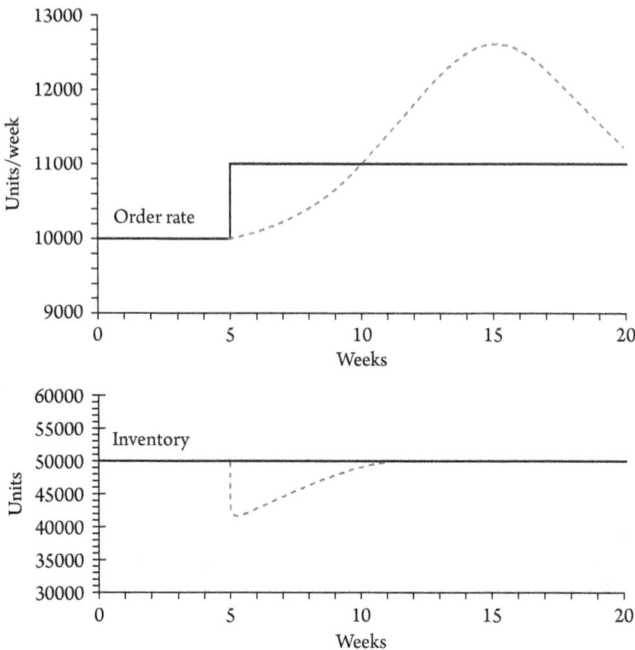

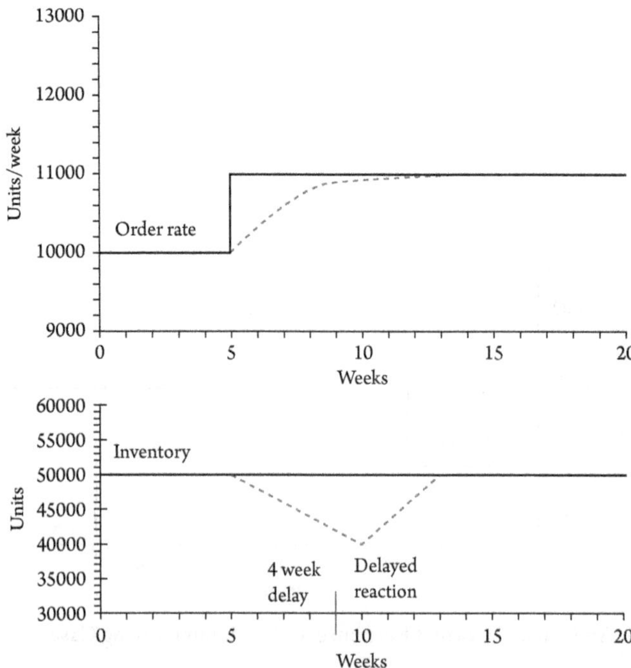

Figure 11.9 Typical Incorrect Responses to the Manufacturing Case

The subject shows inventory falling linearly through about week 10 although, given the production path as drawn, inventory would actually fall at a diminishing rate. Worse, the subject then shows inventory rising even though production equals orders after week 10.

Booth Sweeney and Sterman (2000) explored several variants of the task. In one, participants were asked to sketch the paths for both production and inventory (as in figure 11.7). In another, participants were asked only to sketch the trajectory of production (as in figure 11.8). Booth Sweeney and Sterman hypothesized that requiring participants to draw the path for inventory would help them realize the need for production to overshoot customer orders (so as to rebuild inventory to the target level). Overall performance in the inventory graph condition, however, was significantly worse than in the no inventory graph condition ($t = 5.11, p < .0001$). Only 23% of those in the inventory graph condition correctly showed production overshooting orders, compared to 63% of those in the no inventory graph condition.

Overall, 89% of the participants drew production trajectories that violated conservation of material, showing no production overshoot or an overshoot whose area does not equal the area of the production undershoot they drew. The failure to conform to conservation of mass has been repeatedly demonstrated in similar experiments, with different cover stories, including greenhouse gases accumulating in the atmosphere, receipts, and disbursements accumulating in a bank account, and even water filling a bathtub (Sterman and Booth Sweeney 2000; Sterman and Booth Sweeney 2007; Sterman 2008; Cronin et al. 2009; Sterman 2010).

The experimental evidence shows that many people, including many with extensive training in science, technology, engineering, and mathematics (STEM), do not understand the most basic principles of accumulation. Inventory control and supply chain management depend fundamentally on accumulations: inventories accumulate production less shipments, backlogs accumulate orders less fulfillment and cancellations, and so on. If people do not understand the basic principles of accumulation, it should be no surprise that we continue to observe dysfunctional dynamics in supply chains across a wide variety of industries and products.

LEARNING ACTIVITY

The simulation of the stock management structure above explains the origin of amplification and phase lag, but does not exhibit oscillations. How do oscillations arise? Oscillations can arise only when there are time delays in the negative feedbacks controlling the state of the system (Sterman 2000, chapter 4). The mere existence of a supply line and acquisition lag, however, does not necessarily lead to oscillations. In the manufacturing model above, there is an eight-week delay between the start and completion of the manufacturing process, yet the system does not oscillate (with the estimated parameters). In that model, managers fully account for the stock of WIP—the supply line of units in production but not yet received, and reduce orders as soon as they have initiated enough new production to bring inventory up to the desired level even though those units have not yet entered the finished goods inventory.

To oscillate, the time delay must be (at least partially) ignored. The manager must continue to initiate corrective actions in response to the perceived gap between the desired and actual state of the system, even after sufficient corrections to close the gap are in the pipeline. But do managers ignore these time delays and the supply line of corrective actions? In many settings, shockingly, the answer is yes.

The Beer Distribution Game

The Beer Distribution Game illustrates how oscillations arise.[7] The game is a role-playing simulation of a supply chain originally developed by Jay Forrester in the late 1950s to introduce students of management to the concepts of system dynamics and computer simulation. The game has been played all over the world, by tens of thousands of people ranging from high school students to chief executive officers and senior government officials.

The game is played on a board portraying a typical supply chain (figure 11.10). Markets and chips represent orders for and cases of beer. Each brewery consists of four sectors: retailer, wholesaler, distributor, and factory (R, W, D, F). One or two people manage each sector. A deck of cards represents customer demand. Each

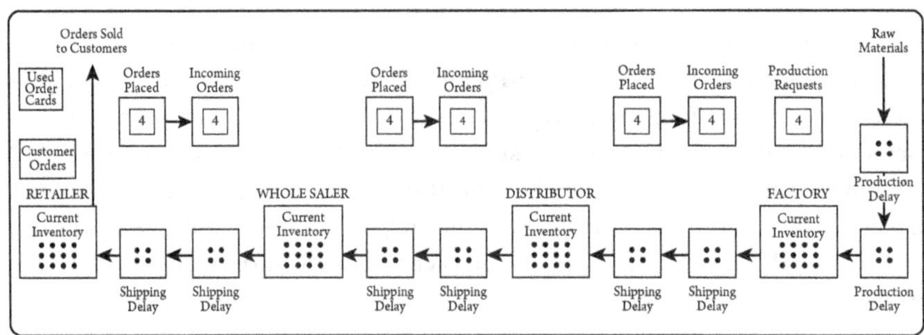

Figure 11.10 The Beer Distribution Game
The game is a role-play simulation. Each player manages one of the links in the distribution chain from Retailer to Factory. In the game, chips of various denominations represent cases of beer and move through the supply chain from Raw Materials to Customers. Customer Orders are written on a deck of cards. Each week players place orders with the supplier on their left, and the factory sets the production schedule. The orders, written on slips of paper, move upstream (left to right). The initial configuration is shown.

7. The game is described in detail in Sterman (1989a). Information and materials are available from the System Dynamics Society at system.dynamics@albany.edu. There is no real beer in the Beer Game, and it does not promote drinking. When the game is used with, e.g., high school students, it is easily recast as the "apple juice game." Many firms have customized the game to represent their industry.

week, customers demand beer from the retailer, filling the order out of inventory. The retailer in turn orders beer from the wholesaler, who ships the beer requested from wholesale stocks. Likewise the wholesaler orders and receives beer from the distributor, who in turn orders and receives beer from the factory. The factory produces the beer. At each stage there are order-processing and shipping delays. Each link in the supply chain has the same structure.

The players' objective is to minimize total costs for their company. Inventory holding costs are typically set to \$0.50 per case per week, and stockout costs (costs for having a backlog of unfilled orders) to \$1.00 per case per week. The task is a clear example of the stock management problem. Players must keep their inventories as low as possible while avoiding backlogs. Incoming orders deplete inventory, so players must place replenishment orders and adjust their inventories to the desired level. There is a delay between placing and receiving orders, creating a supply line of unfilled orders.

The standard game is played with a very simple pattern for customer demand. Starting from equilibrium, there is a small, unannounced one-time increase in customer orders, from four to eight cases per week. The game is far simpler than any real supply chain. There are no random events—no machine breakdowns, transportation problems, or strikes. There are no capacity constraints or financial limitations. The structure of the game is visible to all. Players can readily inspect the board to see how much inventory is in transit or held by their teammates.

Further, the main operational factors that can make amplification rational do not apply in the beer game: as in the simulation model in figures 11.4 and 11.5, the operational factors cited by Lee, Padmanabhan, and Whang (1997) that may lead to demand amplification are absent. There are no quantity discounts that could make order batching rational, no price variations that could make forward buying rational, and no horizontal competition among customers for limited supply that could make phantom ordering or inventory hoarding rational.

Despite the simplicity of the game, however, people do extremely poorly. Among first-time players average costs are typically an astonishing 10 times greater than optimal (Sterman 1989a). Figure 11.11 shows representative results. In all cases customer orders are essentially constant (except for the small step increase near the start). In all cases, the response of the supply chain is unstable. The oscillation, amplification, and phase lag observed in real supply chains are clearly visible in the experimental results. The period of the cycle is 20–25 weeks. The average amplification ratio of factory production relative to customer orders is a factor of four, and factory production peaks some 15 weeks after the change in customer orders.

Most interesting, the patterns of behavior generated in the game are remarkably similar (there are, of course, individual differences in magnitude and timing). Starting with the retailer, inventories decline throughout the supply chain, and most players develop a backlog of unfilled orders (net inventory becomes negative). In response, a wave of orders move through the chain, growing larger at each stage. Eventually, factory production surges, and inventories throughout the

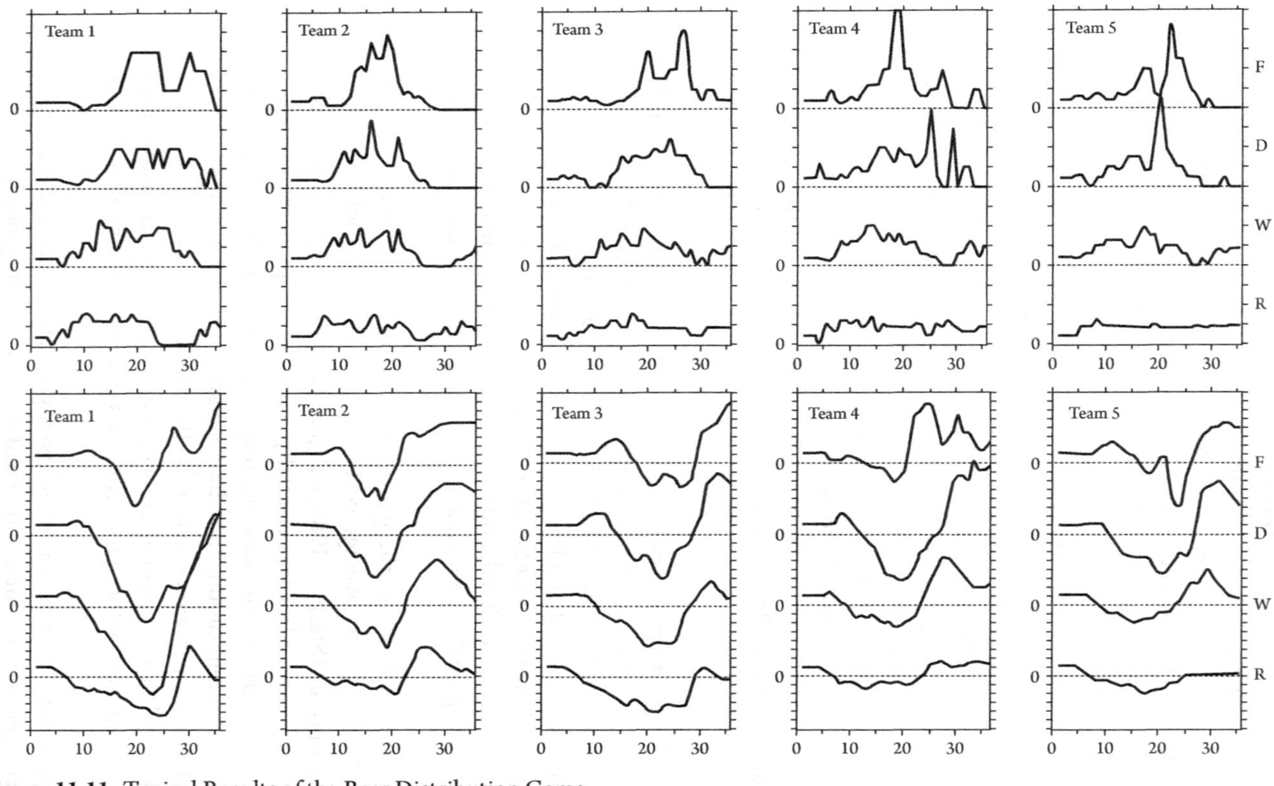

Figure 11.11 Typical Results of the Beer Distribution Game
Top: Orders. Bottom: Net inventory (Inventory—Backlog). Graphs show, bottom to top, Retailer, Wholesaler, Distributor, and Factory. Vertical axis tick marks denote 10 units. Note the characteristic oscillation, amplification, and phase lag as the change in customer orders propagates from retailer to factory.
SOURCE: Sterman 2000.

supply chain start to rise. But inventory does not stabilize at the cost-minimizing level near zero. Instead, inventory significantly overshoots. Players respond by slashing orders, often cutting them to zero for extended periods. Inventory eventually peaks and slowly declines. These behavioral regularities are all the more remarkable because there is no oscillation in customer demand. The oscillation arises as an endogenous consequence of the way the players manage their inventories. Though players are free to place orders any way they wish, the vast majority behave in a remarkably uniform fashion.

Modeling Managerial Behavior: Misperceptions of Feedback

To understand the origin of oscillations more formally, Sterman (1989a) tested the decision rule for customer orders described above against the order decisions of players in the game. Orders placed are given by the anchoring and adjustment rule used in the stock management structure developed above. Participants are assumed to anchor on their belief about expected incoming orders (the loss rate from their inventory), then adjust their orders based on the adequacy of their on-hand inventory and supply line of on-order inventory:

$$OR = MAX(0,\ D^e + A_S + A_{SL}), \tag{11.12}$$

where D^e is expected demand, that is, the participant's belief about what the next incoming order will be. Sterman (1989a) assumes that expected incoming orders are formed by exponential smoothing of customer orders or demand, D, given in discrete time by

$$D_t^e = \theta D_t + (1-\theta) D_{t-1}^e, \tag{11.13}$$

where θ is the smoothing parameter.

Clark and Scarf (1960) showed that managers should give as much weight to on-order inventory (the supply line, SL) as on-hand inventory (the stock, S). If so, orders become

$$OR = MAX\left(0,\ D^e + \left(\left(S^* - S\right) + \left(SL^* - SL\right)\right)/\tau_S\right). \tag{11.14}$$

However, participants might not fully account for the supply line of orders placed but not yet received. Even if participants can keep track of the supply line, the supply line is likely to be given less weight than on-hand inventory because on-hand inventory is the direct determinant of costs, is highly salient, and is right in front of the players, while the supply line has none of these attributes. If participants underweight the supply line, the ordering rule becomes

$$OR = MAX(0,\ D^e + ((S^* - S) + \beta(SL^* - SL))/\tau_S), \tag{11.15}$$

where $\beta = \tau_S/\tau_{SL}$ is the fraction of the supply line adjustment taken into account: when people underweight or ignore the supply line, τ_{SL} will be longer than the stock adjustment time; if the supply line adjustment is completely ignored, then

$\tau_{SL} \rightarrow \infty$, which implies $A_{SL} \rightarrow 0$ (Sterman 1989a; 2000). Collecting terms and defining $S' = S^* + \beta SL^*$ yields

$$OR = MAX(0, D^e + (S' - (S + \beta SL))/\tau_S \quad (11.16)$$

Assuming that the desired stock and desired supply line are constant and including an additive error term yields the system of equations to be estimated:

$$ORt = MAX(0, D_t^e + \alpha(S' - (S_t + \beta SL_t)) + \varepsilon_t) \quad (11.17)$$

$$D_t^e = \theta D_t + (1-\theta) D_{t-1}^e, \quad (11.18)$$

where $\alpha = 1/\tau_S$ is the fraction of the perceived inventory discrepancy ordered each week. There are four parameters to be estimated: the forecast updating time, $0 \leq \theta \leq 1$; the fraction of the perceived inventory discrepancy ordered each week, $0 \leq a \leq 1$; the fraction of the supply line of unfilled orders taken into account, $0 \leq \beta \leq 1$; and the desired stock of on-hand and on-order inventory, $0 \leq S'$.

Sterman (1989a) estimated equations (11.17–11.18) by nonlinear least squares for a sample of 44 players. Overall, the decision rule worked quite well, explaining 71% of the variance in participants' order decisions. The estimated parameters showed that most participants used grossly suboptimal cue weights. The average weight on the supply line was only 0.34. Only 25% of the participants considered more than half the supply line, and the estimated value of β was not significantly different from zero for fully one-third. To illustrate, figure 11.12 compares simulated and actual behavior for the factory in an actual game. The estimated fraction of the inventory discrepancy ordered each week is 0.8—the player reacted aggressively to inventory shortfalls, ordering nearly the entire inventory shortfall

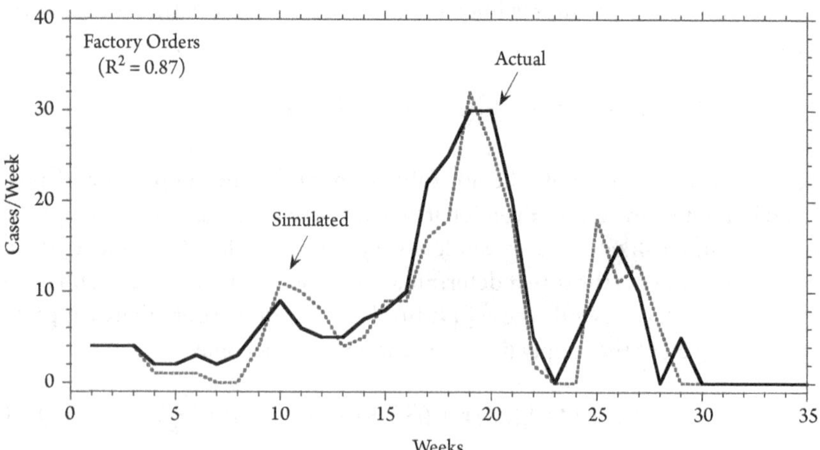

Figure 11.12 Estimated versus Actual Behavior in the Beer Game
Parameters: $\theta = 0.55$, $S' = 9$, $a = 0.80$, $\beta = 0$.
SOURCE: Sterman 1989a.

each week. At the same time, the estimated fraction of the supply line taken into account is zero—this participant completely ignored the supply line of orders placed but not yet received. As you would expect, aggressively reacting to current inventory shortfalls while completely ignoring the supply line leads to severe instability and high costs. Because it takes three weeks to receive production requested today, the player effectively orders almost three times more than needed to correct any inventory shortfall.

Other experiments with the beer game and similar stock management systems (for example, Sterman 1989b; Diehl and Sterman 1995; Brehmer 1992; Paich and Sterman 1993; Kampmann and Sterman 2014; Croson and Donohue 2006; Croson et al. 2013) show that the tendency to ignore time delays and underweight the supply line is robust. In many of these experiments the supply line was prominently displayed to participants yet ignored anyway. The information we use in decision-making is conditioned by our mental models. If we don't recognize the presence of a time delay or underestimate its length, we are unlikely to account for the supply line even if the information needed to do so is readily available.

Many players find these results disturbing. They argue that they took a wide range of information into account when placing orders and that their subtle and sophisticated reasoning cannot be captured by a model as simple as the anchoring and adjustment decision rule described here. After all, the decision rule for orders only considers three cues (incoming orders, inventory, and the supply line)—how could it possibly capture the way people place orders? Actually, players' behavior is highly systematic and is explained well by the simple stock management heuristic. The cue weights people tend to use are grossly suboptimal and lead to very poor performance, including the oscillation, amplification, and phase lag seen in both the game and real supply chains. People often are surprised how well simple decision rules can mimic their behavior.

In fact, one of the games shown in figure 11.11 is a simulation, not the actual play of real people. The simulation uses the decision rule in equations (11.17–11.18), with the parameters, for all four players, set to the average estimated values over the full sample in Sterman (1989a). A small amount of random noise was added to the order rate. Can you tell which is the simulation?[8]

DISCUSSION

Recognizing and Accounting for Time Delays

The Beer Game clearly shows it is folly to ignore the time delays in complex systems. Consider the following situation: You are involved in an automobile

8. Simulated orders were generated by eqs. (11.17–11.18) with $\theta = 0.36$, $S' = 17$ units, $\alpha = 0.26$/week, and $\beta = 0.34$. The error term was iid normal with mean zero and standard deviation set to the average of the standard errors of the estimated order equation over the full sample.

accident. Thankfully, no one is hurt, but your car is a total loss. Insurance settlement in hand, you visit a dealer and select a new car. You agree on a price, but the model you want is not in stock—delivery will take four weeks. You pay your deposit and leave. The next morning, noticing that your driveway is empty—*Where's my car!*—you go down to the dealer and buy another one. Ridiculous, of course. No one would be so foolish as to ignore the supply line. Yet in many real-life situations people do exactly that. Consider the following examples (table 11.1 shows how they map into the stock management structure):

- You cook on an electric range. To get dinner going as soon as possible, you set the burner under your pan to "high." After a while you notice the pan is getting quite hot, so you turn the heat down. But the supply line of heat in the glowing coil continues to heat the pan even after the current is cut, and your dinner is burned anyway.
- You are surfing the World Wide Web. Your computer did not respond to your last click. You click again, then again. Growing impatient, you click on other buttons—any buttons—to see if you can get a response. After a few seconds, the system executes all the clicks you stacked up in the supply line, and you end up far from the page you were seeking.
- You arrive late and tired to an unfamiliar hotel. You turn on the shower, but the water is freezing. You turn up the hot water. Still cold. You turn the hot up some more. Ahhh. Just right. You step in. A second later you jump out screaming, scalded by the now too-hot water. Cursing, you realize that once again, you've ignored the time delay for the hot water to get to your shower.
- You are driving on a busy highway. The car in front of you slows slightly. You take your foot off the gas, but the distance to the car in front keeps shrinking. Your reaction time and the momentum of your car create a delay between a change in the speed of the car ahead and a change in your speed. To avoid a collision, you have to slam on the brakes. The car behind you is forced to brake even harder. You hear the screech of rubber and pray you won't be rear-ended.
- You are young and experimenting with alcohol for the first time. Eager to show your friends you can hold your liquor, you quickly drain your glass. You feel fine. You drink another. Still feeling fine. You take another and another. As consciousness fades and you fall to the floor, you realize—too late—that you ignored the supply line of alcohol in your stomach and drank far too much.[9]

How often you have fallen victim to one of these behaviors? Few of us can say we've never burned our dinner or been scalded in the shower, never drunk too much or been forced to brake hard to avoid a collision.

9. Tragically, young people die every year from alcohol poisoning induced by aggressive drinking (a short stock adjustment time, τ_s, and failure to account for the supply line of alcohol they've already ingested, $\beta \approx 0$).

Recognizing and accounting for time delays is not innate. It is behavior we must learn. When we are born, our awareness is limited to our immediate surroundings. Everything we experience is *here* and *now.* All our early experiences reinforce the belief that cause and effect are closely related in time and space: When you cry, you get fed or changed. You keep crying until mother or father appears, even when you hear your parents say, "We're coming" (i.e., despite knowledge that your request for attention is in the supply line). As all parents know, it takes years for children to learn to account for such time delays. When my son was two he might ask for a cup of juice: "Juice please, Daddy." "Coming right up," I'd say, taking a cup from the shelf. Though he could see me getting the cup and filling it up, he'd continue to say, "Juice, Daddy!" many times—ever more insistently—until the cup was actually in his hand.

Learning to recognize and account for time delays goes hand in hand with learning to be patient, to defer gratification, and to bear short-run sacrifice for long-term reward. These abilities do not develop automatically. They are part of a slow process of maturation. The longer the time delays and the greater the uncertainty over how long it will take to see the results of your corrective actions, the harder it is to account for the supply line.[10]

You might argue that by the time we become adults we have developed the requisite patience and sensitivity to time delays. There may be no cost to saying "juice" a dozen times, but surely when the stakes are high we would quickly learn to consider delays. You don't burn yourself in your own shower at home—you've learned where to turn the hot water faucet to get the temperature you like and to wait long enough for the water to warm up. Most people learn to pay attention to the supply line of alcohol in their system and moderate their drinking. The conditions for learning in these systems are excellent. Feedback is swift, and the consequences of error are highly salient (particularly the morning after). There is no doubt in either case that it was the way you made decisions—the way you set the faucet or drank too fast—that caused the problem. These conditions are frequently not met in business, economic, environmental, and other real-world systems. In the real world, cause and effect are obscure, creating ambiguity and uncertainty. The dynamics are much slower, and the time required for learning often exceeds the tenure of individual decision-makers.

The French economist Albert Aftalion recognized in the early 1900s how failure to account for the time delays could cause economic cycles. Using the familiar fireplace as an analogy, his description explicitly focuses on the failure of decision-makers to pay attention to the supply line of fuel:

10. More subtly, our childhood experiences reinforce the idea that there is no cost to ignoring the supply line. Though my son may have said, "Juice, Daddy" 10 times before I could fill his order, I brought him only one cup. He didn't take the supply line into account, but I did. In that situation, there is no cost to overordering, while patience might not work (dad might get distracted and forget to bring the juice). In many real stock management situations, there is no central authority to account for the time delays and prevent over-ordering.

> If one rekindles the fire in the hearth in order to warm up a room, one has to wait a while before one has the desired temperature. As the cold continues, and the thermometer continues to record it, one might be led, if one had not the lessons of experience, to throw more coal on the fire. One would continue to throw coal, even though the quantity already in the grate is such as will give off an intolerable heat, when once it is all alight. To allow oneself to be guided by the present sense of cold and the indications of the thermometer to that effect is fatally to overheat the room. (Haberler 1964, 135–136)

While Aftalion argued that "the lessons of experience" would soon teach people not to "continue to throw coal," he argued that business cycles in the economy arose because individual entrepreneurs focused only on current profitability and failed to account for the lags between the initiation of new investment and its realization, leading to collective overproduction.

Yet even if individuals can't learn effectively, shouldn't the discipline imposed by the market quickly weed out people who use suboptimal decision rules? Those who ignore the supply line or use poor decision rules should lose money and go out of business or be fired, while those who use superior decision rules, even by chance, should prosper. The selective pressures of the market should quickly lead to the evolution of optimal decision rules.

The persistent cycles in a wide range of supply chains presented at the start of this chapter suggest Aftalion was right. Learning and evolution in real markets appear to be slow, at best, despite decades of experience and the huge sums at stake, as illustrated by the persistence of business cycles and speculative bubbles such as the bubble in housing construction in the early 2000s that culminated in the financial crisis of 2008 and the Great Recession. People tend to discount the experience of prior decades as irrelevant, arguing that the world has changed since the last crisis.

Although individual firms usually do not ignore the supply lines of materials on order or capital under construction, the problem is one of aggregation. The individual firm tends to view itself as small relative to the market and treats the environment as exogenous, thereby ignoring all feedbacks from prices to supply and demand. The individual firm may not know or give sufficient weight to the supply lines of all firms in the industry or the total capacity of all plants under construction. Firms tend to continue to invest and expand as long as profits are high today, even after the supply line of new capacity under construction is more than sufficient to cause a glut and destroy profitability. Each investor takes market conditions as exogenous, ignoring the reactions of others. When all investors react similarly to current profit opportunities, the result is overshoot and instability.

SUMMARY

Supply chains are fundamental to a wide range of systems, and many exhibit persistent instability and oscillation. Every supply chain consists of stocks and the policies used to manage them. These management policies are designed to keep the stocks at their target levels, compensating for usage or loss and for unanticipated environmental disturbances. Often there are important delays between the initiation of a control action and the result, creating a supply line of unfilled orders.

This chapter developed a generic model of the stock management structure and shows how it can be customized to various situations. The model explains the sources of oscillation, amplification, and phase lag observed in supply chains. These patterns of behavior are fundamental to the basic physical structure of stock management systems and supply chains. Oscillation arises from the combination of time delays in negative feedbacks and decision-maker failure to take the time delays into account. Field and experimental studies show that people often ignore the time delays in a wide range of systems.

There is no one single cause for the failure to account for time delays and the supply line. A range of factors, from information availability to individual incentives, all contribute. But behind these apparent causes lies a deeper problem. True, the supply line often is inadequately measured, but if people understood the importance of the supply line, they would invest in data collection and measurement systems to provide the needed information. True, compensation incentives often encourage people to ignore the delayed consequences of today's actions, but if investors understood the structure and dynamics of the market, they could redesign compensation incentives to focus on long-term performance. Our mental models affect the design of our institutions, information systems, and incentive schemes. These, in turn, feed back to our mental models. The failure to account for the supply line reflects deeper defects in our understanding of complex systems. Ignoring time delays is one of the fundamental misperceptions of feedback that leads to poor performance in systems with high dynamic complexity. Failure to understand the role of time delays worsens the instability we face and leads to more unpleasant surprises, reinforcing the belief that the world is inherently capricious and unpredictable and strengthening the short-term focus still more.

References

Anderson, E., Fine, C., Parker, G. 2000. Upstream volatility in the supply chain: The machine tool industry as a case study. Production and Operations Management 9 (3), 239–261.

Armony, M., Plambeck, E. 2005. The impact of duplicate orders on demand estimation and capacity investment. Management Science 51 (10), 1505–1518.

Bendoly, E., Croson, R., Gonçalves, P., Schultz, K. 2010. Bodies of knowledge for research in behavioral operations. Production and Operations Management 19 (4), 434–452.

Booth Sweeney, L., Sterman, J. 2000. Bathtub dynamics: Initial results of a systems thinking inventory. System Dynamics Review 16 (4), 249–294.

Boudreau, J., Hopp, W., McClain, J., Thomas, L. 2003. On the interface between operations and human resources management. Manufacturing and Service Operations Management 5 (3), 179–202.

Brehmer, B. 1992. Dynamic decision making: Human control of complex systems. Acta Psychologica 81, 211–241.

Cachon, G., Lariviere, M. 1999. Capacity choice and allocation: Strategic behavior and supply chain performance. Management Science 45 (8), 1091–1108.

Clark, A., Scarf, H. 1960. Optimal policies for a multi-echelon inventory problem. Management Science 6, 475–490.

Cronin, M., Gonzalez, C., Sterman, J. 2009. Why don't well-educated adults understand accumulation? A challenge to researchers, educators, and citizens. Organizational Behavior and Human Decision Processes 108 (1), 116–130.

Croson, R., Donohue, K. 2006. Behavioral causes of the bullwhip and the observed value of inventory information. Management Science 52 (3), 323–336.

Croson, R., Donohue, K., Katok, E., Sterman, J. 2013. Order stability in supply chains: The impact of coordination stock. Production and Operations Management 23 (2), 176–196.

Cyert, R., March, J. 1963. A Behavioral Theory of the Firm. Englewood Cliffs, NJ: Prentice-Hall. 2nd ed., Cambridge, MA: Blackwell, 1992.

Diehl, E., Sterman, J. 1995. Effects of feedback complexity on dynamic decision making. Organizational Behavior and Human Decision Processes 62 (2), 198–215.

Forrester, J. W. 1961. Industrial Dynamics. Cambridge, MA: MIT Press.

Gino, F., Pisano, G. 2008. Toward a theory of behavioral operations. Manufacturing and Service Operations Management 10 (4), 676–691.

Haberler, G. 1964. Prosperity and Depression. London: George Allen and Unwin.

Kahneman, D., Slovic, P., Tversky, A. 1982. Judgment under Uncertainty: Heuristics and Biases. Cambridge: Cambridge University Press.

Kampmann, C., Sterman, J. 2014. Do markets mitigate misperceptions of feedback? System Dynamics Review 30 (3), 123–160.

Lee, H., Padmanabhan, V., Whang, S. 1997. Information distortion in a supply chain: The bullwhip effect. Management Science 43 (4), 546–558.

Lo, A., Repin, D. 2002. The psychophysiology of real time financial risk processing. Journal of Cognitive Neuroscience 14 (3), 323–339.

McCarthy, J., Hocum, C., Albright, R., Rogers, J., Gallaher, E., Steensma, D., et al. 2014. Biomedical system dynamics to improve anemia control with darbepoetin alfa in long-term hemodialysis patients. Mayo Clinic Proceedings 89 (1), 87–94.

Morecroft, J. 1985. Rationality in the analysis of behavioral simulation models. Management Science 31 (7), 900–916.

Paich, M., Sterman, J. 1993. Boom, bust, and failures to learn in experimental markets. Management Science 39 (12), 1439–1458.

Rudolph, J., Repenning, N. 2002. Disaster dynamics: Understanding the role of stress and interruptions in organizational collapse. Administrative Science Quarterly 47, 1–30.

Senge, P. 1980. A System dynamics approach to investment-function specification and testing. Socio-Economic Planning Sciences 14 (6), 269–280.

Shah, A., Mullainathan, S., Shafir, E. 2012. Some consequences of having too little. Science 338, 682–685.

Simon, H. 1982. Models of Bounded Rationality. Cambridge, MA: MIT Press.

Sterman, J. 1989a. Modeling managerial behavior: Misperceptions of feedback in a dynamic decision making experiment. Management Science 35 (3), 321–339.

Sterman, J. 1989b. Misperceptions of feedback in dynamic decision making. Organizational Behavior and Human Decision Processes 43 (3), 301–335.

Sterman, J. 2000. Business Dynamics: Systems Thinking and Modeling for a Complex World. Boston: Irwin/McGraw-Hill.

Sterman, J. 2008. Risk communication on climate: mental models and mass balance. Science 322, 532–533.

Sterman, J. 2010. Does formal system dynamics training improve people's understanding of accumulation? System Dynamics Review 26 (4), 316–334.

Sterman, J., Booth Sweeney, L. 2007. Understanding public complacency about climate change: Adults' mental models of climate change violate conservation of matter. Climatic Change 80 (3–4), 213–238.

Sterman, J., Dogan, G. 2014. "I'm not hoarding, I'm just stocking up before the hoarders get here": Behavioral causes of phantom ordering in supply chains. Working paper, MIT Sloan School of Management, Cambridge, MA.

Tversky, K., Kahneman, D. 1974. Judgment under uncertainty: Heuristics and biases. Science 185, 1124–1131.

CHAPTER 12

Kicking the "Mean" Habit

Joint Prepositioning in Debiasing Pull-to-Center Effects

JAIME A. CASTAÑEDA AND PAULO GONÇALVES

OVERVIEW

This chapter addresses the newsvendor pull-to-center effect. We examine the effect within the context of preposition decisions (where supplies are installed prior to an emergency event) in preparation for emergencies and explore a debiasing strategy based on joint newsvendor order decisions or a newsvendor portfolio. First analyzed in Schweitzer and Cachon's (2000) seminal newsvendor experiment, the pull-to-center effect reflects biased inventory orders for newsvendor-type items. Specifically, when the costs associated with an item and its demand process call for small orders (a low-profit or high-cost item), people tend to order more than is optimum. In contrast, when the costs associated with an item and its demand process call for large orders (a high-profit or low-cost item), people tend to order less than is optimum.

Evidence of the pull-to-center effect in real-world managerial settings is limited. Beyond anecdotal examples of the effects in fashion skiwear and maps (Ren and Croson 2013), the bulk of the work on the pull-to-center effect has been experimental (e.g., Bolton and Katok 2008; Bostian, Holt, and Smith 2008; Kremer, Minner, and van Wassenhove 2010; Schweitzer and Cachon 2000). To a lesser extent, it also has been analytical (e.g., Schweitzer and Cachon 2000; Su 2008). Evidence of the effectiveness of debiasing strategies in real managerial settings also is lacking.

The pull-to-center effect has primarily been studied in traditional profit-based inventory systems (e.g., Bolton and Katok 2008; Bostian, Holt, and Smith 2008). Beyond analytical work applying the newsvendor framework to preposition decisions—where emergency supplies are placed in context prior to their need / ultimate deployment (e.g., Campbell and Jones 2011; Lodree and Taskin 2008), the pull-to-center effect has remained largely unexplored in less traditional, non-profit-based inventory systems. In addition, a common criticism of experimental work in operations management and in experimental economics generally has focused on the typical subject pool. Undergraduates' decisions do not arguably represent those of operations managers. Nonetheless, experimental newsvendor research reveals that both students (both undergraduate and graduate) and managers are prone to the pull-to-center effect (Bolton, Ockenfels, and Thonemann 2012).

Notwithstanding its experimental nature, this chapter contributes to the pull-to-center literature by exploring the bias in preposition decisions in preparation for emergencies, a rather unexplored newsvendor setting. We also explore the effect among humanitarian practitioners, broadening the scope of pull-to-center effect research. In addition, by exploiting the joint nature of preposition decisions and of inventory order decisions in general as a debiasing strategy, this chapter also aims to broaden the scope of pull-to-center effect debasing research.

THEORETICAL PERSPECTIVE

The pull-to-center effect refers to underordering in high-profit or low-cost newsvendor systems, and to overordering in low-profit or high-cost newsvendor systems. For example, Fisher and Raman (1996) examined the inventory decisions of a firm selling fashion skiwear and observed that managers consistently underordered and that profits would have increased by 60% had they ordered optimally. Operationally, the bias can be defined as the average tendency to order between the newsvendor normative solution and mean customer demand (Bostian, Holt, and Smith 2008). To date, there is no clarity regarding what actually drives pull-to-center effect behavior. Different modeling approaches have been proposed to explain it, such as ex post inventory error minimization (Schweitzer and Cachon 2000), overconfidence (Croson et al. 2011, cited in Ren and Croson 2013), random errors (Su 2008), and reference dependence (Ho, Lim, and Cui 2010), among others, making it difficult to develop effective debiasing strategies.

The pull-to-center effect has been replicated in several experiments since it was first analyzed by Schweitzer and Cachon (2000) (e.g., Bolton and Katok 2008; Bolton, Ockenfels, and Thonemann 2012; Bostian, Holt, and Smith 2008). Given the prevalence of the bias and its adverse economic performance consequences, subsequent experimental work has proposed several debiasing strategies. Under the idea that biases are consistent with the fact that "people are adaptive" and "have limited information processing capacity," some experimental work has explored modifications to experience and feedback "known to improve adaption or information processing" (Bolton and Katok 2008, 522).

Some research has emphasized the role played by extended experience, allowing decision-makers to make inventory order decisions for multiple rounds. For example, Bostian, Holt, and Smith (2008) provided participants with 30 decision rounds, whereas Bolton and Katok (2008), Bolton, Ockenfels, and Thonemann (2012), and Benzion and coauthors (Benzion et al. 2008; Benzion, Cohen, and Shavit 2010) provided 100 decision rounds. Others have sharpened payoff differentials to mitigate impediments to learning stemming from the flatness of the newsvendor expected profit function around the optimum (e.g., small expected payoff differences between orders around the optimum's neighborhood). For example, Bolton and Katok (2008) and Feng, Keller, and Zheng (2011) sharpened payoff differentials by reducing the number of ordering options, whereas Bostian, Holt, and Smith (2008) made the economic consequences of under- and overstocking more severe. Still others have provided decision-makers with improved outcome feedback. For example, Bolton and Katok (2008) presented individuals with payoffs of forgone options and reduced decision frequency, requiring them to maintain the same order for 10 rounds. Similarly, Bostian, Holt, and Smith (2008) reduced decision frequency to once every five rounds. In a further manipulation, outcome feedback itself also was limited to once every five rounds. Finally, Lurie and Swaminathan (2009) decoupled feedback frequency from decision frequency by fixing decision frequency and varying outcome feedback frequency to separate their effects.

Results from these approaches are inconclusive. Some studies show trends in the direction of optimal inventory orders when individuals are provided with extended experience (Benzion et al. 2008; Bolton and Katok 2008; Bostian, Holt, and Smith 2008), whereas others reveal no trends (Benzion, Cohen, and Shavit 2010; Bolton, Ockenfels, and Thonemann 2012). Similarly, some studies show no systematic positive effect associated with sharpening payoff differentials (Bolton and Katok 2008; Bostian, Holt, and Smith 2008), while the results from Feng, Keller, and Zheng's (2011) study suggest the opposite when extremeness aversion concerns are accounted for. Likewise, results associated with modification of the frequency of decision and outcome feedback are mixed. For example, Bolton and Katok (2008) found that reducing decision frequency is critical, while Bostian, Holt, and Smith (2008) and Lurie and Swaminathan (2009) found that it is not. Likewise, while Lurie and Swaminathan (2009) found that reducing outcome feedback frequency plays a role, results reported by Bostian, Holt, and Smith (2008) suggest that these reductions have no effect. Finally, Lurie and Swaminathan's (2009) study suggests that outcome feedback frequency may matter more than decision frequency. In the literature as a body, no conclusive patterns have emerged to date.

Other experimental work has explored modifications akin to established empirical patterns of human behavior. The idea behind such modifications is not to eliminate a behavioral effect, but rather to make it more salient in order to influence behavior in an intended direction. For example, building on reference dependence, Ho, Lim, and Cui (2010) added disutilities of under and overstocking to a multilocation newsvendor model. In addition, drawing on the idea that people experience psychological disutilities, they manipulated the relative salience of overstock disutilities in a low-profit system to drive orders downward. They also manipulated the relative salience of understock disutilities in a high-profit system to drive orders upward. Compared to nonsalient disutilities baselines, they observed an experimental reduction in the pull-to-center effect. Following a similar approach, Castañeda (2014) manipulated the relative salience of lost sales (under stock) by placing them in the backlog. He observed better performance in terms of both profits and product availability in a low-profit system compared to the traditional newsvendor model, and better performance in terms of product availability in a high-profit system.

Drawing on mental accounting, Chen, Kök, and Tong (2013) added prospective accounting—underweighting of either outgoing (negative) or incoming (positive) payments (utilities), whichever occurs first—to the newsvendor model. They posited that having an incoming payment before the demand realization (scheme C: receive a projected revenue or a revenue-based loan) drives orders downward, whereas having an outgoing payment before the demand realization (scheme O: standard wholesale price contract) drives orders upward. They observed that scheme O reduces the pull-to-center effect in high-profit systems, whereas scheme C reduces bias in low-profit schemes.

Experimental evidence suggests that effective debiasing strategies in newsvendor systems may increase the salience of behavioral effects. Strategies should be designed to account for inherently boundedly rational behavior and incorporate mechanisms that drive inventory orders either upward or downward according to managers' intentions.

CASE EXAMPLE

Relief agencies often preposition a range of emergency supplies (e.g., water, blankets, and vaccines) in preparation for emergencies. Maintaining adequate amounts of prepositioned emergency items can have a significant impact on the success of relief operations. Prepositioning emergency supplies is not an easy task. Relief agencies must make these preposition decisions without knowledge of beneficiary demand because demand materializes after an emergency strikes. Related evidence from several manufacturing and retail firms provides an illustration. For example, several firms experienced stock outs in 2004 because they were not prepared to meet the demand caused by the multiple hurricanes that struck the southeastern United States. In 2005, these firms again experienced stock outs because of the extreme demand surge caused by Hurricane Katrina. These experiences motivated firms to be more aggressive in their approach to stocking supplies the following year. However, because of an inactive hurricane season in 2006, numerous firms experienced excess inventory (Taskin and Lodree 2010).

In addition, a cost-effective use of funds is critical given pressure exerted by donors (Thomas 2003; Thomas and Kopczak 2005; van der Laan, de Brito, and Vergunst 2009). Prepositioning emergency supplies brings economic benefits to communities, builds resilience, and facilitates high-speed, low-cost delivery.

Prepositioning can increase effectiveness. A tarpaulin serves as a useful example—the price of a US$12 tarpaulin can rise to as much as US$90 once it becomes necessary to hire cargo planes, which means relief agencies spend a lot of money, and suppliers lose credibility (Roopanarine 2013).

By having uncertainty in beneficiary demand, and cost-effectiveness metrics, the newsvendor model can inform preposition decisions (e.g., Campbell and Jones 2011; Lodree and Taskin 2008). For example, assume q prepositioned items are purchased at unit cost w. After an emergency strikes, beneficiary demand D is realized. If q exceeds D, then there are $q - D$ excess items, which incur a unit handling cost s in addition to w already incurred. For simplicity, and following previous newsvendor experiments (e.g., Bolton and Katok 2008; Schweitzer and Cachon 2000), we assume $s = 0$. That is, unit overordering cost equals w.[1] If, instead, D exceeds q, then there are $D - q$ items in short supply, which must be expedited to meet remaining beneficiary demand at an additional unit cost x. That is, unit underordering cost equals x. Assuming stationarity of both beneficiary demand and preposition costs, the above structure resembles the well-known newsvendor problem. That is, the optimal preposition quantity relates the cumulative distribution function of beneficiary demand to over- and underordering costs in the well-known critical fractile. The challenge is thus to find a balance or an adequate trade-off between beneficiary demand coverage and preposition costs.

By the same token, humanitarian practitioners making preposition decisions also may be prone to the pull-to-center effect. On the one hand, underordering behavior in a low-cost preposition system would lead to stock outs. These could strongly impact the success of a relief operation because "all" necessary emergency supplies to alleviate suffering and prevent the loss of human life would be unavailable. In addition, this would ramp up costs because short-supply emergency supplies would need to be expedited at additional cost. In contrast, overordering behavior in a high-cost preposition system would lead to excess inventory. Although all necessary emergency supplies are available, this could also ramp costs up because of handling costs associated with the excess inventory.

To influence the pull-to-center effect in preposition decisions in intended directions, we stress the importance of emergency supplies in order to make them more salient relative to other emergency supplies. This is done by taking advantage of two widely observable trends. First, preposition decisions and inventory order decisions in general have a joint nature. Managers usually place inventory orders for several products at the same time. That is, they manage a portfolio of products (Abdel-Malek and Montanari 2005b). Second, emergency supplies differ in their perceived importance for preventing loss of life. For example, safe drinking water is arguably more important than a blanket (e.g., Global WASH Cluster 2009).

1. Perishability is not a necessary condition to apply the newsvendor framework. What is required is that excess items do not carry over to future periods or, in this case, emergencies. For example, a relief agency operating in a particular location could ship any unused supplies to other locations or back to a main hub.

In linking two emergency supplies that differ in their perceived importance we expect the *more* important item to be more salient to humanitarian practitioners than the less important item. This should induce larger orders for the more important item, relative to a separate preposition decision associated with the same item. For a high-cost, high-importance item, this would imply a strengthening of the pull-to-center effect. However, more important items would be available. For a low-cost, low-importance item, this would imply a weakening of the pull-to-center effect. Therefore, more important items would be available.

This approach is consistent with the expressed view that debiasing strategies should not focus on eliminating a behavioral effect. Rather, strategies should emphasize the salience of behavioral effects to influence decision-making in intended directions. By making an important emergency item more salient, we seek either to strengthen or to weaken the pull-to-center to increase the availability of more critical emergency supplies.

LEARNING ACTIVITY

The activity consists of two games. In the first game, humanitarian practitioners[2] make preposition decisions for low- and high-importance emergency items separately. In the second game, humanitarian practitioners make preposition decisions for low- and high-importance items jointly. Importance is operationalized through the use of the characterizing phrases *critical-to-life* and *nice-to-have*. These phrases refer to high-importance and low-importance emergency supplies in a humanitarian context, respectively (Gonçalves and Castañeda 2013). Below, we provide details of both games.

Separate Decisions Game

Humanitarian practitioners are divided into two groups: those who play an "inconsistent" cost-importance game and those who play a "consistent" cost-importance game. In both games there are high- and low-cost items. For the high-cost item, the purchasing or preposition cost is 9 francs and the additional expediting cost is 3 francs. For the low-cost item, the purchasing or preposition cost is 1 franc and the additional expediting cost is 3 francs. Demand for all types of items follows a uniform distribution $D \sim U[1, 100]$. Different noise seeds are used for "critical-to-life" and "nice-to-have" items to control similar preposition patterns due to demand-chasing effects (Bolton and Katok 2008; Schweitzer and Cachon 2000). Thus, the mean beneficiary demand is 50 items and the optimal preposition quantities in the high- and low-cost systems are 25 and 75 items, respectively.

2. The activity is intended originally for humanitarian practitioners. However, the activity could be played by anyone.

"Inconsistent" Cost-Importance Game

In this game, humanitarian practitioners individually play a preposition game for a high-cost, critical-to-life item for 30 rounds and an additional preposition game for a low-cost, nice-to-have item for 30 rounds. From the newsvendor structure, humanitarian practitioners should order small amounts of the critical-to-life item (25 items in optimality) and large amounts of the nice-to-have item (75 items in optimality) regardless of their importance. However, given the pervasiveness of the pull-to-center effect, we expect preposition decisions to exhibit the bias. Prepositioning should fall between 25 and 50 items, on average, for the critical-to-life item and between 50 and 75 items on average for the nice-to-have item.

The order of the preposition tasks is randomized to control order-of-presentation effects. http://forio.com/simulate/castanej/emergency2 presents first the high-cost, critical to-life preposition task and then the low-cost, nice-to-have task, whereas http://forio.com/simulate/castanej/emergency2a presents first the low-cost, nice-to-have preposition task and then the high-cost, critical-to-life task. These links are randomly assigned to participants.

"Consistent" Cost-Importance Game

In this game, humanitarian practitioners individually play a preposition game for a low-cost, critical-to-life item for 30 rounds and an additional preposition game for a high-cost, nice-to-have item for 30 rounds. Again, from the newsvendor structure, humanitarian practitioners should order large amounts of the critical-to-life item (75 items in optimality) and small amounts of the nice-to-have item (25 items in optimality) regardless of their importance. However, we expect preposition decisions to exhibit the bias—between 50 and 75 items on average for the critical-to-life item and between 25 and 50 items on average for the nice-to-have item.

The order of the preposition tasks is randomized to control order-of-presentation effects. http://forio.com/simulate/castanej/emergency1 presents first the low-cost, critical-to-life preposition task and then the high-cost, nice-to-have task, whereas http://forio.com/simulate/castanej/emergency1a presents first the high-cost, nice-to-have preposition task and then the low-cost, critical-to-life task. These links also are randomly assigned to participants.

Joint Decisions Game

Here the group that played the "inconsistent" cost-importance game in the separate decisions part again plays an "inconsistent" cost-importance game. The group that played the "consistent" cost-importance game in the separate decisions part again plays a "consistent" cost-importance game. Demand for all types of items follows a uniform distribution $D \sim U[1, 100]$ with different noise seeds for critical-to-life and nice-to-have items. In addition, these noise seeds are different from those used in the separate decisions games to control for similar preposition patterns between separate and joint decisions due to demand-chasing effects. Ideally, the joint decisions game should be played a day or two following the separate decision games to control learning effects. Notice that, by design, the joint decisions game is always played after the separate decisions game. This is done to avoid priming participants with a reference that could affect separate preposition decisions and thus allows us to run a clean test of the joint decisions debiasing strategy.

"Inconsistent" Cost-Importance Game

In this game, humanitarian practitioners individually play a joint preposition game for a high-cost, critical-to-life item and a low-cost, nice-to-have item for 30 rounds. Participants make 60 preposition decisions in 30 rounds.

Participants should order small amounts of the critical-to-life item (25 items in optimality) and large amounts of the nice-to-have item (75 items in optimality). However, by providing a low-importance item that arguably serves as a reference to compare decisions, we expect the high-importance item to be more salient, potentially leading to larger prepositioned quantities for the high-importance item if compared to the separate preposition decisions. Therefore, we expect the pull-to-center effect to exhibit a strengthening for the critical-to-life item. The link for the game is as follows: http://forio.com/simulate/castanej/emergency4.

"Consistent" Cost-Importance Game

In this game, humanitarian practitioners individually play a joint preposition game for a low-cost, critical-to-life item and a high-cost, nice-to-have item for 30 rounds, making 60 preposition decisions in 30 rounds.

Participants should order large amounts of the critical-to-life item (75 items in optimality) and small amounts of the nice-to-have item (25 items in optimality). In addition, by providing a low-importance item that arguably serves as a reference to compare decisions, we expect the high-importance item to be more salient, potentially leading to larger prepositioned quantities for the high-importance item if compared to the separate preposition decisions. Therefore, we expect the pull-to-center effect to exhibit a weakening for the critical-to-life item. The link for the game is as follows: http://forio.com/simulate/castanej/emergency3.

Game's Setup

An outline of the game's setup is shown in figure 12.1.

Note-taking tables for players to record their thoughts regarding factors influencing their decision-making are presented in table 12.1. The note-taking table for the **Separate decisions game** is filled in twice, one for each decision task (individuals are given two tables).

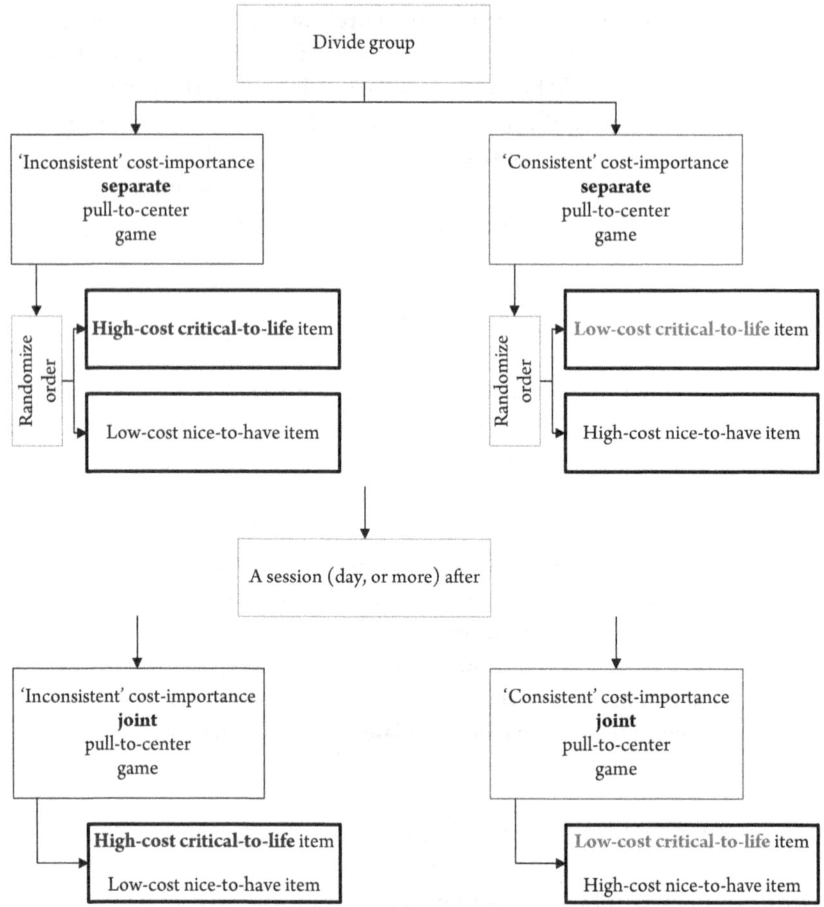

Figure 12.1 Game's Setup

The wording preceding the note-taking table is as follows:

Please fill the following table as you make decisions. If you use the same rationale to arrive at your decisions in all rounds, please describe it once only. However, if you change the rationale during the course of the game, the table should reflect this. Please also mention whether you think decisions are successful and why.

Table 12.1. Note-Taking Table, Separate Decisions Game

Rd	Decision	Rationale behind decision	Was the decision successful? Why?
1			
2			
3			
...	...	...	...
30			

Table 12.2. NOTE-TAKING TABLE, JOINT DECISIONS GAME

Rd	Decision critical-to-life	Decision nice-to-have	Rationale behind decisions	Were the decisions successful? Why?
1				
2				
3				
...	...	...	...	...
30				

The wording preceding the note-taking table for the **Joint Decisions Game** remains the same. However, the table changes (table 12.2).

DISCUSSION

The separate preposition tasks are structurally equivalent to the well-known newsvendor problem. Thus, it is expected that participants playing these games will exhibit the pervasive pull-to-center effect. Newsvendor research also has shown an asymmetry in the pull-to-center effect. Specifically, the bias tends to be stronger in low-profit systems (e.g., Bolton and Katok 2008; Bostian, Holt, and Smith 2008; Schweitzer and Cachon 2000). Hence, it is possible to expect a stronger pull-to-center effect for high-cost items, regardless of whether they are of high or low importance. Preliminary evidence suggests that participants exhibit the pull-to-center effect, while no clear asymmetries have been observed (Gonçalves and Castañeda 2013).

The joint preposition game portrays a newsvendor portfolio that corresponds to newsstand problems with no resource constraints, that is, they reduce to solve a newsvendor problem for each item. However, the emphasis on items' importance within the context of relief operations adds a little-explored issue within newsvendor order decision-making. In providing a low-importance item that arguably serves as a reference to compare both preposition decisions, we expect that high-importance items will be more salient, leading to larger prepositioned quantities relative to separate decisions. For the high-cost, high-importance item, this would represent a strengthening of the pull-to-center effect. For the low-cost, high-importance item, this would represent a weakening of the bias. Preliminary evidence suggests this pattern adheres, and to a greater extent for the high-cost, high-importance item (Gonçalves and Castañeda 2013).

It also may be important to consider the cost issue in the preposition task. Newsvendor experiments have traditionally focused on profit-based systems. In contrast, the preposition task in the learning activity does not have any cost metric related to revenue, making the system cost-based. The learning activity may lead to results with dynamics not observed in previous revenue-focused problems. In addition, the introduction of an additional goal—to prevent loss of life—may create conflict with cost minimization or profit-maximization goals.

Special attention should be paid when comparing the results of this learning activity to traditional behavioral newsvendor research. The goal of the activity is to highlight the role of items' perceived importance in joint newsvendor order decisions. What ultimately is most relevant is the comparison between separate and joint order decisions in the learning activity.

The dynamics in preposition patterns stemming from the learning activity may offer framing recommendations. Within the context of relief operations, a "consistent" cost-importance joint decision frame for cheap critical items may be implemented, combining decisions for critical items with noncritical items. Both decisions would be joined to reduce the pull-to-center effect for critical items, increasing not only decisions' cost-effectiveness but also items' availability during emergencies. An "inconsistent" cost-importance joint decision frame for expensive critical items may be implemented as well. Both decisions would be joined to increase the pull-to-center effect for critical items. Although cost-effectiveness would decrease, items' availability during emergencies would increase.

In industrial settings, a "consistent" cost-importance joint decision frame can be implemented any time a high-profit product is perceived as more important than a low-profit product. Both decisions would be joined to increase profits achieved on the high-profit product. In addition, an "inconsistent" cost-importance joint decision frame may be implemented when a strategic item is costly but critical (e.g., low-profit parts with long replenishment delays) in order to increase availability and customer service satisfaction. Joining newsvendor order decisions also is presumably easier and less costly to implement than strategies to align multiple partners and coordinate their decisions (e.g., buyer-supplier alignment and relief operation coordination across multiple organizations).

The proposed joint newsvendor framework has seen little attention in the operations management literature. The framework has been addressed mostly from an analytical perspective in modeling studies of the Newsstand problem (with resource constraints). Hence, most of the work addresses solution methodologies (e.g., Abdel-Malek and Montanari 2005a; Erlebacher 2000; Lau and Lau 1996). However, these modeling studies are in general parsimonious and do not incorporate behavioral factors such as individuals' perceptions about items' importance; an exception is the modeling of risk preferences in the newsstand problem (Zhou et al. 2008). Importantly, these models have not been tested behaviorally.

Consequently, little is known about how individuals actually make decisions in these more realistic joint newsvendor frameworks, either with or without resource constraints. An exception is the study of reference dependence effects on ordered quantities within a portfolio of newsvendor products, which exploits cost or profitability condition comparisons to influence ordered quantities (Tong and Song 2011). Although preliminary evidence suggest items' perceived importance influences joint inventory order decisions (Gonçalves and Castañeda 2013), more systematic evidence is needed to assess the effects of items' perceived importance on these decisions, and the behavioral factors driving such behavior. For example, arguments developed building on attribution theory, cognitive dissonance, and/or reference dependence could provide insight into the likely effects of items' perceived importance on joint inventory order decisions. Further research should explore what behavioral factors are likely to influence order behavior in joint newsvendor frameworks, analyzing the extent that individuals are influenced by such factors, improving existing analytical models (Katok 2010).

References

Abdel-Malek, L. L., Montanari, R. 2005a. An analysis of the multi-product newsboy problem with a budget constraint. International Journal of Production Economics 97 (3), 296–307.

Abdel-Malek, L. L., Montanari, R. 2005b. On the multi-product newsboy problem with two constraints. Computers and Operations Research 32 (8), 2095–2116.

Benzion, U., Cohen, Y., Peled, R., Shavit, T. 2008. Decision-making and the newsvendor problem: An experimental study. Journal of the Operational Research Society 59 (9), 1281–1287.

Benzion, U., Cohen, Y., Shavit, T. 2010. The newsvendor problem with unknown distribution. Journal of the Operational Research Society 61 (6), 1022–1031.

Bolton, G. E., Katok, E. 2008. Learning by doing in the newsvendor problem: A laboratory investigation of the role of experience and feedback. Manufacturing and Service Operations Management 10 (3), 519–538.

Bolton, G. E., Ockenfels, A., Thonemann, U. W. 2012. Managers and students as newsvendors. Management Science 58 (12), 2225–2233.

Bostian, A. A., Holt, C. A., Smith, A. M. 2008. Newsvendor "pull-to-center" effect: Adaptive learning in a laboratory experiment. Manufacturing and Service Operations Management 10 (4), 590–608.

Campbell, A. M., Jones, P. C. 2011. Prepositioning supplies in preparation for disasters. European Journal of Operational Research 209 (2), 156–165.

Castañeda, J. A. 2014. Inventory order decisions in a single echelon: The effect of backorders. Working paper, Center for Transportation and Logistics, MIT, Cambridge, MA.

Chen, L., Kök, A. G., Tong, J. D. 2013. The effect of payment schemes on inventory decisions: The role of mental accounting. Management Science 59 (2), 436–451.

Croson, R., Croson, D., Ren, Y. 2011. The overconfident newsvendor. Working paper, University of Texas at Dallas, Richardson, TX.

Erlebacher, S. J. 2000. Optimal and heuristic solutions for the multi-item newsvendor problem with a single capacity constraint. Production and Operations Management 9 (3), 303–318.

Feng, T., Keller, L. R., Zheng, X. 2011. Decision making in the newsvendor problem: A cross-national laboratory study. Omega 39 (1), 41–50.

Fisher, M., Raman, A. 1996. Reducing the cost of demand uncertainty through accurate response to early sales. Operations Research 44 (1), 87–99.

Global WASH Cluster. 2009. The Human Right to Water and Sanitation in Emergency Situations: The Legal Framework and a Guide to Advocacy. New York, NY: Global WASH Cluster.

Gonçalves, P., Castañeda, J. A. 2013. Impact of joint decisions and cognitive dissonance on prepositioning (newsvendor) decisions. Working Paper 5021-5013, Sloan School of Management, MIT, Cambridge, MA.

Ho, T.-H., Lim, N., Cui, T.-H. 2010. Reference dependence in multilocation newsvendor models: A structural analysis. Management Science 56 (11), 1891–1910.

Katok, E. 2010. Using laboratory experiments to build better operations management models. Foundations and Trends in Technology, Information and Operations Management 5 (1), 1–84.

Kremer, M., Minner, S., van Wassenhove, L. N. 2010. Do random errors explain newsvendor behavior? Manufacturing and Service Operations Management 12 (4), 673–681.

Lau, H.-S., Lau, A. H.-L. 1996. The newsstand problem: A capacitated multiple-product single-period inventory problem. European Journal of Operational Research 94 (1), 29–42.

Lodree Jr., E. J., Taskin, S. 2008. An insurance risk management framework for disaster relief and supply chain disruption inventory planning. Journal of the Operational Research Society 59 (5), 674–684.

Lurie, N. H., Swaminathan, J. M. 2009. Is timely information always better? The effect of feedback frequency on decision making. Organizational Behavior and Human Decision Processes 108 (2), 315–329.

Ren, Y., Croson, R. 2013. Overconfidence in newsvendor orders: An experimental study. Management Science 59 (11), 2502–2517.

Roopanarine, L. 2013. How pre-positioning can make emergency relief more effective. The Guardian, January 17. http://www.theguardian.com.

Schweitzer, M. E., Cachon, G. P. 2000. Decision bias in the newsvendor problem with a known demand distribution: Experimental evidence. Management Science 46 (3), 404–420.

Su, X. 2008. Bounded rationality in newsvendor models. Manufacturing and Service Operations Management 10 (4), 566–589.

Taskin, S., Lodree, E. J., Jr. 2010. Inventory decisions for emergency supplies based on hurricane count predictions. International Journal of Production Economics 126 (1), 66–75.

Thomas, A. S. 2003. Humanitarian logistics: Enabling disaster response. White paper, Fritz Institute, San Francisco, CA.

Thomas, A. S., Kopczak, L. R. 2005. From logistics to supply chain management: The path forward in the humanitarian sector. White paper, Fritz Institute, San Francisco, CA.

Tong, J., Song, J.-S. 2011. Reference prices and transaction utility in inventory decisions. Working paper, Fuqua School of Business, Duke University, Durham, NC.

van der Laan, E. A., de Brito, M. P., Vergunst, D. A. 2009. Performance measurement in humanitarian supply chains. International Journal of Risk Assessment and Management 13 (1), 22–45.

Zhou, Y.-J., Chen, X.-H., Wang, Z.-R. 2008. Optimal ordering quantities for multi-products with stochastic demand: Return-CVaR model. International Journal of Production Economics 112 (2), 782–795.

CHAPTER 13

Sharing the Risk

Understanding Risk-Sharing Contracts from the Supplier's Perspective

KAREN DONOHUE AND YINGHAO ZHANG

OVERVIEW

A critical decision for suppliers engaged in business-to-business (B2B) interactions is what contract terms to offer buyers. The most common, hands-off, approach is to simply list products at a set wholesale price. From suppliers' perspective, this is a simple contract to administer, requiring only setting one contract parameter (the wholesale price) and no monitoring of buyers' behavior following the purchase. However, research on the performance of different supplier contracts reveals that suppliers may be leaving money on the table offering such contracts. This is particularly true if suppliers' customers face substantial demand uncertainty when placing orders. It has been well documented (Cachon 2003) that in such situations wholesale price contracts lead buyers to order less than optimal amounts from a channel perspective. As a consequence, the combined profit of buyers and suppliers is lower than it would be if retailers ordered more. This is one of the early lessons in most teaching modules on supply chain contracting and serves as a motivator for why "risk sharing" contracts may be a useful alternative to wholesale price contracts.

Risk-sharing contracts are contracts that allow suppliers to absorb some of the cost of demand uncertainty buyers face. Examples include buyback, revenue sharing, quantity-flexibility, option contracts, and sales rebates. Table 13.1 provides a brief description of these contracts and industries that tend to use them. A common characteristic of risk-sharing contracts is that the monies suppliers are

Table 13.1. Types of Risk-Sharing Contracts

Contract type	Contract feature	Industry examples
Buyback	Supplier buys back excess inventory	Book, CD, apparel, high tech, pharmaceutical
Revenue sharing	Supplier shares revenue for each item the buyer sells	Video rental, movie exhibition, aircraft MRO
Quantity Flexibility	Supplier allows the buyer to adjust order quantity once demand is known	Computer, European automotive
Option contract	Supplier gives buyer option to purchase additional items later	High tech, textile, plastic
Sales rebate	Supplier gives buyer rebates for units sold above a threshold	Hardware, software, automotive

paid are tied to the final demand buyers experience with their own customers, so suppliers share the risk associated with buyers' excess inventory and/or lost sales. These contracts are more complex to administer (compared with wholesale price contracts), requiring suppliers to monitor buyers' demand levels and how these impact sales and inventory. However, these contracts offer the potential benefit of higher expected profit for suppliers and the channel as a whole.

The purpose of this classroom activity is to give students experience with risk-sharing contracts and insight into the potential challenges associated with their implementation. The activity also helps students appreciate differences in risk-sharing contracts and why some are more appropriate in specific settings. The activity and accompanying lecture materials build from recent behavioral research, particularly the experimental study described in Zhang, Donohue, and Cui (2014). Specific questions explored throughout the activity include the following:

1. Are all risk-sharing contracts equivalent to suppliers?
2. How does the type of product (e.g., whether it has a high or low margin) influence the relative benefit of these contracts?
3. What challenges and trade-offs arise in pricing risk-sharing contracts?
4. Which types of risk-sharing contracts provide a higher profit level after accounting for behavioral factors that potentially influence pricing decisions?

For simplicity, the activity focuses on comparing two representative risk-sharing contracts: buyback and revenue sharing. These two contracts are traditionally grouped together and viewed as equivalent in terms of suppliers' potential profits. In this activity, students will experience that this is not always true. When students are asked to choose between the two contracts and to price them, their answers reveal that the contracts perform differently when profit margins are high versus low. One of the reasons for this discrepancy is a common behavioral phenomenon known as loss aversion (Kahneman and Tversky 1979), as well as a newer concept known as prospective accounting (Prelec and Loewenstein 1998). The activity offers an opportunity to introduce these behavioral concepts and discuss why their influence should be considered when designing supply contracts.

This activity was designed for a senior undergraduate Supply Chain Strategy capstone course, but would also be appropriate for an undergraduate or MBA elective focused on supply chain management or strategic sourcing. We provide guidance for adapting the activity in larger classes of 60 or more students, as well as smaller classes of roughly 30 students. The activity consists of two exercises where students adopt the role of suppliers. In the first exercise, suppliers are asked to choose between offering a buyback or revenue-sharing contract. In the second exercise, suppliers are asked to set contract parameters for one of these contracts. After each exercise, students discuss their answers and debrief on how the patterns that emerge map to more realistic situations. The students come away from the activity with a deeper understanding of how risk-sharing contracts work, what trade-offs exist between different types of contracts, and how behavioral factors—such as loss aversion and prospective accounting—influence contract performance.

THEORETICAL PERSPECTIVE

The design and performance of risk-sharing contracts has been an active area of research within supply chain management for the past 15 years. Cachon (2003) provides an excellent introduction to prior literature on risk sharing and other types of supplier contracts. One of the primary benefits of risk-sharing contracts is that they encourage more risk taking so both suppliers and buyers can be better off from an expected profit perspective. Some risk-sharing contracts also have been shown to be "channel optimal," maximizing the combined profits of suppliers and buyers.

Much of the literature on risk-sharing contracts has focused on single-period settings characteristic of seasonal or short life cycle products, such fashion apparel, toys, and some consumer electronics. This single-period setting also is typical of perishable products, such as bakery goods or produce. In these settings, buyers must decide on a single order quantity to cover demand for the products' entire life cycle. This makes the order quantity decision risky for buyers since it must be placed while the demand forecast is highly uncertain. Our activity adopts a single-period setting within the context of a bakery that manufactures cheesecakes ordered by a retailer each week and sold from inventory to retail customers.

We focus on buyback and revenue-sharing contracts because these risk-sharing contracts are both commonly used in industry and have been shown to be equivalent in terms of the maximum profit each can achieve for suppliers and buyers. Revenue-sharing contracts have been utilized most notably within the video-rental industry. Here suppliers set a low initial wholesale price but receive a split in any revenue buyers earn from customers. From suppliers' perspective, the initial wholesale price may not cover manufacturing costs, and so they maintain a negative cash flow until buyers sell a sufficient number of items.

Buyback contracts have been adopted by a wider range of industries, including publishing, high tech, and fashion apparel. Here, buyers also initially pay suppliers a wholesale price for each item. However, rather than providing suppliers with a second payment stream, buyers now receive payments from their suppliers for items remaining at the end of the season. This payment takes the form of a unit buyback price for each unsold item. Compared with revenue-sharing contracts, buyback contracts offer suppliers an initial, short-lived flush of cash. Suppliers must be ready to give some of this money back to buyers at the end of the season.

Table 13.2 summarizes the financial transactions before (i.e., at order) and after market demand is realized for the two contracts using mathematical notation. The contract parameters for buyback include the unit wholesale price w_b and the unit buyback price b for each unsold item, while the parameters for revenue sharing include the unit wholesale price w_r and the revenue share r received from buyers for each item sold. Also included is notation for the total number of units purchased by buyers, Q, and final customer demand realized during the selling season, D.

Cachon and Lariviere (2005) established that buyback and revenue-sharing contracts are equivalent in terms of earnings achieved by each channel member for any given demand realization D, when $r = b$ and $w_r = w_b - b$.[1] This implies that suppliers should be indifferent to the choice of buyback versus revenue-sharing contract if maximization of expected profit is the objective. However, these contracts do exhibit differences in terms of how their cash flows are framed. Table 13.2 highlights how the timing and magnitude of losses and gains differ, even though their sum (i.e., total profit) is the same when the contract parameters are set optimally. Note here that loss is defined relative to the reference point of current wealth, which is typical in behavioral economics.

Buyback contracts start with a certain gain followed by an uncertain loss that occurs following the realization of the market demand. In contrast, revenue sharing begins with a sure loss followed by an uncertain gain. Research in both behavioral economics and psychology indicates that human preferences pertaining to financial transactions are sensitive to payment framing (Tversky and Kahneman 1981).

Table 13.2. FINANCIAL TRANSACTIONS FOR THE TWO CONTRACTS

	At order	After demand
Buyback	$(w_b - c)\, q$ Gain	$-b \max(q - D, 0)$ Loss
Revenue sharing	$(w_r - c)\, q$ Loss	$r \min(q, D)$ Gain

NOTE: $w_r < c$.

1. This claim can be easily verified by substituting $r = b$ and $w_r = w_b - b$ into the supplier's profit function. For instance, the supplier's profit under revenue sharing contract is $\pi_{RS} = (w_r - c)\, Q + r \min(q, D) = (w_b - c)\, Q - b\, (Q - \min(Q, D)) = (w_b - c)\, Q - b \max(Q - D, 0)$, which is equivalent to the supplier's profit under the buyback contract.

Two behavioral regularities that commonly emerge are that people exhibit *loss aversion* and *prospective accounting.* Loss aversion refers to the phenomena where people weigh the cost of a perceived unit loss more heavily than the benefit of a unit gain (Kahneman and Tversky 1979). Prospective accounting theory predicts that the "pain of paying" is buffered by thoughts of future gains, and that the benefit of a current gain is dampened by thoughts of future repayments (Prelec and Loewenstein 1998), leading decision-makers to discount prior transactions.

In a recent experimental study, Zhang, Donohue, and Cui (2014) examined whether and how behavioral tendencies influence suppliers' contract decisions. They found that individual characteristics, such as an individual's level of loss aversion and prospective accounting, influence the performance of buyback and revenue-sharing contracts in different ways. This leads to the contracts providing different profit outcomes once they are parameterized by human decision-makers. Specifically, human suppliers appear to achieve higher profit levels under revenue-sharing contracts, particularly for high profit margin products (i.e., products where is it optimal for the buyer to maintain a relatively high service level to avoid lost sales). They also find that when contract parameters are set optimally (in terms of maximizing expected profit), suppliers prefer revenue sharing for high profit margin products but shift their preference to buyback for low profit margin products.

The classroom activity is designed to naturally uncover some of these behavioral factors as students compare and price these contracts. The exercises feature a range of product types, with different profit margins. This allows students to see how their preferences and pricing behaviors compare with predictions offered by prior behavioral research. Students also learn how their pricing strategies differ from profit-maximizing recommendations offered by normative research.

CASE EXAMPLE

Before going into the specifics of the two exercises in the next section, here we provide an overview of the case context common to both exercises. AmazinCake is a family-owned cake factory located in Salisbury, Maryland. The factory produces several kinds of cakes, including tortes, cupcakes, soufflés, cheesecakes, and specialty wedding and birthday cakes. AmazinCake has been in business for 25 years and is well known for its high-quality products. The manager of the cheesecake line recently retired and has hired you to take over his position.

Cheesecakes are sold to consumer through a local retail store called M-Mart. M-Mart places orders for cheesecakes each Friday for next Monday delivery. The factory then makes cheesecakes during the weekend, and delivers them to the store. Since the cheesecake is freshly baked and preservative-free, it has only a one-week shelf life. At the end of the week, any unsold cakes are thrown away and have no salvage value.

AmazinCake has been using a simple wholesale price contract with M-Mart. That is, M-Mart pays AmazinCake a fixed unit wholesale price for each cheesecake when placing its Friday order. As the manager, you have heard about the benefits of risk-sharing contracts and would like to explore using such a contact in place of the current wholesale price contract. After some research you have decided to adopt either a buyback or revenue-sharing contract, but are still not sure which one would work better for your business.

The market conditions experienced by your customer, M-Mart, are fairly stable across the year. M-Mark charges its customers $20 per unit for cheesecake, and its average demand is 50 units per week with a range of 1 to 100 units. More precisely, weekly customer demand is equally likely to be any integer from 1 to 100 (i.e., there is a 1/100 chance that D will be any one of the integers from 1 to 100).

To help you better understand the trade-offs between these options, you will take part in two exercises. In the first exercise, you will be shown a revenue-sharing and a buyback contract option (with preset contract terms) and asked which option you prefer. In the second exercise, you will be asked to set contract terms for a given contract. You will have a chance to discuss your experience after each exercise and compare your answers with other participants who made similar decisions under different product contexts.

LEARNING ACTIVITIES

In exercise 1, students are introduced to the dynamics of buyback and revenue-sharing contracts and given the opportunity to choose which they prefer for a specific product type. This information is conveyed in a survey format. The exercise allows students to become familiar with the terms involved in each contract (e.g., wholesale price, buyback price, revenue-sharing level) and see how their contract preferences differ from those of their classmates. This leads to the discovery that profit margin may contribute to different perceptions of the benefits of each contract. It also leads to the discovery that behavioral factors may affect preferences. The survey portion of the exercise takes about 10 minutes, followed by 20 minutes for discussion.

In exercise 2, students learn what challenges and trade-offs supply managers face when pricing a risk-sharing contract. This exercise requires a computer for each student and is executed using Microsoft Excel. To keep the exercise manageable, students are asked to set only the wholesale price for either a buyback or revenue-sharing contract. Other contract parameters are optimized automatically based on students' input wholesale price. This exercise takes about 30 minutes, followed by another 20 minutes for discussion. We recommend running both exercises in the same class session and allowing about 90 minutes in total.

Exercise 1: Students are first presented with background information about the AmazinCake case, as outlined in the previous section. They are then handed a paper survey describing two contracts and asked to pick which they prefer. The contract terms for the contracts are set so their expected profit is identical. This control on expected profits allows students to focus on the framing differences between the contracts. The survey is implemented in two formats, with half of the students receiving format A, and other half format B. Both formats are included in appendix A.

The two versions of the survey differ in their description of profit margin. In survey A, the cheesecake costs \$1 to produce and is sold at \$20. This is the high profit margin case. Students familiar with the newsvendor model can be informed that this implies an overage cost of c_o = \$1 and an underage cost of c_u = \$20 – \$1 = \$19. This further implies that if retailers wish to maximize local profit, they should set the order quantity so that the probability of not stocking out is $c_u/(c_u + c_o)$ = \$19/\$20 = .95. In this case, it is optimal to order 95 cheesecakes. If students are not familiar with the newsvendor model, they can be told that the retailer sets order quantity to maximize expected profit and that this order quantity is 95 cheesecakes.

In survey B the unit production cost is set at \$17, resulting in overage and underage costs of c_o = \$17 and c_u = \$20 – \$17 = \$3. This is the low profit margin case. If retailers wish to maximize expected profit in this case, order quantity should be set so that the probability of not stocking out is $c_u/(c_u + c_o)$ = \$3/(\$3 + \$17) = .15. This implies that 15 cheesecakes should be ordered. Again, if students are not familiar with the newsvendor model, they can simply be informed that the retailer sets order quantity to maximize expected profit, and that in this low margin case the associated order quantity supporting this objective is 15 cheesecakes.

Once students have completed the survey, the instructor can ask one member from each group to tally the results, including the percentage of the group that preferred each contract type. The instructor can then list these statistics on the board by group and ask the students if they see any patterns. They should see that for survey A, a higher percentage indicated revenue sharing as their preference, while for survey B a higher percentage chose buyback.

The instructor can then ask the students what they think is driving this pattern. It may help here to pick a few students from each group who chose the predicted contract (i.e., revenue sharing chosen in group A and buyback chosen in group B) and ask them why they had this preference. The instructor can list the various reasons given for the preferences for buyback or revenue sharing across the two groups. This can lead to the class generating some theories about what changes take place between high- and low-profit products. The issue of loss aversion (Kahneman and Tversky 1979) should naturally arise in this discussion, although students are unlikely to refer to this behavioral phenomenon directly. The issue of whether the loss occurs first or second may also be mentioned, suggesting that prospective accounting (Prelec and Loewenstein 1998) may contribute to these preferences. If these ideas are brought up by students, the instructor can use this opening to give a brief lecture on these two behavioral factors and how they reinforce the tendency to prefer revenue sharing for high-margin products and buyback for low-margin products.

If these ideas are not brought up directly, the instructor may need to probe to find out what is driving students' preferences. For example, asking students what the cash flows look like for each contract under the two profit margin conditions and then writing these cash flows on the board, separated by period (before and after demand is known). This should reveal that the magnitude of loss changes across the two contracts, even though the sum of the loss and gain is the same. In the high profit margin condition (survey A), loss is lower under the revenue-sharing contract, while in the low profit margin condition (survey B), loss is lower under the buyback contract. Theory predicts that people who are loss averse should prefer the contract that exhibits the lower loss level. Once these behavioral factors are pointed out, the instructor should transition to exercise 2.

Exercise 2: In this second exercise, students have an opportunity to price the contracts. Students assigned survey A in exercise 1 will continue to work with the high profit margin context and students assigned survey B will likewise continue to work with the low profit margin context. However, the production cost is now set to $5 for the high profit margin group and $13 for the low profit margin group. If the class size is larger than 40 students, each group can be further divided into two subgroups (groups A1 and A2; B1 and B2) as shown in table 13.3. Here subgroups A1 and B1 are asked to price the buyback contract, while groups A2 and B2 are asked to price the revenue-sharing contract. For smaller classes, students in each group A or B can price both buyback and revenue-sharing contracts. The number of students for each type of contract should be at least 10 to allow for a reasonable comparison. An Excel file is provided to students to help compute values. Students also need to manually record these values on the worksheet provided in appendix B.

Once students are assigned to groups, they can begin their work. The students continue to take the role of the cheesecake manager for AmazinCake, but now set the contract parameters. The store, M-Mart, will decide how many units of cheesecake to order, given the terms being offered, and then sell cheesecakes to the market. In this exercise, the store is automated. In other words, the store has been preprogrammed to place orders to maximize its own expected profit subject to the terms being offered. The students' task is to set the contract terms to maximize their total profit.

To simplify the task, students are only asked to set the wholesale price (w) for each contract. The associated optimal buyback price (b) or revenue-sharing price (r) is then provided by the Excel program once a desired

Table 13.3. Breakdown of Groups

	High margin (c = $5)	Low margin (c = $13)
Buyback	A1	B1
Revenue sharing	A2	B2

wholesale price is chosen. The optimal b and r are determined such that the store's expected profits remain unchanged, regardless of the wholesale price chosen by the students. To provide a fair comparison, we also ensure the store obtains the same amount of profit under the two contracts. In other words, the store will not benefit if one contract is chosen over the other, or if a different wholesale price is selected. Once a set of contract parameters is established, the Excel program will display the store's order quantity (which changes with the wholesale price), the realized market demand at the store, and final profit. The students will price the contract 20 times, representing 20 weeks. During each week, students should keep track of the following information provided on the Excel spreadsheet:

1. Wholesale price decision (w)
2. Associated buyback price (b) *or* revenue-sharing price (r)
3. Store's order quantity (Q)
4. Realized market demand (D), generated by the program
5. Unit leftover (for buyback) *or* unit sold (for revenue sharing)
6. Cash flow at the beginning and at the end of the week, which can be computed using table 13.2
7. Total profit for the week

Appendix B contains a table (table 13.4) that should be handed out to students to record this information. After finishing the exercise, students can use this table to calculate their average profit across the 20 weeks. The instructor will then collect average profit information from students within each group (i.e., within each treatment listed in table 13.3) and calculate the average profit for each group. These group-based averages can be reported to the class and used as a catalyst for discussion.

To assist students in making decisions and calculating important values, two Excel workbooks are provided, one each for the buyback and revenue-sharing contracts. In each workbook, there are two spreadsheets for the high profit margin and low profit margin products, respectively. Before the exercise, the instructor must make sure the students use the correct file, based on the group to which they are assigned (table 13.3).

Figure 13.1 provides a screenshot of the Excel spreadsheet for the buyback contract. The revenue-sharing contract uses a similar interface. A scrollbar is used to choose initial wholesale price (A). Once a value is chosen, the optimal value for the buyback price is displayed (B). The spreadsheet also displays the store's order quantity, initial profit at the beginning of the week, and possible buyback costs at the end of the week (C). Because buyback costs depend on customer demand, which is not revealed during the decision stage, the screen only displays the highest and lowest possible buyback costs (i.e., $b \times Q$ and 0, respectively). This provides students with some knowledge of the range of possible buyback costs at the end of the week. For revenue-sharing contracts, the screen will display the highest and lowest revenue share (i.e., $r \times Q$ and 0).

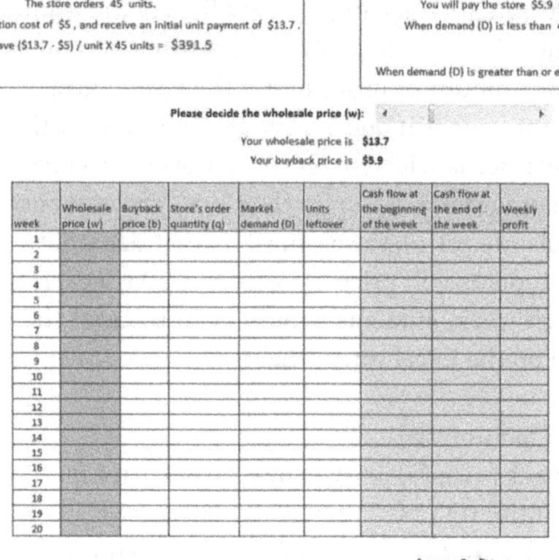

Figure 13.1 Spreadsheet for the Buyback Contract

After deciding on a wholesale price, students will input this price into the second column of the spreadsheet (shaded in orange) next to the proper week index (D). After inputting a wholesale price, the spreadsheet will show demand realization and automatically calculate the earnings at the beginning and end of the week, as well as total profits for the week. At this point, students record information for the week into their worksheet (table 13.5 in appendix B). After finishing all 20 weeks, the average total profit is calculated and displayed on the bottom of the spreadsheet. Having students manually enter these values allows them to internalize the impact of their decisions more than if this information were collected on the Excel spreadsheet. It also provides an aide for class discussion, since students can refer back to their decisions and form opinions about the resulting performance.

Once students have completed the exercise, the instructor should ask one student in each group to collect information on expected profit achieved by each group member and write these numbers on the board, along with a grand average. The instructor can then add the maximum expected profit level that could be achieved ($422 for the high-margin product and $92 for the low profit margin product). Once this information has been posted, the instructor can start by asking students if they notice any patterns in the profit levels achieved across contract types within profit margin conditions. They should observe that expected profit is higher for the revenue-sharing contract, particularly with high profit margins. The difference should be lower for the low profit margin condition. The instructor should ask the students why revenue sharing leads to higher profits.

The answer lies in the biases students introduce when making the wholesale price decision under the two contracts. The instructor can reveal the optimal wholesale price for each contract assuming the objective is to maximize expected profit. For the high profit margin case, this will be $w_r^*(H) = 1.3$ and $w_b^*(H) = 16.3$ (with associated $r = b = 15$), while in the low profit margin case, this will be $w_r^*(L) = 3.3$ and $w_b^*(L) = 18.3$ (with $r = b = 15$). The instructor can then turn to groups that evaluated buyback contracts (groups A1 and B1) and ask how their wholesale prices compare to these "optimal" values. The instructor can ask for a show of hands of who set the wholesale price consistently below this target. This percentage should be quite high. The instructor can follow up by asking students why they think this is the case. Students may identify that by setting the wholesale price lower they reduce buyback price in the second period and so reduce this loss—loss aversion is in play.

The instructor can next call out groups that evaluated the revenue-sharing contract (groups A2 and B2) and ask how many priced w_r higher than $w_r^*(H)$ and $w_r^*(L)$. The instructor can point out that this also is due to loss aversion. Here a higher wholesale price leads to a lower loss in the first period (before demand is realized). This also is an opportunity to ask students which contract they prefer now that they can see the biases that occur in setting the wholesale price. Students should notice that these biases impact the buyback contract more in the high profit margin condition and lead to the revenue-sharing contract dominating in terms of the average profit achieved. The instructor should point out that when choosing a contract type, a supply manager should consider who will be setting contract parameters, for example, whether the prices are set by a human supply analyst, who may introduce behavioral biases, or by a software support system that uses a preprogrammed algorithm.

DISCUSSION

These two exercises together give students an appreciation for how risk-sharing contracts work and the trade-offs between different contract types. The students observe firsthand how the contracts perform under different profit margin conditions. They discover the surprising result that supply managers may prefer revenue-sharing contracts for high profit margin products yet switch to buyback contracts for low profit margin products. They also discover that when behavioral factors, such as loss aversion and prospective accounting, are accounted for in the contract-pricing decisions, the wholesale price will be set lower than "optimal" under the buyback contract and higher than "optimal" under the revenue-sharing contract. These biases lead to the revenue-sharing contract performing better than the buyback, particularly for high-margin products.

In practice, behavioral influences are not normally considered when choosing between risk-sharing contract types. In that sense, this activity exposes students to the results of cutting-edge research and provides an opportunity to discuss how experimental studies can be used more broadly to help inform supply chain practice. As part of the debrief, students should be asked to summarize how these new insights change the way they think about risk-sharing contracts and what advice they would offer a supply manager who is likely unfamiliar with these patterns. They also can be asked to think of what other environmental factors (besides profit margin) might influence the performance of these two contracts, and how this could be tested experimentally.

Much of the existing supply chain contract literature has focused on identifying optimal pricing policy when decision-makers are able to optimize and wish to maximize their own expected profit. Incorporating the impact of other utility functions, as well as possible decision errors, is fairly novel in this field. We predict that behavioral research will become an important subarea of the supply contract literature because people normally make contract choices and sign off on contract prices. To move the recommendations of prior research closer to practice, it is essential to understand how performance changes when these decisions are made by people.

Loss aversion and prospective accounting have been identified in a wide range of decision contexts, including finance, marketing, consumption, and health. It is not surprising that these behavioral factors also are present in a supply chain contracting context. What is more novel are the types of financial flows that emerge in risk-sharing contracts and the opportunity this represents for new comparisons. For example, buyback and revenue-sharing contracts differ in terms of the magnitude of the loss and gain between periods, as well as the timing of losses. They also differ in whether the loss or gain is uncertain (e.g., loss is uncertain in the buyback contract, while gain is uncertain in the revenue-sharing contract). This combination of differences in how loss is presented is quite unique and has not been studied in the prior behavioral economics research. In that sense, this activity also offers an opportunity to teach students in the behavioral economics field more about how loss aversion and prospective accounting arise in real industry contexts. The richness of the framing comparison in this activity also provides a platform for thinking about how financial flows that involve losses and gains should be evaluated more generally in light of behavioral factors.

Appendix A

Survey A

As the cheesecake manager, you are considering which contract, buyback or revenue sharing, to offer to the store. The two contracts are described below. Under both contracts, you will incur a production cost of $1 for each cheesecake produced and the store will sell these cheesecakes purchased from you at a unit price of $20. No matter which contract you choose, the store will always order 95 units. Recall that the market demand at the store is equally likely to be any integer from 1 to 100, with a mean of 50.

> *Buyback*: At the beginning of each week, the store pays you $15.25 per cheesecake, so you receive an initial profit of $15.25 – $1 = $14.25 for each unit the retailer orders. During the week, demand occurs. At the end of the week, if there is any leftover inventory, you will buy back any unsold cheesecakes for $15 per unit.
>
> *Revenue sharing*: At the beginning of each week, the store pays you $0.25 per cheesecake, so you initially incur a cost of $0.25 – $1 = –$0.75 for each unit the retailer orders. During the week, demand occurs. At the end of the week, the store will give you $15 for each cheesecake sold.

Which option do you prefer (check one)?	Buyback	Revenue Sharing
	☐	☐

Please briefly explain why:

Survey B

As the cheesecake manager, you are considering which contract, buyback or revenue sharing, to offer to the store. The two contracts are described below. Under both contracts, you will incur a production cost of $17 for each cheesecake produced and the store will sell these cheesecakes purchased from you at a unit price of $20. No matter which contract you choose, the store will always order 15 units. Recall that the market demand at the store is equally likely to be any integer from 1 to 100, with a mean of 50.

> *Buyback*: At the beginning of each week, the store pays you $19.25 per cheesecake, so you receive an initial profit of $19.25 – $17 = $2.25 for each unit the retailer orders. During the week, demand occurs. At the end of the week, if there is any leftover inventory, you will buy back any unsold cheesecakes for $15 per unit.

Revenue sharing: At the beginning of each week, the store pays you $4.25 per cheesecake, so you initially incur a cost of $4.25 – $17 = –$12.75 for each unit the retailer orders. During the week, demand occurs. At the end of the week, the store will give you $15 for each cheesecake sold.

Which option do you prefer (check one)? Buyback ☐ Revenue Sharing ☐

Please briefly explain why:

Appendix B

Table 13.4. Worksheet for Buyback Contract

Week	Wholesale price (w)	Buyback price (b)	Store's order quantity (Q)	Market demand (D)	Units left over	Cash flow at the beginning of the week	Cash flow at the end of the week	Weekly profit
1								
2								
3								
4								
5								
6								
7								
8								
9								
10								
11								
12								
13								
14								
15								
16								
17								
18								
19								
20								
							Average profit	

Table 13.5. Worksheet for Revenue-Sharing Contract

Week	Wholesale price (w)	Revenue share (r)	Store's order quantity (Q)	Market demand (D)	Unit sold	Cash flow at the beginning of the week	Cash flow at the end of the week	Weekly profit
1								
2								
3								
4								
5								
6								
7								
8								
9								
10								
11								
12								
13								
14								
15								
16								
17								
18								
19								
20								
							Average profit	

References

Cachon, G. 2003. Supply chain coordination with contracts. S. Graves, T. de Kok (eds.) in Supply Chain Management: Design, Coordination and Operation. Boston: Elsevier.

Cachon, G., Lariviere, M. 2005. Supply chain coordination with revenue sharing contracts. Management Science 51 (1), 30–44.

Kahneman, D., Tversky, A. 1979. Prospect theory: An analysis of decision under risk. Econometrica 47 (2), 263–291.

Prelec, D., Loewenstein, G. 1998. The red and the black: Mental accounting of savings and debt. Marketing Science 17 (1), 4–28.

Tversky, A.,Kahneman, D. 1981. The framing of decisions and the psychology of choice. Science 211, 453–458.

Zhang, Y., Donohue, K., Cui, T. -H. 2014. Contract preferences and performance for the loss averse supplier: Buyback versus revenue sharing. Working paper, University of Minnesota.

CHAPTER 14

A Chain of Hands

Prosocial Integration in a Coffee Supply Chain Setting

TUNG NHU NGUYEN AND KHUONG NGOC MAI

OVERVIEW

The value chain of coffee is used to illustrate issues of unequal revenue distribution. The case focuses on Vietnam, the world's second largest coffee exporter, which moves coffee beans to Europe, Canada, and the United States. This value chain would deserve no criticism if coffee farmers benefited fairly from coffee revenues, to compensate for their hard work in coffee plantations. The welfare distribution inequality is scrutinized from both operations management and behavior science perspectives. Pedagogically, the teaching activity is a role-play involving different parties in the coffee value chain. Participants explore the causes of this social injustice, and theorists can revisit traditional frameworks in their own discipline, that is, operations management or behavior science, for any key assumptions that need to be challenged and what lessons they can learn.

From a sociological perspective, resolution of social injustice in the coffee value chain requires action from consumers, businesses, social enterprises, and nonprofit organizations. A World Bank report predicted that consumption tendency would be shifted from nonsustainable to sustainable coffee (World Bank 2004). The reasons for this paradigm shift are attributed to enabling environments, including national policies, multilateral agreements, and new business environments where buyers (i.e., traders, roasters, retailers) increasingly create sustainability standards of their own (World Bank 2004). Importantly, consumers have become more concerned about ethical and environmental issues.

Consumers in developed countries in North America, Western Europe, and Japan tend to purchase sustainable coffee (World Bank 2004). In a market where consumers can choose from many product varieties, prosocial consumers tend to select product varieties certified with ethical production standards and accept premiums for coffee certified as fair trade (Galarraga and Markandya 2004). Leading coffee companies increasingly purchase coffee with ethical sources, for example, fair-trade certified coffee. They also partner with nonprofit organizations to design and implement their own "equity" practice programs. For example, CAFE (Coffee and Farmer Equity) Practices programs implemented by Starbucks in partnership with Conservation International help to increase income and improve working conditions for coffee farmers. In 2013 over 90% of Starbucks coffee was ethically sourced (Starbucks 2014). The fair-trade movement for coffee no doubt helps to improve working conditions and income for coffee farmers in tropical or subtropical countries, but fair-trade certification may lead to marginalization of small-scale farmers with no access to fair-trade programs (Bacon 2005). Sustainability initiatives from nonprofit organizations, social enterprises, and corporate entities include fair-trade certification, the Rainforest Alliance, Smithsonian Migratory Bird Center (SMBC) Bird Friendly certification, the Common Code for Coffee Community Code of Conduct, Starbucks CAFE Practices, and the Nestle Initiative among others.

From an operations management perspective, the accuracy of demand forecasting is a problem for coffee growers. They cannot produce exact quantities of coffee because of demand fluctuations from downstream to upstream in the supply chain. This phenomenon is called the "bullwhip" effect, which is defined in detail in the next section. For example, retailers may order more than the real demand from consumers, possibly because they want quantity discounts or to avoid stock-out costs. The same psychological behavior may also be found among coffee importers, who place overestimated orders with exporters. By the time orders arrive at the farms, deviation from real demand is substantial, and farmers just grow a lot of coffee. When coffee prices fall, they take a big loss on the raw coffee inventory in stock. Nevertheless, this inventory-related cost problem, or bullwhip effect, has not been studied in much literature on the coffee supply chain. According to a World Bank report, farmers grow too much coffee because they receive no signal on falling prices, or learn of them too late, or even are given false information on demand and market price (World Bank 2004). So when the real demand for coffee is low, raw coffee gets stuck in farmers' barns or trading companies' warehouses, increasing holding costs.

In addition, the shipping costs of raw coffee from farms in tropical countries to roasters in other countries account for a high percentage of sales revenues. An Oxfam report on the coffee chain found that a coffee grower in Uganda sold raw coffee at 14 cents per kilogram, and after being transported by traders, coffee arrives at the roaster factory at a price of US$1.64 per kilo (Oxfam 2002). The price difference (US$1.50, or 91%) is used to pay shipment costs, traders' margin, taxes, and any costs related to the supply chain. A cost analysis report found that 60%–70% of Starbucks' operating costs were to cover transportation and other costs related to the supply chain (Cooke 2010). Using these facts, educators have an opportunity to educate participants on the uneven coffee welfare distribution, the bullwhip effect, and supply chain economics.

THEORETICAL PERSPECTIVE

Supply chain management (SCM) focuses on the flow of materials and information. Traditional SCM theories postulate that information, communication, cooperation, and trust are critical to "attain the level of synchronization that will make it more responsive to customer needs while lowering costs" (Russel and Taylor 2009, 334). This chapter explores two classic operations management (OM) concepts: bullwhip effects caused by imperfect information flow and their impact on inventory costs.

The bullwhip effect represents ill-serving ordering dynamics, often driven by delays and misperceptions, that give rise to systematic and exacerbated deficiencies and excessive stockpiles in a supply chain (Lee et al. 1997). Consequently, inventory costs and logistics costs increase and decrease profitability (Heizer and Render 2008). Bullwhip effects in the supply chain are discussed to highlight distorted information, which flows long distances through multiple members. This effect influences the decision-making effectiveness of members in the global supply chain. Bullwhip effects lead to increased inventory costs due to high inventory levels at all stages of the chain.

Economic order quantity models and just-in-time assumptions are challenged in this chapter. The objective of these inventory models is to minimize inventory-related costs. The economic order quantity model assumes that demand and lead time are known and constant. In case of variability, the model is adjusted to add safety stock on the assumption that the probability distribution is normal. In fact, moving raw materials over long distances, involving multiple parties, complicates inventory modeling. Obstacles in general and specific business environments hamper the accuracy of the inventory models. These models also fail to account for "the impact of perceived fairness on purchase behavior" (Bendoly, Donohue, and Schultz 2006, 740). Another driver of demand is the change in buying behavior of "ethical" users, who may boycott products violating human rights. This can collapse the whole supply chain.

Power of Suppliers and Consumers

Operations management theorists have tended to ignore social and behavioral factors in classical linear inventory models in traditional textbooks. In fact, the accuracy of inventory is challenged by the commitment made by suppliers and consumers, who as humans are influenced by individual, social, and environmental factors. Bendoly, Donohue, and Schultz (2006) argued that supplier selection models assumed the relatively static nature supplier relationships. Local supply contexts, economic conditions, business philosophy, decision rationality, and education, not to mention political dynamics, differ by region. Nonperformance of supply contracts on the supplier side may emerge as a consequence of on-the-spot dynamics. For example, coffee traders may postpone the delivery of exports as promised because they expect coffee can be exported to new markets for higher selling price.

The operations management literature discusses ethical issues because they are critical to long-term success of organizations (Heizer and Render 2008). Today, multinationals have to attend to codes of conduct because nonprofit organizations and watchdogs monitor how well and fairly local workers are treated.

However, OM theory does not detail the dynamics of corporation, consumer, and cause in transforming corporate social responsibility (CSR) inputs into outcomes. Behavior theories can help to explain when, why, and how consumers respond to corporate social initiatives through the contingent framework of CRS (Bhattacharya and Sen 2004). According to this framework, when firms invest in CSR activities, external outcomes include sales revenue, reputation (word-of-mouth), consumer behavior modification, and contribution to a cause (Bhattacharya and Sen 2004). The traditional OM literature has failed to account for or assess the impact of consumers' and suppliers' power on the supply chain.

Organizational behavior theories can help to bridge this gap by exploring factors influencing consumer demand and supplier trust. According to the model of informed decision, factors influencing consumers' decision-making include knowledge and affect toward a particular product variety (Bekker et al. 1999). This frame reflects the cognitive process, starting from an understanding of product quality and the degree to which it satisfies consumers' wants, to the formation of affect toward the product. These factors lead to the choice of the product. According to utility theory, consumers can derive utility from a variety of characteristics of goods. Each consumer's utility depends on observed product characteristics, which may be, for example, fair trade or SA8000 certification, but "consumers may differ in how they evaluate different product characteristics" (Hiscox et al. 2011, 5). The utility model is expressed in the form of an equation as follows.

$$U_{ijt} = U(x_{it}\xi_{jt}, v_{it})\theta,$$

where
U_{ijt}: consumer i's utility from buying the jth good in market t
x_{it}: observed product characteristics
ξ_{jt}: unobserved product characteristics
v_{it}: unobserved differences in consumer tastes
θ: how sensitive a consumer is to each of the observed product characteristics

The utility model explains why an individual, mostly in advanced countries, decides to buy an ethically labeled product that is slightly more expensive than a nonlabeled product. This decision is consistent with the value he expects from the outcome of his decision. For example, when he has bought fair-trade coffee, he may feel more pleasant because he knows that his action helps give more income to coffee growers. The interesting thing for the utility model for coffee products is that consumers are willing to pay, not for their own utilities, but for the utilities of farmers in remote, developing countries. However, the classical utility theory considers only personal preference and attitude, and it is not sufficient, particularly with regard to truly informed decisions (Bekker et al. 1999). Informed decision theorists supplement it with the factors of knowledge on and affect toward a particular product as predictors to buying decision (Bekker et al. 1999). Also, most recently, the theory of planned behavior—by which intention to buy is influenced by attitudes, social norms, and behavioral control—has been used to frame utility in this context. According to the theory of planned behavior, the intention to buy depends on attitudes toward a particular behavior, subjective norms associated with the behavior, and perceived behavioral control. For example, when customers are aware that their buying behavior may support unfair trade—which they oppose—they may not buy any more of the product in question. Without customers in the supply chain, the chain collapses. Therefore, it is essential that operations practitioners recognize the power of customers in choosing what they support and pay for.

The demand for fair labor voiced by ethical users has been so strong recently that standards for fair labor have been established and used to monitor performance in terms of social sustainability in businesses (Hutchins and Sutherland 2008). According to these authors, it is essential to account for indicators for social sustainability, which include the following factors.

- **Labor equity**: if we consider a supply chain as an integrated input-output system, all workers engaged in the process should receive fair compensation and benefits. A simple comparison between the hourly wage of a coffee farmer in a developing country and that of an employee in the United States may be misleading because of purchasing power parity (PPP) issues. One US dollar can buy a meal in Vietnam or other poor countries, but cannot pay for a hamburger in the United States. Regardless of inherent PPP distinctions, there should be nonsignificant differences in hourly wages. The minimum wage in rural areas (Region IV) in Vietnam in 2013 is stipulated by law to be about $90 per month, or less than $5 per working day or less than $1 per working hour (www.amchamvietnam.com). In contrast, the minimum hourly wage of an employee in the United States is about $7 (www.dol.gov), which represents a significant gap!
- **Healthcare**: the ratio of company-paid healthcare expenses per employee to the market capitalization per employee.
- **Safety**: the ratio of average days not injured to the total days worked (per employee).
- **Philanthropy**: the ratio of charitable contributions to market capitalization.

CASE EXAMPLE

Coffee Value Chain

Today, multinational corporations (MNCs) are expanding their reach to the farthest corners of the world, where input costs, such as raw materials and labor, are cheap. They shop from country to country as a shopper moves from store to store to buy all the necessary materials to make a product. In this global supply chain, the benefit to farmers from developing countries is just a small portion of the added value of their agricultural product. The most outstanding instance of the disparity in benefits can be seen in the case of coffee, which is among the most traded agricultural products in the world. The ideal circumstance for farmers who take pains to grow coffee in their tropical countries would be to accrue the biggest cut of added value. In reality, they do not.

A great deal has been written on unfair trade in the coffee supply chain. Sociologists refer to it as social injustice in international trade ("Cups of Coffee Filled with Injustice" 2002; Jaffee 2007). The distribution of the added value of coffee is not evenly shared among farmers, traders, shippers, roasters, and retailers. In specific terms, farmers share only 10% of the added value, traders 3%, shippers 4%, roasters 70%, and retailers 13%. Both economic and social sustainability are critical issues in this process. These two dimensions of sustainability in combination with environmental issues form the foundation for the construct of sustainability. From an ethical standards perspective, it is critical that multinational corporations pay more attention to these issues of sustainability because people at the bottom of the pyramid (BOP) in developing countries need their support to improve their health and economic conditions. The Millennium Development Goals of the United Nations urge corporations, for the purpose of sustainability, to take action to "promote meeting more basic needs through reductions in poverty [and] improvements in human health and eco-system protection" and to further "quality of life" and "equity" (United Nations 2000). Evidence pointing to the absence of social sustainability in the coffee chain is that farmers who work hard in poor working conditions on their coffee farms share the smallest cut. They are also vulnerable to falling price shocks. The Oxfam report found that in the early 2000s when coffee prices significantly slumped, sales revenues received by small coffee growers in Dak lak Province in Vietnam were enough to cover about 60% of production cost (Oxfam 2002). Historical data indicate that coffee commodity prices on exchanges were volatile over time, and so were green coffee bean futures prices (USDA 2007). Aside from supply-demand imbalance, the unpredictability of coffee futures price is increasingly affected by price speculators who reflect their expectation of future events that may significantly impact the coffee industry (Lewin, Giovannucci, and Varangis 2004; World Bank 2004).

Vietnam: The World's Top Robusta Coffee-Farming Country

The French introduced coffee to Vietnam in 1857. In 2012 with 500,000 hectares of farms used to produce coffee and 25.47 million 60 kg bags exported, Vietnam is the world's second largest producer and exporter of coffee, after Brazil. Up to 95% of its total output is accounted for by robusta coffee. In 2012, Vietnam's coffee export value was up to a record US$3.7 billion (Ipsos 2013). Brazil is the number one coffee exporter, but it produces Arabica coffee, which is more expensive than Vietnam's robusta. In July 2013, a kilogram of arabica cost US$1.25, compared to

US$0.8 for robusta. Coffee production stagnated during the Vietnam War period from 1954 to 1973. When the Vietnam War ended in 1975, Vietnam initiated an aggregate agricultural production plan for its focal agricultural crops, including rice, tea and robusta coffee. Its robusta coffee supply led the world in 2000. Since then, US multinational organizations, such as Mondelēz International, the world's second largest coffee brand, with 2012 revenue of $35 billion, have consumed Vietnam's robusta coffee.

History Lessons of Coffee Supply and Sustainability Initiatives

Until the 1990s, Ivory Coast and Cameroon were the world's leading robusta suppliers. In the early 1990s, young people in these countries left the countryside for cities, significantly decreasing their coffee production volume. This phenomenon also started to occur in Vietnam, where the younger generation preferred factories to rice fields, where work is tougher but generates more income. Three family members can earn less than US$4,000 per year from coffee farming, while a single worker can earn more than US$6,000 per year in Hanoi City in a factory (Cong 2013). Selling prices are set by brokers or traders who buy coffee from farmers and sell it to exporting companies for margin. It is these intermediaries who benefit the most within the coffee supply chain. Typically, these brokers sell fertilizers on credit to farmers short on cash and buy coffee from them at predetermined low prices (Cong 2013).

MNCs such as Mondelēz International (United States), Nestle, and Ecome (Switzerland) are assisting Vietnam's coffee farmers with multi-million-dollar programs primarily for improved cultivation techniques. For example, in 2013 Mondelēz International opened a training center in Lam Dong Province and plans to invest $200 million through 2020. It is a modern building, surrounded by small pieces of land farmed with many varieties of robusta coffee. Here, a range of subjects are taught, including grafting, fertilizer use, watering control, and even price negotiation ("Mondelēz International Helps Coffee Farmers" 2013). That is one way to invest in the future of the coffee industry. No nation but Vietnam can satisfy the booming demand for robusta coffee (Cong 2013).

LEARNING ACTIVITY

Duration: about 30 minutes
Ask the Group:

- What is the most-traded agricultural commodity in the world?—coffee
- Where is it grown?—near the equator
- Where is most coffee consumed?—United States, Canada, Europe
- What is the (general) chain of people that coffee goes through to get from the places near the equator where it is grown to consumers in the United States, Canada, and Europe?—growers/farmers, traders, shippers, roasters, retailers

Ask for seven volunteers, each of whom will play one role. These roles represent the people occupying these positions in the chain leading from the point at which the coffee is grown to the point at which it is sold to the consumer. Ask the volunteers to line up in the middle of the space in order: the three growers/farmers next to each other, then the trader, shipper, roaster, and retailer. Have each one read his or her character card aloud (the card describes the work done by the character). See Figure 14.1 for typical role and group layouts.

Have the rest of the group split themselves in half (roughly evenly) and stand on opposite sides of the space with the "actors" in between them. Hand out one set of coins or buttons to each half of the group; each person should take some. Explain that there are 100 coins on each side and that each represents 1 cent of a dollar spent on coffee.

Designate one side to be the "Ideal World" and the other to be the "Real World." Ask each side to distribute their coins among the different actors (put in the appropriate bowl). The "Ideal World" group should distribute their coins/buttons as they think that they *should* be distributed in a just world, based on the difficulty of the work, its importance in the coffee process, the role holder's needs/costs, and so on. The "Real World" group should distribute their coins/buttons as they think that they *actually* are distributed in the world today, based on the difficulty of the work, its importance in the coffee process, the role holder's needs/costs, and so on. As the coins are being distributed, the "actors" should make their case as to how much their particular role should get (both for the just- and the real-world cases), emphasizing their importance in the process, their costs, and so on.

When both groups are satisfied with how their coins are distributed, ask them briefly why they chose to distribute the coins the way that they did, whom they gave the most and least coins to and why. Ask each actor how many coins he or she has in each bowl, "Ideal World" bowl first, then "Real World" bowl. Ask: How do these discrete patterns of resource distribution compare? What do the actors think of the amount they got (in both the ideal- and real-world cases)? Is the resource distribution as it "should" be? Is it different? Why? Reveal how many coins each character should have in the "Real World" bowl to be accurate.

Ask: Why the difference? What values do you see projected in your resource allocation decisions? Hard work? Education? Expenses? How do these values affect your spending habits in your own life?

In the actual distribution, the three growers share 10 coins, the trader gets three, the shipper four, the roaster 70, the retailer 13.

- Reactions: Are you surprised?

From this learning activity, students are—or become—aware that welfare distribution is not as just as they might have expected looking at variance 2 in table 14.1. At this point the instructor should point out this injustice as a problem

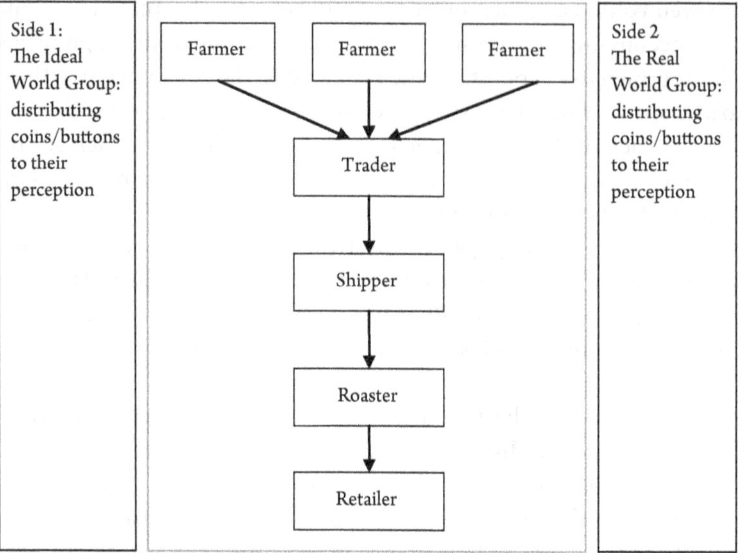

Figure 14.1 Layout of the Two Groups in the Game
NOTE: The arrow represents the stream of the coffee process.

Table 14.1. SPREADSHEET FOR RECORDING VARIANCES

Member in the chain	Number of coins/ buttons allocated by participants in Ideal World Group	Number of coins/ buttons allocated by participants in Real World Group	Actual welfare distribution	Variance 1 (difference between Ideal World and actual distribution)	Variance 2 (difference between Real World and actual distribution)
Farmers (× 3)			10%		
Trader			3%		
Shipper			4%		
Roaster			70%		
Retailer			13%		
				= SUM(ABOVE)	= SUM(ABOVE)

NOTE: actual welfare distribution figures calculated from International Coffee Organization sources.

caused by several factors. A fish-bone chart can be used to determine possible causes. Let participants speak to the causes and allow the facilitator to record those causes in a relevant category (lack of information, value-added product, tax policies, different cost of living, etc.).

The smaller variance 2 is, the better the participant understands the differences in revenue distribution among members in the supply chain.

DISCUSSION

The following captures what participants are likely to have observed in the learning activity.

Value Increase in a Supply Chain

Raw coffee growers are paid 10% of sales revenues, whereas roasters get 70%. Participants can think of activities in the chain that add more value to the product, such as roasting, packaging, and flavoring.

Understanding Based on Imperfect Information Flow in a Global Supply Chain

Having participants sit so as to see the back of the previous member in the chain limits their communication or leads to ineffective communication. Participants can observe that members (the coffee growers) sitting in the first row cannot see the end consumer in the last row. They may also observe that consumer behaviors (i.e., a change in consumer demand) cannot be seen by the growers.

Awareness of Farmers' Vulnerability to Price Shocks

Participants see that the coffee supply chain may stretch over long distances and involve many members. This lengthy and multistep process is not financially beneficial to coffee growers because potential profits have to be cut into smaller portions for all members of the supply chain. Coffee growers are apportioned the smallest cut of the profit for their manual farming. They also are vulnerable to coffee price shocks. In 2013, the average price of raw coffee paid to farmers dropped to less than 40,000 Vietnam dongs per kilogram (or less than $2). In an interview with Vietnam Television (VTV) broadcast on November 7, 2013, a Vietnamese coffee farmer said that his one hectare of coffee generated an annual profit of only 30 million Vietnam dongs, or about US$1,428 for a whole year of farming hardship. Things get worse for his household economy when coffee is the sole source of income for his seven-member family, and his five children are still of school age. One reason for the fall of the global coffee price is that coffee is bought and sold by investors and price speculators as a tradable commodity on the New York Stock Exchange, a "paper market." Sometimes the world coffee price is not that low, but the price bid to farmers is low for other reasons. First, because the bullwhip effect (explained below), farmers have magnified information bearing on coffee shortages, and many of them switch to growing coffee until its price slumps. Second, traders and exporters want to earn big profits on buying green coffee by paying farmers below-market price and keeping a large margin percentage for themselves. Third, farmers have no access to information on market demand and price, so they accept whatever price they are offered if they want to generate some cash return on their investment and do not want to see coffee stack up in their warehouses.

Coffee Supply Chain Requiring an Integrated and Committed System

The whole chain can collapse not only through slumping consumer demand but also though lack of supplier commitment. Participants see that coffee is grown in countries near the equator, meaning that raw material sources of supply depend totally on these countries. Being hungry for cash, farmers may sell their harvests to any parties who bid for higher prices, and exporters abandon their traditional customers to shake hands with traders in new markets such as China for higher profits. In some cases suppliers unilaterally have failed to perform on their signed supply contracts to US and European markets. They sold materials at new high prices to other new markets, for example, China. Certainly, excuses such as natural disasters, poor crops, inflation, high input costs, and so on, emerge. Importers tend to be angry about supply disruptions because they do not have supplies to bring to markets as committed. Consequently, importers sometimes take suppliers to international courts based on contract nonperformance. This game is most likely to be won by importers because they base themselves on contracted terms on quantities and prices. Rarely are the exporters successful in asking for modified higher selling price. Worse, vendors' credibility can be lost.

Now consider a scenario of low coffee demand. Farmers assume that the previous coffee demand hike is real, so more farmers grow more coffee. When coffee demand is lower than their expectations, and there is oversupply, the selling price goes down. This time traders jump in and bargain for a good price. With pressures of investment payback and bank interests, farmers have little choice but sell raw coffee at the new lower price. The beneficiary member in the chain is now the trader. The above threats require global coffee businesses to integrate raw materials suppliers into their system, creating a trust-based and commitment-based supplier-customer relationships rather than arm's-length linkages. It also is critical to provide realistic coffee demand information to farmers, develop support policies such as floor-prices, consumption contracts and training for farmers on legal issues and business plans.

Fairer View of Profit Distribution among Members in the Supply Chain

In the actual real-world distribution, roasters get 70% of the money spent on coffee, while farmers receive roughly 10%. On first inspection, this revenue distribution is unfair in consideration of the hard work and toil put in by the growers. However, there are additional considerations to account for. First, this difference in percentage may be misleading if we do not examine differences in the cost of living between countries involved in the supply chain. As noted above, while one US dollar can buy a meal in Vietnam, it cannot pay for a hamburger in the United States. Second, expenses incurred by US roasters are huge. They spend much a great deal in packaging and product marketing. A high corporate income tax and sales tax in the United States also place pressure on the selling price. Therefore, the income net of these expenses for roasters is not as high as might be thought by an outsider observer. This learning activity also raises critical issues such as that investments in value-added activities, that is, packaging or augmented services by roasters, can raise the selling price. This lesson can be learned by producers in poorer countries seeking higher profit. Because of a lack of knowledge and support, these farmers do not add value to their raw products, which results in lower selling prices.

Knowledge on Economical Inventory Models

The classical inventory model determines the economic order quantity where total holding costs and total ordering costs cross over. In practice, roasters or shippers may want to order a large shipment to reduce total ordering costs, because transportation costs from country to country are very high. But the trade-off is that they have to pay more inventory-holding costs, which may explain why the coffee value is significantly added at the roasting step. The learning activity can generate discussion of the significance of supply chain costs. Overordering phenomena can distort demand information flowed upstream, inducing farmers to grow too much, until they reach the point at which traders stop buying raw coffee because of falling prices, and farmers bear the financial losses.

Learning Best Practices in Social Corporate Responsibility

This learning activity also offers the opportunity to introduce the initiatives of multinational corporations, such as the Nestlé Plan, by which Nestlé guarantees to buy coffee from farmers and also to provide them with technical assistance and best practices. This is a good example of multinational corporate social responsibility helping with fair trade.

Risk of Collapse of the Coffee Supply Chain

The above discussion reveals the power of end coffee consumers in deciding what to buy. Without customers in the supply chain, the whole chain collapses. US coffee drinkers may not be sensitive to price, but they are more and more focused on issues of ethics. If they realize that coffee margins are not fairly shared among members in the supply chain, or discover that farmers' rights are violated in developing countries, they may boycott various coffee brands. This kind of product boycott occurred to Nike products in the 1990s when Vietnamese workers were reported to work in sweatshops. Consequently, sales revenues decreased, leading to reduced tax collections for importing countries. Operations managers should focus on the development of risk management plans to respond to this potential risk.

Sustainability in Global Coffee Supply Chain

Multinational corporations also are attentive to economic, environmental, and social sustainability. Social responsibility relates to the areas of sustainability and ethics as they pertain to the communities where the organization does business. A recent study showed that 80% of likely consumers surveyed said they were willing to pay more for an item if they could be assured it was made under good working conditions (Elliot and Freeman 2003, 29–35). Galarraga and Mankandya (2004) gathered data on retail prices of coffee sold in major supermarkets in Britain and estimated that an average premium of around 11% was charged for coffee with a "green" label (they combined fair-trade, organic, and shade-grown labels in this category). Operations managers in the coffee supply chain should pay attention to fair-trade and SA8000 certificated products, which both help improve farmers' working conditions and increase sales revenues.

Supply Contract Management

Contract nonperformance is another concern for coffee traders, which may lead to supply chain collapse. When coffee farmers realize that their portion of potential profit is unfair, they may discontinue raw coffee supply. Their excuses may be poor crops, natural disasters, inflation, high production costs, or another cause as they seek a price increase on previously committed-to prices. In some cases, supply becomes rare because producers sell raw materials at better prices to other markets with high demand in other emerging markets. This pattern may affect not only coffee supplies, but also other tropical raw materials such as cashews, which become artificially scarce, disrupting the flow of supplies to importers. Coffee traders are intermediaries who have committed a fixed contract price and delivery date to US wholesalers. A price adjustment with farmers would require the importers to negotiate with the wholesalers for new prices as well, which is almost unviable, as wholesalers would insist on contract price. In practice, as negotiation has failed, importers have brought raw materials suppliers to court for not performing the contract. As discussed earlier, importers usually win and exporters compensate them for any damages that occur.

Business Environmental Factors and the Power of Consumers

To determine a reorder point or an optimal order point requires estimation of quantities demanded. Deterministic inventory models are used when demand and lead time are constant, while probabilistic models for inventory cost minimization are applied in case of variability in demand and lead time. Based on the probabilities of previous stock-out occurrences, a safety stock is recommended to minimize stock-out costs. Nevertheless, in a global supply chain, when materials flow from country to country over long distances, environmental factors can unexpectedly affect lead time and demand. For example, at the level of general business environment, export-import policies involving countries or watchdog organizations for human rights can push or pull supplies. In a specific business environment, change in consumer knowledge, utilities, and affect can lead to the decision to buy a product or not. Current inventory models are too generic to cover a particular product with unique properties like coffee (i.e., long lead time, required imports, etc.).

A Challenge to Following a Just-in-Time Approach

It is true that the just-in-time approach for inventory has not been adopted in the global coffee supply chain. The World Bank (2004) indicates that the world's top coffee-exporting countries—Brazil, Vietnam, and Columbia—which account for 61% of total coffee production, do not follow demand-pulled approaches, and consequently in recent years there have been instances of oversupply. The World Bank report also points out that causes of oversupply include policy failures, market failures, lack of access to realistic information, and willingness to supply by farmers. The learning activity can help participants recognize that there are multiple members in the supply chain and because of "push" approaches, coffee inventory must accrue for some members. The World Bank report found that roasters do not want to hold too much inventory and push logistical demands that are just-in-time, down to their suppliers. Therefore, inventory pileup may occur at the warehouses of shippers or traders. Future research needs to further explore the inventory problems of shipping and trading corporations and whether increased holding costs influence their business performance.

Sociologists postulate that communication effectiveness may be distorted by factors such as cultural differences, absence of feedback, improper channels, physical distractions, status effects, and semantic problems. Literature in communications should explore how those factors affect communication in global supply chains. When information has to flow across many individuals or parties with different interests, especially asymmetrically across long distances, such as in the global supply chain, information distortion, called the bullwhip effect, can occur.

The Bullwhip Effect Caused by Individualism

Traditional decision models in the behavioral sciences assume that decision-makers are rational and provided with all necessary knowledge for decisions. In fact, people make decisions in some cases under conditions with only limited or distorted information. In the supply chain, the information distortion is referred as a bullwhip effect. Existing communication models ignore this psychological effect, also attributed in part to individual behavior, driven by personal interest maximization. This phenomenon should be explored in future human decision-making research. For example, retailers may place a slightly larger coffee order, possibly to maximize their sales revenues because of sudden local demand increase, or to minimize total ordering costs by reducing the number of orders. The roaster thinks that the demand is truly increasing (actually he has no knowledge of the true demand for coffee in the retailer's locality). As he does not want to run out of coffee the next time, the roster places an even larger order to the shipper. The shipper then orders a little extra coffee from the trader. Many "little" quantities accumulate to a substantial quantity. This effect is relayed from retailers to suppliers. This means that it is not until several weeks or even months after the extra order from the retailer that coffee farmers are aware of it. Worse, the farmers assume that the demand increase is true without knowing that it is due to the one-time intention of the retailer for the sake of local profit maximization. In this situation, a purchase officer or material planning officer should carefully analyze the issue and control ordering quantities by sharing information with all members in the supply chain and using information technology (e.g., computer-aided ordering).

Marginalization of Small-Scale Producers

Regardless of its cause, fair-trade or SA8000 certification may have some side effects. Coffee multinationals implement fair-trade coffee as part of their corporate social responsibilities but also for differentiating premium coffee products for the ethical customer segment, and for higher sales revenues. They broadcast fair-trade programs in developing countries for thousands of farmers. However, with thousands of coffee farmers in need, the dynamics of these programs "threaten exclusion of small-scale farmers and create further marginalization of the poor in developing countries" (Perez-Aleman and Sandilands 2008, 35). These small-scale farmers may be entitled to their programs, which advocate stringent quality and social and environmental norms. This impact deserves future research consideration.

References

Bacon, C. 2005. Confronting the coffee crisis: can fair trade, organic, and specialty coffees reduce small-scale farmer vulnerability in northern Nicaragua? World Development 33 (3), 497–511.

Bekker, H., Thornton, J., Airey, C., Connelly, J., Hewison, J., Robinson, M., et al. 1999. Informed decision making: an annotated bibliography and systematic review. Health Technology Assessment 3 (1), 1–156.

Bendoly, E., Donohue, K., Schultz, K. L. 2006. Behavior in operations management: Assessing recent findings and revisiting old assumptions. Journal of Operations Management 24 (6), 737–752.

Bhattacharya, C. B., Sen, S. 2004. Doing better at doing good: When, why and how consumers respond to Corporate Social Initiatives. California Management Review 47 (1), 10.

Cong, T. D. 2013. Bao Phap Le Point: Vietnam xuat khau ca phe hang dau the gioi. Cong an Thanh pho Ho Chi Minh. September 5. Retrieved from http://congan.com.vn/?mod=detnews&catid=1120&id=502575.

Cooke, J. A. 2010. From bean to cup: how Starbucks transformed its supply chain. Retrieved from http://www.supplychainquarterly.com/topics/Procurement/scq201004starbucks/

Cups of coffee filled with injustice. World Notes. 2002, 2002/10/06/. Catholic New Times, 26, 8.

Elliott, K.A., Freeman, R.B. 2003. Can labor standards improve under globalization? Washington: Institute for International Economics.

Galarraga, I., Markandya, A. 2004. Economic techniques to estimate the demand for sustainable products: a case study for fair trade and organic coffee in the United Kingdom. Economía Agraria y Recursos Naturales (Agricultural and Resource Economics), 4(7), 109–134.

Heizer, J. H., Render, B. 2008. Operations management (Vol. 1). Delhi, India: Pearson Education India.

Hiscox, M., Broukhim, M., Litwin, C., Woloski, A. 2011. Consumer Demand for Fair Labor Standards: Evidence from a Field Experiment on eBay. Available at SSRN 1811788.

Hutchins, M. J., Sutherland, J. W. 2008. An exploration of measures of social sustainability and their application to supply chain decisions. Journal of Cleaner Production 16 (15), 1688–1698.

Ipsos. 2013. Vietnam's Coffee Industry.

Jaffee, D. 2007. Brewing Justice: Fair Trade Coffee, Sustainability, and Survival. Columbia and Princeton: University Presses of California.

Lee, H. I., Padmanabhan, V., Whang, S. 1997. The bullwhip effect in supply chains. Sloan Management Review 38 (3), 93–102.

Lewin, B., Giovannucci, D., Varangis, P. 2004. Coffee markets: New paradigms in global supply and demand, World Bank Agriculture and Rural Development Discussion Paper.

Mondelēz International Helps Coffee Farmers in Vietnam to Become More Successful Entrepreneurs. 2013. http://www.mondelezinternational.com/Newsroom/Multimedia-Releases/Mondelez-International-Helps-Coffee-Farmers-in-Vietnam-to-Become-More-Successful-Entrepreneurs.

Oxfam. 2002. Mugged: Poverty in your cup. http://www.oxfam.org.nz/resources/mugged.pdf.

Perez-Aleman, P., Sandilands, M. 2008. Building value at the top and bottom of the global supply chain: MNC-NGO partnerships and sustainability. California Management Review 51 (1), 24–49.

Russel, R. S., Taylor, B. W. 2009. Operations Management: Along the Supply Chain. Hoboken, NJ: John Wiley and Sons.

Starbucks. 2014. We take a holistic approach using responsible purchasing practices, farmer loans and forest conservation programs. http://www.starbucks.com/responsibility/sourcing/coffee.

United Nations. 2000. United Nations Millennium Declaration.

United States Department of Agriculture (USDA). 2007. Cost pass-through in the U.S. coffee industry.

World Bank. 2004. Coffee markets: New paradigms in global supply and demand. World Bank.

CHAPTER 15

Supply Chain Negotiator

A Game of Gains, Losses, and Equity

YOUNG K. RO, YI-SU CHEN, THOMAS CALLAHAN, AND TSAI-SHAN SHEN ■

OVERVIEW

One of the most important elements of operations management/supply chain management (OM/SCM) is the negotiation of relationships between supply chain members (buyers and suppliers). These relationships are critical as supply chain members are interdependent, working together to coordinate tasks and share information in production and service settings. Supply chain activities can be successful if these relationships are based on trust, commitment, and fairness. However, supply chain efforts are likely to be unfruitful when firm relationships break down. Since successful management of firm-level within-supply chain relationships requires the management of relationships across a complex network of organizations, several behavioral phenomena, including trust, conflict, contracting, and negotiation, are salient.

Firms involved in supply chain relationships regularly interact through business exchanges and transactions. During the course of these interactions, negotiation and conflict resolution are likely to be necessary as buyers and suppliers often retain divergent interests. As a result, it is critical that firms become familiar with various bargaining and conflict management strategies, along with their respective advantages and disadvantages, in order to maximize the probabilities associated with goal attainment.

The activity introduced in this chapter presents five negotiation strategies from the academic literature with the goal of familiarizing participants with them through the practice of negotiation. These strategies are accommodating, avoiding, collaborating, competing, and compromising (Thomas and Kilmann 1978). The purpose of this activity is to highlight how bargaining behavior can impact negotiation outcomes within supply chain contexts. Applications for both prospect theory and equity theory also can be illustrated through the use of this activity.

State of Management Practice

As firms engage in joint activities with other firms, conflicts are almost inevitable. Conflict can be defined as "an expressed struggle between at least two interdependent parties who perceive incompatible goals, scarce rewards, and (potential) interference from the other party in achieving their goals" (Hocker and Wilmot 1985, 23). It also is reflective of an "interactive process manifested in incompatibility, disagreement, or dissonance within or between social entities" (Rahim 1992, 16). Given inherent incompatibilities between parties involved in conflict, not all differences or disagreements can be resolved employing the same strategies. It is a critical issue to understand how to manage conflicts in an effective and appropriate way.

Thomas and Kilmann (Thomas 1974) proposed five categories for the classification of conflict management styles, along two dimensions: cooperativeness (involving concern for others) and assertiveness (involving concern for self). Depending on whether a cooperative or an assertive approach is adopted, one of the five conflict management styles will be employed. With the *avoiding* strategy individuals seek to bypass confrontation and withdraw from conflict. With the *accommodating* strategy, individuals will acquiesce to the demands of others. With the *competing* strategy, individuals stress winning conflicts. With the *collaborating* strategy, individuals will integrate ideas and generate alternative options in an effort to achieve win-win solutions. Finally, with the *compromising* strategy, individuals utilize a give-and-take approach to resolve the conflict, simultaneously sacrificing and gaining in the negotiation.

When facing a conflict, both conflict resolution and conflict management should be the end goal. Conflict resolution entails buyer and supplier firms agreeing upon a solution. Conflict management, in contrast, extends to the management of relational issues with partner firms. Interparty conflict and negotiation has been a major research focus in the management literature for several decades. The conflict resolution and negotiation strategies covered in this chapter and exercise are broadly represented in the literature (Thomas and Kilmann 1978; Wall and Blum 1991; Vliert and Kabanoff 1990).

It is important to recognize that there is no one "best" conflict management style—each has its strengths and weaknesses. While the avoiding strategy may provide more time to reconsider focal issues, it also allows conflicts to simmer, setting the stage for potential volatility later in time. While the accommodating strategy may demonstrate reasonableness and a willingness to resolve issues, it also fosters an undertone of resentment or signals a lack of power. The competing strategy may facilitate decisive and quick resolutions, yet it also may lead to conflict escalation. These trade-offs bear on all of the conflict styles. Thus, because no single conflict management style is appropriate across all situations, the correct approach to adopt is contingent on the outcomes one seeks (Beebe, Beebe, and Redmond 2007). Since all five strategies vary in the extent to which they reflect two value dimensions—the value of the relationship versus the value of the goal—the effectiveness of each strategy depends on the relative weight given to these two dimensions. For example, if relationship preservation and goal accomplishment are both of high importance, the collaborating strategy may be most appropriate. As a result, the conflict management concepts presented in this chapter are critical elements in the training and practice of supply chain professionals.

THEORETICAL PERSPECTIVE

The traditional OM/SCM literature provides that strategic buyer-supplier relationships are "win-win," trust-based, and collaborative (e.g., Benton and Maloni 2005; Dyer 1996; Lambert and Cooper 2000). Under this premise, a range of supply network activities benefit from deeper supplier integration. Growing trends, including vendor managed inventory (VMI), early supplier involvement (ESI) in product development, and collaborative planning, forecasting, and replenishment (CPFR) in collaborative logistics exemplify modern firm focus on enhanced coordination between buyer-supplier activities.

Many studies have focused on the benefits associated with the coordinated efforts of supply chain organizations, frequently citing benefits such as faster product development time, better product quality, and leaner inventory stocks (e.g., Aviv 2001; Waller, Johnson, and Davis 1999; Petersen, Handfield, and Ragatz 2005). When problems associated with these joint activities arise, both parties share responsibility for solving the problems together. With the increasing need for integrated activities, all five of the negotiation strategies (i.e., accommodating, avoiding, collaborating, competing, compromising) illustrated in this chapter and exercise are relevant.

The negotiation exercise incorporates important concepts from the decision-making literature, including prospect theory (Tversky and Kahneman 1981) and equity theory (Adams 1965). Prospect theory is a descriptive theory that specifically predicts decision-making behaviors under different perceptions of risk. Prospect theory holds that in situations where decision outcomes are associated with losses, individuals exhibit a risk-seeking preference, and where decision outcomes are associated with gains, individuals exhibit risk-averse behaviors (Kahneman and Tversky 1979). Kahneman and Tversky (1979) posit that decision-makers experience more displeasure with losses than the pleasure they experience with gains of equal value, making decision-makers loss-averse. Even when the expected value of a decision outcome is the same, individuals behave differently when choices are framed as losses instead of gains. Kahneman and Tversky (1979) maintain that decisions made under varying conditions of risk are transformed into subjective values representing the pleasure associated with decision outcomes. These subjective values are then weighted by the impact of probabilities on choice (Holmes et al. 2011). The condition of risk requires that individual decision-makers have knowledge of the potential outcomes of each decision option as well as the probabilities associated with those outcomes (Holmes et al. 2011). According to Holmes, R. M. and coauthors (2011), the value function explains how individuals develop subjective values of outcomes as well as the probability weighting (i.e., certainty) function. This defines the relationship between decision weights and probabilities. These two functions are central to the application of prospect theory.

Equity theory (Adams 1963; 1965) provides a framework for understanding individual perceptions of fairness. Equity theory holds that individuals compute the ratio of their perceived organizational contributions (inputs) to perceived organizational rewards (outcomes). Individuals then compare that ratio to the ratios of others in their work environments to assess equity or fairness (Siegel, Schraeder, and Morrison 2008). As an equilibrium theory, equity theory predicts that in instances in which fairness is not perceived, individuals will attempt to change attitudes and/or behaviors to establish equity and thereby restore psychological equilibrium (Adams 1965). When the ratio is less than 1, individuals are likely to believe that a condition of underbenefit exists. Conversely, when the ratio is greater than 1, individuals experiences a condition of overbenefit. Both conditions create attitudinal and behavioral consequences (Siegel, Schraeder, and Morrison 2008). Adams (1965) explained that underbenefit conditions will lead to more limited inputs, higher demand for outcomes, or even disruptive behaviors. In contrast, overbenefit conditions will lead to increased inputs or attempts to lower levels of outcomes. Most research suggests that the affective and behavioral consequences of underbenefit are stronger than those of overbenefit. Also, feelings of equity and fairness are critical within negotiations contexts. In their review of the empirical literature, Siegel, Schraeder, and Morrison (2008) concluded that perceptions of equity are associated with diminished strain, workplace violence, and increased organizational commitment. Perceptions of inequity are associated with increased turnover and decreased organizational commitment (Harmon 1997).

This chapter's exercise involves separate negotiations for cost-sharing and gain-sharing. By separating these two negotiation stages, the behaviors, attitudes, and perceptions of participants are measurable at each stage of the negotiation. Negotiation training in the supply chain area should benefit through the identification of participants behaviors and attitudes at both stages.

CASE EXAMPLES

There are several real-world case examples of high-profile disputes between two *former* supply chain partners. The sport utility vehicle (SUV) tire crisis of 2000 involving Ford Motor Company and the Firestone Tire and Rubber Company was a well-publicized conflict between the automotive original equipment manufacturer (OEM) and one of its long-standing suppliers that ultimately destroyed the relationship. The former Ford-Firestone relationship was once the longest standing buyer-supplier relationships in the automotive industry. The strategic business relationship started in 1906 and was strengthened with the marriage of the granddaughter of Harvey Firestone to the grandson of Henry Ford in 1947. Before the relationship was dissolved in 2001, Ford was Firestone's top customer, and 41% of Ford's vehicles used Firestone tires as original equipment.

The crisis involved faulty Firestone tires mounted on the Ford Explorer SUV. The tires were designed for the Explorer, a reflection of early supplier involvement present in the relationship. Evidence suggests that both firms were aware of the problem and tried to conceal information. Up to this point, the relationship was intact and both parties shared the same goal—to conceal information regarding the faulty products.

When the issue became public knowledge in February 2000, conflicts between these two former partners surfaced. Initially, both firms were able to work together, as the traditional OM/SCM literature would suggest—they jointly announced a massive recall in August 2000. Their dispute centered on which company was at fault, and the situation escalated to the point where both companies testified at several congressional hearings. By that point, the goal of each party appeared to be, at worst, to shift responsibility to the other, or at best, to maintain public confidence in their respective products.

Firestone maintained that consumers should have confidence in Firestone tires because other brands of vehicles had no such issue. In contrast, Ford argued that consumers should have confidence in Ford vehicles because other brands of tires on Explorers did not have a similarly high failure rate. The firms began finger-pointing in the press, a reflection of their conflicting goals. In hindsight, the ESI practice had adversely planted seeds for dispute, in the event of product problems. Eventually the tension between achieving their respective goals and maintaining the relationship became critical and the relationship was dissolved. The five conflict management styles covered in this chapter provide a rich foundation to explain the evolution of the interactions between these two former partners over time.

There are other notable examples of conflict between supply chain partners in recent years. For example, when Toyota Motor Corporation began transplanting its automotive factories in the United States in the 1980s and 1990s, domestic automotive suppliers were essentially forced, reluctantly, to adopt just-in-time (JIT) production in order to keep doing business with Toyota. In the retail industry, suppliers commonly complain of the difficulties of doing business with Wal-Mart. These difficulties extend to the point that some suppliers actually refuse to do business with Wal-Mart altogether. In the consumer electronics industry, both Apple and Samsung Electronics compete and collaborate together on various projects, leading to frequent disputes. With the prevalence of such conflict in supply chain relationships, coupled with the increasing prevalence of more intense firm partner involvement in supply chain activities, it is critical for managers to engage in successful negotiation and conflict management strategies.

LEARNING ACTIVITIES

The purpose of this chapter's activity is to introduce five negotiation strategies and familiarize students with these strategies through practice exercises. The activity is comprised of two parts. The first part (part 1) involves participant behavior assessment. The second part (part 2) is the negotiation exercise (broken into three phases). In the first phase of part 2, five strategies are introduced. In the second and third phases of part 2, students are provided the opportunity to apply these strategies in different bargaining situations. The following is a descriptive outline of the exercise.

EXERCISE OUTLINE

Part 1: Behavior Assessment

Personality test (based on Thomas-Kilmann negotiation/bargaining style instrument)

- Every student completes a personality inventory to assess negotiation/bargaining style. This is done at the outset of the activity to avoid priming effects.

Part 2: Setup and Game Rules for Each Phase

Phase 1: The purpose of this phase is to introduce the five conflict management/negotiation strategies and prepare for phases 2 and 3.

- Setup: The class is divided into groups of three. Within each group, each student has one 0.5-point extra credit certificate.
- Activity: Students within each group of three will negotiate (for ~10 minutes) with each other and try to attain as many 0.5-point extra credit certificates as possible.
- Game rules:
  - One person must leave the negotiation with nothing (i.e., no extra credit).
  - Extra credit points may *not* be split up; cannot split the certificates.
  - One person may walk away with all the points.
  - *No* chance procedures are allowed—drawing straws, flipping a coin.
  - However, "bribery" is acceptable—paying money, giving movie tickets, washing cars . . .

Setting for phases 2 and 3: The class is divided into two. Half of the students will keep the same team and negotiate with the same players in both phases 2 and 3. Each player assumes the same role in both phases 2 and 3. The other half of the class will play the game with different players (but will keep the same role) in phases 2 and 3.

Phase 2 (cost-sharing negotiations)

- Setup: The class is divided into groups of three.
    - Each group represents a three-tier supply chain: one supplier, one manufacturer, one dealer.
    - All supply chain team members adopt the ERP system in order to continue their business relationships.
    - The ERP adoption costs $6 million upfront and includes three main modules: the PO (purchase order) module costs $3 million, the A/P module costs $2 million, and the CRM module costs $1 million.
    - The ERP system is customized for your company and your current supply chain partners. Changes in any supply chain partner(s) will invalidate this customized ERP system.
    - If the business relationship continues, the projected cost saving per year is $2 million for all three supply chain partners to share.
- Game rules:
    - Every player in each group of three starts out with five poker chips. Each chip represents 0.1% potential extra credit. Therefore, every player begins phase 2 with 0.5% of potential extra credit value in chips. These are all the chips for phases 2 and 3. Players will negotiate with these chips and trade them for potential cost savings/sharing. Chips may be carried over from phase 2 to phase 3.
    - By the end of the game, if a team cannot reach a conclusion, they have only two choices: (1) each pays $6 million to install ERP modules in order to continue their business, or (2) the business relationships are dissolved. See individual information sheet for current business revenue and other information.
    - Adoption of ERP requires installment of *all* three modules to make it work.
    - The cost of each module cannot be split.
    - One person may walk away without incurring any ERP adaptation costs.
    - *No* chance procedures are allowed—drawing straws, flipping a coin.
    - However, one can offer different contract terms in exchange. See individual information sheet for current and available contract terms.

Phase 3 (sharing of cost-savings negotiations)

- Setup: The class is divided into groups of three.
    - Each group represents a three-tier supply chain: one supplier, one manufacturer, one dealer.
    - The ERP adoption costs $6 million upfront and includes three main modules: the PO (purchase order) module that costs $3 million, the A/P module that costs $2 million, and the CRM module that costs $1 million.

- The ERP system is customized for your company and your current supply chain partners. Changes in any supply chain partner(s) will invalidate this customized ERP system.
- The projected cost saving per year is $2 million for all three supply chain partners to share. The cost saving sharing is possible as long as the business relationship continues.

- Game rules:
  - By the end of the game, if a team cannot reach a conclusion, they have only two choices: (1) appeal to the court to rule for allocation of cost saving. However, the litigation process is estimated to cost $2 million per firm and it is uncertain as to when a ruling will occur, or (2) dissolve the business relationships. See individual information sheet for current business revenue and other information.
  - One can withdraw from the business relationship. But any withdraw will automatically break down the entire supply chain.
  - One person may walk away with all projected cost savings.
  - *No* chance procedures are allowed—drawing straws, flipping a coin.
  - However, one can offer different contract terms in exchange. See individual information sheet for current and available contract terms.

For phase 2 and phase 3: Each participant will receive a copy of the information package that includes specific information pertaining to the role participants assume, the task, and questions to answer before and after the negotiation game.

See appendices for complete versions of forms used in the game. An overview is provided here for guidance:

RELEVANT FORMS AND WORKSHEETS

The following section contains forms and worksheets used throughout the exercise. The documents appear in the following sequence:

1. Supply Chain Negotiation Game—Master
   - This file contains the Behavior Assessment (used in part 1) as well as the forms for participants (used in part 2).
   - [Advanced versions of the rules and details are indicated if the facilitator/instructor desires to enhance the exercise].
2. Supply Chain Negotiation Game (Supplement)—Supplier
   - This file contains the forms for the Supplier role (used in part 2).
   - [Advanced versions of the rules and details are indicated if the facilitator/instructor desires to enhance the exercise].
3. Supply Chain Negotiation Game (Supplement)—Manufacturer
   - This file contains the forms for the Manufacturer role (used in part 2).
   - [Advanced versions of the rules and details are indicated if the facilitator/instructor desires to enhance the exercise].
4. Supply Chain Negotiation Game (Supplement)—Dealer
   - This file contains the forms for the Dealer role (used in part 2).
   - [Advanced versions of the rules and details are indicated if the facilitator/instructor desires to enhance the exercise].
5. Supply Chain Negotiation Game—Worksheets
   - This file contains the blank worksheets, along with key, for the facilitator/instructor to enter data (used after part 2 is completed).

DISCUSSION

Upon completion of the exercise, aspects of prospect theory and equity theory should be evident. The exercise presented in this chapter requires two separate negotiation sessions, one involving costs (i.e., the loss frame) and the other, potential cost-saving sharing (i.e., the gain frame). Previous research involving prospect theory has confirmed that individuals become more risk averse when encountering a gain frame and more risk seeking when encountering a loss frame (Holmes et al. 2011; Kühberger, Schulte-Mecklenbeck, and Perner 1999). As a result, it can be expected that participants may behave differently and adopt different strategies for phase 2 (a loss frame) and phase 3 (a gain frame), with more risk-seeking behaviors being displayed in phase 2 than phase 3 and more risk-averse behaviors being displayed in phase 3 than phase 2.

Relevant discussion questions for prospect theory:

1. *What negotiation strategies did you employ during each phase of the exercise?*
2. *What was your primary or initial strategy?*
3. *What were the costs and benefits of your strategy? Was your strategy effective?*
4. *Did your attitude toward risk change during the exercise?*

Moreover, equity theory provides that individuals tend to try to balance input-outcome ratios. As equity theory predicts, when individuals perceive they under-benefited (overbenefited) in an earlier negotiation encounter (e.g., phase 2), they will either reduce their inputs or attempt to enlarge their outcomes in a later encounter (e.g., phase 3). Equity theory, in this regard, helps predict the strategies likely to be adopted when entering phase 3 of our exercise.

After phases 2 and 3, the negotiation results are recorded for each team. The results indicate the dollar ($) amount allocated to each supply chain partner. In phase 2, the dollar amount represents the one-time only implementation cost, whereas in phase 3, the dollar amount represents the annual cost savings given a continuing relationship. Following phases 2 and 3, participant report on the "fairness" of each supply chain partner, including their own company as well as the other two supply chain partners.

Relevant discussion questions for equity theory:

1. *Was the outcome of the negotiations fair from your point of view? Was the outcome of the negotiations fair from your partners' point of view?*
2. *Do you think you were under-/overbenefited in phase 2 (phase 3)? Do you feel your partners were under-/overbenefited in phase 2 (phase 3)?*
3. *Did your negotiation style differ between phases 2 and 3? Why or why not?*

The application of equity theory as a theoretical lens yields itself to two possible comparisons. First, a within-team comparison can be conducted. If each team represents a unique supply chain, insights can be generated regarding potential differences in perceived fairness of the negotiations from each participant's perspective as well as the supply chain partners' perspective. The buyer-supplier relationship literature has reported perceptual differences on various issues between the two sides (e.g., Ellram and Hendrick 1995; Kim, Park, and Kim 1999; Ro, Liker, and Fixson 2008; Lettice, Wyatt, and Evans 2010; Nyaga, Whipple, and Lynch 2010; Geiger et al. 2012). Findings from our exercise can expand our understanding of perceptual differences from a dyad to a triad context (i.e., supply chain or supply network), complementing the OM/SCM literature.

Second, a within-subject comparison also is possible in this exercise. As equity theory predicts, individuals who perceive that they underbenefited (overbenefited) in phase 2 may be more (less) aggressive in their bargaining style in phase 3 so that the input-outcome (i.e., cost saving / cost incurred) ratio between both phases remains rather balanced. The within-subject comparisons can provide empirical validation to such a prediction and have important implications. If such a prediction is empirically validated, it highlights the importance of reciprocity in business exchanges since incurred costs and benefits often occur across time. Reciprocity facilitates continuity of business exchanges. In contrast, failure of empirical validation necessitates further exploration to identify causes resulting in deviation. In either case, new insights to the practice and literature of negotiations are generated.

Learning Outcomes

The primary purpose of this exercise is to create self-awareness of learners' negotiation styles and behaviors. In a postexercise disclosure phase, the facilitator asks participants to compare their perceptions of which Thomas-Killman negotiation style they relied on during the exercise with their style preference measures from phase 1, noting any patterns or departures from the styles. Similarly, participants also should reflect on the influence of predictions from prospect theory on their negotiation styles during phases 2 and 3. Specifically, what strategies or styles did they rely on in loss/gain situations? Do they agree or disagree that their behaviors agreed with prospect theory's predictions? Participants also should reflect on the fairness of the outcomes in phases 2 and 3 at both the personal and group levels. What do they believe about the fairness of the outcomes based on their own personal inputs? What do they believe about the fairness of the outcomes for the group they represent? Finally, participants should reflect on what they have learned about distributive bargaining and win-win solutions. Overall, how would they categorize their solutions in phases 2 and 3 in the win-win typology? What factors aided or obstructed coming to a win-win solution?

As any review of the OM/SM area theory and practice reveals, negotiations are a core supply chain activity. Understanding negotiation strategies and the factors that influence them can have a strong impact on individuals' careers and the success of the organizations these individuals represent. This exercise provides an experiential opportunity for learners to explore and understand their negotiation styles, the factors that influence their reliance on these styles, and potential consequences associated with their behavior.

Appendix 1. Introduction and Part 1

INTRODUCTION

The purpose of this activity is to introduce five different negotiation strategies and familiarize students with these five strategies through negotiation practices.

The activity has three phases; the first phase is to introduce these five strategies. The second and third phases are to provide students opportunities to apply those strategies in different bargaining situations.

In all phases, the class is divided into groups of three. In phases 2 and 3, each group of three players represents a three-echelon supply chain with each player assuming a certain role: one supplier, one manufacturer, and one dealer. Players assume the same role in both phases 2 and 3.

- Phase 1: the purpose for this phase is to introduce the five conflict management/ negotiation strategies and prepare for phases 2 and 3.
- Phase 2: In this phase, each group negotiates the allocation of costs associated with an ERP implementation.
- Phase 3: In this phase, each group negotiates the allocation of cost savings resulting from the ERP implementation.

Thank you in advance for your participation!
If you are interested in the results of this study, please feel free to give me your business card or contact information.

BEHAVIOR ASSESSMENT

Before going into the next round, consider situations in which you find your goals or wishes differing from those of another person. How do you usually respond to such situations? Listed in table 15.1 are several statements describing possible behavioral responses. Please rate each of the following statements to the extent that they describe your behavioral tendencies as an individual (1 = strongly disagree and 7 = strongly agree; please circle one for each item).

Table 15.1. Instrument for Assessment of Negotiation Orientation

A1: There are times when I let others take responsibility for solving the problem.	Strongly disagree	1	2	3	4	5	6	7	Strongly agree
A2: I might try to soothe the other's feelings and preserve our relationship.	Strongly disagree	1	2	3	4	5	6	7	Strongly agree
A3: I attempt to get all concerns and issues immediately out in the open.	Strongly disagree	1	2	3	4	5	6	7	Strongly agree
A4: I try to win my position.	Strongly disagree	1	2	3	4	5	6	7	Strongly agree
A5: I try to postpone the issue until I have had some time to think it over.	Strongly disagree	1	2	3	4	5	6	7	Strongly agree
A6: I sometimes sacrifice my own wishes for the wishes of the other person.	Strongly disagree	1	2	3	4	5	6	7	Strongly agree
A7: I attempt to immediately work through our differences.	Strongly disagree	1	2	3	4	5	6	7	Strongly agree
A8: I make some effort to get my way.	Strongly disagree	1	2	3	4	5	6	7	Strongly agree
A9: I feel that differences are not always worth worrying about.	Strongly disagree	1	2	3	4	5	6	7	Strongly agree
A10: I try not to hurt the other's feelings.	Strongly disagree	1	2	3	4	5	6	7	Strongly agree
A11: I am very often concerned with satisfying all our wishes.	Strongly disagree	1	2	3	4	5	6	7	Strongly agree
A12: I am firm in pursuing my goals.	Strongly disagree	1	2	3	4	5	6	7	Strongly agree
A13: I try to do what is necessary to avoid tensions.	Strongly disagree	1	2	3	4	5	6	7	Strongly agree
A14: In approaching negotiations, I try to be considerate of the other person's wishes.	Strongly disagree	1	2	3	4	5	6	7	Strongly agree
A15: I usually seek the other's help in working out a solution.	Strongly disagree	1	2	3	4	5	6	7	Strongly agree
A16: I try to convince the other person of the merits of my position.	Strongly disagree	1	2	3	4	5	6	7	Strongly agree

Appendix 2-A. Phase 1: Cost Sharing

NOTES FOR INSTRUCTOR ON SETUP OF PHASE 1 OF NEGOTIATION GAME

- Setup: The class is divided into groups of three. Within each group, each student has one 0.5-point (points can be changed and are subject to instructors' discretion) extra credit certificate.
- Activity: Students within each group of three will negotiate (for ~10 min.) with each other and try to attain as many 0.5-point extra credit certificates as possible.
- Game rules:
    - One person must leave the negotiation with nothing (i.e., no extra credit).
    - Extra credit points may *not* be split up; cannot split the certificates.
    - One person may walk away with all the points.
    - No chance procedures are allowed—drawing straws, flipping a coin, etc.
    - However, "bribery" is acceptable—paying money, giving movie tickets, washing cars . . .

Appendix 2-B. Phase 2: Cost Sharing

NOTES FOR INSTRUCTOR

- Each group represents a three-tier supply chain: one supplier, one manufacturer, one dealer.
- All supply chain team members must adopt the ERP system in order to continue their business relationships.
- The ERP adoption costs $6 million upfront and includes three main modules: the PO module costs $3 million, the A/P module costs $2 million, and the CRM module costs $1 million.
- The ERP system is customized for your company and your current supply chain partners. Changes in any supply chain partner(s) will invalidate this customized ERP system.
- If the business relationship continues, the projected cost savings per year is $2 million for all three supply chain partners to share.

PREACTIVITY QUESTIONS TO ALL STUDENTS

1. Before going into the next round, what is the dominant negotiation strategy you anticipate to take? Check **one** that best fits your anticipated dominant strategy.

	Avoidance	Accommodation	Competition	Collaboration	Compromise
Anticipated dominant negotiation strategy	☐	☐	☐	☐	☐

2. Choose *one and only one* from each of the following pairs: (ask this before playing the game?)

   a. Choose between the two risky bets, A or B: ________________
      A. Win $2,500 with probability of .33, win $2,400 with a probability of .66, and win $0 (nothing) with a probability of .01
      B. Win $2,400 with certainty

   b. Choose between the two risky bets, A or B: ________________
      A. Win $2,500 with probability of .33, and win $0 with a probability of .67
      B. Win $2,400 with probability of .34 and win $0 with a probability of .66

   c. Choose between the two risky bets, A or B:
      A. Lose $2,500 with probability of .33, lose $2,400 with a probability of .66, and lose $0 (nothing) with a probability of 0.01
      B. Lose $2,400 with certainty

d. Choose between the two risky bets, A or B: ________________
  A. Lose $2,500 with probability of .33, and lose $0 with a probability of .67
  B. Lose $2,400 with probability of .34 and lose $0 with a probability of .66

GAME RULES

- Every player in each group of three starts out with five poker chips. Each chip represents 0.1% of potential extra credit. Therefore, every player begins phase 2 with 0.5% of potential extra credit value in chips. These are all the chips for phases 2 and 3. Players will negotiate with these chips and trade them for potential cost savings/sharing. Chips may be carried over from phase 2 to phase 3.
- By the end of the game, if a team cannot reach a conclusion, they have only two choices: (1) each pays $6 million to install the ERP modules in order to continue their business, or (2) dissolve the business relationships. See individual information sheet in the supplement for current business revenue and other information.
- Adoption of ERP requires installment of ALL three modules to make it work.
- The cost of each module cannot be split.
- One person may walk away without incurring any ERP adoption costs.
- *No* chance procedures may be used—drawing straws, flipping a coin, etc.
- [Advanced] However, one can offer different contract terms in exchange. See individual information sheet for current and available contract terms.

OBJECTIVE

Your task is to negotiate with your supply chain partners to share the costs associated with the ERP implementation. You will need to get your supervisor's approval if you recommend dissolving any existing business relationships that you currently manage.

[Students Now Read Role-Specific information (see supplement in appendix 2-M2 or 2-S2)]

[Engage in Phase 2 Activity]

POSTACTIVITY QUESTIONS FOR STUDENTS

You are the purchasing manager of the **dealer** Fisher Co.:

1. How would you characterize the relationship between your company and

	Arm's length 1	2	Partnership I 3	4	Partnership III 5
a. the Manufacturer Inc.	☐	☐	☐	☐	☐

2. What is the conclusion reached by your team? Please indicate the dollar amount allocated to each supply chain partner, and changes, if any, in contract terms in exchange for such allocation.

Supplier	is responsible for $____________________ of the implementation cost
Manufacturer Inc.	is responsible for $____________________ of the implementation cost
Dealer	is responsible for $____________________ of the implementation cost

[Advanced] Changes in contract terms (please specify)

____

☐ Check if your team could not reach agreement.

3. When playing the game: (check one that best describes your perceptions)

	Strongly disagree 1	2	Neutral 3	4	Strongly agree 5
a. I feel the time pressure	☐	☐	☐	☐	☐
b. The cost of no agreement for me personally is huge	☐	☐	☐	☐	☐
c. The cost of no agreement for my company is huge	☐	☐	☐	☐	☐

4. Out of the five following choices, which one best fits your dominant strategy?

	Avoidance	Accommodation	Competition	Collaboration	Compromise
Early in the game	☐	☐	☐	☐	☐
Middle of the game	☐	☐	☐	☐	☐
Later in the game	☐	☐	☐	☐	☐

5. In your perception, how fair do you think the result is?

	(1) Underbenefit	(2)	(3) Fair	(4)	(5) Overbenefit
	One gives up much more than one gains.		One gains about the same as one gives up.		One gains much more than one gives up.
a. Supplier	☐	☐	☐	☐	☐
b. Manufacturer	☐	☐	☐	☐	☐
c. **Dealer**	☐	☐	☐	☐	☐

APPENDIX 2-C. Phase 3: Cost-Saving Sharing

NOTES FOR INSTRUCTOR

- In this phase, each group represents a three-tier supply chain: one supplier, one manufacturer, one dealer.
- The ERP adoption costs $6 million upfront and includes three main modules: the PO (purchase order) module that costs $3 million, the A/P module that costs $2 million, and the CRM module that costs $1 million.
- The ERP system is customized for your company and your current supply chain partners. Changes in any supply chain partner(s) will invalidate this customized ERP system.
- The projected cost saving per year is $2 million for all three supply chain partners to share. The cost-saving sharing is possible as long as the business relationship continues.

PREACTIVITY QUESTIONS TO ALL STUDENTS

1. Before going into the next round, what is the dominant negotiation strategy you anticipate to take? Check **one** that best fits your anticipated dominant strategy.

	Avoidance	Accommodation	Competition	Collaboration	Compromise
Anticipated dominant negotiation strategy	☐	☐	☐	☐	☐

2. Before going into the next round, what is the perceived importance in your opinion?

	Very unimportant 1	2	Neutral 3	4	Very important 5
a. Maintaining relationships with partners	☐	☐	☐	☐	☐
b. Influence from previous negotiation experience with partners	☐	☐	☐	☐	☐
c. Personal relationship with the counterparts	☐	☐	☐	☐	☐

GAME RULES

- Assume the ERP implementation was successful.
- By the end of the game, if a team cannot reach a conclusion, they have only two choices: (1) appeal to the court to rule for allocation of cost saving. However, the litigation process is estimated to cost $2 million per firm and it is uncertain as to when a ruling will occur, or (2) dissolve the business relationships. (See individual information sheet in the supplement for current business revenue and other information).
- One can withdraw from the business relationship. But any withdrawal will automatically break down the entire supply chain.
- One person may walk away with all projected cost savings.
- *No* chance procedures may be used—drawing straws, flipping a coin, etc.
- [Advanced] However, one can offer different contract terms in exchange. See individual information sheet in the supplement for current and available contract terms.

OBJECTIVE

Your task is to negotiate with your supply chain partners to share the cost savings resulting from the successful ERP implementation. You will need to get your supervisor's approval if you recommend dissolving any existing business relationships that you currently manage.

[Students Now Read Role-Specific information (see supplement in appendix 2-M3 or 2-S3)]

[Engage in Phase 3 Activity]

POSTACTIVITY QUESTIONS FOR STUDENTS

You are the purchasing manager of the **dealer** Fisher Co.:

1. How would you characterize the relationship between your company and

	Arm's length 1	2	Partnership I 3	4	Partnership III 5
a. the Manufacturer Inc.	☐	☐	☐	☐	☐

2. What is the conclusion reached by your team? Please indicate the dollar amount allocated to each supply chain partner, and changes, if any, in contract terms in exchange for such allocation.

Supplier	will enjoy $____________ out of the projected $2 million annual cost saving.
Manufacturer	will enjoy $____________ out of the projected $2 million annual cost saving.
Dealer	will enjoy $____________ out of the projected $2 million annual cost saving.

[Advanced] Changes in contract terms (please specify)

____

☐ check if your team could not reach agreement.

3. When playing the game: (check one that best describes your perceptions)

	Strongly disagree 1	2	Neutral 3	4	Strongly agree 5
a. I feel the time pressure	☐	☐	☐	☐	☐
b. The cost of no agreement for me personally is huge	☐	☐	☐	☐	☐
c. The cost of no agreement for my company is huge	☐	☐	☐	☐	☐

4. Out of the five following choices, which one best fits your dominant strategy?

	Avoidance	Accommodation	Competition	Collaboration	Compromise
Early in the game	☐	☐	☐	☐	☐
Middle of the game	☐	☐	☐	☐	☐
Later in the game	☐	☐	☐	☐	☐

5. In your perception, how fair do you think the result is?

	(1) Underbenefit	(2)	(3) Fair	(4)	(5) Overbenefit
	One gives up much more than one gains.		One gains about the same as one gives up.		One gains much more than one gives up.
a. Supplier	☐	☐	☐	☐	☐
b. Manufacturer	☐	☐	☐	☐	☐
c. **Dealer**	☐	☐	☐	☐	☐

Appendix 2-S2. Supplemental Material for Supplier Role in Phase 2

Your name ________________

You must answer *all* questions to get the points.

Phase 2: Cost Sharing
In this phase, each group negotiates allocation of costs associated with the ERP implementation.

1. Before going into the next round, what is the dominant negotiation strategy you anticipate to take? Check **one** that best fits your anticipated dominant strategy.

	Avoidance	Accommodation	Competition	Collaboration	Compromise
Anticipated dominant negotiation strategy	☐	☐	☐	☐	☐

2. Choose *one and only one* from each of the following pairs: (ask before playing?)
   a. Choose between the two risky bets, A or B: ________________
      A. Win $2,500 with probability of .33, win $2,400 with a probability of .66, and win $0 (nothing) with a probability of .01
      B. Win $2,400 with certainty
   b. Choose between the two risky bets, A or B: ________________
      A. Win $2,500 with probability of .33, and win $0 with a probability of .67
      B. Win $2,400 with probability of .34 and win $0 with a probability of .66
   c. Choose between the two risky bets, A or B: ________________
      A. Lose $2,500 with probability of 0.33, lose $2,400 with a probability of .66, and lose $0 (nothing) with a probability of .01
      B. Lose $2,400 with certainty
   d. Choose between the two risky bets, A or B: ________________
      A. Lose $2,500 with probability of .33, and lose $0 with a probability of .67
      B. Lose $2,400 with probability of .34 and lose $0 with a probability of .66

Wait for instruction.

Please do not turn to the next page until further instruction is given.

Phase 2: Cost sharing

- Each group represents a three-tier supply chain: one supplier, one manufacturer, one dealer.
- All supply chain team members must adopt the ERP system in order to continue their business relationships.
- The ERP adoption costs $6 million upfront and includes three main modules: the PO module costs $3 million, the A/P module costs $2 million, and the CRM module costs $1 million.
- The ERP system is customized for your company and your current supply chain partners. Changes in any supply chain partner(s) will invalidate this customized ERP system.
- If the business relationship continues, the projected cost saving per year is $2 million for all three supply chain partners to share.

Phase 2: Cost sharing

- Game rules:
    - Every player in each group of three starts out with five poker chips. Each chip represents 0.1% of potential extra credit. Therefore, every player begins phase 2 with 0.5% of potential extra credit value in chips. These are all the chips for phases 2 and 3. Players will negotiate with these chips and trade them for potential cost savings/sharing. Chips may be carried over from phase 2 to phase 3.
    - By the end of the game, if a team cannot reach a conclusion, they have only two choices: (1) each pays $6 million to install ERP modules in order to continue their business, or (2) dissolve the business relationships. See individual information sheet for current business revenue and other information.
    - Adoption of ERP requires installment of *all* three modules to make it work.
    - The cost of each module cannot be split.
    - One may walk away without incurring any ERP adaptation costs.
    - *No* chance procedures may be used—drawing straws, flipping a coin, etc.
    - [Advanced] However, one can offer different contract terms (as well as chips, as aforementioned) in exchange. See individual information sheet for current and available contract terms.
- Your task is to negotiate with your supply chain partners to share the costs associated with the ERP implementation. You will need to get your supervisor's approval if you recommend dissolving any existing business relationships that you currently manage.

Wait for instruction.

Please do not turn to the next page until further instruction is given.

Please do not show this to your team members (supply chain partners).

Information Sheet: Supplier

You are the account manager working for Zeta LLC. Your job is to keep your major customers satisfied and you are responsible for contract management.

Current business with the Manufacturer Inc. accounts for about 35% of total sales, that is, purchasing approximately $300 million worth of components from your company. Besides your company, there are three other suppliers who are capable of providing the same components to the Manufacturer. Your company is the leading company in the industry.

The Manufacturer Inc. is your top customer. Besides the Manufacturer Inc., your company also sells the same items to two of the Manufacturer Inc.'s major competitors, Sigma and Phi. Total sales for Sigma and Phi account for 30% and 25%, respectively. Other smaller players together account for 10% of the total sales.

Your company has been in business with the Manufacturer for 12 years. The industry median for a relationship is seven years.

As far as you are concerned, the Manufacturer Inc. adopts a multiple sourcing strategy and also sources the same components from Supplier Alpha and Supplier Beta.

[The following contract terms can be negotiated if using the Advanced version of the exercise:]

The current contract terms are as follows:

- Level of quality: 1.5% defective rate or less. The industry median is a 3% defective rate.
- Delivery term: 30 days. The industry median is 45 days.
- Payment term: 45 days. The estimated account receivable (related to the Manufacturer Inc.) is $37.5 million. The industry norm is 1 month (30 days).
- Shipment priority: Top.
- Last-minute order change fee: None. The Manufacturer Inc. is solely responsible for any additional costs that are incurred due to any last-minute change in the order by the Manufacturer Inc.

Other contract terms that your company provides for smaller customers are as follows:

- Delivery term: 45 and 60 days.
- Payment term: month (30 days). The estimated account receivable (related to the Manufacturer Inc.) is $25 million.
- Shipment priority: Second (to the Manufacturer Inc. major competitors 1-Sigma and 2-Phi).

- Last-minute order change fee: In addition to the additional costs incurred due to any last minute order change, your company also charges 0.25% of the newly changed order as a penalty fee. The industry median for this penalty fee is 0.5%. In the past 12 years, last-minute order changes occurred only twice.

Wait for instruction.

Please do not turn to the next page until further instruction is given.

You are the account manager of the **supplier** Zeta:

1. How would you characterize the relationship between your company and

	Arm's length 1	2	Partnership I 3	4	Partnership III 5
a. the Manufacturer Inc.	☐	☐	☐	☐	☐

2. What is the conclusion reached by your team? Please indicate the dollar amount allocated to each supply chain partner, and changes, if any, in contract terms in exchange for such allocation.

Supplier Zeta LLC.	is responsible for $ ____________________ of the implementation cost
Manufacturer Inc.	is responsible for $ ____________________ of the implementation cost
Dealer Fisher Co.	is responsible for $____________________ of the implementation cost

[advanced] Changes in contract terms (please specify)

____

☐ Check if your team could not reach agreement.

3. When playing the game: (check one that best describes your perceptions)

	Strongly disagree 1	2	Neutral 3	4	Strongly agree 5
a. I feel the time pressure	☐	☐	☐	☐	☐
b. The cost of no agreement for me personally is huge	☐	☐	☐	☐	☐
c. The cost of no agreement for my company is huge	☐	☐	☐	☐	☐

4. Out of the five following choices, which one best fits your dominant strategy?

	Avoidance	Accommodation	Competition	Collaboration	Compromise
Early in the game	☐	☐	☐	☐	☐
Middle of the game	☐	☐	☐	☐	☐
Later in the game	☐	☐	☐	☐	☐

5. In your perception, how fair do you think the result is for each supply chain partner?

	(1) Underbenefit	(2)	(3) Fair	(4)	(5) Overbenefit
	One gives up much more than		One gains about the same as one		One gains much more than one
a. **Supplier Zeta LLC.**	☐	☐	☐	☐	☐
b. Manufacturer Inc.	☐	☐	☐	☐	☐
c. Dealer Fisher Co.	☐	☐	☐	☐	☐

Wait for instruction.

Please do not turn to the next page until further instruction is given.

Appendix 2-M2. Supplemental Material for Manufacturer Role in Phase 2

Your name ________________

You must answer *all* questions to get the points.

Phase 2: Cost Sharing
In this phase, each group negotiates allocation of costs associated with the ERP implementation.

1. Before going into the next round, what is the dominant negotiation strategy you anticipate to take? Check **one** that best fits your anticipated dominant strategy.

	Avoidance	Accommodation	Competition	Collaboration	Compromise
Anticipated dominant negotiation strategy	☐	☐	☐	☐	☐

2. Choose *one and only one* from each of the following pairs: (ask this before playing the game?)

   a. Choose between the two risky bets, A or B: ________________
      A. Win $2,500 with probability of .33, win $2,400 with a probability of .66, and win $0 (nothing) with a probability of .01
      B. Win $2,400 with certainty

   b. Choose between the two risky bets, A or B: ________________
      A. Win $2,500 with probability of .33, and win $0 with a probability of .67
      B. Win $2,400 with probability of .34 and win $0 with a probability of .66

   c. Choose between the two risky bets, A or B: ________________
      A. Lose $2,500 with probability of .33, lose $2,400 with a probability of .66, and lose $0 (nothing) with a probability of .01
      B. Lose $2,400 with certainty

   d. Choose between the two risky bets, A or B: ________________
      A. Lose $2,500 with probability of .33, and lose $0 with a probability of .67
      B. Lose $2,400 with probability of .34 and lose $0 with a probability of .66

Wait for instruction.

Please do not turn to the next page until further instruction is given.

Phase 2: Cost sharing

- Each group represents a three-tier supply chain: one supplier, one manufacturer, one dealer.
- All supply chain team members must adopt the ERP system in order to continue their business relationships.
- The ERP adoption costs $6 million upfront and includes three main modules: the PO module costs $3 million, the A/P module costs $2 million, and the CRM module costs $1 million.
- The ERP system is customized for your company and your current supply chain partners. Changes in any supply chain partner(s) will invalidate this customized ERP system.
- If the business relationship continues, the projected cost saving per year is $2 million for all three supply chain partners to share.

Phase 2: Cost sharing

- Game rules:
    - Every player in each group of three starts out with five poker chips. Each chip represents 0.1% of potential extra credit. Therefore, every player begins phase 2 with 0.5% of potential extra credit value in chips. These are all the chips for phases 2 and 3. Players will negotiate with these chips and trade them for potential cost savings/sharing. Chips may be carried over from phase 2 to phase 3.
    - By the end of the game, if a team cannot reach a conclusion, they have only two choices: (1) each pays $6 million to install ERP modules in order to continue their business, or (2) dissolve the business relationships. See individual information sheet for current business revenue and other information.
    - Adoption of ERP requires installment of *all* three modules to make it work.
    - The cost of each module cannot be split.
    - One may walk away without incurring any ERP adaptation costs.
    - *No* chance procedures may be used—drawing straws, flipping a coin, etc.
    - [Advanced] However, one can offer different contract terms (as well as chips, as aforementioned) in exchange. See individual information sheet for current and available contract terms.
- Your task is to negotiate with your supply chain partners to share the cost associated with the ERP implementation. You will need to get your supervisor's approval if you recommend dissolving any existing business relationships that you currently manage.

Wait for instruction.

Please do not turn to the next page until further instruction is given.

Please do not show this to your team members (supply chain partners).

Information Sheet: Manufacturer

You are the senior supply chain manager working for Manufacturer Inc. Your responsibility is to ensure products assembled by your company are delivered to end customers on time. This includes identifying suppliers who sell key components to your company and managing dealers from whom the end customers purchase the products of your company.

Current business with the supplier Zeta LLC. accounts for about 35% of the total revenue for your company. Besides the supplier Zeta LLC., there are three other suppliers who are capable of providing the same components to your company. From among these three other suppliers, your company also sources the same items from Supplier Alpha and Supplier Beta. Your company is a leading company in the industry.

The dealer Fisher is the major dealer for the product lines that you are responsible for. Thirty-five percent of the sales of your products come from Fisher. Besides Fisher, two other dealers (Delta and Gamma) also carry your products, with each carrying 30% and 25%, respectively. There are a few other dealers but they are relatively small players in the dealership market.

Your company has been in business with the supplier Zeta LLC. for 12 years and with the dealer Fisher Co. for 10 years. The industry median for both types of relationships is seven years.

As far as you are concerned, supplier Zeta LLC. also sells the same items to two of your major competitors, Sigma and Phi. Likewise, dealer Fisher Co. also carries these two major competitors' products.

[The following contract terms can be negotiated if using the Advanced version of the exercise:]

The current contract terms with Zeta LLC. are as follows:

- Level of quality: 1.5% defective rate or less. The industry median is a 3% defective rate.
- Delivery term: 30 days. The industry median is 45 days.
- Payment term: 45 days. The estimated account payable to Zeta is $37.5 million. The industry norm is one month (30 days).
- Your company is solely responsible for any additional costs that are incurred due to any last-minute change in the order initiated by your company. The Supplier does not charge any additional fee.

The current contract terms with Fisher are similar:

- Payment term: 45 days. The estimated account receivable (from Fisher) is $55.5 million.

- Delivery term: 30 days.
- Options of buyback contract: Yes. Fisher can return unsold products to your company.

Other contract terms that your company has with other suppliers are as follows:

- Delivery term: 45 and 60 days. The estimated cost savings (due to delivery premium savings) is $6 million and $12.5 million, respectively.
- Payment term: 30 days. The estimated account payable (related to Zeta) will be $25 million.
- Shipment priority: First.

Other contract terms that your company provides to other dealers:

- Payment term: 1 month (30 days)
- Options of buyback contract: No such option
- Shipment priority: Second, meaning you will fulfill orders from Delta and Gamma before Fisher

Wait for instruction.
Please do not turn to the next page until further instruction is given.

You are the supply chain manager of the **Manufacturer Inc.**:

1. How would you characterize the relationship between the Manufacturer Inc. and the

	Arm's length 1	2	**Partnership I** 3	4	**Partnership III** 5
a. Supplier Zeta LLC.	☐	☐	☐	☐	☐
b. Dealer Fisher Co.	☐	☐	☐	☐	☐

2. What is the conclusion reached by your team? Please indicate the dollar amount allocated to each supply chain partner, and changes, if any, in contract terms in exchange for such allocation.

Supplier Zeta LLC.	is responsible for $ ______________________ of the implementation cost
Manufacturer Inc.	is responsible for $ ______________________ of the implementation cost
Dealer Fisher Co.	is responsible for $ ______________________ of the implementation cost

[Advanced] Changes in contract terms (please specify)

____

☐ check if your team could not reach agreement.

3. When playing the game: (check one that best describes your perceptions)

	Strongly disagree 1	2	Neutral 3	4	Strongly agree 5
a. I feel the time pressure	☐	☐	☐	☐	☐
b. The cost of no agreement for me personally is huge	☐	☐	☐	☐	☐
c. The cost of no agreement for my company is huge	☐	☐	☐	☐	☐

4. Out of the 5 following choices, which one best fits your dominant strategy?

	Avoidance	Accommodation	Competition	Collaboration	Compromise
Early in the game	☐	☐	☐	☐	☐
Middle of the game	☐	☐	☐	☐	☐
Later in the game	☐	☐	☐	☐	☐

5. In your perception, how fair do you think the result is for each supply chain partner?

	(1) Underbenefit	(2)	(3) Fair	(4)	(5) Overbenefit
	One gives up much more than		One gains about the same as one		One gains much more than one
a. Supplier Zeta LLC.	☐	☐	☐	☐	☐
b. **Manufacturer Inc.**	☐	☐	☐	☐	☐
c. Dealer Fisher Co.	☐	☐	☐	☐	☐

Wait for instruction.

Please do not turn to the next page until further instruction is given.

Appendix 2-S3. Supplemental Material for Supplier Role in Phase 3

Your name _________________

You must answer *all* questions to get the points.

Phase 3: Cost-saving sharing
In this phase, each group negotiates allocation of costs associated with the ERP implementation.

1. Before going into the next round, what is the dominant negotiation strategy you anticipate to take? Check **one** that best fits your anticipated dominant strategy.

	Avoidance	Accommodation	Competition	Collaboration	Compromise
Anticipated dominant negotiation strategy	☐	☐	☐	☐	☐

2. Before going into the next round, how important is each of the following in your opinion?

	Least important 1	2	Neutral 3	4	Most important 5
a. Maintaining (business) relationships with partners	☐	☐	☐	☐	☐
b. Influence from previous negotiation experience with partners	☐	☐	☐	☐	☐
c. Personal relationship with the counterparts	☐	☐	☐	☐	☐

Wait for instruction.

Please do not turn to the next page until further instruction is given.

Phase 3: Cost-saving sharing

- Each group represents a three-tier supply chain: one supplier, one manufacturer, one dealer.
- The ERP adoption costs $6 million upfront and includes three main modules: the PO (purchase order) module that costs $3 million, the A/P module that costs $2 million, and the CRM module that costs $1 million.
- The ERP system is customized for your company and your current supply chain partners. Changes in any supply chain partner(s) will invalidate this customized ERP system.
- The projected cost saving per year is $2 million for all three supply chain partners to share. The cost saving sharing is possible as long as the business relationship continues.

Phase 3: Cost-saving sharing

- Game rules:
  - Assume the ERP implementation was successful.
  - By the end of the game, if a team cannot reach a conclusion, they have only two choices: (1) appeal to the court to rule for allocation of cost saving. However, the litigation process is estimated to cost $2 million per firm and it is uncertain as to when a ruling will occur, or (2) dissolve the business relationships. See individual information sheet for current business revenue and other information.
  - One can withdraw from the business relationship. But any withdrawal will automatically break down the entire supply chain.
  - One may walk away with all projected cost savings.
  - *No* chance procedures may be used—drawing straws, flipping a coin, etc.
  - [Advanced] However, one can offer different contract terms (as well as chips that you carry from phase 2) in exchange. See individual information sheet for current and available contract terms.
- Your task is to negotiate with your supply chain partners to share the cost savings resulting from the successful ERP implementation. You will need to get your supervisor's approval if you recommend dissolving any existing business relationships that you currently manage.

Wait for instruction.

Please do not turn to the next page until further instruction is given.

Please do not show this to your team members (supply chain partners).

Information Sheet: Supplier

You are the account manager working for Zeta LLC. Your job is to keep your major customers satisfied and you are responsible for contract management.

Current business with the Manufacturer Inc. accounts for about 35% of total sales, i.e., purchasing approximately $300 million worth of components from your company. Besides your company, there are three other suppliers who are capable of providing the same components to the Manufacturer. Your company is the leading company in the industry.

The Manufacturer Inc. is your top customer. Besides the Manufacturer Inc., your company also sells the same items to two of the Manufacturer Inc.'s major competitors, Sigma and Phi. Total sales for Sigma and Phi account for 30% and 25%, respectively. Other smaller players together account for 10% of the total sales.

Your company has been in business with the Manufacturer for 12 years. The industry median for a relationship is seven years.

As far as you are concerned, the Manufacturer Inc. adopts a multiple sourcing strategy and also sources the same components from Supplier Alpha and Supplier Beta.

[The following contract terms can be negotiated if using the Advanced version of the exercise:]

The current contract terms are as follows:

- Level of quality: 1.5% defective rate or less. The industry median is a 3% defective rate.
- Delivery term: 30 days. The industry median is 45 days.
- Payment term: 45 days. The estimated account receivable (related to the Manufacturer Inc.) is $37.5 million. The industry norm is 1 month (30 days).
- Shipment priority: Top.
- Last-minute order change fee: None. The Manufacturer Inc. is solely responsible for any additional costs that are incurred due to any last-minute change in the order by the Manufacturer Inc.

Other contract terms that your company provides for smaller customers are as follows:

- Delivery term: 45 and 60 days.
- Payment term: 1 month (30 days). The estimated account receivable (related to the Manufacturer Inc.) is $25 million.
- Shipment priority: Second (to the Manufacturer Inc. major competitors 1-Sigma and 2-Phi)

- Last-minute order change fee: In addition to the additional costs incurred due to any last minute order change, your company also charges 0.25% of the newly changed order as a penalty fee. The industry median for this penalty fee is 0.5%. In the past 12 years, last minute order changes occurred only twice.

Wait for instruction.

Please do not turn to the next page until further instruction is given.

You are the account manager of the **supplier Zeta**:

1. How would you characterize the relationship between your company and

	Arm's length 1	2	**Partnership I** 3	4	**Partnership III** 5
a. the Manufacturer Inc.	☐	☐	☐	☐	☐

2. What is the conclusion reached by your team? Please indicate the dollar amount allocated to each supply chain partner, and changes, if any, in contract terms in exchange for such allocation.

Supplier Zeta LLC.	will enjoy $ ______________ out of the projected $2 million annual cost saving.
Manufacturer Inc.	will enjoy $ ______________ out of the projected $2 million annual cost saving.
Dealer Fisher Co.	will enjoy $ ______________ out of the projected $2 million annual cost saving.

[advanced] Changes in contract terms (please specify)

____

☐ Check if your team could not reach agreement.

3. When playing the game: (check one that best describes your perceptions)

	Strongly disagree 1	2	Neutral 3	4	Strongly agree 5
a. I feel the time pressure	☐	☐	☐	☐	☐
b. The cost of no agreement for me personally is huge	☐	☐	☐	☐	☐
c. The cost of no agreement for my company is huge	☐	☐	☐	☐	☐

4. Out of the five following choices, which one best fits your dominant strategy?

	Avoidance	Accommodation	Competition	Collaboration	Compromise
Early in the game	☐	☐	☐	☐	☐
Middle of the game	☐	☐	☐	☐	☐
Later in the game	☐	☐	☐	☐	☐

5. In your perception, how fair do you think the result is for each supply chain partner?

	(1) Underbenefit	(2)	(3) Fair	(4)	(5) Overbenefit
	One gives up much more than		One gains about the same as one		One gains much more than one
a. **Supplier Zeta LLC.**	☐	☐	☐	☐	☐
b. Manufacturer Inc.	☐	☐	☐	☐	☐
c. Dealer Fisher Co.	☐	☐	☐	☐	☐

Appendix 2-M3. Supplemental Material for Manufacturer Role in Phase 3

Your name ________________

You must answer *all* questions to get the points.

Phase 3: Cost-saving sharing
In this phase, each group negotiates allocation of costs associated with the ERP implementation.

1. Before going into the next round, what is the dominant negotiation strategy you anticipate to take? Check **one** that best fits your anticipated dominant strategy.

	Avoidance	Accommodation	Competition	Collaboration	Compromise
Anticipated dominant negotiation strategy	☐	☐	☐	☐	☐

2. Before going into the next round, how important is each of the following in your opinion?

	Least important 1	2	Neutral 3	4	Most important 5
a. Maintaining (business) relationships with partners	☐	☐	☐	☐	☐
b. Influence from previous negotiation experience with partners	☐	☐	☐	☐	☐
c. Personal relationship with the counterparts	☐	☐	☐	☐	☐

Wait for instruction.

Please do not turn to the next page until further instruction is given.

Phase 3: Cost-saving sharing

- Each group represents a three-tier supply chain: one supplier, one manufacturer, one dealer.
- The ERP adoption costs $6 million upfront and includes three main modules: the PO (purchase order) module that costs $3 million, the A/P module that costs $2 million, and the CRM module that costs $1 million.
- The ERP system is customized for your company and your current supply chain partners. Changes in any supply chain partner(s) will invalidate this customized ERP system.
- The projected cost saving per year is $2 million for all three supply chain partners to share. The cost saving sharing is possible as long as the business relationship continues.

Phase 3: Cost-saving sharing

- Game rules:
  - Assume the ERP implementation was successful.
  - By the end of the game, if a team cannot reach a conclusion, they have only two choices: (1) appeal to the court to rule for allocation of cost saving. However, the litigation process is estimated to cost $2 million per firm and it is uncertain as to when a ruling will occur, or (2) dissolve the business relationships. See individual information sheet for current business revenue and other information.
  - One can withdraw from the business relationship. But any withdrawal will automatically break down the entire supply chain.
  - One may walk away with all projected cost savings.
  - *no* chance procedures—drawing straws, flipping a coin, etc.
  - [Advanced] However, one can offer different contract terms (as well as chips that you carry from phase 2) in exchange. See individual information sheet for current and available contract terms.
- Your task is to negotiate with your supply chain partners to share the cost savings result from the successful ERP implementation. You will need to get your supervisor's approval if you recommend dissolving any existing business relationships that you currently manage.

Wait for instruction.

Please do not turn to the next page until further instruction is given.

Please do not show this to your team members (supply chain partners).

Information Sheet: Manufacturer

You are the senior supply chain manager working for Manufacturer Inc. Your responsibility is to ensure products assembled by your company are delivered to end customers on time. This includes identifying suppliers who sell key components to your company and managing dealers from whom the end customers purchase the products of your company.

Current business with the supplier Zeta LLC. accounts for about 35% of the total revenue for your company. Besides the supplier Zeta LLC., there are three other suppliers who are capable of providing the same components to your company. From among these three other suppliers, your company also sources the same items from Supplier Alpha and Supplier Beta. Your company is a leading company in the industry.

The dealer Fisher is the major dealer for the product lines that you are responsible for. Thirty-five percent of the sales of your products come from Fisher. Besides Fisher, two other dealers (Delta and Gamma) also carry your products, with each carrying 30% and 25%, respectively. There are a few other dealers but they are relatively small players in the dealership market.

Your company has been in business with the supplier Zeta LLC. for 12 years and with the dealer Fisher Co. for 10 years. The industry median for both types of relationships is seven years.

As far as you are concerned, supplier Zeta LLC. also sells the same items to two of your major competitors, Sigma and Phi. Likewise, dealer Fisher Co. also carries these two major competitors' products.

The current contract terms with Zeta LLC. are as follows:

- Level of quality: 1.5% defective rate or less. The industry median is a 3% defective rate.
- Delivery term: 30 days. The industry median is 45 days.
- Payment term: 45 days. The estimated account payable to Zeta is $37.5 million. The industry norm is 1 month (30 days).
- Your company is solely responsible for any additional costs that are incurred due to any last-minute change in the order initiated by your company. The Supplier does not charge any additional fee.

[The following contract terms can be negotiated if using the Advanced version of the exercise:]

The current contract terms with Fisher are similar:

- Payment term: 45 days. The estimated account receivable (from Fisher) is $55.5 million.

- Delivery term: 30 days.
- Options of buyback contract: Yes. Fisher can return unsold products to your company.

Other contract terms that your company has with other suppliers are as follows:

- Delivery term: 45 and 60 days. The estimated cost savings (due to delivery premium savings) is $6 million and $12.5 million, respectively.
- Payment term: 30 days. The estimated account payable (related to Zeta) will be $25 million.
- Shipment priority: First.

Other contract terms that your company provides to other dealers:

- Payment term: 1 month (30 days)
- Options of buyback contract: No such option
- Shipment priority: Second, meaning you will fulfill orders from Delta and Gamma before Fisher

Wait for instruction.
Please do not turn to the next page until further instruction is given.

You are the supply chain manager of the **Manufacturer Inc.**:

1. How would you characterize the relationship between the Manufacturer Inc. and the

	Arm's length 1	2	**Partnership I** 3	4	**Partnership III** 5
a. Supplier Zeta LLC.	☐	☐	☐	☐	☐
b. Dealer Fisher Co.	☐	☐	☐	☐	☐

2. What is the conclusion reached by your team? Please indicate the dollar amount allocated to each supply chain partner, and changes, if any, in contract terms in exchange for such allocation.

Supplier Zeta LLC.	will enjoy $ ______________ out of the projected $2 million annual cost saving.
Manufacturer Inc.	will enjoy $ ______________ out of the projected $2 million annual cost saving.
Dealer Fisher Co.	will enjoy $ ______________ out of the projected $2 million annual cost saving.

Changes in contract terms (please specify)

____

☐ Check if your team could not reach agreement.

3. When playing the game: (check one that best describes your perceptions)

	Strongly disagree 1	2	Neutral 3	4	Strongly agree 5
a. I feel the time pressure	☐	☐	☐	☐	☐
b. The cost of no agreement for me personally is huge	☐	☐	☐	☐	☐
c. The cost of no agreement for my company is huge	☐	☐	☐	☐	☐

4. Out of the five following choices, which one best fits your dominant strategy?

	Avoidance	Accommodation	Competition	Collaboration	Compromise
Early in the game	☐	☐	☐	☐	☐
Middle of the game	☐	☐	☐	☐	☐
Later in the game	☐	☐	☐	☐	☐

5. In your perception, how fair do you think the result is for each supply chain partner?

	(1) Underbenefit	(2)	(3) Fair	(4)	(5) Overbenefit
	One gives up much more than		One gains about the same as one		One gains much more than one
a. Supplier Zeta LLC.	☐	☐	☐	☐	☐
b. **Manufacturer Inc.**	☐	☐	☐	☐	☐
c. Dealer Fisher Co.	☐	☐	☐	☐	☐

References

Adams, J. S. 1963. Towards an understanding of inequity. Journal of Abnormal and Social Psychology 67 (5), 422.

Adams, J. S. 1965. Inequity in social exchange. Advances in Experimental Social Psychology 2, 267–299.

Aviv, Y. 2001. The effect of collaborative forecasting on supply chain performance. Management Science 47 (10), 1326–1343.

Beebe, S. A., Beebe, S. J., Redmond, M. V. 2007. Interpersonal Communication: Relating to Others. Boston: Allyn & Bacon.

Benton, W. C., Maloni, M. 2005. The influence of power driven buyer/seller relationships on supply chain satisfaction. Journal of Operations Management 23 (1), 1–22.

Dyer, J. H. 1996. How Chrysler created an American keiretsu. Harvard Business Review 14 (2), 128–129.

Ellram, L. M., Hendrick, T. E. 1995. Partnering characteristics: A dyadic perspective. Journal of Business Logistics 16 (1), 41–64.

Geiger, I., Durand, A., Saab, S., Kleinaltenkamp, M., Baxter, R., Lee, Y. 2012. The bonding effects of relationship value and switching costs in industrial buyer-seller relationships: An investigation into role differences. Industrial Marketing Management 41 (1), 82–93.

Harmon, H. A. 1997. A gender blind system for promotion in the salesforce. Marketing Intelligence and Planning 15 (1), 28–31.

Hocker, J. L., Wilmot, W. W. 1985. Interpersonal Conflict. 2nd ed. Dubuque, IA: Wm. C. Brown.

Holmes, R. M., Bromiley, P., Devers, C. E., Holcomb, T. R., McGuire, J. B. 2011. Management theory applications of prospect theory: Accomplishments, challenges, and opportunities. Journal of Management 37 (4), 1069–1107.

Kahneman, D., Tversky, A. 1979. Prospect theory: An analysis of decision under risk. Econometrica 47 (2), 263–291.

Kim, B., Park, K., Kim, T. 1999. The perception gap among buyer and suppliers in the semiconductor industry. Supply Chain Management 4 (5), 231–241.

Kühberger, A., Schulte-Mecklenbeck, M., Perner, J. 1999. The effects of framing, reflection, probability, and payoff on risk preference in choice tasks. Organizational Behavior and Human Decision Processes 78 (3), 204–231.

Lambert, D. M., Cooper, M. C. 2000. Issues in supply chain management. Industrial Marketing Management 29 (1), 65–83.

Lettice, F., Wyatt, C., Evans, S. 2010. Buyer-supplier partnerships during product design and development in the global automotive sector: Who invests, in what and when? International Journal of Production Economics 127 (2), 309–319.

Nyaga, G. N., Whipple, J. M., Lynch, D. F. 2010. Examining supply chain relationships: Do buyer and supplier perspectives on collaborative relationships differ? Journal of Operations Management 28 (2), 101–114.

Petersen, K. J., Handfield, R. B., Ragatz, G. L. 2005. Supplier integration into new product development: Coordinating product, process and supply chain design. Journal of Operations Management 23 (3), 371–388.

Rahim, M. A. 1992. Managing Conflict in Organizations. 2nd ed. Westport, CT: Praeger.

Ro, Y. K., Liker, J. K., Fixson, S. K. 2008. Evolving models of supplier involvement in design: The deterioration of the Japanese model in US auto. IEEE Transactions on Engineering Management 55 (2), 359–377.

Siegel, P. H., Schraeder, M., Morrison, R. 2008. A taxonomy of equity factors. Journal of Applied Social Psychology 38 (1), 61–75.

Thomas, K. W. 1974. Thomas-Kilmann Conflict Mode Instrument. Tuxedo, NY: Xicom.

Thomas, K. W., Kilmann, R. H. 1978. Comparison of four instruments measuring conflict behavior. Psychological Reports 42 (3c), 1139–1145.

Tversky, A., Kahneman, D. 1981. The framing of decisions and the psychology of choice. Science 211, 453–458.

Van de Vliert, E., Kabanoff, B. 1990. Toward theory-based measures of conflict management. Academy of Management Journal 33 (1), 199–209.

Wall, J. A., Blum, M. W. 1991. Negotiations. Journal of Management 17 (2), 273–303.

Waller, M., Johnson, M. E., Davis, T. 1999. Vendor-managed inventory in the retail supply chain. Journal of Business Logistics 20 (1), 183–204.

CHAPTER 16

ERP Simulator

Examining Competitive Supply Chain Team Dynamics

DAVID E. CANTOR AND PAMELA MANHART ■

OVERVIEW

Individuals, teams, firms, and industries experience change. Firms experience change in terms of the nature of marketplace competition. Because sustainable competitive advantage is elusive, firms must constantly evolve and periodically update/change strategic priorities to protect market position. As Joseph Schumpeter pointed out, firms are constantly engaging in "creative destruction." For example, Coke and Pepsi are aware of each other's manufacturing and product packaging strategies and continually attempt to respond to each other's competitive environmental moves (Hofer, Cantor, and Dai 2012).

An important strategic weapon enabling firms to respond to competition is information. Firms leverage data and information to stay alert to rivals' competitive acts. In so doing firms become aware of dynamic marketplace changes. Examples of dynamic change include a rival's introduction of new products, a supplier's poor delivery performance, and customer needs. Firms gain access to this type of competitive information through business analytics tools available in enterprise software systems. Indeed, enterprise software systems such as SAP and Oracle are increasingly being adopted by many Fortune 500 companies. These technologies enable managers to analyze changes in the marketplace and engage in a rapid response.

Employees also must adapt to organizational changes in the hypercompetitive marketplace. Organizational changes occur because management reconfigures the firm in response to market dynamics. Thus employees must adapt to different roles within teams and departments for firms to respond effectively to rivals' competitive actions. Moreover, employees must adapt to the increased presence of information technology tools used to coordinate firms' responses. Employees and their team members rely on the data and information available through enterprise software to make collaborative decisions.

Cross-functional supply chain teams make critical business decisions that can affect competitive advantage. Cross-functional teamwork is commonly found in supply chains. Examples of supply chain teamwork activities include sales and operations planning, new product development, total quality management, sourcing, assembly tasks, and enterprise resource planning implementations (Wu, Loch, and Ahmad 2011). Easton and Rosenzweig (2012) offer an example of how the characteristics of team members affect the success of total quality management projects.

The purpose of this chapter is to examine dynamic team behavior within the context of a competitive SAP enterprise system gaming environment. This is an important topic because work in the SAP enterprise resource planning (ERP) environment is inherently a team-based activity. Supply chain teams rely on up-to-date information to run manufacturing operations. For example, if supply chain teams have completed a Plan for Every Part (PFEP), the entire plan output can be stored in SAP, primarily the material master. This enables every member of the organization to know what others are doing with regard to this plan for each part. In completing a PFEP, it is critical for supply chain teams to consider the impact of this planning process on inventories, so firms can compete.

Teams can leverage information stored in SAP to analyze historical information on inventory balances. These can be used with upstream and downstream work centers (run by teams) to determine setups, lot sizing, and inventory impact (quantities, investment dollars, and space). Working with upstream and downstream work center teams is crucial for integrating work centers and the whole organization to create flow within the supply chain. Understanding of the big-picture dynamics leads to greater capabilities in improving project performance (Bendoly 2014).

This chapter describes how supply chain student teams adapt to change in the context of a SAP enterprise resource planning (ERP) software simulation program. We examine how differentiated supply chain team roles impact team performance in a competitive gaming SAP situation. In the SAP simulation game, teams are comprised of differentiated supply chain roles in a supply chain decision-making task. Each supply chain team is responsible for selling different products in a hypercompetitive simulated marketplace. At first, the supply chain teams are tasked with making decisions, such as determining the prices of each bottled water product, investing in advertising, monitoring inventory levels, and reviewing the average market price for each product. The team's next set of tasks expands (i.e., stretch work) to include three new tasks. The goal of this chapter is to explain how supply chain teams can successfully overcome the flux in team coordination caused by stretch work and how their ability to adapt to change affects their competitive behavior.

THEORETICAL PERSPECTIVE

Schumpeterian Economics

Before describing the supply chain software simulation exercise, we offer theoretical insights as to the importance of supply chain competition. Here we draw on Schumpeterian economics. Schumpeter (1934; 1942) argued that firms respond to the competitive actions taken by their rivals to create and erode sources of competitive advantage (Grimm and Smith 1997). In so doing, firms seek to enhance their own performance. Firms recognize that markets are in constant flux and that rivals are motivated to respond to actions that would otherwise erode their ability to earn profit potential (Grimm and Smith 1997). Examples include changing prices, marketing investments, capital and equipment investments, research and development investments, and new product innovations (Chen and MacMillan 1992; Miller and Chen 1994; Smith et al. 1991). In the supply chain literature, Hofer, Cantor, and Dai (2012) showed that firms can leverage environmental practices to engage in competitive moves and countermoves.

Schumpeterian economics also sheds light on the vital role of information in facilitating competitive moves in the supply chain. An important characteristic of market disequilibrium in the Schumpeterian view is imperfect information, in contrast to the neoclassical assumption that all market participants have full access to information. Information is not fully shared among firms or between firms and their customers. Acquisition and dissemination of information is of critical importance, as firms compete primarily via innovation. In fact, both firms and individuals require an enormous amount of time and effort to collect, organize, and process information (Cantor and Macdonald 2009).

Supply Chain Information-Processing Perspectives

Supply chain scholars have explored how information sharing represents an important driver of both individual and team-level supply chain decision-making behavior (Cantor and Macdonald 2009). In fact, a steady stream of supply chain research has examined how information affects supply chain decision-making. For example, Lee, Padmanabhan, and Whang (1997) pointed out that poor information-sharing practices can lead to the bullwhip effect, and thus it is critical that firms implement improved information dissemination practices such as CPFR (collaborative planning, forecasting, and replenishment) and part-planning practices in manufacturing settings. Beyond information technology tools and collaborative practices, misperception of feedback (information) also affects decision-making within and across firms (Sterman 1989). Subsequent studies have examined how improved information sharing can improve supply chain decision-making behavior.

For example, Steckel, Gupta, and Banerji (2004) examined how sharing point-of-sale (POS) data led to improvements in supply chain performance. Croson and Donohue (2006) examined how the flow and direction of information sharing (e.g., dynamic inventory information) provided greater benefits to supply chain decision-making. Adopting a social psychology approach, Cantor and Macdonald (2009) drew on construal-level theory (Liberman and Trope 2008) to show how the consideration of either an abstract or concrete view of information affects decision-making behavior. Relatedly, Mortiz, Hill, and Donohue (2012) utilized cognitive reflection theory (Frederick 2005) to explain why individuals with higher cognitive reflection exhibited a lower tendency to chase demand in a newsvendor task. Tokar and coauthors (2013) examined how individuals react to demand shocks in simple replenishment tasks. More broadly, Sanders (2007) points out how e-business technology leads to improved intraorganizational and interorganizational information sharing/collaboration and overall firm performance.

While the above-mentioned scholars have made important contributions to the literature, scant research has considered how team structure and collaboration affect supply chain decision-making in competitive contexts. Teams are responsible for making competitive decisions in supply chains. Teams must adapt to vast amounts of information to make competitive decisions. Below, we examine how dynamic team roles can affect supply chain decision-making using the theory of the strategic core as our theoretical lens (Summers, Humphrey, and Ferris 2012).

Theory of Strategic Core

The characteristics of teams affect team performance (Humphrey, Morgeson, and Mannor 2009). In supply chains, Easton and Rosenzweig (2012) point out that team familiarity and individual and organizational experiences drive the success of Six Sigma projects. More generally, research suggests that some roles have a more prominent impact on organizational performance than others (Delery and Shaw 2001). We adopt the theory of strategic core to explain how certain role holders in teams can have a greater influence on competitive performance (Summers, Humphrey, and Ferris 2012; Humphrey, Morgeson, and Mannor 2009). Following Summers, Humphrey, and Ferris (2012) and Humphrey Morgeson, and Mannor (2009), we define the strategic core as the role or roles on a team that (*a*) encounter more of the problems that need to be overcome in the team, (*b*) have a greater exposure to the tasks that the team is performing, and (*c*) are more central to the workflow of the team. Moreover, Humphrey, Morgeson, and Mannor (2009) pointed out that a strategic core role can be thought of as a continuum: The more that a role meets these criteria, the more "core" the role is to the team.

In supply chains, there are team members who encounter more of the problem the team needs to overcome. For example, project managers need to reconcile competing subordinate perspectives in new product development activities (Wouters et al. 2009). Project managers (leaders) also seek buy-in and resources necessary for achieving project success (Linderman, Shroeder, and Choo 2006). Undoubtedly, competing perspectives arise because some team members are more familiar with the business challenges associated with bringing new products to market. Other team members are concerned with technical hurdles. Thus, project leaders/project managers reconcile these views and seek to facilitate critical supply chain business decisions (Bendoly, Perry-Smith, and Bachrach 2010). Scott-Young and Samson (2008) illustrated some of the critical success factors that project leaders need to address that can impact project cost, schedule, and operability.

In supply chains, some team members have a greater exposure to the tasks that need to be performed to enhance supply chain team performance. Because of the vital role of information, supply chain core team members need to have access to business intelligence tools such as dashboards in order to make critical business decisions. Indeed, Johnson and coauthors (2007) provided insight as to how customer supply chain teams leverage e-business technologies more than other supply chain teams to make important supply chain decisions.

CASE EXAMPLE

To illustrate the nature of how teams dynamics affects supply chain performance, we describe an inventory and planning problem that BigCo Company faced in its supply chain. To illustrate, the heat-treat work center at BigCo, in Galesburg, Illinois, determined that it can easily gain efficiencies by minimizing setups and running each product only once per month. The supervisor (e.g., project leader) reviewed forecast information and produced the number of parts forecast for the next month each time the plant set up to heat-treat housings. The supply chain team decided that it was best to store excess inventory in the Galesburg warehouse until the downstream work center at BigCo's Ames, Iowa, plant placed an order for its turning operation. Because the lead time to the Ames plant is one month, it placed an order for housings at least one month in advance of forecast need. The Ames warehouse contained inventory to cover forecast demand during the long lead time. When BigCo's customer GiganticCorp placed a large order, it scheduled more production, but would not have enough heat-treated housings to turn. Ames would place an order to the Galesburg plant that would be out of stock, and because of the large runs already scheduled, it would not currently have capacity to heat-treat housings for weeks.

Each batch ahead of the housings would be large enough to create warehouse stores even while customer sales were waiting. Although BigCo carried large amounts of inventory, it was not the correct mix. It carried too much of the wrong things and not enough of the right things. The efficiency-maximizing behavior of each operation created a unit price benefit at a particular work center while leading toward backorder dollars for the firm and the customer. In addition, storage was required at every step of the process and large queues would slow responsiveness to changes in demand. Operations would generally blame the sales department and/or the customer for not providing better SKU (stock keeping unit) level forecasts. Clearly, poor team dynamics was an issue.

Shortly after a substantial investment in SAP, BigCo's supply chain team decided to improve cross-functional team dynamics because they wanted to create a PFEP plan for every part. Given that forecasts are only good at the aggregate level and less accurate toward SKU-level detail, a PFEP could help bridge the gap. The firm also wanted to utilize its new SAP capabilities to help lower costs and improve throughput. A competitor, SpendCo, had recently installed additional capacity that had allowed it to offer reduced lead times.

SpendCo had reduced prices in an attempt to increase volumes and utilize the extra capacity. BigCo needed a competitive response to maintain its market share and felt that an investment in SAP including a PFEP would allow the company to strategically cut both inventories and lead times. A cross-functional team was created to develop the PFEP with members from planning, purchasing, operations, engineering, information technology, and the continuous improvement team. Cross-functional teams were an integral part of the deployment strategy.

Analysts, operators, supervisors, and management levels from multiple sites were represented. They brainstormed and decided they could capture all of the parts and relevant issues by categorizing them in a matrix of volume, variation, and cost. Through business intelligence queries in SAP, they accessed demand information of several key parts representing various value streams. Considering volume, variation, maximums, and minimums against timing intervals (smooth, lumpy, or trend), they categorized multiple patterns. Definitions of each parameter were described. Each section of the matrix represented a build frequency and lot size strategy. To determine optimal settings, a simulation was designed. Phony parts were created with mock bills of materials in the SAP test database. Demand imitating the categorized patterns was reproduced in the test database. Beginning and ending inventory levels were captured across the various replenishment schemes proposed. After observing the results for three months, the team agreed the optimal solution was the one in each scenario representing the lowest inventory without going negative. The winning schemes were populated into the corresponding blocks of the matrix. These parameters would be suggested default settings for materials flowing through BigCo.

To roll out the implementation, a member of the Ames turning operation, its planner, and its buyer all went to Galesburg to meet with three corresponding members from the heat-treat operation. Half of these were members of the PFEP matrix team. Through queries in SAP, the implementation team accessed demand information. They reviewed the demand patterns and timing intervals of all the heat-treated parts flowing from Galesburg to Ames as well as the number and duration of stockouts at each level. SAP has a unique feature of being able to go back in history and take a snapshot of inventory on a past date. Pulling this information for the last two years, they could calculate the average quantity of inventory held for each item. Pairing these data with the material master to multiply quantity by costs obtained average dollar values invested in inventory. From the inventory snapshot, aging can also be determined. In addition, they pulled transactional detail of time from order to completion.

Even though BigCo intended to produce batch sizes of one month of forecast, the implementation team realized that was seldom the case. Forty percent of the time, sales did not materialize to consume the full production run, and inventories aged for an average of three months prior to moving. Inventory turns can hide slow-moving inventory if there are enough faster-moving materials to compensate. By looking at SKU-level items, the team determined the actual range of performance and identified SKU's warranting a change in strategy. In contrast, 40% of the time sales exceeded forecasts and stockouts occurred prior to the next planned production run. When the forecast was short, there was not enough flexibility in production to respond. They were shocked to learn that only 30% of sales shipped complete to customer due date. After reviewing all of the data, they went on a plant tour of the heat-treat operation to help add some context to the data and fully understand the limitations and capabilities of the work center.

After analyzing the data and touring the work center, they began assigning parts to the matrix and developed a plan for each section. Both teams had to give and take to arrive at a winning compromise. This required a shift in perspective from looking at work centers individually to viewing the supply chain as a whole. The strategy agreed upon was that the Ames plant would take possession of the entire run that the Galesburg plant produced. All of the inventory would be consolidated at the point of consumption. In return, Galesburg agreed to reduce their production runs and lead time. Galesburg would be willing to set up a production run each week in a small batch quantity. The cost of extra setups was offset by the benefits of saving thousands of dollars invested in inventory, as well as substantial warehouse space and corresponding handling costs. In addition, the Galesburg group planned a kaizen event to speed up changeover times for further savings. The inventory at the Ames plant did not increase, even though the plant accepted ownership of each Galesburg production run because the batch sizes were smaller. Consolidation also provided improved visibility of the total number of housings in the system.

Highly variable parts would no longer have buffers to cover demand variation. Galesburg would run only what was needed, as often as needed. The most expensive parts were to carry only minimal amounts of inventory to reduce inventory investment. However, some inventory would be necessary to prevent high-dollar orders from stocking out. In addition, only minimal inventories were needed for the stable parts. Short-term forecast errors tended to offset each other; slightly low sales one period were often followed by slightly higher sales the following period. Stable inventory is low risk and helped to minimize unnecessarily frequent production runs. By reducing lot sizes, quantity decisions were made within a shorter horizon, which increased accuracy. Trying to predict demand in longer-term horizons required using inaccurate data, which led to investments in the wrong products, creating inefficiencies for the overall supply chain.

The team-based collaboration created flow through the supply chain between the two work centers, which was replicated throughout BigCo. It established expectations, boundaries, and flexibility. By utilizing business intelligence SAP information, working effectively in teams, and looking at the bigger picture, lead times and costs were reduced while service levels improved. In addition to lot size and frequency of build decisions, each pair of links in the supply chain also reviewed other part-specific information such as packaging, dedicated storage, dual sources, and quality controls to complete the PFEP. These efforts enabled BigCo to lower prices and lead times while maintaining profit margins and growing market share. The company's competitive supply chain reactions to SpendCo were successful.

LEARNING ACTIVITY

To illustrate supply chain team dynamics concepts within the classroom, we utilize the SAP enterprise resource planning (ERP) software bottled water simulation program, which was developed by the faculty at HEC Montreal. The ERP simulation game involves three-person teams that are composed of differentiated team roles on a supply chain decision-making task. In groups of three participants, each team operates a bottled water distribution company. Each team has access to standard reports to make business decisions to ensure the profitability of their operation. Further, each supply chain SAP ERP team is responsible for selling six different products in three different regions of a hypercompetitive simulated German marketplace. The market size is about 6,000 euros per team (company) per day. The six different bottled water products are offered in 1 liter or 500 ml versions. See figure 16.1 for more details of the products that each team manages.

All students are provided additional details of the ERP simulation game. They are instructed that the game lasts 60 minutes. Each round of the game runs 20 minutes. After each round, all student teams are provided with information regarding where they rank in the game as well as other team performance information (e.g., profitability metrics). See figure 16.2 for an example of an end-of-round

Product Code	Product Description	Units in box	Cost of boxes
$$-B01	1L ClearPure	12 bottles	11.99
$$-B02	1L Spritz	12 bottles	14.99
$$-B03	1L Lemon Spritz	12 bottles	16.99
$$-B04	500mL ClearPure	24 bottles	16.99
$$-B05	500mL Spritz	24 bottles	19.99
$$-B06	500mL Lemon Spritz	24 bottles	22.99

Figure 16.1 Team Manages Six Bottled Water Products

Team	Credit ratings	Interest Rate (%)	Rank	Cumulative Net Income	Total sales	Gross Margin (%)	Net Margin (%)	ROE (%)	RSA (%)	D/E (%)	Mktg/S (%)
I	AA-	5.75	1	12,263.41	109,599.94	11.189	11.189	2.394	2.394	0	0
H	AA-	5.75	2	10,093.66	144,658.92	11.148	8.803	1.979	1.979	0	2.344
J	AA-	5.75	3	9,426.69	94,634.89	9.961	9.961	1.85	1.85	0	0
A	AA-	5.75	4	8,238.71	88,172.75	11.726	9.344	1.621	1.621	0	2.382
E	AA-	5.75	5	8,006.17	113,096.50	8.534	7.079	1.576	1.576	0	1.455
D	AA-	5.75	6	4,223.37	101,998.71	4.92	4.141	0.838	0.838	0	0.779
C	AA-	5.75	7	-11,013.60	110,788.92	10.26	-9.941	-2.252	-2.252	0	20.201
F	AA-	5.75	8	-49,164.43	102,794.88	11.047	-47.828	-10.905	-10.905	0	58.875
B	BBB+	7.25	9	-323,043.94	103,793.33	4.704	-311.24	-182.56	-154.15	18.429	315.807

Figure 16.2 End of Round Financial/Ranking Report

Cost, inventory & initial pricing

Material	$$-B01	$$-B02	$$-B03	$$-B04	$$-B05	$$-B06
Name	1L Clear Pure	1L Spritz	1L Lemon Spritz	500mL ClearPure	500mL Spritz	500mL Lemon Spritz
Size	1L	1L	1L	500mL	500mL	500mL
Number of bottles in package	12	12	12	24	24	24
Cost	€11.99	€14.99	€16.99	€16.99	€19.99	€22.99
Initial price	€14.99	€17.99	€19.99	€19.99	€22.99	€25.99
Initial stock	1,000	1,000	1,000	1,000	1,000	1,000

Figure 16.3 Initial ERP Simulation Game Settings

financial/ranking report. The student teams also are instructed that decisions in one round carry over to the next round, including their current inventory position. The students can only sell product(s) that they have in stock. The students are explicitly told that they are competing against other teams in the simulation. The goal of the simulation is to maximize profit. All teams are provided with the initial cost, inventory, and pricing information, as shown in figure 16.3.

Each team competes against the other teams in the SAP ERP bottled water simulation game for three rounds. See figure 16.4 for the game layout. The winning

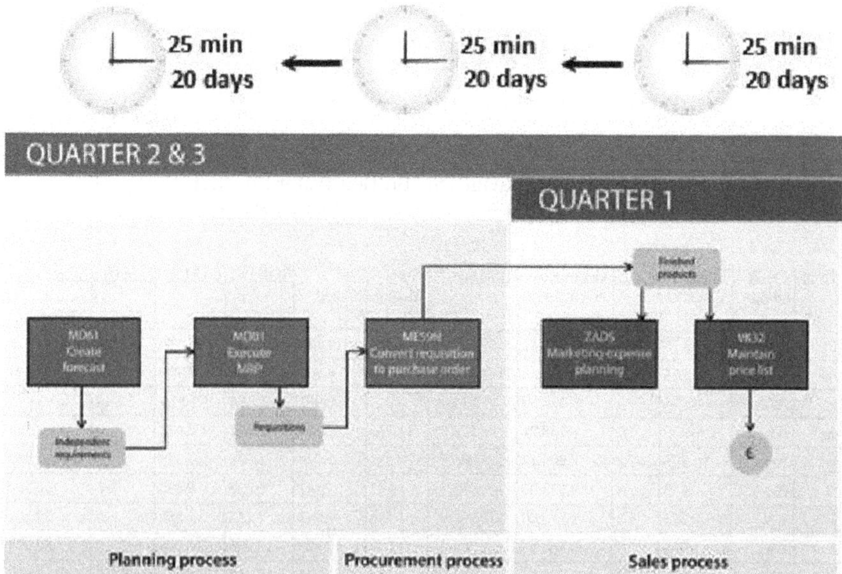

Figure 16.4 SAP ERP Simulation Game Layout

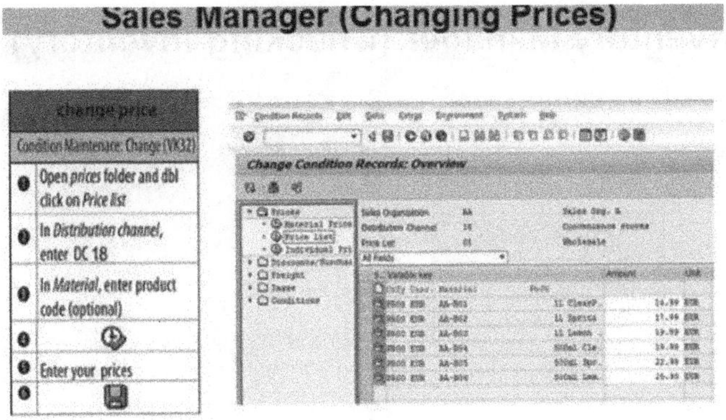

Sales Manager (Changing Prices)

change price

Condition Maintenance: Change (VK32)

1. Open prices folder and dbl click on Price list
2. In Distribution channel, enter DC 18
3. In Material, enter product code (optional)
4.
5. Enter your prices
6.

Figure 16.5 Sales Manager's SAP Price Changing Screen

team (most profitable team) is awarded a cash prize (e.g., BigCo versus SpendCo as illustrated in the previous section). Another randomly selected team also is awarded a cash prize. Every student who volunteers to participate in the simulation exercise is awarded extra credit.

Initially, the supply chain teams are tasked with making decisions such as determining the prices of each bottled water product, investing in advertising, monitoring inventory levels, and reviewing the average market price for each product. Specifically, in the first round, each team is responsible for managing the sales process. Every team member is provided a functional task. One team member is responsible for carrying out sales activities, which include monitoring the sales market report and making pricing changes. See figure 16.5 for the sales manager's SAP changing price screen. The inventory manager is responsible for monitoring the inventory levels of the six bottled water products. See figure 16.6 for the inventory manager's SAP screen. The marketing manager is responsible for investing in marketing in any of the three geographical regions of the game across the six bottled water products. See figure 16.7 for the marketing manager's SAP screen.

At the completion of each round, following an approach utilized by Cantor, Summers, and Humphrey (2014) the students are presented with a set of survey questions to assess their perception of the team dynamics. See Table 16.1 for full details. The first set of team dynamic questions relates to the type of information that the team accessed to make competitive decisions and subsequent nature of their competitive pricing actions (e.g., proactive or reactive pricing decisions). Examples of these team dynamic questions include the following:

- We changed the prices on our products in reaction to what we saw other teams doing.
- We changed the prices of our products before other teams changed their prices.

It also is important to examine team coordination in the SAP ERP simulation game. The following are sets of questions we have utilized to examine intrateam coordination behavior.

Inventory Manager (Checking Inventory)

System Help

stock levels
Inventory report(ZMB52)
Shows all stock levels.

Inventory Report

Warehouse Capacity

Finished Goods:	6,000 /	250,000
Raw Materials:	0 /	250,000
Packaging:	0 /	1,000,000

Inventory Report: Quarter 1 Day 01

SLoc	Material	Material Description	Stock	Unit
04	AA-B01	1L ClearPure	1,000	ST
	AA-B02	1L Spritz	1,000	ST
	AA-B03	1L Lemon Spritz	1,000	ST
	AA-B04	500mL ClearPure	1,000	ST
	AA-B05	500mL Spritz	1,000	ST
	AA-B06	500mL Lemon Spritz	1,000	ST

Figure 16.6 Inventory Manager's SAP Screen

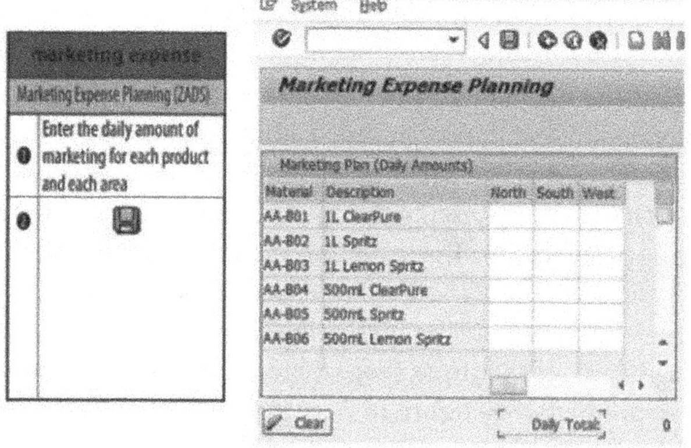

Figure 16.7 Marketing Manager's SAP Screen

- Our team worked together in a well-coordinated fashion.
- Our team had very few misunderstandings about what to do.
- We accomplished the task smoothly and efficiently.

Although the assigned sales manager role has more responsibilities than the other team members, it is possible that another team member emerges as the team leader. Therefore, it is interesting to ask each team member:

- Did a leader emerge during the first round (or other round of the game)?
- If yes, which position emerged as the leader?

Beginning in the second round of the competitive, the team's set of tasks expands (i.e., stretch work) to include three new tasks (Cantor et al. 2014; Summers,

Humphrey, and Ferris 2012). Students are instructed that *only* the sales manager takes on new responsibilities, which include (1) running production (MRP); (2) running procurement (convert purchase requisitions to purchase orders); and (3) replenishing inventory / forecasting. Students are told that it will take up to three days to replenish inventory. The other team members are instructed to continue following their previous job responsibilities. Recall that the goal of this exercise is to examine how teams can successfully overcome the flux in team coordination caused by stretch work to remain competitive.

Specifically, in this round, the sales manager will continue to change prices of one or more products and monitor the price market report. The inventory manager will continue to check inventory status, and the marketing manager will continue to focus on advertising. Sales managers are provided with specific instructions on how to carry out their additional task duties (Cantor et al. 2014). For example, we demonstrate and provide documentation to the sales manager on how to run MRP in SAP.

We explain to the sales manager that the default forecast is for 1,000 units for each of the six products (e.g., default setting in quarter 1). Participants are instructed to double-click on "MRP Run" from the SAP Home Page. See figure 16.8. The sales manager is instructed to click on the green check-mark button (two times).

After the MRP runs, the sales manager will see an MRP output screen. This step does not directly replenish inventory (e.g., bottles of water). The sales manager

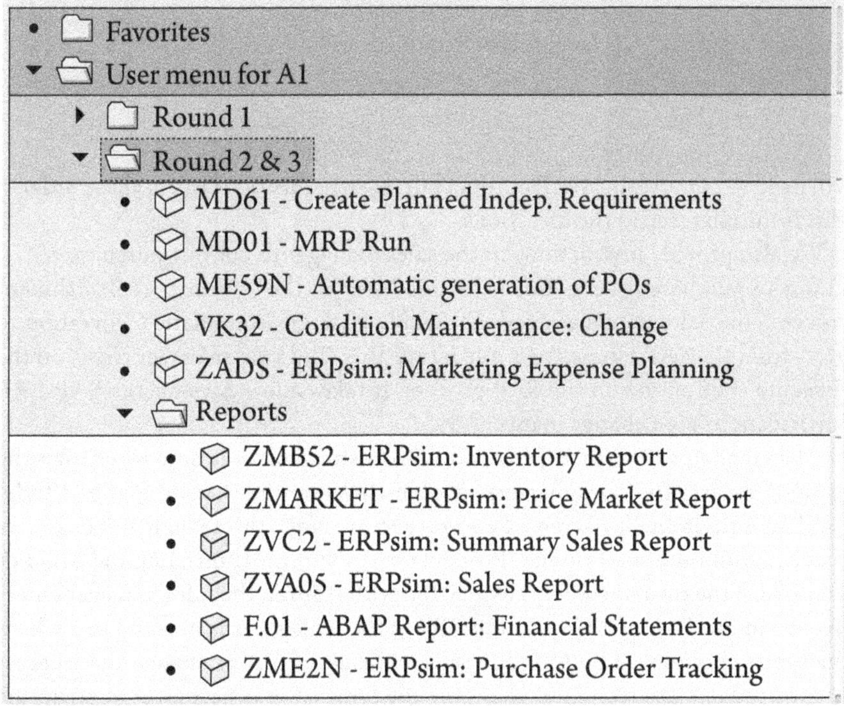

Figure 16.8 Running MRP from Main SAP Screen

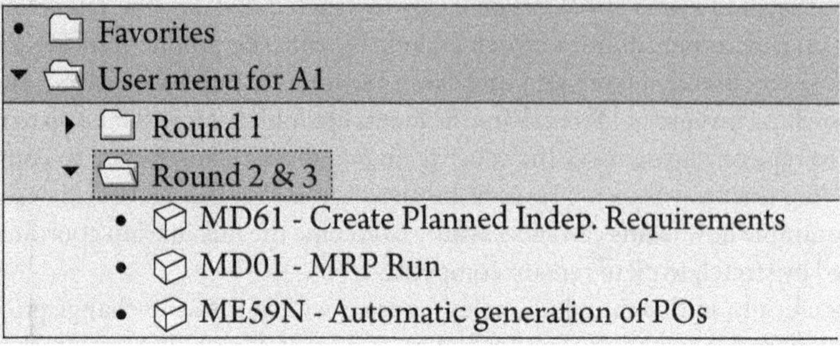

Figure 16.9 Generation of POs

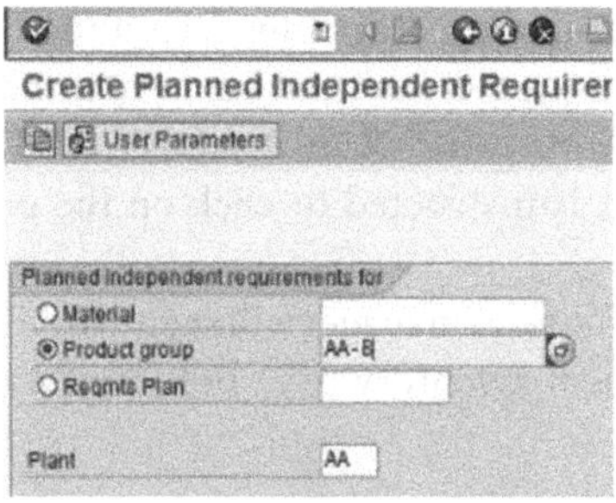

Figure 16.10 Creating Planned Independent Requirements

will need to convert the MRP output (purchase requisitions to purchase orders). This is the next step in the directions.

We also provide instructions to the sales manager to convert purchase requisitions to purchase orders. This is the final step in the inventory replenishment process. The sales manager needs to double-click on "Automatic Generation of POs" from the SAP Home Page. See figure 16.9. The sales manager clicks on the "Execute" button to run the SAP process. It takes a few days for the SAP ERP participant to see a change in inventory.

Sales managers are then provided with instructions on how to change the team's forecast. The sales manager double-clicks on the "Create Planned Independent Requirements" screen. See figure 16.10. Next, this team member selects product group and enters in the "Product Group" box the team name and "-B." For example, if the team member is associated with team A, the sales manager enters "AA-B" in the "Product Group" box. The sales manager is instructed to click on the green check-mark button. The sales manager can now change the forecast of the products desired. After changing the forecast, it is necessary to rerun the MRP process.

DISCUSSION

The purpose of this chapter is to examine dynamic team behavior within the context of a competitive SAP enterprise system gaming environment. As illustrated in the BigCo versus SpendCo example, this is an important topic because work in a SAP ERP environment is inherently team-based. Supply chain teams rely on up-to-date business intelligence information from systems such as SAP in order to run their supply chain operations. High-performing teams rely on access to competitive information to respond to dynamic market conditions where rivals seek to increase their position in the marketplace.

We adopt multiple perspectives to explain the complex nature of supply chain competition. We introduced the Schumpeterian view of competition to shed light on why organizations are motivated to engage in complex competitive moves and countermoves to maintain and improve on their market position. Undoubtedly, the Schumpeterian perspective helps to explain why firms cannot rest on their "laurels." We also incorporated information processing theoretical perspectives from the supply chain literature to provide insight as to how supply chain scholars have considered the important role of information in the decision-making literature. Clearly, in competitive markets, access to knowledge and information is critical. Rivals need access to real-time information in order to become aware of both external market and internal organizational conditions that affect their ability to make competitive moves. We also incorporate the theory of the strategic core. The theory of the strategic core helps to explain how certain team members are more critical than others in supply chain decision-making. A change in a strategic core team member can potentially more negatively affect teams' ability to make quality decisions than changes in noncore membership. Top management needs to be aware of how to minimize disruptions of specific team members. Otherwise, dysfunctional team dynamics can hinder firms' ability to engage in competitive actions.

The SAP ERP simulation game is a classroom software tool that can be adopted to investigate team dynamics. We observed that it is typical for members to act individually, focusing on maximizing their own job responsibilities (e.g., sales, marketing, and inventory). Based on previous uses of the game, we have observed that a necessary ingredient for high-performing teams is strong leadership. Strong leaders can align members into a cohesive unit. Each team member will have different motivations. Some will participate in the game because of intrinsic motivation (e.g., an internally driven motivation to learn). Others are more concerned with winning the game to get a higher grade in the course. Therefore we expect to see variation in effort and stress related to the gaming exercise.

As members begin to realize their task interdependencies, it is common for their attention to shift to others. Some will engage leadership for direction. Others will seek awareness of what others are doing, and some may attempt to better understand the system capabilities. A good strategic core member (e.g., leader) will align members and delegate responsibilities to the other team members to create efficiencies in coordination and decision-making. Strategic core members will coordinate available external and internal information so that the team can make strong competitive moves.

Although the goal of profit maximization is clearly stated to each team, the strategies that teams pursue to implement that goal can be in conflict with one another. For example, members responsible for watching inventory (e.g., inventory manager) may decide that minimizing inventory is the best strategy to achieve profit. The sales role member may believe the goal is best accomplished through maximizing sales, which can only be transacted if inventory is on hand prior to the sale. The strategic core member (e.g., sales manager) will need to enact leadership behaviors to help the teams decide how to best coordinate and realize their goals. We implemented a survey at the end of each round to capture teams' information-processing and game-playing strategy, to better understand how teams sought to accomplish their performance goals. We also were interested in understanding whether other team members emerged as team leaders even though we instructed the sales manager to carry out the majority of the game-playing activities. An interesting future topic to examine is whether or not our version of the SAP ERP simulation game gives rise to emergent leadership.

We provided each team member with SAP reports that could be used to improve the team's supply chain decision-making. For example, we shared with each team where it ranked in terms of overall game performance. Indeed, we believe that displaying the team rank information at the end of each round of the game adds competitive pressure. Teams who are ahead will be motivated to maintain their lead. Lower-ranked teams will feel pressure to improve their performance. This will be dependent on their comprehension of key game activities. Again, a strong core team member (or emergent leader) is critical to avoid unconstructive blaming, motivate dissimilar members, and take unified steps toward improving the team's performance in the game. This may come from the appointed leader or from the emergence of an informal leader. The SAP ERP simulation game contains several reports that teams can use to improve their levels of intrateam coordination (e.g., sales market report, inventory report, financial report, etc.). In other versions of the game (e.g., advanced manufacturing HEC Montreal SAP game), teams have access to business intelligence tools that provide real-time reporting information that also can improve decision-making performance.

We hope that this book chapter has provided new insights into supply chain team dynamics from a competition perspective. Examining team-level behavior is important because effective supply chain management requires inter- and intra-organizational collaboration enabled by information technology systems such as enterprise resource planning systems. In addition, it can be argued that organizations are leaner and flatter than in the past, thus raising the profile of insight into the cross-coordination of within-team member behavior.

Appendix

Table 16.1. Team Dynamic Worksheet

	1 Strongly agree	**2 Agree**	**3**	**4 Disagree**	**5 Strongly disagree**	**Notes/ reactions**
Information (awareness) strategy						
The team accessed external available information—price market report before making any game-related decisions.	1	2	3	4	5	
The team accessed internally available information—sales and inventory levels—before making any game related decisions	1	2	3	4	5	
Other comments: 1. Please identify specific SAP reports that you used. 2. Did any of these reports affect your level of motivation in the game?						
Team proactiveness strategy						
We changed the prices on our products in reaction to what we saw other teams doing.	1	2	3	4	5	
We changed the prices of our products before other teams changed their prices.	1	2	3	4	5	
Other comments: Please comment on other strategies (actions) that your team implemented to improve the competition position of your team.						

Table 16.1. (Continued)

	1 Strongly agree	2 Agree	3	4 Disagree	5 Strongly disagree	Notes/ reactions
Team coordination						
Our team worked together in a well-coordinated fashion.	1	2	3	4	5	
Our team had very few misunderstandings about what to do.	1	2	3	4	5	
We accomplished the task smoothly and efficiently.	1	2	3	4	5	
Our team needed to backtrack and start over a lot.	1	2	3	4	5	
Other comments: Please describe any barriers that prevented your team from making effective decisions in the SAP game.						
Information exchange						
I interacted frequently with my other team members.	1	2	3	4	5	
I exchanged information with my other team members.	1	2	3	4	5	
I kept information from my other team members.	1	2	3	4	5	
Other comments: Were there certain team members that you interacted with more than others? Who emerged as the team leader?						

References

Bendoly, E. 2014. Systems dynamics understanding in project execution: information sharing quality and psychological safety. Production and Operations Management 23 (8), 1352–1369.

Bendoly, E., Perry-Smith, J. E., Bachrach, D. G. 2010. The perception of difficulty in project-work planning and its impact on resource sharing. Journal of Operations Management 28 (5), 385–397.

Cantor, D. E., Macdonald, J. R. 2009. Decision-making in the supply chain: Examining problem solving approaches and information availability. Journal of Operations Management 27 (3), 220–232.

Cantor, D. E., Summers, J. K., Humphrey, S. E. 2014. An examination of team dynamics in a competitive environment. Working paper, Iowa State University.

Chen, M.-J., MacMillan, I. C. 1992. Nonresponse and delayed response to competitive moves: The roles of competitor dependence and action irreversibility. Academy of Management Journal 35 (3), 539–570.

Croson, R., Donohue, K. 2006. Behavioral causes of the bullwhip effect and the observed value of inventory information. Management science 52 (3), 323–336.

Delery, J. E., Shaw, J. D. 2001. The strategic management of people in work organizations: Review, synthesis, and extension. Research in Personnel and Human Resources Management 20, 165–197.

Easton, G. S., Rosenzweig, E. D. 2012. The role of experience in Six Sigma project success: An empirical analysis of improvement projects. Journal of Operations Management 30 (7–8), 481–493.

Frederick, S. 2005. Cognitive reflection and decision making. Journal of Economic Perspectives 19 (4), 25–42.

Grimm, C. M., Smith, K. G. 1997. Strategy as Action: Industry Rivalry and Coordination. Cincinnati: South-Western College Pub.

Hofer, C., Cantor, D. E., Dai, J. 2012. The competitive determinants of a firm's environmental management activities: Evidence from US manufacturing industries. Journal of Operations Management 30 (1), 69–84.

Humphrey, S. E., Morgeson, F. P., Mannor, M. J. 2009. Developing a theory of the strategic core of teams: A role composition model of team performance. Journal of Applied Psychology 94 (1), 48.

Johnson, P. F., Klassen, R. D., Leenders, M. R., Awaysheh, A. 2007. Utilizing e-business technologies in supply chains: The impact of firm characteristics and teams. Journal of Operations Management 25 (6), 1255–1274.

Lee, H. L., Padmanabhan, V., Whang, S. 1997. Information distortion in a supply chain: The bullwhip effect. Management Science 43 (4), 546–558.

Liberman, N., Trope, Y., 1998. The role of feasibility and desirability considerations in near and distant future decisions: A test of temporal construal theory. Journal of Personality and Social Psychology 75 (1), 5–18.

Linderman, K., Schroeder, R. G., Choo, A. S. 2006. Six Sigma: The role of goals in improvement teams. Journal of Operations Management 24 (6), 779–790.

Miller, D., Chen, M.-J. 1994. Sources and consequences of competitive inertia: A study of the US airline industry. Administrative Science Quarterly 39 (1), 1–23.

Moritz, B. B., Hill, A. V., Donohue, K. 2012. Individual differences in the newsvendor problem: Behavior and cognitive reflection. Journal of Operations Management 31 (1–2), 72–85.

Sanders, N. R. 2007. An empirical study of the impact of e-business technologies on organizational collaboration and performance. Journal of Operations Management 25 (6), 1332–1347.

Schumpeter, J. A. 1934. The Theory of Economic Development: An Enquiry into Profits, Capital, Credit, Interest, and the Business Cycle. Cambridge, MA: Harvard University Press.

Schumpeter, J. A. 1942. Capitalism, Socialism and Democracy. London: Routledge.

Scott-Young, C., Samson, D. 2008. Project success and project team management: Evidence from capital projects in the process industries. Journal of Operations Management 26 (6), 749–766.

Smith, K. G., Grimm, C. M., Gannon, M. J., Chen, M.-J. 1991. Organizational information processing, competitive responses, and performance in the US domestic airline industry. Academy of Management Journal 34 (1), 60–85.

Steckel, J. H., Gupta, S., Banerji, A. 2004. Supply chain decision making: Will shorter cycle times and shared point-of-sale information necessarily help? Management Science 50 (4), 458–464.

Sterman, J. D. 1989. Modeling managerial behavior: Misperceptions of feedback in a dynamic decision making experiment. Management Science 35 (3), 321–339.

Summers, J. K., Humphrey, S. E., Ferris, G. R. 2012. Team member change, flux in coordination, and performance: effects of strategic core roles, information transfer, and cognitive ability. Academy of Management Journal 55 (2), 314–338.

Tokar, T., Aloysius, J., Williams, B., Waller, M. 2013. Bracing for demand shocks: An experimental investigation. Journal of Operations Management 32 (4), 205–216.

Wouters, M., Anderson, J. C., Narus, J. A., Wynstra, F. 2009. Improving sourcing decisions in NPD projects: Monetary quantification of points of difference. Journal of Operations Management 27 (1), 64–77.

Wu, Y., Loch, C., Ahmad, G. 2011. Status and relationships in social dilemmas of teams. Journal of Operations Management 29 (7), 650–662.

CHAPTER 17

The Fresh Connection

Cross-Functional Integration in Supply Chain Management

SANDER DE LEEUW, MICHAÉLA C. SCHIPPERS, AND STEFAN J. HOOGERVORST

INTRODUCTION

Supply chain management games have proven to be useful tools to facilitate operations management learning in classroom environments (Mehring 2000) and learning among practitioners (Sterman 1989), and as a source of input for academic research (Steckel et al. 2004). Several supply chain games have been developed in support of one or more of these goals, with the Beer Game probably being the best known. In this chapter we focus on the use of one particular game: The Fresh Connection (abbreviated as TFC), a web-based supply chain management learning environment built around a cross-functional business simulation. The focus of the game is on the experiential learning of various aspects of supply chain management.

THEORETICAL PERSPECTIVE

Games have long been used in academic settings to support teaching the principles of logistics and supply chain management (Sweeney et al. 2010). The use of games is common in many fields, including medicine, chemistry and physics, and construction (for a review see Pasin and Giroux 2011). Games in management studies can be traced back to the 1950s (Wells 1993; see Pasin and Giroux 2011). The use of games as a learning tool in the operations management domain has increased considerably over the past several decades (Lewis and Maylor 2007). In the operations management domain, games and simulations represent a dominant focal area in journal articles related to teaching operations management (Medina-Lopez, Alfalla-Luque, and Marin-Garcia 2011).

One of the primary advantages associated with the use of games is that many are cross-functional in nature. Traditionally, study programs have been set up in functional units, yet most of the problems in the corporate world are far from discrete and require the use of multiple skills. Further, games also offer a means to connect learning motivation, cognitive growth, and social growth in a competitive environment (Chang et al. 2010). Van Houten and colleagues (2005) defined requirements for successful supply chain games. According to their research, supply chain management games need to be useful, implying that the game context should be credible to those playing it. Further, games should be usable; Van Houten and colleagues (2005) argued that this requires a web-enabled interface together with a continuous advancement of the game rather than a turn-based (i.e., play week by week, for example) system. Given the success of the Beer Game in both research and teaching (see below) this requirement is perhaps somewhat strongly formulated.

Among the early papers focused on the use of the Beer Game in research Sterman (1989) argued that inefficiencies in supply chains could be related to the inability of decision-makers to account for the long delays in time between placing orders and receiving them. In Lee, Padmanabhan, and Whang (1997) paper on the "bullwhip effect," these authors delimit the causes of these ordering patterns to four aspects: batch sizing of orders, shortage gaming and rationing (which occurs in cases of potential shortages), demand forecast updating (where frequent forecast updates lead to nervousness because of the resulting frequent updates of planned orders), and price fluctuations (because of promotional actions).

In fact, a large part of the experimental research in supply chains involves issues related to the bullwhip effect (Bendoly, Donohue, and Schultz 2006). Steckel, Gupta, and Banerji (2004) used the Beer Game as a basis to argue that speeding up cycle times is actually more beneficial than sharing point-of-sale information. Croson and Donohue (2006) also based their conclusion that suppliers further upstream in the supply chain benefit more from point-of-sale data sharing than those closer to demand on experiments leveraging the Beer Game.

In teaching, the Beer Game has seen considerable popularity for introducing students to supply chain management issues (Sparling 2002). The Beer Game often is used to show the bullwhip effect and also is an excellent tool for providing students opportunity to experience this effect firsthand. Obviously, because of its simplifications the game cannot reveal the true complexities of a supply chain, though that simplicity also is a strong point in terms of its educational value. However, because of this functional compromise, the translation to practice is somewhat cumbersome. For example, the game does not provide a good setting for students to work through solutions to deal with the problems identified in the Beer Game (Sparling 2002).

Over time, several other games also have emerged. Mehring (2000) described a game focused on experiential learning. The game can be used to show the effects of dependencies in the supply chain (and therefore the need for coordination among supply chain entities), and also to analyze the effects of coordination methods in the supply chain.

Other often used supply chain games include the Distributor Game (Van Houten et al. 2005) and games developed by Littlefield Technologies (cf. Feng and Ma 2008). Lewis and Maylor (2007) compared several operations games and concluded that (other than the Beer Game) most games have considerable complexity. The Beer Game is in fact a rather simple and intuitive game with basically one decision to make: how much to order from a direct supplier each round for one type of product assuming unlimited capacities. Later computer-based games encompass multiple products, capacity limitations, or financial aspects (e.g., depreciation of stock value over time to represent the fact that older stock has less market value).

The supply chain game that we describe in this chapter is The Fresh Connection game.[1] Developed in the Netherlands, this game was originally conceived in 2008. The first format of The Fresh Connection was a national Supply Chain Management Competition, in which both companies and universities participated. After six qualification rounds the best teams of the various competition pools were invited to a national final, during which the teams had to cope with new events and elements. This national competition was so successful that a supply chain management training-and-development program was developed around the game. Consequently, the level of complexity and the supply chain themes of the game were designed to be configurable to firm-specific training and development needs, available time, the level of the participants, and so on. Starting in 2009, this training and development program was deployed on a worldwide scale within both commercial firms and universities and business schools. The current status of the program is that more than 10,000 professionals from over 500 companies located in 25+ countries and more than 5,000 students from 40+ universities in 20 + countries have participated in The Fresh Connection game.

LEARNING ACTIVITY

A drawback of operation management pedagogy is that it often teaches students that decisions can be optimized and that they can solve operations management issues using formal mathematical modeling. A simulation game can serve as a powerful tool for teaching operation management principles against such a deterministic mindset (Pasin and Giroux 2011). During such games, students can learn that decisions are interlinked, and often that decisions involve multiple stakeholders with discrete goals. Such games strengthen students' "cognitive-recognition architecture" and inspire learning through achievement (Chang, Peng, and Chao 2010). By reflecting on their decisions and possible mistakes, students can learn more and improve over time (Dahling, Whitaker, and Levy 2009; Pasin and Giroux 2011; Rosenorn and Kofoed 1998). If a game is integrated

1. See www.thefreshconnection.eu.

across the length of a course, students can receive regular feedback and learn to integrate and apply the theories taught in the program of which the course is a part. The Fresh Connection has been designed to be played in a time frame between three and six weeks (i.e., two or one rounds per week, respectively). The authors have experience with both frequencies and both work equally well. Each round requires about eight hours of preparation per person.

The Fresh Connection

The Fresh Connection (TFC) is a supply chain management game in which four participants take up a role in a new management team for a (virtual) company that is making a loss. They can either be a VP Purchasing (covering the areas Supplier Management and Total Cost of Ownership), a VP Sales (covering the areas Demand and Portfolio Management), a VP Operations (covering the areas Capacity and Production Management) or a VP Supply Chain (covering the areas Inventory Management and Value Chain Management). See table 17.1 for role descriptions used. Participants make strategic and tactical supply chain-related decisions for the company The Fresh Connection, a virtual producer of fruit juices.

The game is played in three to six rounds (dependent on students' training and development needs). Each round represents a decision horizon of six months. The focus of the game is on strategic and tactical supply chain decisions. The game is offered in an open competition format where hundreds of teams compete with each other simultaneously. It also is used in-house in companies and universities alike. An example of the main screen of the game is shown in figure 17.1.

TFC is different from many other supply chain games as it mimics a real company in terms of scope and complexity of decisions that need to be taken. The goal is to foster cross-disciplinary teamwork and break down functional silos as

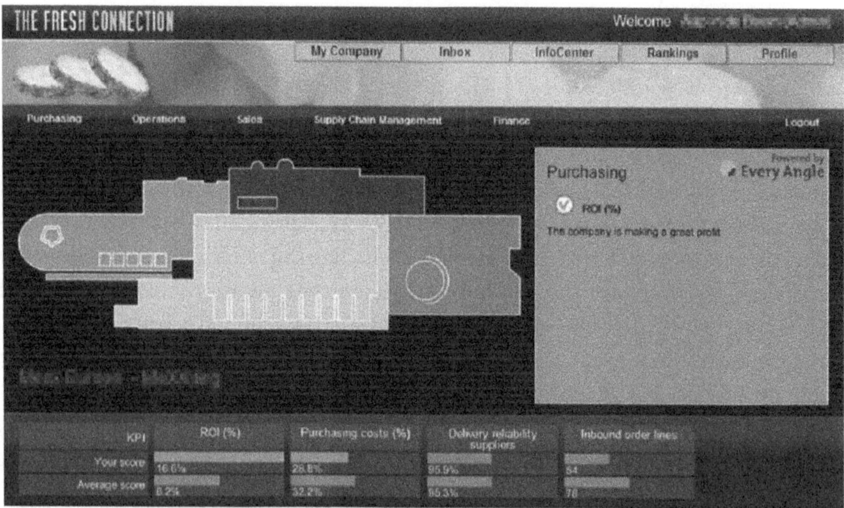

Figure 17.1 Main Screen of the Business Simulation with an Overview of Results

Table 17.1. Roles in TFC

Role	*Description*
VP Sales	Product sales are overseen by the VP Sales. He/she negotiates The Fresh Connection's terms of delivery with the customers. Service levels, order deadlines, shelf life agreements, and promotional pressures are all negotiable. The VP Sales plays an extremely important role in the game and his/her bargaining can result in a high sales price—as long as The Fresh Connection can keep its promises. And sales are, of course, the launch pad for profits.
VP Supply Chain	The VP Supply Chain is the glue that holds the other roles together. By devising a supply chain strategy and undertaking intelligent inventory planning, the VP Supply Chain plays a decisive role in the team. He/she can ensure that unreliable suppliers or production facilities are covered by strategically deployed safety stock, ensuring that the company keeps its promises to the customer.
VP Operations	The VP Operations is in charge of the production facilities and the warehouses. He/she orchestrates the work shifts and ensures that the staff is trained. The VPO also decides on the space and manpower deployed in the warehouses. The VP Operations can make or break the game for the entire team. By ensuring that the production system remains flexible, production costs are low, and reliability high, the VP Operations ensures total production costs are controlled while product availability is high.
VP Purchasing	The VP Purchasing is responsible for purchasing the components. He/she negotiates the terms of supply and the price with suppliers, and can terminate existing contracts and conclude new ones. The VP Purchasing plays a crucial role in the game. By choosing suppliers who offer favorable terms, low prices, and a high level of reliability, the VP Purchasing ensures that total purchasing costs are kept under control, stocks stay low, and reliability of delivery for components to production is high.

participants can only take decisions in their respective areas of responsibility. In TFC strategic and tactical decisions also are explicitly in focus (instead of, for example, individual operational decisions that are more emphasized in the Beer Game). The team has the assignment to make the company profitable again by realizing the highest possible return on investment. The participants do this by making strategic and tactical supply chain decisions that affect the complete value chain of TFC.

The Fresh Connection products are stored on pallets in the finished goods warehouse. They stay there until a delivery is made, or until their shelf life has expired. The finished goods have, from the moment of production, a shelf life of 20 weeks. The customers claim a significant part of these 20 weeks, usually between 60% and 80%. This leaves The Fresh Connection with a total shelf life between 20% and 40% of these 20 weeks. If the shelf life expires, the product has to be destroyed. The Fresh Connection does not have a fleet to deliver product to its customer's distribution centers, and instead outsources transportation to a partner. The Fresh Connection manufactures all the products it sells in house. The fruit juices are mixed in a mixer and immediately bottled on a bottling line. Mixer and bottling line are part of The Fresh Connection's production equipment. There are a variety of packaging formats, and these are all bottled on the same line. A finished product consists of two primary components—packaging and concentrated fruit juice. A bill of materials identifies the quantities of each component in a finished product.

The components are purchased from suppliers. The packaging material is bought from local and regional suppliers. Concentrated fruit juice is acquired either from fruit traders or producers from across the globe. Each supplier has its own characteristics regarding, for example, price, lead times, and reliability. The components delivered to The Fresh Connection cannot always be immediately used in production, which is why the company has a raw materials warehouse. Packaging material is delivered on pallets and stored in the raw materials warehouse. The warehouse also stores concentrated fruit juice if it is delivered in drums or integrated bulk containers. The concentrated fruit juice that arrives in tank trucks is pumped into a tank yard. The concentrated fruit juice has a limited shelf life, and after the expiration date the concentrated fruit juice has to be destroyed.

Objectives and Game Play

The objective for each team is to achieve the best return on investment (ROI). The sole aim is not simply to make as much money as possible—managing investments in a proper way also is critical. In addition to the team score there also is an individual score. These individual scores do not count toward the team score, but do allow participants to gauge their performance relative to peers in other (competing) teams. After each round participants can check their performance and compare with other teams in the competition.

These objectives should be clearly communicated with the students in the course manual and during the first meeting. Students play one round every week. This can be accompanied by theoretical lectures on behavioral aspects and decision-making in teams as well as several interactive workshops. It also is important to hold a kickoff session, where the lecturer helps familiarize students with the game, the types of decisions made, and the interface used. This often is done with a so-called voting session.

In a voting session students are confronted with typical decision problems from the game. Using multiple choice answers, students can vote for an answer to a problem posed. In this way students get to practice game decisions.

Then the students establish teams of four, although the lecturer or students themselves may have also done this before the session. Lecturer selection of teams provides the opportunity to use the game to study behavioral effects. In one case the authors have assembled teams based on students' personality characteristics, identified through a questionnaire filled out before the voting session. Students receive questionnaires on team dynamics every round. We investigated their social network and recorded team interactions on video (cf. Lehman-Willenbrock et al. 2014).

An overview of the rounds involved in the full game is provided in table 17.2. Students preferably play the first round in a computer room. The teacher and/or teaching assistants familiar with the game are present to answer questions. The first round typically takes up to three hours (the first rounds may take slightly more than the subsequent rounds because student need to learn how to work with the game interface). For every round, the game input (i.e., the decisions made) has to be entered before a deadline. At the deadline decisions are calculated (takes about 10 minutes) and the outcomes of the decisions are revealed so that teams can progress to the second round.

Many decisions are made when playing The Fresh Connection. A trade-off is incorporated into every decision, so a decision will not only have positive effects, but negative effects as well. The key is to assess these consequences and to balance them against each other. Because The Fresh Connection is a tactical and strategic supply chain management experience, teams are assessed on the long-term effects of their decisions. Given that the results are measured in terms of their long-term effects, teams don't suffer negative consequences resulting from poor decisions in earlier rounds as performance in each round is calculated independently. The advantage of this is that the business can be organized in a new way every round, without accounting for fading-in and fading-out effects from previous rounds. On the other hand, by analyzing results from previous rounds closely teams can start making improvements in subsequent rounds.

Lectures and Feedback Sessions Behavioral Operations Management

The objectives of this game partly relate to supply chain theory and partly to behavioral aspects of working in cross-functional teams. We thus provide the students with background in behavioral operations management during separate lectures. In these lectures we identify how behavioral operations relate to the Fresh Connection game (and other games, such as the Beer Game). This background is important for students to write their assignment report (see below). During the game the lecturer also has the option to organize feedback sessions (2–3 during the course of the game). During the first week students may be asked to draw a supply chain map with key performance indicators (e.g., lead times or service levels). During these lectures students also may be confronted with the effects of their decisions. For example, in the game, increasing inventory levels often has negative impacts on financial performance because the key products

Table 17.2. Learning Activities by Round in The Fresh Connection

Topic	**Building block**	**Remarks**
Student preparation documents	0. Introduction PDFs	
Kickoff	1. Kick off TFC	
Round 1, The Fresh Connection		
Feedback round 1	3. Feedback round	Supervisor shows scores and debriefs
Supply chain mapping	4. Supply chain mapping	Exercise in class or home assignment
Component characteristics and TCO (total cost of ownership)	5. Component characteristics and TCO	Exercise in class or home assignment
Round 2, The Fresh Connection		
Feedback round 2	See 3. Feedback round	Supervisor shows scores and debriefs
Basic understanding	8. Basic understanding	Focus on shelf life and inventory management
Trade-off exercise	9. Trade-off exercise	Including team presentation
Round 3, The Fresh Connection		Participants can select their own KPIs (key performance indicators) in TFC
Feedback round 3	See 3. Feedback round	Supervisor shows scores and debriefs
Supply chain strategy introduction	12. Supply chain strategy introduction	Lecture on supply chain strategy
Exercise Strategy into action	13. Exercise strategy into action	Align KPIs to strategy and set targets
Round 4, The Fresh Connection		Theme S&OP is added
Feedback round 4	See 3. Feedback round	Supervisor shows scores and debriefs
S&OP intro & exercise	16. S&OP intro and exercise	Lecture on S&OP and exercise S&OP
Round 5, The Fresh Connection		External collaboration elements are added
Feedback round 5	See 3. Feedback round	Supervisor shows scores and debriefs

Table 17.2. (Continued)

Topic	Building block	Remarks
Collaboration intro	19. Collaboration intro	Also show effect of promotion horizon
Exercise inflate PET bottles (polyethylene terephthalate)	20. Exercise inflate PET	Calculations and business case
Buyer and supplier view	21. Buyer and supplier view	Determine chances for successful collaboration
Round 6, The Fresh Connection		
Feedback round 6	See 3. Feedback round	Supervisor shows scores and debriefs

managed are perishable. Initially, students do not necessarily understand how increasing inventory may actually deteriorate delivery performance. In feedback lectures, the effects of such decisions may be discussed. A good method to employ here is to draw causal loop diagrams with students in class around themes. Students may not always bring up themes themselves. It is advisable to prepare discussion topics that a lecturer can use to probe students.

Assignment and Grading

The students are given an assignment in which they have to reflect on their experiences in the game. Ideally, the course consists of five different parts:

1. Progressive difficulty
2. Strategy report (see appendix 1)
3. Feedback classes
4. Log of activities (see appendix 2)
5. Evaluation report (see appendix 3)

The main outcome of the game (ROI) could be used as part of the total class grade. It is advised to not make this part too big (between 10% and 20% of the grade students can get for the game); in that way the students have the idea that they can still experiment with the game. We make this explicit in the course manual and during our lectures.

Progressive Difficulty

Each round the players learn more and have to make progressively more difficult decisions. The Fresh Connection can be configured to the training and development needs of the company or university. Therefore the level of complexity and the supply chain themes are designed in a modular way to allow customizing the learning experience to the learning objectives of the training or course. The core of The Fresh Connection is the need to break down functional silos and to implement the chosen supply chain strategy in a coherent way across the different functional areas. These elements are the basis for the first three levels in The Fresh Connection, as indicated in table 17.3.

After having played two to three rounds on these levels, different supply chain themes can be added, such as Supply Chain Risk Management, External Collaboration, Sustainability via so-called extensions (table 17.4).

By adding levels and extensions the complexity can be gradually increased during the course of the game; in this way the learning experience can be built up gradually. To allow participants to reflect on their decisions, their decision-making process, and how consistently they implement their strategy, a learning cycle has been developed around The Fresh Connection to enhance the learning experience for the participants, and to allow them to link theoretical frameworks to practice. For that purpose, supporting learning materials and exercises have been developed to further enhance the learning experience and to create a deeper and more-lasting understanding of the interaction between decisions for the participants (see table 17.2 as well).

Strategy Report

In the strategy report, students reflect on the strategy they think works well. They thus have to reflect on a strategy before they start, which can give them a head

Table 17.3. LEVELS IN THE FRESH CONNECTION

	Theme	Sales	SCM	Operations	Purchasing
Level 1	Reliability	Service level Order deadline Shortage rule	Safety stocks	# Shifts # Pallet locations # FTE	Delivery window Delivery reliability
Level 2	Batches and frequencies	Shelf life Trade unit	Lotsizing in production and purchasing	SMED Increase speed	Trade unit
Level 3	Speed and quality	Payment terms	Frozen period	Intake time Preventive maintenance Solve breakdowns training Raw materials inspection	Supplier selection Payment terms Quality Transport mode

Table 17.4 Extensions on The Fresh Connection

Nr:	Theme	Sales	SCM	Operations	Purchasing
A	S&OP	Promotional pressure Category management Forecasting	Production interval tool	Resource selection	Dual sourcing
B	External collaboration	Promotion horizon VMI		Outsourcing warehouse (MCC) Inflate PET	VMI Supplier development
C	CO2 footprint Sustainability	CO2 Service Level Agreements		Decrease of water usage Decrease of energy usage Decrease of start-up productivity loss	
D	KPIs and targets	KPI selection	KPI selection	KPI selection	KPI selection
E	Supply chain risk management	Risk events Relaunch (horizon)	Scenario planner	Tracking and tracing Quarantine Risk events Pooling warehouse	Contract duration Supplier development Dual sourcing Risk events

start into the game (cf. (Hackman and Morris 1975). In addition, having a clear strategy may guide students' decisions as well as serve as a way to make sense of the myriad of decisions they have to make (see appendix 1). In this report, due after round 1, students describe in which markets they want to be active and why/how, what the criteria of supply chain success for their company will be, and what choices they intend to make (and why) for the different areas, such as sourcing and supply management, inventory management, manufacturing, and so on.

Log of Activities

After each round students hand in a log of activities, in which they reflect on what went well, what could be improved, and what they have decided (see appendix 2, and Table 17.5). These logs can be used as part of the team assignment and form input for the final evaluation report. These logs also may be used to flag team problems to the lecturer.

Feedback Classes

Feedback classes can be scheduled so that students can ask questions bearing on how to improve their team's performance. Time and a computer lecture room can be reserved in the student lecture schedule for the course so that students can make decisions for the game together in a computer room. This is an ideal moment to discuss game progress. A good way to review progress is by means of developing impact diagrams such as the one depicted in figure 17.2. Students tend to have difficulties in the beginning of the game developing an overview of what is going on because of the large number of variables present during play. Developing an overview of how the key aspects of the game relate to each other is very helpful.

Evaluation Report

Finally, students write an evaluation report (see appendix 3). This is a report on bearing on how they made decisions, on the relation between their decisions and supply chain theory and behavioral operations management, and on how they could improve as a team. Depending on the content of the course, the focus of this report can be more on operations management or more on behavioral aspects of team interaction. In the appendix we give an example of such an assignment, but many variations are possible. We ask the teams to reflect, specifically, on how they performed and how could improve as a team. The teams need to identify what went well and what did not. They need to come up with concrete examples and suggestions for improvement. They also are asked to reflect on how they made decisions for each round and why they were made that way. For instance, were all team members involved, or did one team member make all the decisions? This

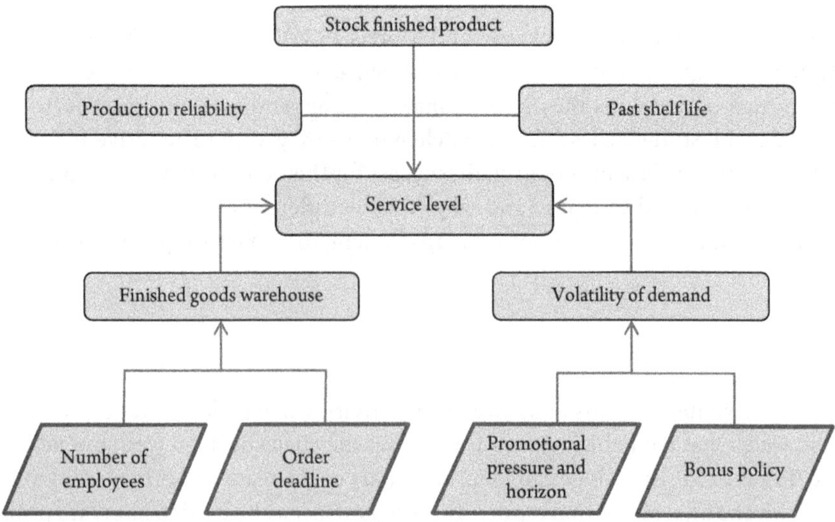

Figure 17.2 Example of Impact Diagram on Service-related Variables in the Game

can make a difference in the outcome, also in combination with clarity of leadership (Schippers 2014). Finally, students are asked to make a connection to supply chain theory and theories from behavioral operations management. The students have to use these theories to illustrate how they could have increased the team's performance. In doing this, students are required to use specific examples from the game, rather than resorting to reflection on generic theory. This last requirement often proves the most difficult for students. Whenever possible, it would be best if the students could hand in an initial concept report, receive extensive feedback, and then improve after using this feedback (Dahling et al. 2009; Schippers, Homan, and van Knippenberg 2013).

Maximizing the Learning Effect

In order to create an even larger learning effect, it would be ideal if the teams could reflect on their composition and team processes to see how these affect the team outcomes (cf. Dahling et al. 2009; Pasin and Giroux 2011). In the past few years, we have sent out questionnaires to the teams participating in the game, surveying factors such as regulatory focus, and team processes such as psychological safety, and team reflexivity (i.e., the extent to which teams reflect on and improve team functioning (Rook, Van de Velde, and Schippers 2014; Schippers, Den Hartog, and Koopman 2007; Schippers, Rook, and Van de Velde 2014). Questions may also be asked about how decisions are made and clarity of leadership, factors shown to interact in predicting the ROI that teams achieve in the game (Schippers 2014). The information from the questionnaires could be fed back to the teams and can form the basis for reflection on how decisions were made as a team and the biases and errors that the team made (or team information processing failures) (Schippers, Edmondson, and West 2014). At the same time, the information can be used as a basis for scientific research, after students sign a consent form. Even more direct feedback can be given by videotaping the team interaction (e.g., Lehmann-Willenbrock, Allen, and Kauffeld 2013) and feeding this information back to the team. This could potentially maximize the learning effect, especially when used in combination with questionnaires. Also, this setup allows for a productive combination with research.

DISCUSSION

We have found that TFC is an active and inspiring way to teach and for students to learn. There is room to experiment as participants are confronted with the results of their decisions. They can actively create their own insights and knowledge. Participants experience what it is like to deal with conflicting interests and trade-offs between the four different roles in the game. They are hence challenged to make joint decisions in a complex situation with many variables. As participants can only take decisions in their own functional area, adherence to a selected supply chain strategy, cooperation between the functional disciplines, and aligning decisions turn out to be key factors to successfully play TFC. As such, The Fresh Connection is very suitable for team building and for getting insight into group processes. As the game is able to align goals, it may also help mitigate the often-found negative effects of diversity on performance (Schippers et al. 2003; for a review see van Knippenberg and Schippers 2007).

Similar to the game described by Mehring (2000), playing TFC reveals to participants the complexities and multitude of ways to manage a supply chain. It can be used to illustrate several key supply chain concepts. Playing TFC, for example, shows that the sales and operations planning process is key to company success and encompasses more than the supply chain department, which is in line with earlier findings of Oliva and Watson (2011).

In conclusion, the game is a useful addition to conceptual learning. In classroom settings it provides a hands-on, experiential way to apply course theory in an interactive way. Students who have played the game testify that playing the game is not only fun, but enhances learning on how to strategize and how to collaborate in a supply chain setting. Students learn in lectures that supply chain strategy is relevant but often have little imaginative power to understand how supply chain strategy works in practice. In the game students can experience what works and what does not work and hence learn by experience why and how supply chain strategy is important. This also gives an opportunity to combine playing TFC alongside conceptual lectures. Students often are very positive about playing the game itself, and its learning effects, even if they did not generate a good ROI. The game also supports academic research. It can be used to analyze team behavior over time. Research on playing a game with virtual teams by Phadnis and coauthors (2013) is a good example of this, as is the work of Schippers, Rook, and Van de Velde (2014). The decision data from the game provide a wealth of information about decision behavior, which can be used for research on, for example, issues that relate behavior to performance criteria. With these data we can, for example, investigate to what extent teams that are performing poorly make decisions in a different ways than teams that are winning the game. TFC thus provides a challenging learning environment together with a great opportunity to do behavioral research.

Appendix 1. Supply Chain Strategy Report for The Fresh Connection

You need to write supply chain strategy report for your team that focuses on the following questions:

1. Which markets do we want to be active and why/how?
2. What are criteria of supply chain success for our company?
3. What choices do intend to you make (and why) for:
   - Sourcing and supply management?
     - Examples: sourcing locations, alternative suppliers
   - Inventory management?
     - Examples: stock products, inventory targets
   - Manufacturing?
     - Examples: focus on flexibility vs efficiency, investments
   - Delivery?
     - Examples: outsourcing
   - Customer management?
     - Examples: number of products offered, delivery priority
   - Sustainability?
     - Examples: trade-off costs versus sustainability, focal areas

The strategy report should focus on each question noted above; the examples under point 3 are illustrative. Please use what you consider appropriate for your case, but remember you need to evaluate it in your final report! Enclosures do not really belong to a strategy report, so refrain from using them. Use references where you think it is appropriate. A strategy needs to be concise, so the page limit is five (excluding title page but including references).

Appendix 2. Log of Activities

The following log of activities is used.

Table 17.5. Log of Activities

(i) LOG OF ACTIVITIES	
(ii) ROUND NO:	*(iii) DATE:*
Objectives of previous rounds: • • • •	
Describe key decisions made in these rounds and why: • • •	
Describe how well you achieved your objectives of previous rounds and why • • •	
Explain objectives of coming rounds and expected results • • • •	
Total time the team spent on preparing decisions per round (avg. per person) •	
Issues to be resolved by the team: • • •	

Appendix 3. Evaluation Report

You need to write an evaluation for your team performance and each role in the team. In this report you need to address the following questions:

- *As a whole team*:
    - How well did you perform as a team? Identify what went well and what went not so well.
    - How could you have improved team performance? Make concrete suggestions.
    - How did you make your decisions for each round, and why did you make them in that way?
    - How could supply chain theory and theories from behavioral operations management have helped you to (further) improve? Use these theories to illustrate how you could have increased your performance. Please use specific examples from the game; just reflecting on generic theory will not be sufficient.

Make sure you write your report in **maximum XXX words *everything included* (from title page to references)**. You hand this report in as a team. Please provide proper referencing when referring to resources.

The structure of your report should be as follows:

- *Chapter 1: team performance*
    - What went well
    - What could be improved

- *Chapter 2: strategy evaluation*
    - Explain: What was your strategy, how well did you execute this, and what should you have done differently in hindsight? **Use literature** to support your analysis.

- *Chapter 3: individual performance*
    - For each of the roles: a brief overview of the process of how you set key decisions
    - For each of the roles: an overview of potential improvements of these decisions **based on literature**; consult appropriate resources on your area of expertise (not necessarily articles only; also use books!)

GRADING CRITERIA:

- Quality of your review
- Quality of explaining actions
- Extent to which you base improvements in theory
- Reporting and presentation quality

References

Bendoly, E., Donohue, K., Schultz, K. L. 2006. Behavior in operations management: Assessing recent findings and revisiting old assumptions. Journal of Operations Management 24 (6), 737–752.

Chang, Y. C., Peng, H. Y., Chao, H. C. 2010. Examining the effects of learning motivation and of course design in an instructional simulation game. Interactive Learning Environments 18 (4), 319–339.

Croson, R., Donohue, K. 2006. Behavioral causes of the bullwhip effect and the observed value of inventory information. Management Science 52 (3), 323–336.

Dahling, J. J., Whitaker, B. G., Levy, P. E. 2009. The development and validation of a new Machiavellianism Scale. Journal of Management 35 (2), 219–257.

Feng, K., Ma, G. 2008. Learning supply chain management with fun: An online simulation game approach. California Journal of Operations Management 6 (1), 41–48.

Hackman, J. R., Morris, C. G. 1975. Group tasks, group interaction process, and group performance effectiveness: A review and a proposed integration. L. Berkowitz (ed.) in Advances in Experimental Social Psychology. New York: Academic Press.

Lee, H. L., Padmanabhan, V., Whang, S. 1997. The bullwhip effect in supply chains. Sloan Management Review 38 (3), 93–102.

Lehmann-Willenbrock, N., Allen, J. A., Kauffeld, S. 2013. A sequential analysis of procedural meeting communication: How teams facilitate their meetings. Journal of Applied Communication Research 41 (4), 365–388.

Lehmann-Willenbrock, N., Schippers, M. C., De Leeuw, S., Koroleva, K. 2014. Team interaction and team performance in a supply chain decision making context. Working paper, Free University, Amsterdam.

Lewis, M. A., Maylor, H. R. 2007. Game playing and operations management education. International Journal of Production Economics 105, 134–139.

Medina-Lopez, C., Alfalla-Luque, R., Marin-Garcia, G. A. 2011. Research in operations management teaching: Trends and challenges. Intangible Capital 7 (2), 507–548.

Mehring, J. S. 2000. A practical setting for experiential learning about supply chains: Siemens brief case game supply chain simulator. Production and Operations Management 9 (1), 56–65.

Oliva, R., Watson, N. 2011. Cross-functional alignment in supply chain planning: A case study of sales and operations planning. Journal of Operations Management 29 (5), 434–448.

Pasin, F., Giroux, H. 2011. The impact of a simulation game on operations management education. Computers and Education 57 (1), 1240–1254.

Phadnis, S., Perez-Franco, R., Caplice, C., Sheffi, Y. 2013. Educating supply chain professionals to work in global virtual teams. Working paper, MIT.

Rook, L., Van de Velde, S. L., Schippers, M. C. 2014. Regulatory focus as a moderator for the newsvendor "pull-to-center" effect: Experimental evidence. Working paper, Erasmus University Rotterdam.

Rosenorn, T., Kofoed, L. B. 1998. Reflection in learning processes through simulation/gaming. Simulation and Gaming 29 (4), 432–440.

Schippers, M. C. 2014. Majority decision making and team performance: The moderating role of shared task representations and leadership clarity. Working paper, Erasmus University Rotterdam.

Schippers, M. C., Den Hartog, D. N., Koopman, P. L. 2007. Reflexivity in teams: A measure and correlates. Applied Psychology 56 (2), 189–211.

Schippers, M. C., Den Hartog, D. N., Koopman, P. L., Wienk, J. A. 2003. Reflexivity and diversity in teams: The moderating effects of outcome interdependence and group longevity. Journal of Organizational Behavior 24 (6), 779–802.

Schippers, M. C., Edmondson, A. C., West, M. A. 2014. Team reflexivity as an antidote to information processing failures. Small Group Research 45 (6), 731–769.

Schippers, M. C., Homan, A. C., van Knippenberg, D. 2013. To reflect or not to reflect: Prior team performance as a boundary condition of the effects of reflexivity on learning and final team performance. Journal of Organizational Behavior 34 (1), 6–23.

Schippers, M. C., Rook, L., Van de Velde, S. 2014. Team reflexivity and regulatory focus can enhance sales and operations planning effectiveness: Evidence from a business simulation. Paper presented at the Ninth Annual Behavioral Operations Conference, June, Cologne, Germany.

Sparling, D. 2002. Simulations and supply chains: Strategies for teaching supply chain management. Supply Chain Management 7 (2), 334–342.

Steckel, J. H., Gupta, S., Banerji, A. 2004. Supply chain decision making: Will shorter cycle times and shared point-of-sale information necessarily help? Management Science 50 (4), 458–464.

Sterman, J. 1989. Modeling managerial behavior: Misperceptions of feedback in a dynamic decision making experiment. Management Science 35 (3), 321–339.

Sweeney, D., Campbell, J., Mundy, R. 2010. Teaching supply chain and logistics management through commercial software. International Journal of Logistics Management 21 (2), 293–308.

Van Houten, S. P., Verbraeck, A., Boyson, S., Corsi, T. 2005. Training for today's supply chains: An introduction to the distributor game. Proceedings of the 2005 Winter Simulation Conference, Orlando, FL, 2338–2345.

van Knippenberg, D., Schippers, M. C. 2007. Work group diversity. Annual Review of Psychology 58, 515–541.

Wells, R. A. 1993. Management games and simulations in management development: An introduction. Journal of Management Development 9 (2), 4–6.

CHAPTER 18

Wrapping It Up

Behavior and Decision-Making Revealed in Business Simulation Games

ARTURO OROZCO AND MIGUEL ESTRADA

OVERVIEW

Simulation is a powerful tool that through the use of computational-theoretical modeling emulates real-world conditions. It also efficiently facilitates assessment of potential solutions within complex systems. Its application within classroom settings also facilitates student learning, offering engaging near-to-life experiences that allow students to evaluate the impact of their decisions within defined contexts. IPADE Business School (El Instituto Panamericano de Alta Dirección de Empresa) has run a successful Business Simulation course for the past two decades. The course consistently receives among the highest evaluations within the MBA program. Most participants tend to agree that the course allows them to learn not only basic operations management concepts but also critical real-world insights applicable in managerial contexts.

In this business simulation game, participants manage a company with an emphasis on generating profits by the end of the one-week course. The course is taught at IPADE's full-time MBA program as well as other business schools in Latin America and Spain. The goal of the course is achievement of a developed understanding of a company by simulating its operations and relationships with other functional areas, and an integrated vision of a company.

Although a core objective is to test basic operations management concepts (production and supply planning, capacity management, inventory management), in order to apply these concepts, it is critical that students establish an atmosphere of collaboration and objectivity, facilitating effective decisions. Doing so depends on the definition of common team objectives and students' unique beliefs and biases.

In this chapter we describe the simulation game introduced above in detail. We also seek to contribute to the literature by reporting observed game dynamics and insights generated through students' experiences. First, we offer theoretical framing and a literature review of learning activities in behavioral operations management. We then broadly describe the business simulation game and connections with real-world situations. A detailed description of our Business Simulation course and how it has been deployed follows, with teaching plan suggestions. We then discuss findings and observations from running the simulation over the last years. We conclude with a description of those findings from individual, team, and group perspectives.

THEORETICAL PERSPECTIVE

This chapter describes a business simulation game in which teams (companies) compete, beginning the competition with identical financial results, operating rules, and market share. Further, all participants operate with similar theoretical frameworks, technical tools, and concepts. In light of this common point of departure, one would expect teams to finish the game with similar results, in neck-and-neck competition. However, there tends to be significant interteam variation in the end-of-game results. Central to our focus on behavioral operations management, we maintain that in most instances these performance differences emerge not as a consequence of randomness or participants' technical preparation, but rather from the human factor functioning as a significant driver of those differences.

The human factor in operations management has been identified in many contexts (Lee, Padmanabhan, and Whang 1997). These authors examined role-played employee information sharing as a driver of supply chain coordination effectiveness. Along similar lines, Gino and Pisano (2007) argued that behavioral operations can increase understanding of the underlying drivers of system performance, including frequent "pathologies" such as excess inventory and late product development projects. Insight into behavioral operations management thus has the potential to improve supply chain operations by identifying appropriate general management interventions.

Consistent with this position, Eckerd and Bendoly (2013) argued that the core focus of the field of behavioral operations is an "improved understanding of the anomalies resulting from human deviation from normative theory. It looks specifically at the human variable to explain breakdowns and failures of operation systems, as well as differences in performance that result from social, psychological, and cultural root causes." These authors also identify simulation as a foundational methodological approach used to develop insight into behavioral operations in this research.

Roth (1993) highlighted a deficiency in modern economic through the use of behavioral experiments testing the presence of nonrational behavior. The results from these experiments demonstrate the presence of the behavioral patterns in isolation. Bendoly, Donohou, and Schultz (2006) pointed out that behavioral economists are now developing generalizations of neoclassic economic theory by the addition of normative psychological or regularized behavioral patterns. The authors also note that despite ongoing research into the implications of behavioral phenomena, no developed theories have been established integrating classical and neoclassical propositions.

Loch and Wu (2007) reflect on the fact that although development in the fields of operations management and behavioral operations has been progressive and independent way, conceptually both fields are intertwined. The set of theories undergirding behavioral operations include those focused on individual decision-making, behavior, social preferences, status, reciprocity, relationships, and group identity. Cultural models also have been recognizes as a critical pillar in the development of the field.

Experimental simulations have seen extensive use in the literature, particularly in supply chain research. Croson and Donohue (2005), for example, showed the impact of information sharing using a controlled version of the Beer Distribution Game. They found that the bullwhip effect is not only mitigated by sharing information, but by behavioral factors related to decision-making authority. Croson and Donohue (2006) continue the exploration of these issues, with the use of simulations to identify behavioral drivers. They reflect on the value of information, proposing an additional behavioral cause of the bullwhip effect they call the coordination risk, which emerges from assumptions made about others' behavior. Kimborough, Wu, and Zhong (2002) investigated whether artificial agents achieve higher performance than human agents. They found that artificial agents effectively played the Beer Game, tracking demand, eliminating the bullwhip effect, identifying optimal policies, and good policies under complex scenarios where analytical solutions are not available.

Most simulation-based experiments described in the literature have been designed to test one or more specific behavioral phenomena in operation management settings. To our knowledge, little or no broad behavioral research, of the kind encompassed by business simulation games, has emerged.

Del Pozo and coauthors (1998), based on ten years of research, argued that business simulation represents a viable alternative teaching modality, insisting that games based on system dynamics models should be transparent-box business simulations. In 1997, these authors offered evidence regarding the utility of electronic data interchange (EDI) and a computerized Internet-based version of the Beer Game as a way to enhance supply chain coordination.

In business game simulations, participants can make decisions using analytical tools. However, given inherent complexities and time pressures, these tools often are replaced by heuristics, rules of thumb, intuitive judgments, or "common sense." In practice, we have observed how such heuristic-driven decisions free resources that are allocated to robust situational diagnosis and strategic game analysis. In such cases, the use of heuristics potentially represents an asset rather than a liability, as suggested by Katsikopoulos, K. V. and Gigerenzer (2013). These authors identified conditions under which heuristics may be counted as an asset, rather than the liability they are commonly assumed to be in classic theory.

CASE EXAMPLE

The business simulation game in focus in this chapter, SimEmp,[1] is a web-based simulation requiring students to assume different roles within teams of four to six members. Apendix 1 (Figures 18.1 and 18.2) shows a snapshot of the simulation's web interface. Each team competes against four to five different teams (companies) for market demand. The one-week length of the course makes for a very intensive competition, as teams have very limited time to make operations decisions for their company.

The simulation is run in periods of four months. At the start of each period, teams decide how the company is going to compete in terms of production, logistics, marketing, and finance. Because there are more than 300 decision variables, there is too much work for a single person. Thus, the organization of the teams becomes a critical aspect of the course. Besides the time pressure to make decisions and manage the team, the course also includes role-playing experiences such as negotiations with union leaders, negotiations with credit executives from the bank, and results presentations to a board.

The business game runs for six periods, that is, two years. This allows teams to experience at least two complete demand seasons. Each country (market) is arranged in five different zones or regions (north, west, east, south, and center). Demand is different across regions, with two different customer segments (high and low). Product life cycle also is different across regions. All teams have historical data, which provides insight into market size and functional characteristics.

Teams compete against all other teams in the same country (market) in a dynamic way. The simulation only establishes the web platform and the rules, but teams decide about how to use their resources to generate zero-sum market share. Team performance is a direct function of their own—and other teams'—decisions.

Simulation Platform

The simulation platform encompasses two basic types of users. The first is teams responsible for making decisions about the company. Teams are allowed to enter their decisions into the system, but can't execute the simulation. The second type of user is instructors, who can view teams' decisions, edit decisions if required, and most importantly run a simulation period.

In each period the simulation is run in two phases. First, once teams have entered their decisions (price, ads expense, sales force, etc.), the instructor can execute the market assignment. In this phase the simulator confronts teams' marketing decisions and assigns a potential demand to be fulfilled by each team.

Once potential demand has been assigned, the instructor can run the second phase, in which the simulation determines teams' capacity to fulfill potential demand based on their production, distribution, purchasing, and financial decisions. In

1. SimEmp stands for *Simulacion Empresarial* in Spanish. This same course in other business schools is known as ES2 or ExSim.

this phase, the platform simulates materials in-flow, calculating remaining stocks or stock outs while simultaneously determining cash flows, and financials such as short- and long-term credits, investments, charges, and payments. Appendix 2, Figure 18.3, illustrates these two phases of the simulation. Figures 18.4–5 provide snapshots of the reporting capabilities of SimEmp in support of decision making in this activity.

Although the simulation runs across two sequential phases, students make all their decisions during the first phase. This requires developed intrateam coordination to accurately forecast required cash flows to operate the company. Inaccurate forecasts result in the need for high-interest, emergency loans that penalize teams for ineffective planning. When teams make accurate forecasts, and match product demand at the right time and location, companies can sell their products, generating a flow of goods and money into the company. It is important to recall at this point that all teams begin the game with an equivalent operating position, two years in the market, equivalent inventory, machinery, labor, financial results, and market share.

The inherent complexity associated with the game results in an interesting behavioral pattern. The pressure to make fast decisions and to get a good grade generates a "second-level" experience, which exposes students to the real-world complexity inherent to the management of a team of individuals with their own beliefs and preconceptions, and the necessity of finding the best way to work together to win the game.

As a consequence of these second-level behavioral patterns, this course allows us to observe some analogies with real-world situations where effective navigation of the behavioral component is critical. These analogies are reflected in structural organization, teamwork coordination, decision-making process, errors, learning, and leadership.

Students are assigned to teams and are not allowed to choose their own members. Thus, it is essential that they first define each member's function, the team's goals, and the means to integrate and coordinate members' contributions. Members must define their roles, which include the following:

- **Sales/marketing director**: responsible for defining the company's marketing strategy to increase its market share. Students in this role need to understand the dynamics of the market to determine pricing strategy and define an appropriate marketing budget for advertising. Marketing directors' performance is measured by market share of the company.
- **Finance director**: students in this position decide how much money is going to be invested and taken out as loans. The finance director needs strong coordination skills to accurately forecast cash flows in order keep running its operations. The performance of students in this role is measured by the ratio of financial expenses to total sales.
- **Distributor director**: in charge of shipping the product between factories and distribution centers. Students in this role decide the appropriate means (train, truck, airplane) to transport product to the warehouses as well as warehouse size. The performance of students in this role is evaluated using a service-level indicator.

- **Production director**: the most complex role in the business game, deals with line-balancing issues, capacity management, resource utilization, and supply. Some teams decide to assign two individuals to execute these responsibilities. A production director decides production orders, workers to be hired/fired, equipment to be bought/sold, assignment of workers, and raw material requirements. As it is possible to have a factory in every region of a country, those in this role need to make decisions for every region where the firm is located. The performance of production managers is measured by unit cost.
- **CEO**: this is perhaps the most demanding role in the simulation. Students playing this role define company strategy and the company's overall objectives and coordinate the execution of these objectives. The CEO is ultimately responsible for company profitability, and this is the basis on which the CEO's performance is evaluated. For instructors, CEOs serve as the principal conduit for communication with teams, as they serve as the "face" of the company.

LEARNING ACTIVITIES

Business Simulation is a core MBA course and is taught during the third trimester of the program immediately prior to students' going into their summer internships, and following their core courses in operations, marketing, and finance. Other business schools have implemented SimEmp as an elective course with very good results as well.

The course begins on Monday morning and ends on Friday afternoon. It is an intensive week, with work schedules extending beyond a regular eight-hour day. Total dedication is required to complete the course successfully. We ask students the previous week to avoid scheduling any activities outside of school in order to maintain game focus.

The business game has the following general objectives:

- Develop managerial skills, including teamwork, problem-solving, negotiation, definition of common objectives, and working under pressure
- Facilitate student reflect on about decision-making processes with scarce resources and limited information
- Analyze processes and relationships among production, logistics, marketing, and finance
- Develop a "sense of business": how and why companies make money

Preparing and delivering the course requires a heavy burden of work for instructors. Below, we describe the activities that have to be completed before starting the game and during play.

Before the Game

A week prior to the start of the business game, students receive three documents: (1) a business case describing the operation of the company in all functional areas, (2) the bankruptcy rules of the game (companies that lose more than one-third of their initial equity), and (3) a welcome letter to the course.

The business case is critical in the game, describing in great detail how things work in the company. This includes the flow of materials, the cost of transactions (hiring/firing salesmen and workers, purchasing raw materials and equipment, transportation, advertising, etc.), and the business rules of the simulation. The case also provides financial statements for the first two years (six periods) of operations of the company students are now running.

After the students have read and understood the case, the simulation platform and its functionality are more easily assimilated.

During the Game

Appendix 4, Figure 18.6, shows a typical work schedule for the business game course. A day-to-day plan of activities might proceed as follows.

Day 1

The first day of the simulation is one of the most critical parts of the course. It is an intensive day for both students and instructors. The day starts by providing a general introduction to the simulation platform, delivered to the entire group of students. This includes game objectives, an explanation of how the simulation works (market assignment and operations simulation), and how team performance is evaluated. Student teams are assigned during this introduction.

Following the introductory presentation, students are given some time (30 minutes) to start teamwork activities and define members' roles. Students are asked to elaborate an organization chart, which they hand in at the end of the day. At this point, teams also are assigned rooms to facilitate their work during the course.

Once students have decided their roles for the course, a detailed explanation of the different functional areas is provided. We ask only students playing a particular role to attend the explanation of their corresponding responsibilities, that is, marketing directors attend the marketing meeting, production directors attend the production meeting, and so on. We recommend students playing the CEO role attend all of these meetings as well. This takes approximately half of a workday.

During the rest of the day, once all students understand their responsibilities and have defined their personal objectives, teams prepare for the first period of simulation (or period 7 in the life of the company). In order to accelerate their learning curve, we dedicate the afternoon block to respond to questions and clarify doubts, while allowing teams to do some simulation trials in order to perform "what-if" analysis. This also provides the opportunity for instructors to become familiar with teams and the way in which they have organized their work.

Day 2

By day 2, most teams have begun to understand the business game rules well and have worked in spreadsheets allowing them to forecast sales, material flows, and cash flows. We ask teams to turn in the strategy they intend to follow during the game, as well as their strategic objectives. The strategy of each team is written in a document, which is accessible to all board members.

During the morning block of day 2, we formally run the first period of the simulation, which is the first moment of truth (among many) for the students. While instructors are running the simulation, the web platform blocks access to edit decisions and view reports. After instructors run the simulation, students are allowed to view reports and check their results.

The reports provided by the platform are extensive (appendix 3 provides a sample report). Students are able to choose from a wide variety of reports, from general financial reports as results statements, balance sheets, and biweekly cash flows to production or logistics reports that show the flow of material, finished goods, stocks on hand, stock in transit, and so on. There is a summary report showing the financial results of all companies in the country, as well as a market report that shows prices and market share in the different segments and regions of the country. Students appreciate both reports, as they represent a way to compare their own results against the competition.

After the analysis of results, teams begin preparing the next period of the simulation and for their first board meeting. The board meeting is a role-play activity in which teams present their results and their strategy for the course to the board (the board is a team composed of two to three professors and business professionals). As in a real-world board meeting, students are usually required to present commitments (e.g., return on investment, sales targets, etc.).The workday ends with teams preparing their decisions for period 8 and likely making some changes to their strategy. By this point, questions to instructors become less technical and more strategic.

Day 3

The third day of the course is perhaps one of the most exhausting for students. At the end of this day, higher-performing teams have developed a deep understanding of the business game rules, and intrateam dynamics start to play an important role here.

The instructors run periods 8 and 9 of the simulation on day 3. Instructors put pressure on students to make fast decisions, and it is common to observe multiple teams struggling to enter decisions minutes before the scheduled official simulation. Coordination and definition of good decision-making processes becomes crucial at this point.

This third day of the course also incorporates another role-playing experience, which is negotiation with bank executives (a role usually played by a professor or a real-world CFO). Some teams realize that they need to increase their investments in assets (new facilities, new equipment, etc.) while substantially increasing their short- or long-term debts as well. Thus, teams need to negotiate terms with a virtual bank to have access to debts, including interest rates, payment periods, and supporting assets.

Day 4

By day 4, most if not all teams have become experts in the simulation platform. Most teams now master their spreadsheets and are able to forecast with some degree of accuracy the expected material and cash flows of the company. They can test and evaluate several scenarios, and competition between teams becomes tougher. For many students, the business game starts to look like a chess game.

On day 4, we pack two formal period simulations together: periods 10 and 11, which actually represent the start of the second year of operations. This day also includes two role-playing activities. First, before the simulation of period 11, teams must again meet with the board. By this time, a complete year has passed, and this offers a good opportunity to discuss the results of their strategy and reflect on how well the team performed in terms of the commitments made at the start of the simulation.

Day 4 also is the day for unions. This recommended role-playing activity is optional. In many cases, after four simulation periods, most teams haven't touched the salaries of their workers. Nevertheless, some teams have created their jobs and have increased their salaries proportionate with the increase in sales or profits. Now is a good chance for instructors to introduce the union leader, whose role is to try to push teams to improve the living standards of the union's affiliates. This role is usually given to a real union leader, so negotiations with this person are in many cases quite tough. The activity can take place just before the end of day 4, and it is not necessary to call on all teams. The instructor might prefer to focus on those teams with the lowest salary levels in the market.

Day 5

This is the final day of the course, and if everything has developed according to plans, teams arrive at this day with high expectations as to winning the business game. By the end of the week, most teams know more about the company than the instructors themselves know. Thus, simulation of the last period is basically a war of strategic moves.

As teams are evaluated according to accumulated net profits, teams typically look for any alternative way to generate income. In order to prevent selling the company out, we recommend running the last period of the game with one additional rule in mind: teams are not allowed to sell equipment or facilities. The reason to do this is to keep up the level of competition level and maintain sustainable into the future.

Once period 12 has been simulated, the final activity of the course is the wrap-up. It is suggested instructors close the activity in the classroom with all teams together and a discussion of the learning points of the week. In order to maintain certain degree of healthy excitement, we disable the access to all simulation reports, and final results are shown after this discussion. Typical questions to address these learning points are the following:

- What did you learn during this week?
- What difficulties did you experience?
- What surprised you?
- How did you define objectives and commitments to your team?
- How well did the team perform?

- How did you organize and coordinate the decision-making process?
- What is the role of a CEO? How well did your CEO perform?

A good discussion of these topics can take as long as 40–50 minutes. After addressing the main learning points of the week, we reflect on students' final results. At this point, students might be a little nervous and excited, and it is very convenient to maintain tension until the very last moment.

Interactions between Instructors and Participants

Throughout the course, instructors have a number of good opportunities to interact with students in a variety of ways. Before teams make their final decisions prior to the end of period simulation, instructors are able to observe the team's dynamics as well as the way the CEO leads his or her team. Particularly during the first days of the game, students look for instructors to get some advice on basic operations, marketing, or finance concepts. As the game progresses, questions from students become more strategic and instructors can help them to evaluate the benefits and costs of possible decision vectors.

After a period has been simulated, instructors also have the opportunity to talk with teams about what went wrong—particularly in teams with problems, what criteria were used to make decisions, and if teams had a clear view of how the game functions. This is a good moment for teams to reflect about the way they organized workload and compare themselves against the competition.

Ethic Analysis during Business Simulation

This business simulation allows us to observe the ethical behavior of the participants and their impact in the decision-making process. During the simulation, the instructor can observe, from an external position, how individual and collective will is modified by the growing pressure to achieve results within the team's level of competence, increasing the desire to break rules with covenants intended to achieve unfair benefits. Some participants even use their own teammates as mere instruments, forgetting their human dignity.

Another advantage of this aspect of the simulation is that it allows instructors to make the participants aware that what they are doing involves ethical acts. Instructors as external witnesses can discuss with participants how cultural differences influence moral human interactions, and provide feedback. After participants are aware of the effects of their actions, some decisions no longer appear irrational, becoming moral acts that are willingly and consciously made.

Evaluation of the Course

The course is a capstone activity and a very popular activity within the MBA program. Nevertheless, it is also a core course required to fulfill academic requirements. The final course grade depends on three components. First, team performance, the total equity achieved by teams during the simulation, accounts for 70% of the final grade. Individual performance, which is measured according to the role students played in the simulation, accounts for 20% of the final grade. We also give a weight of 10% to the team's performance in the board meetings. This component is clearly subjective and depends on the board's perception of the work done by the team. Nevertheless, it encourages students to offer substantial analysis of the situation and go through a real-world experience in a safe environment.

Activity Log

During the week, students are asked to complete a short survey about their perceptions of the work done by the team. This is a questionnaire (see appendix 5) that is applied on day 2 (after period 7 simulation), on day 3 (after period 9 simulation), and on day 5 (at the end of the course and before students know their final results).

The purpose of this questionnaire is twofold. First, students realize while filling out this questionnaire how much their perceptions have changed during the simulation. In many cases, they are able to capture those differences. Second, the questionnaire also becomes a tool for students to reflect with their teammates about their work, and their coordination and integration within the team.

DISCUSSION

Although the real world is more complex, the business simulation allows us to introduce a sufficient level of complexity to observe the range of behavioral phenomena in a controlled context.

In this section, we would like to describe experiences and insights from playing this game for the past 25 years at IPADE Business School. We have seen how the "human variable" influences not only those decisions related to operations, but those relating to finance or marketing as well. When a rational decision is expected, teams find themselves making biased decisions, using intuition or taking unnecessary risks in order to achieve their goals.

First, below, we describe our observations from an individual perspective, that is, how an individual's own biases and preconceptions can influence the execution of his or her role in the simulation. We then list insights bearing on team processes, which is in fact a group of individuals making decisions for the team's sake but each with different possible interests. Finally, we analyze the performance of teams as members that interact and compete with other teams under similar conditions, pointing out the gap between rationality and the resulting context when behavioral variables are present.

Insights Related to Individual Performance

All participants arrive to the first day of the course sharing similar theoretical frameworks. Those frameworks are extensive and range from operations topics to strategy, marketing, finance, and organizational behavior. In many cases, students have experience in management positions leading teams. Thus, it is valid to assume that participants would be ready to assume their role in the simulation and rapidly establish rules for their work as a team.

Nevertheless, in many cases organization and coordination of the team becomes a difficult task as a result of individuals' biases and expectations. One of the first is students trying to optimize their own area of control without accounting for other members' needs. As the game progresses, they realize that their decisions are completely intertwined with others' decisions. Although they are individually measured during the simulation, they realize that in order to achieve common goals compromises are necessary.

Participants in the role of the CEO are of particular relevance. All start with the selection of the individual that plays this role. In many cases, the CEO volunteers to do the job, but in others, nobody wants to take on the responsibility of the role—although they are playing in relatively safe environment. In either case, CEOs often think that managing a team of highly trained and competitive people will be an easy task. It is very common to see CEOs in the first two days of the simulation very relaxed as they think their colleagues are doing a good job. However, sooner or later they realize that they need to lead the team and look for ways to facilitate the decision-making process.

Decision-making is precisely one of the points of dissonance within the teams, particularly at the start of the simulation. First, although familiar with a variety of management theories, members don't know what should be the starting point of their job. It is very common to have, for example, students playing the role of CEOs, asking instructors about what to do first and how to do it. Another common issue is the difficultly associated with the allocation of their own resources, including their time. Students tend to spend a lot of time performing deep analysis of the different situations while delaying the decision-making process. As a result, in the first few days of the course they devote little time entering their decisions into the system and validating them. In this sense, this becomes one of the primary sources of error in the simulation.

As the game progresses, it is very easy to observe which students are better at handling frustration than others. Individuals who are not well equipped to do this tend to isolate themselves and finish working as separate entities from the rest of the team. They even end up working in a different room in order to concentrate on their decisions. In such situations, students point out analogies with organizations that operate in silos. As expected, when those situations emerge, team performance tends to be worse than that of the other teams. It is in these situations where the role of the CEO gains in importance, with a focus on dealing with these conflicts.

Insights Related to Team Performance

Students agree that maintaining good communication and integration within the team is crucial for performance. Nonetheless, they also agree that this is not easy task, particularly when good results are difficult to get and frustration emerges.

The first important insight here bears on how teams manage errors and create a learning environment. In general, it seems that weak performance is directly related to the way in which teams work under pressure and time their decisions. Teams that rush in the final minutes to enter their decisions tend to have lower performance. Although they know that this dynamic plays against them, teams in this situation usually don't do anything to correct this misappropriation of their time. Other teams, of course, organize themselves and are able to establish a structured procedure to enter their decisions. They even fill out improvised forms that allow the team, and the CEO, to be informed of all decisions suggested by different individuals.

The physical arrangement of their work spaces also reveals a lot about the teams' personality. As in real-world companies, teams with higher performance tend to work in a more compact way. Students work close to each other, sharing lot of information and suggestions about decisions. In such teams, the CEO goes from one individual to another, trying to develop a complete picture of the game. They ask, challenge, and ultimately lead the team in making the appropriate decisions. In contrast, teams with lower performance tend to work in relatively isolated mini-teams. It is common to see production and distribution directors working together but ignoring the work of finance or marketing. Some students point out that biases or preconceptions suggests that CEOs tend to overweight certain areas while neglecting others.

Insights Related to Interactions between Teams

The course establishes a competition among teams of highly trained people. As all teams start in a state of relative equilibrium, one would expect a close competition as the game progresses. Nonetheless, there is always a clear separation between high and low performers.

As this separation becomes clearer, lower performers end up assuming more risks (e.g., significantly decreasing prices to gain market share) than higher performers. Although sometimes the rewards associated with assuming risks is good (often given by some sort of lucky strike), in most cases lower performers make decisions under the pressure of the results of higher performers. Lower performers also are less likely to assess the risks they take from different perspectives, and in many times end up deviating from the strategies that they initially prepared.

Importance of Observed Dynamics

The business simulation is able to show the dynamic nature of participants and the influence of individuals over decisions in a real-world way. The observation of those variables in a controlled setting is important for researchers as well as for practitioners.

For practitioners, this type of activity facilitates reflection on the core values and foundation of collaborative work. Clearly, good performance is not based merely on the level of expertise or technical knowledge of the individuals involved. Sometimes, willingness to cooperate within the team becomes a stronger performance driver than technical expertise. A better understanding of team and individual expectations is critical toward building this willingness.

In the case of operations management, we tend to think that simulation based learning activities helps to better understand the impact of operational decisions on overall firm performance and whether interventions are feasible or practical to implement. In this sense, business game settings offer a viable framework to compare market-driven strategies versus efficiency-driven strategies and the role played by operations in each approach. For researchers, this also represents a viable opportunity to further investigate the key obstacles and constraints in the design and implementation of an operations strategy.

The use of criteria based on heuristics (rule of thumb, intuition, etc.) is an important issue developed during the course. The use of heuristics becomes an asset in the team decision-making process as it accelerates the diagnosis and the definition of the company's strategic orientation. Further, the transparent logic used in the business simulation allows participants to validate their approaches based on decision outcomes.

For disciplines other than operations management, there also are clear opportunities for research. Organizational behavior researchers might find this type of activity useful to test and contrast different theories bearing on teamwork. Psychologists might find the business game interesting for how individuals manage frustration and how the internal/external factors influence individual responses. The dynamics observed in the simulation can also potentially serve as an anthropological laboratory to develop better understanding of the differences and motivations in the act of directing a company.

Furthermore, the business simulation provides a great source of data to analyze high and low performers under particular contexts and competition. The analysis of these data can lead to the development of models that bear on existing gaps in performance and ultimately forecast team/individual behavior in the decision-making process.

In parallel to the research objectives of this type of alternative, simulation represents an alternative way for participant-centered learning methods, as it provides a more transparent and integrated approach to reveal the implications of behavioral issues in scenarios closer to real-world experiences.

Appendix 1. Business Game Simulation Interface

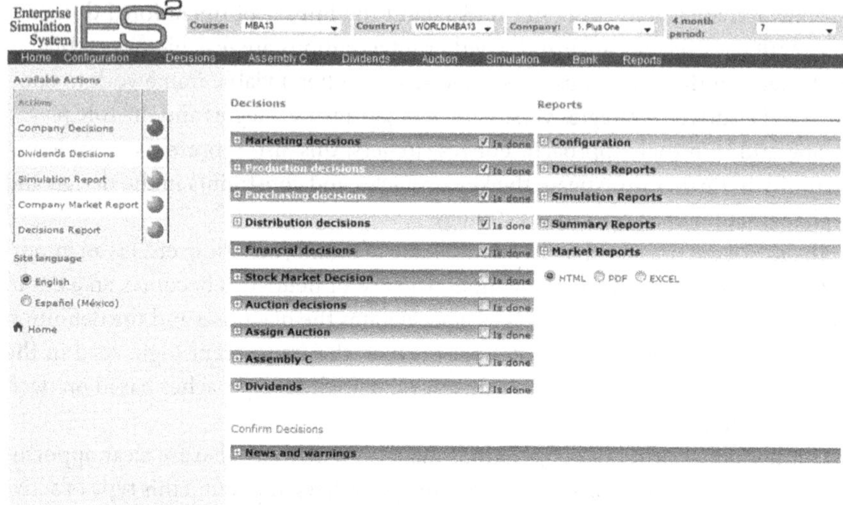

Figure 18.1 Business Game Simulation Interface A

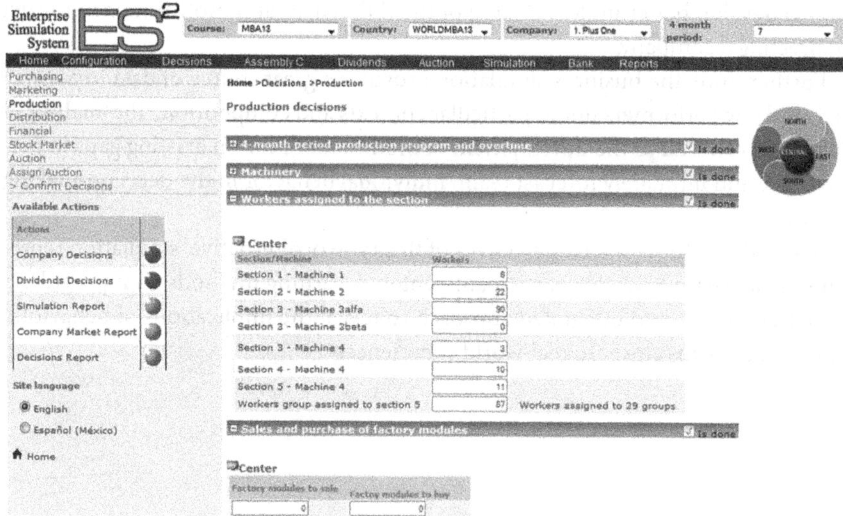

Figure 18.2 Business Game Simulation Interface B

Appendix 2. Two-Phase Procedure for Executing Simulation in SimEmp

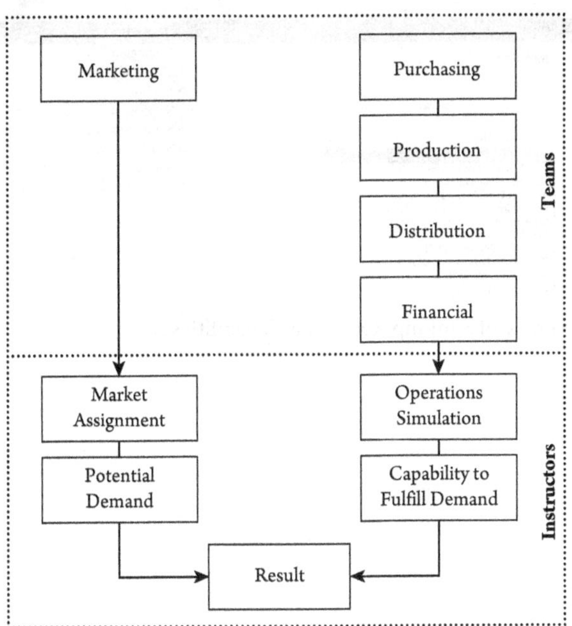

Figure 18.3 Two-Phase Procedure for Executing Simulation in SimEmp

Appendix 3. Sample of SimEmp Reporting Capabilities

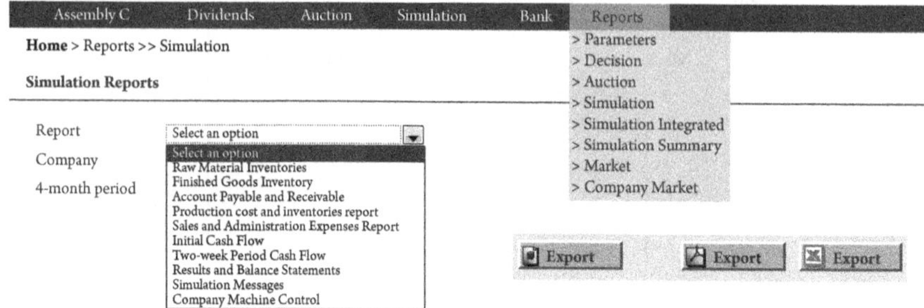

Figure 18.4 Sample of SimEmp Reporting Capabilities A

Appendix 4. Typical Work Plan of the Business Game Course

	Day 1. Monday	Day 2. Tuesday	Day 3. Wednesday	Day 4. Thursday	Day 5. Friday
Morning Block	General introduction Teamwork: organization chart Detailed explanation by functional area	Period 7 preparation and testing Simulation Period 7	Period 8 Preparation Simulation Period 8	Period 10 preparation Simulation Period 10 Meeting with union leader	Period 12 preparation Simulation Period 12 Course Wrap-up & Final Results
Afternoon Block	Period 7 preparation and testing	Period 8 and board preparation First board meeting Period 8 preparation	Period 9 preparation Meetings with bank executives Simulation Period 9	Second board meeting Simulation Period 11	

Figure 18.5 Typical Work Plan of the Business Game Course

Appendix 5. Questions Related to Perceptions of the Teamwork

I. GENERAL INFORMATION

- Date:
- Team:
- Role:
- Previous work position before your MBA:

II. TEAM ORGANIZATION

1. How would you evaluate the impact of your previous work experience in the role you have been assigned to this simulation?
2. How would you assess your level of preparation to assume your role in the game?
3. Do you know your functions and responsibilities in your team?
4. Which role do you think is the most important in this simulation?

III. DECISION-MAKING PROCESS

5. Does the team, the CEO, or each individual in his or her area of scope make decisions?
6. How would you evaluate the level of support of the decisions that your team is making?
7. Do you think your CEO leads and coordinates the team in an appropriate way?

IV. TEAMWORK

8. How do you assess communication within your team?
9. Do you think the team has clear and well-defined objectives? Explain why.
10. How would you evaluate interaction and integration of your teammates to fulfill the objectives?
11. How would you evaluate the work environment in your team?

V. EXPECTATIONS

12. How do you assess your performance in the game so far?
13. What are your expectations about your team results toward the end of the game?

References

Bendoly, E., Donohue, K., Schultz, K. L. 2006 Behavior in operations management. Journal of Operation Management 24 (6), 737–752.

Croson, R., Donohue, K. 2005. Upstream versus downstream information and its impact on the bullwhip effect. System Dynamics Review 21 (3), 249–260.

Croson, R., Donohue, K. 2006. Behavioral causes of the bullwhip effect and the observed value of inventory information. Management Science 52 (3), 323–336.

Del Pozo J., D., Ruiz del Castillo, J. C., Domingo, M. A., González, M. M. 1998. Our ten years of work on transparent box business simulation. Presented to the 16th International Conference of the System Dynamics Society, Quebec, Canada.

Eckerd, S., Bendoly, E. 2013. Behavioral operations. October 30. http://www.scholarpedia.org/article/Behavioral_Operations

Gino, F., Pisano, G. 2007. Toward a theory of behavioral operations. Working paper, April 30.

Katsikopoulos, K. V., Gigerenzer, G. 2013. Behavioral operations management: A blind spot and a research program. Behavioral Operations and Heuristics 49 (1), 1–6.

Kimborough, S. O., Wu, D. J., Zhong, F. 2002. Computers play the beer game: Can artificial agents manage supply chains? Decision Support Systems 33, 323–333.

Lee, H. L., Padmanabhan, V., Whang, S. 1997. Information distortion in a supply chain: The bullwhip effect. Management Science 43 (4), 546–558.

Loch, C. H., Wu, Y. 2007. Behavioral Operation Management. Hanover, MA: Publishers Inc.

Roth, A. E. 1993. On the early history to experimental economics. Journal of the History of Economics Thought 15 (Fall), 161–181.

CHAPTER 19

Behavioral Operations in Practice and Future Work

ELLIOT BENDOLY AND DANIEL G. BACHRACH

Traditionally, management theory has been used as a way to understand and also to define drivers of critical organizational outcomes. Development of a useful, conceptual framework that encompasses any number of a wide range of possible antecedents of these outcomes is influenced at least in part by the belief that these independent antecedents (1) exist and (2) can be measured. Further, typical conceptualization of the dependencies between elements in the theoretical framework relies on assumptions that often do not go beyond linear effects, moderated or mediated by other linear factors (see figure 19.1).

That a functional kind of linearity will emerge is of course the hope (and assumption) underlying variance-focused research. The default operating assumption is that variables fit together in this way. This issue is seeing increased critical attention in the management literature with broader emphasis on, for example, curvilinearity in previously assumed linear associations (Grant and Schwartz 2011; Pierce and Aguinis 2013). Nevertheless, success in the search for stronger linear drivers of variance in critical organizational outcomes is in no way certain. Regrettably, the tendency is for such efforts to take on something of a darts-in-the-dark character. The inertia propelling a traditional focus on "predicting variance" has led to a great deal of incremental empirical research. Researchers build incrementally better models, without necessarily understanding precisely how ("process") a performance measure shifts from one level at a particular point in time to another level at the next point in time, whether these associations have an unmeasured higher-order character that only emerges over time, or whether the nature of the association is stable across periods.

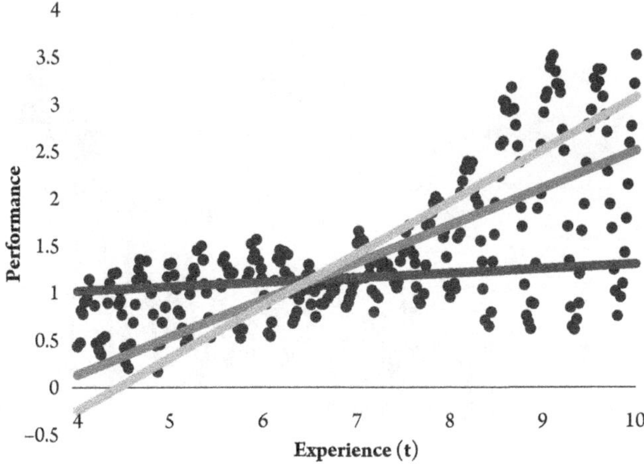

Figure 19.1 Example of Moderated Effect Fit to Data

The gold standard of empiricism is to leverage historical data on predictors to estimate theorized effects on critical outcome variables. An examination of the structure of theoretical arguments demonstrates that there clearly is a common belief that "process" exists in the association between variables. We often encounter theoretical arguments to the effect that "X leads to Y occurring (i.e., 'process'), hence Y goes up as X does (i.e., 'variance')." In other words, "process" is used implicitly to explain variance, but typically it is only variance (and not the process) that ultimately receives systematic empirical attention.

In light of this almost universal faith in the presence of an underlying process mechanism—that a "how" exists to explain variance in outcomes—what is unclear is why empirical management research often stops there (i.e., variance accounting) when going further could be so much more informative. That is, apart from the obvious reason that researchers can still "get away with it" and publish in top-tier journals, there is no sound response to this absence of focus.

In light of the dominant approach in the field, important questions bearing on the mechanics underlying the association between system nodes systematically go left unanswered. For example, why don't we spend more time asking questions like "How much time does it take X to impact Y?" Or, and this gets to questions of empirical operationalization, "Is the time separation between X and Y data sufficient to identify a relationship if one exists?" "Does X always impact Y at the same rate in all contexts for which we've observed data?" "What are the chances that over a sufficient length of time, Y might actually drive future values of X?"

The answers to these kinds of temporal questions have the potential to reveal some surprising empirical relationships that are simply not encompassed by traditional management theory. For example, with the right kind of analysis, it becomes clear that our dependent variables may be much more dependent on themselves than on many of the antecedents derived from an established theoretical framework (see figure 19.2). Although as scholars we typically don't develop conceptualizations that encompass sui generis within-variable self-driven change over

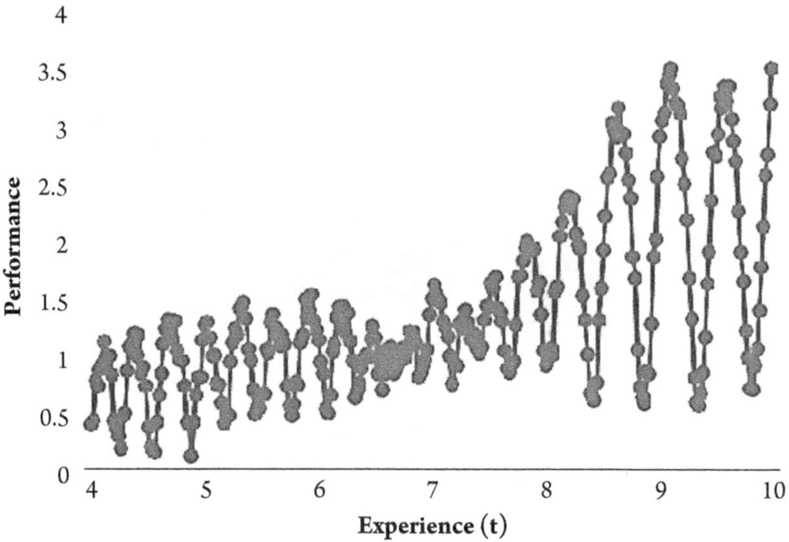

Figure 19.2 Dynamics Driven by a Single Feedback Loop

time, what is clear is that the underlying empirical structure of well-established relationships in the field may well be subject to just this kind of effect.

But, again, these kinds of temporal questions are not often encompassed by traditional theory and so remain unanswered. As even a brief perusal of the top five empirical management journals will quickly reveal, process-focused research is much less prevalent than variance-focused research. Ultimately as a consequence the deep, rich understanding of the relationships between critical variables that could truly serve the practice of management does not tend to emerge. Theoretical discussions of process are present in the literature, but usually only in broad strokes and for the purpose of developing a variance-focused point of departure. This theoretical framing is typically leveraged as a vehicle to support simple variance hypotheses rather than as a framework for process-focused theory testing. However, beyond the issue of academic incentives to focus on questions isomorphic to the constraints of the top journals have been functional constraints on the capacity of academics to reasonably approach and to effectively operationalize questions focused on issues of process. The traditional absence of access to the kind of data that could be used empirically to demonstrate the nature of complex processes also represents a traditional constraint on the systematic development of process theory.

The conditions that have supported this tradition have changed, however. It's time for a new tradition.

A SYSTEMS VIEW OF THEORY

As highlighted at the onset of this text, the truly phenomenal growth in the collection and availability of empirical data has had an indelible impact on what kinds of questions are now available to academic researchers, and the nature of the impact that academic research can have on practice. The greatest fear is that, despite the availability of more (almost unlimited) data, we may simply see more of the same kind of variance focus in the top management journals. It is certainly clear the probability of identifying new, highly correlated antecedents to critical organizational outcomes in variance modeling is going to increase in the new big-data paradigm. Given the risk of encountering spurious relationships (Benjamini 2010; Benjamini and Hochberg 1995), however, these variance models may not necessarily ultimately prove useful to management practice.

What we as a community of researchers and practitioners alike could more directly benefit from is deeper examination of patterns of variation in critical organizational outcomes over time. We need rich visualization of process data revealing the process through which these actions emerge and responses are catalyzed. We need continued rich case study examination, but with particular emphasis on description of detail through which actions translate into outcomes.

These methods used in tandem can offer a powerful mechanism for the germination of new process-focused theory that can open the black "how" box often left closed in traditional management research. Indeed, we argue that best practice for next-generation case analysis should almost certainly require rich visual representation of process data. Done correctly, grounded theory developed from the use of such approaches can further spur the development of new systems models of operational work practice and group dynamics that encompass the mechanics linking variables in traditional variance models. The larger empirical task is to provide parameter estimates toward the validation of these more nuanced process models of activity. It is critical to demonstrate that these kinds of unwrapped process models may not only better capture "variance" in outcomes, but also provide a more developed conceptual bridge linking tactical and higher-level strategic firm performance outcomes. That is, with insight into the nature of the processes linking variables in variance models, researchers and practitioners alike have a more sophisticated set of levers of pull to generate valued outcomes.

Ultimately there is a great deal of potential for rich micro-level research to provide insights for the strategic level of management (Ployhart and Hale 2014). This is an idea that has been embraced by the field of operations strategy for the past two decades. Now, expanding efforts of researchers in the behavioral operations and strategic management (Teece 2007) domain are beginning to provide the mechanisms through which to bridge these levels of analysis.

These bridges are constructed not only from individual theoretical concepts, but also require the simultaneous consideration of multiple theoretical building blocks. In order to bridge from the micro-level of tactical activity to the macro-level of strategic performance, it is essential to view even the tactical world through the lens of macro- or composite phenomena. Systematic and dynamic phenomena such as the bullwhip effect, the behavioral hill, and resonant dissonance/deconstrainment are contemporary exemplars. It is critical to consider the operation of large systems of phenomena operating in conjunction that are likely to be pervasive across operating contexts. In part, the goal of the chapters in this text has been to provide an array of such phenomena and in turn some systematic reflections on their underlying levels of connection.

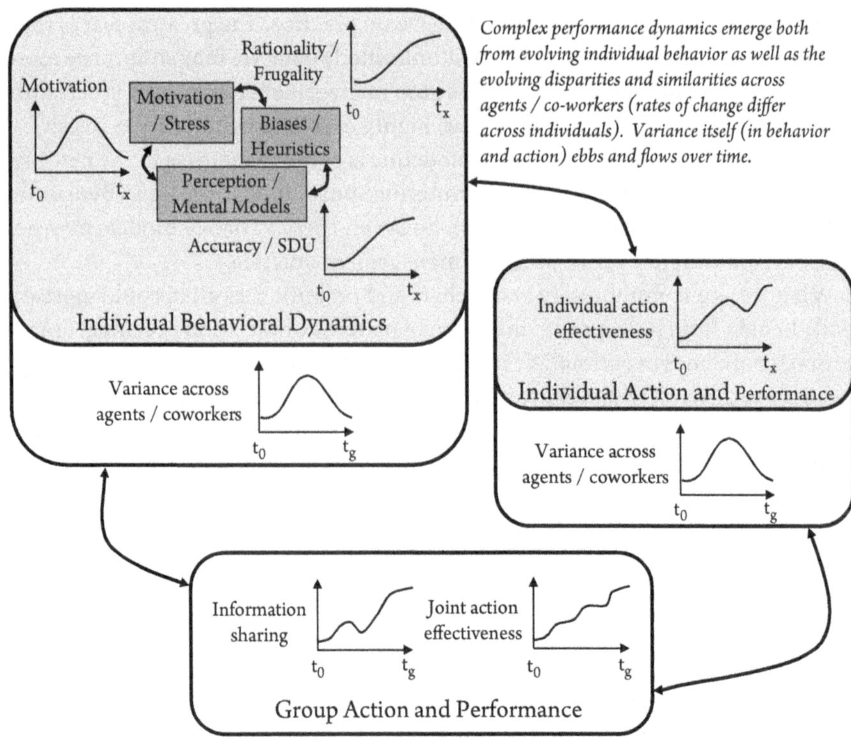

Figure 19.3 A Systems-View of Theory: Multilevel Connections and Evolving Dynamics

The exercise of drawing possible connections between theoretical phenomena is as useful for shaping of future research agenda as is the mapping of real-world processes into systems models of practice. Considering the various phenomena discussed across these chapters in a systematic way, it would be a natural step to confront a larger systems model of theory in general, as follows in figure 19.3.

The depiction in the figure reflects a fairly robust systems view that, apart from emphasizing the multilevel linkages and dynamics present over time in the operations of organizations, allows for a review of the sets of issues covered in this text. It is from this vantage point and motivated by the work from the prior chapters that we next consider broad propositions for future management research.

LOOKING FOR LEARNING IN SYSTEMS OF ACTION

The initial activity chapters reported in this text (chapters 3–7) illustrate how insufficient mental models, and associated biases and heuristics, can lead to seemingly irrational behavioral responses and decisions. Chapters 8 and 9 suggest that rich and thoughtful process considerations can offer a means by which to evolve individuals' mental models to increase perceptual accuracy and frugality in the use of heuristics and decrease susceptibility to the problematic intrusion of decision-making biases. These kinds of psychological adjustments also are broadly believed to be attainable through operational experience gained over time within focal decision-making contexts: albeit at different rates depending individuals' ability to incorporate novel, diagnostic situational information that has the potential to promote these kinds of perceptual and psychological adjustments.

Bendoly and Prietula (2008) further describe shifts in motivation (behavioral hill shifts) as a function of learning and experience with associated adjustments in system actions. Chapters 11 and 12, however, emphasize that adjustments to action need not necessarily be a consequence of adjustments to decision-makers' mental models. Rather, the tendency to adjust action may be driven by even the most stable mental models. Instead, adjustment in action may be a function of a consistent application of heuristics and the systematic impact of biases.

Thus, natural variance in individual action can be emblematic of long-term learning and mental model adjustment, but can also be present systematically in the absence of these learning- induced changes in perception. In order to empirically identify learning that leads to mental model adjustment, we must be able to disentangle such dynamics from systematic adjustments brought on as a consequence of following stable heuristics. Ultimately, in order to be in a position to define and identify changes in what ultimately gives rise to patterns of activity, we must look for patterns in activity to change.

> Proposition 1: The identification of actions associated with mental model adjustment requires the identification of shifts in the systematic patterns of activity driven by the use of stable heuristics.

LOOKING FOR LEADERS IN SYSTEMS OF ACTION

Complicating the development of insight into the mechanisms driving patterns of action and reaction in real-world work contexts, of course, is the presence of multiple agents (as noted from the onset in chapter 1). Chapters 13–16 offer an in-depth consideration of how individual mental models impact individual dispositions to engage in group contexts. However, multiple agents also are characterized by potentially divergent mental models and the fact that evolution in these models occurs at different rates for different actors. How are interactive temporal dynamics within groups complicated by these distinctions in learning rates and concomitant shifts in systemic reaction?

While there is a history of thought regarding the benefits of bringing together individuals with distinct bases of knowledge (Lewis 2003; Lee, Bachrach, and Lewis 2014), the benefits of getting such individuals together are argued theoretically to stem from an embedded capacity to satisfy respective individual gaps. But what if the distinctions in capacity don't manifest solely as a consequence of differences in what people "know," but also as a consequence of differences in what their knowledge leads them to believe is the best course of action (i.e., what should be done moving forward).

Bendoly's (2014) work suggests that distinctions in mental models in group settings can ultimately prove detrimental to information sharing within collective cognitive contexts. This appears to be true even when some members of the group have strong mental models that bear in a coherent way on platonic operational realities and that as a consequence have the potential to achieve relevant conscientiousness. Experienced leaders, through trial and error and experience, can realize that within-team conflicting mental models have the potential to diminish the efficacy and performance potential of otherwise functional group dynamics.

Given this recognition, leaders may actually continue to leverage mental models believed to be less accurate than one they have developed that is more reflective of functional operational contingencies, for the purpose of ensuring that both communication and learning continue. This may persist until followers are "ready" to start thinking about system interrelationships (i.e., they have gained sufficient evidence to support coherent functional thinking) in a more advanced way. Leaders that proceed in this kind of "rationally irrational" way recognize that although practical economies may be available through one mental model, these economies are not practicable until they can be effectively transferred across all constituents subject to their constraints. This suggests a distinct leadership role for conscientious group leaders with an effective mental model distinct from the rest of their group, leading to the following:

> Proposition 2: The most effective mental models are limited in their effectiveness by the distinctions they have from those of others critical to effective work.
>
> Proposition 3: Effective group leaders simultaneously maintain effective mental models and levels of associated conscientiousness, lead the evolution of members' models, and knowingly assimilate suboptimal heuristics and biases when necessary to facilitate group dynamics.

The emergent adoption of increasingly appropriate mental models can be observed by examining patterns of leader action that are distinct from patterns of learned action by others that are led. Only certain leadership-distinguished patterns (and not those most extreme relative to patterns present within the rest of the group) are likely to be associated with increased effectiveness. In these cases, the group affected by leader mental model influence need not be a set of colleagues within the scope of a particular set of intraorganizational tasks, but may just as easily apply to interorganizational activities encompassed by groups of agents that might be essentially competing (or at least in co-opetition) with each other.

LOOKING FOR MULTILEVEL SYNERGIES IN SYSTEMS OF ACTION

Chapter 10 and then chapters 17 and 18 are unique in that they explicitly attempt to provide a mechanism to illustrate systems of theoretical impact. We view these valuable activities as integrative capstone exercises for researchers, practitioners, or students studying the role of behavioral dynamics in operations contexts. They emphasize some of the difficulties that can arise as a consequence of the presence of complexity and task interdependencies across organizational levels. These factors clearly have implications for the formation and (hopefully, eventual) evolution of accurate mental models, on a scale far beyond the challenge faced by simpler contexts (which themselves pose considerable difficulty for human decision-makers; cf. chapter 3). Yet the complexity observed in these integrative scenarios, as in those encountered in the real world, emerges from dynamics at the tactical level where human behavior has the potential to be the most salient. Is it really possible to manage effectively from the "top" without truly understanding—and making relevant changes in—the dynamics at the bottom?

In management research, higher-level organizational (e.g., firm) performance often is viewed as more critical—certainly by key stakeholders such as stock owners and bond-rating agencies—than the performance of any one individual within the firm. Aside from being another somewhat caustic commentary on management research generally (and a clear source of disdain from nonbusiness disciplines), this 50,000-foot point of view is fundamentally flawed. Higher-level firm performance derives from the performance of individuals. Without individuals performing, organizational units and entire firms would fail. More accurately, in order for organizational units to maintain and improve performance, *some portion* of the workers and management population that constitutes them must perform. In any given snapshot of time, one might not be able to find the same individuals consistently driving organizational performance. The same individuals are not necessarily consistently sufficiently motivated to be the drivers of performance. They don't necessarily consistently have the opportunities they need. They don't necessarily consistently learn, improve, or grow in their skills. Any given snapshot in time will not consistently reveal the same individuals leveraging the same mental models or heuristics or safely sidestepping the same detrimental, performance-dampening biases.

Goldratt's classic perspective offers that determining the most critical sources of process limitation (bottlenecks) is absolutely critical to making improvements to operations throughput and ultimately firms' operationally supported strategic advantage. In the presence of system variation over time, the identification of bottlenecks is, of course, made more difficult, as these tend to float around involved processes and workers. As evident from even the simplest exercises, shifts in the nature of constraints can emerge unbeknownst to even careful observers as easily as those just plugging along. As shown in figure 19.4, which provides an illustrative result from the chapter 3 activity, what appears to constrain a system early on need not be as pervasive as system dynamics evolve over time. Facets of a system more highly dependent on others can be more broadly subject to constraining factors and may receive less benefit from buffers (positioned against constraints) than more independent steps. Thus observing individual activities in isolation, and over fairly limited periods, can provide a considerably skewed view of the presence of problems (and opportunities) in larger systems.

This once again this implies that unless well thought out approaches are considered, it is likely to prove extremely difficult to empirically examine any given

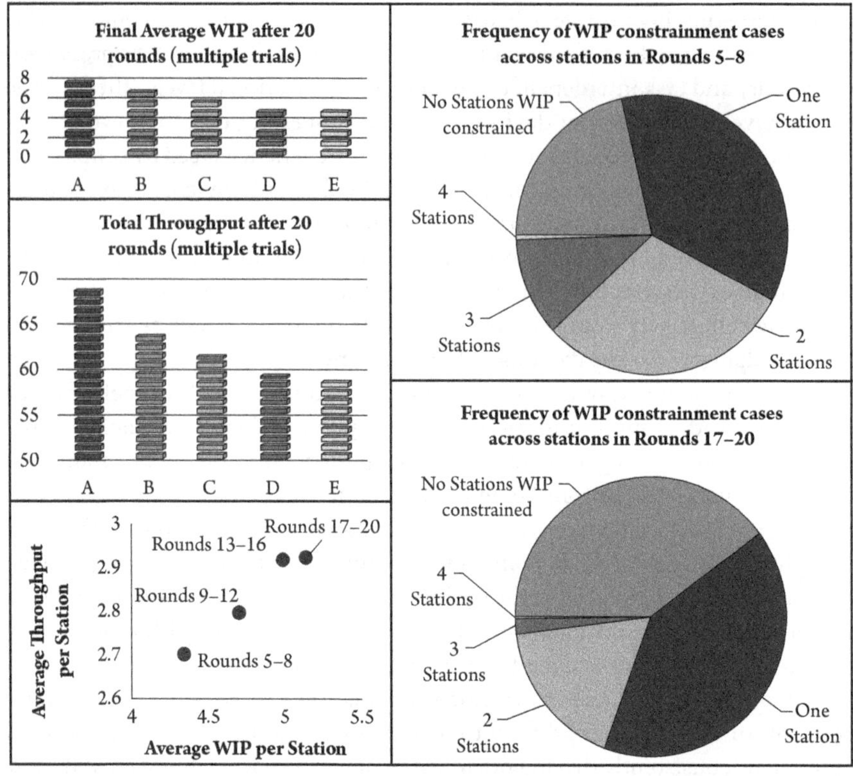

Figure 19.4 Shifts in Constraints in the Synch and Swim Illustration (Chapter 3)

snapshot of tactical activity as an explanatory variable within static models of higher-level performance.

A broader interpretation of bottlenecks (floating or otherwise) would naturally include critical limitations put in place by barriers to learning, and stagnant erroneous mental models, including those created by differential learning rates among agents (as per proposition 3). As learning does ultimately ensue, constraints to further learning are likely to shift. As a consequence, as with so many real-world systems, there is a feedback loop between variability (generated through learning) and the constraints that limit such learning (delaying both the growth and reduction of variability). Just as Goldratt's arguments suggest that reductions in variance can be as effective as constraint management in improving overall performance, minimization of variance in learning should prove useful when such variance isn't otherwise naturally feeding additional learning processes (which it is in fact often not). This is a somewhat novel notion for management research, albeit a clear extension of the Theory of Constraints in the context of learning in multiagent settings.

Of course, determining the nature of bottlenecks within complex operational systems is empirically (and conceptually) quite elusive, particularly if such evaluations start at ground zero with no understanding of extant temporal dynamics. That is where both the current and emerging theory presented in the chapters of this text, and in the systems view of theory (figure 19.3), are most likely to prove useful for both management theory and practice. They not only provide guidelines for the kinds of phenomena that can play out between tactical decisions and higher-level performance, but also speak to the kind of data that would be most useful in searching for and validating such dynamics—as well as ultimately making critical operational and strategic decisions to better govern these dynamics.

> Proposition 4: Firms effectively leveraging customized enterprise data collection to build systems models of tactical-to-strategic dynamics, sensitive to variation in worker behavior, will have a strategic advantage over firms that do not.

Here, as readers have figured out by now, we aren't talking about the vast quantities of marketing-related data that have received so much attention and hype in the growing big-data movement—an artifact that has emerged because we are all consumers and such data are most readily encountered and available for discussion. Not that knowing what people might buy isn't important, but it's only one side of a very big coin. Here we're less focused on external boundary spanning data than on what's happening inside the firm. We are interested in the firm actually looking inward, to what it and all of its constituents do on a regular, ongoing basis. Here we are looking for the flows and barriers to operational cause and high-level effect, over time. An important question that remains unanswered is how much more effective would firms be if they could, simultaneously, understand the best opportunities to pitch to the marketplace as well as the best opportunities for systematic tactical shifts enabling better pitching in the future.

Gnothi seauton—Know thyself—and you'll have an easier time actually using what you know of others.

APPROACHES TO STUDYING SYSTEMS OF ACTION

While the field of behavioral operations has provided strong guidance in the development of research along established methodological lines (cf. Bachrach and Bendoly 2011), until recently there have been few examples in the OM literature of large volumes of semicontinuous activity data being collected or examined. The majority of extant studies that leverage semicontinuous activity data in building rich longitudinal examinations have relied on data collected by single organizations—and not typically with the guidance of researchers. The challenge, therefore, as with all archival research, is knowing whether the data under examination are actually representative of the issues of interest. This is particularly the case when the data represent proxies of issues of interest to research and practice, but not actually the issues themselves.

Fortunately the cost of collecting semicontinuous activity data has gone down substantially over the years, and likely will continue to decrease as the technologies for data collection continue to become more sophisticated. We are now at a cost point for in situ activity collection that makes the customized collection of data at firms collaborating with academic researchers actually possible. Researchers have leveraged an increasing range of such data collection apparatuses and provide some guidance for continued development.

Semicontinuous Tracked and Logged Activity

Records of work activity can include both subjective and objective collections. On the subjective side, real-time employee journaling (Cyboran 2005) and employee self-reporting of job control and cognitive load (e.g., Jackson et al. 1993) can be highly indicative of mental models and their evolution if tracked over time—with the potential of pinpointing real difficulties perceived by key portions of the workforce. However, such subjective assessments certainly have their limitations, in particular the risk that people simply record what they think they are expected to report, contributing to a cycle of self-fulfilling prophecy and opacity in underlying mechanical links.

Less subject to such concerns are objective enterprise captures of work activity, including date/time records of when jobs are received, assigned, and completed, as well as associated costs, errors, rework, and specific resources allocated toward their completion. These extremely detailed and often standardized records are typically event driven, so while perhaps not as continuous as one might desire, are still powerful and relevant. Depending on the nature of the work (e.g., nearly continuous repetitive as opposed to specialized project-based), the frequency of recorded activity may be sufficient to paint a vivid picture of human behavior and system dynamics (cf. Alba et al. 2013).

If more continuous data are desired, or if the nature of the data collected by extant enterprise systems insufficiently captures in-focus activity and behavioral details, adjustments to collection must be made. Options include actually changing the way that the enterprise system collects data, although this is both costly and a not necessarily sufficient approach. Potentially more valuable are *tracked emblematic work studies* (TEWs), which are objective collections of emblematic work activity data across time, in more controlled settings. This can take the form of laboratory explorations of activities, or high-grade facsimiles of real activity. Here we're not talking about garden variety university computer lab experiments. These are experiments designed, with or without realist manipulations, to capture as closely as possible real work environments, often in-fact using real work environments (or adjustments thereof). With such studies come additional empirical perks such as options of biometric measurement (cf. Bendoly 2011; 2013; Carlson 2013).

Analyzing Dialogue around Decision-Making and Action

Apart from physiological indicators, a great deal of rich intelligence can be mined from dialogue that emerges across processes in which actions are decided upon and executed. Today a variety of options are available to firms to facilitate problem/solution dialogue. Capitalizing on the cultural success of social networks, many large firms maintain their own internal discussion forums and heavily leverage electronically facilitated collaborative meeting technologies. All of these settings present trails of information exchange, as well as histories of individual opinions and beliefs that can be critical for developing deeper understanding of the mental models driving complex intrasystem behaviors. As new techniques for parsing text and categorizing commentary emerge, the ability to extract meaning from these dialogues can empower firms with the ability to intervene in ways unavailable in the past, provided of course that doing so is not viewed as overly intrusive, undermining the purpose of these forums.

Systems Thinking / System Dynamics: Understanding Assessments

Accompanying objective natural (or controlled) observations is complementary value in new management assessments that can improve understanding of why the dynamics of observed actions appear to take on a particular form, and why patterns of action vary over time, across circumstances and individuals. These can include short assessments, but often a sufficient understanding of the structure and depth of mental models cannot be generated without exhaustive individual-level evaluation. One approach that has recently proven successful is the System Dynamics Understanding (SDU) assessment used by Bendoly (2014). This 60-minute interview protocol, applied specifically to project teams, follows tools used by Booth-Sweeney and Sterman in their assessment of teacher/student perceptions of system dynamics. Bendoly's recent project team adaptation has proven useful in predicting project performance, particularly when both team-level and intermember variation in System Dynamics Understanding are evaluated simultaneously.

A possible alternative or complementary approach to SDU assessment is *shared factor-map reviews* (SFMRs). In such reviews, managers and workers are given a set of common, well-defined environmental work factors. They are asked to independently use causal loop diagramming approaches to outline associations among the factors, including feedback loops, and to draw out the dynamics in the levels of these factors over time. They also are allowed to suggest up to three additional factors for introduction in subsequent rounds of review. The maps and suggestions are pooled and compared in a group session, and consensus is built around common mappings. Newly recommended factors are defined and rationalized (minimizing conceptual overlap). Subsequent rounds allow individuals to leverage consensus submaps and provide extensions, before reconvening a group review. Used at various points (e.g., twice a year or even quarterly), these sessions can reveal perceived changes in the operational environment and reinforce system thinking among the workforce—with associated benefits.

RECOMMENDATIONS

As a broad summary, given our present understanding of the complex albeit critical role that the evolving mental models of workers and managers have on operational systems, it is clear that much more work is needed to bridge the gap between academic research and practical managerial application. In retrospect, it is clear that this need has long existed. What is new are both the understanding we presently have of salient themes in behavioral operations and the means by which to more rigorously empirically investigate these themes in real-world settings. The activities in this text offer an illustration of behavioral phenomena that clearly emphasize the importance of increasing such understanding. Though it is critical that both managers and management trainers are familiar with these phenomena through such illustration, such awareness is only the starting point for the rigorous investigations that must now follow. With this said, we welcome the collaborative efforts of both the practitioner and academic communities working toward such empirical definition and look forward to the advances that this work will no doubt yield in the future.

References

Alba, C., Salvadore, F., Bendoly, E., Tenhl, A. 2013. Effects of manager's breadth and depth of experience on planning and execution performance. DSI Proceedings. http://www.ner.takushoku-u.ac.jp/anishio/DSI/DSI2013_Proceedings/files/p670090.pdf.

Bachrach, D. G., Bendoly, E. 2011. Rigor in behavior experiments: A basic primer for SCM researchers. Journal of Supply Chain Management 47 (3), 5–8.

Bendoly, E. 2011. Linking task conditions to physiology and judgment errors in RM systems. Production and Operations Management 20 (6), 860–876.

Bendoly, E. 2013. Real-time feedback and booking behavior in the hospitality industry: Moderating the balance between imperfect judgment and imperfect prescription. Journal of Operations Management 31 (1–2), 62–71.

Bendoly, E. 2014. Systems dynamics understanding in project execution: Information sharing quality and psychological safety. Production and Operations Management 23 (8), 1352–1369.

Bendoly, E., Prietula, M. 2008. In "the zone": The role of evolving skill and transitional workload on motivation and realized performance in operational tasks. International Journal of Operations and Production Management 28 (12), 1130–1152.

Benjamini, Y. 2010. Simultaneous and selective inference: Current successes and future challenges. Biometrical Journal 52, 708–721.

Benjamini, Y., Hochberg, Y. 1995. Controlling the false discovery rate: A practical and powerful approach to multiple testing. Journal of the Royal Statistical Society, Series B, 57, 125–133.

Carlson, N. 2013. Physiology of Behavior. 11th ed. Upper Saddle River, NJ: Pearson Education.

Cyboran, V. L. 2005. Moving beyond the training room: Fostering workplace learning through online journaling. Performance Improvement 44, 34–39.

Grant, A. M., Schwartz, B. 2011. Too much of a good thing: The challenge and opportunity of the inverted U. Perspectives on Psychological Science 6, 61–76.

Jackson, P. R., Wall, T. D., Martin, R., Davids, K. 1993. New measures of job control, cognitive demand, and production responsibility. Journal of Applied Psychology 78 (5), 753–762.

Lee, J. Y., Bachrach, D. G., Lewis, K. L. 2014. Social network ties, transactive memory, and performance in groups. Organization Science. Advance online publication. http://dx.doi.org/10.1287/orsc.2013.0884.

Lewis, K. 2003. Measuring transactive memory systems in the field: Scale development and validation. Journal of Applied Psychology 88, 587–604.

Pierce, J. R., Aguinis, H. 2013. The too-much-of-a-good-thing effect in management. Journal of Management 39, 313–338.

Ployhart, R. E., Hale, D., Jr. 2014. The fascinating psychological microfoundations of strategy and competitive advantage. Annual Review of Organizational Psychology and Organizational Behavior 1, 145–172.

Teece, D. J. 2007. Explicating dynamic capabilities: the nature and microfoundations of (sustainable) enterprise performance. Strategic Management Journal 28, 1319–1350.

INDEX